DELINQUENT SAINTS

Number 590

Columbia Studies in the Social Sciences

Edited by the Faculty of Political Science

of Columbia University

DELINQUENT SAINTS

DISCIPLINARY ACTION IN THE EARLY CONGREGATIONAL CHURCHES OF MASSACHUSETTS

by *EMIL OBERHOLZER, Jr.*

AMS PRESS
NEW YORK

COLUMBIA UNIVERSITY
STUDIES IN THE
SOCIAL SCIENCES

590

The Series was formerly known as
Studies in History, Economics and Public Law.

Reprinted with the permission of Columbia University Press
From the edition of 1956, New York
First AMS EDITION published 1968
Manufactured in the United States of America

Library of Congress Catalogue Card Number: 70-76660

AMS PRESS, INC.
NEW YORK, N. Y. 10003

TO MY PARENTS

Preface

Five years ago Professor Richard B. Morris, of Columbia University, suggested that a study of the Puritan attitude on marital and domestic life, based on an examination of the old church records, might prove interesting. This book attempts to present the results of the study which has developed from his suggestion. Although the geographical area covered has been narrowed down to Massachusetts, the subject has been expanded to include all aspects of the churches' disciplinary action. My approach and my interest have been historical, although in the last few pages of chapter XV I have taken the liberty of discussing some aspects of the subject from a theological standpoint. Distinctly skeptical of the methods of some theologians who attempt to exploit the name of Clio for the sake of "theologized" history (as distinguished from the history of theology), I have had no desire, however, to emulate their practices.

At the risk of being a bore, I must acknowledge the help of the acquaintances made in the course of my work, including the Reverend Mrs. Hazel Rogers Gredler and the Reverend Messrs. Adrien R. Aeschliman, Robert S. Balfe, John A. Bembow, Arthur W. Bowler, Eugene Bushong, George E. Cary, Raymond Cosseboom, Arthur C. Cummings, Earl C. Davis, George H. Douglas, J. Edward Elliot, Bradford E. Gale, Perley Grant, Clayton Brooks Hale, Herbert R. Houghton, Jr., Thomas Kidd, Ralph Long, Robert H. MacPherson, Howard A. McDonald, Robert D. Ostle, J. Herbert Owen, Ralph Rowse, Francis C. Schlater, Donald J. Selbie, Thomas A. Sinclair, Donald E. Smith, Earle H. Steeves, John A. Stevens, Charles M. Strydon, Lynne P. Townsend, Pierre du Pont Vuilleumier, William Wakefield, Raymond W. Ward, Henry Blair Whitney, Clyde D. Williams, and Edgar Wolfe, all of whom served churches in Massachusetts while I was engaged in my research. In this connection I must also mention Miss Carrie S. Allen, of Milton; Mrs. Marion C. Billings, of Hatfield; Mrs. George C. Chandler, of Kingston; Mr. Samuel Le Baron Dexter, of Mattapoisett; Dr. George B. Gibson, of Ipswich; Professor William Hall, of Rochester; Mrs. Hiram Harlow, of Shrewsbury; Mrs. Oscar S. Hodkins, of Marblehead; Mr. Waldo C. Hodgson, of Dedham; Miss Elizabeth Jenkins, of West Barnstable; Mrs. Roscoe Johnson, of Barre; Mr. Benjamin May, of Needham; Mr. George E. Mills, of Rockport; Miss Nellie Rist, of Montague; A. Warren Stearns, M.D., of Billerica; Mrs. George G. Swain, Jr., of Marblehead; and Mr. Frank E. Tuit II, of Northampton.

Libraries and historical societies readily extended their facilities and made their holdings available. Their names will be found in the bibliography in the listings of church records consulted. Some special debts, however, must be acknowledged here. Miss Fanny G. Clark, of the Berkshire Athenaeum, Pittsfield; the Reverend John A. Harrer, of the Congregational Library, Boston; Mr. Russell Jackson, of the Essex Institute, Salem; and Mrs. Graham D. Wilcox, of the Stockbridge Library Association, rendered valuable assistance. I am also grateful to Professor (formerly Acting Dean) George H. Williams, of the Harvard Divinity School, for access to the magnificent collection of local history at the Widener Library at Harvard University, to the Columbia University Libraries, and to the library of the Union Theological Seminary in New York. At Union, Professor Robert F. Beach, librarian, and Mrs. Hugh Foster, reference librarian and expert guide to the Seminary's fabulous McAlpin Collection, rendered immeasurable services.

Professors Richard Hofstadter, William E. Leuchtenburg, and Dumas Malone, of the Faculty of Political Science in Columbia University, read the manuscript and offered many helpful suggestions, and Professor Sidney A. Burrell, of Barnard

College, read the first chapter and contributed valuable advice on the section dealing with the Covenant Theology. Helpful hints were also received from Professors Albert T. Mollegen, of the Protestant Episcopal Seminary in Virginia, and Frederick Quentin Shafer, of Claremont College, California, while in residence at Columbia during the summer.

The close connection between Columbia University and Union Theological Seminary, which enabled me to share to some extent in the life and work of the Seminary students, has not only proved invaluable but has been a source of great pleasure. To Professor John T. McNeill, who aroused my interest in the history of the Church, and to Professor John C. Bennett, who opened the door to numerous old records, I am greatly indebted.

Mrs. Nelson Bennett, of Bayonne, New Jersey, and Mrs. Meyer Rosenfield, of Cincinnati, shared in the thankless task of typing the manuscript, as did Miss Susan Anne Davies, of Fort Thomas, Kentucky, who proved to be not only an expert typist but a good friend as well. Professor Jacob R. Marcus, of the American Jewish Archives, Cincinnati, where I was employed during a portion of the time while this book was in progress, kindly permitted some generous adjustments in my working schedule, which in no small part enabled me to complete the work, and to Mr. Charles Reznikoff, of New York, whom I met in Cincinnati, I am grateful for some stylistic advice. Finally I must express my thanks to my many friends in Massachusetts, who made my visits even more enjoyable. Space compels me to restrict myself to mentioning the names of Mr. and Mrs. George H. Genzmer, of Groton, and, above all, that of an old and dear friend, Mrs. Beata Rank, of Cambridge.

To Professor Robert T. Handy, of Union Theological Seminary, I owe an incalculable debt. In addition to reading the entire manuscript at least twice, Professor Handy gave numerous hours of his time offering valuable advice on historical and theological matters.

No words can adequately express my gratitude to Professor

Morris, who guided this work through all its stages, from its inception to its publication. His countless suggestions on the gathering, arrangement, and evaluation of the material, as well as on stylistic matters, are deeply appreciated. Without his constant encouragement, advice, and generous guidance, this book would never have been published. For all errors of fact or interpretation, however, I am alone responsible.

EMIL OBERHOLZER, JR.

December, 1955

Contents

Delinquent Saints

Introduction

Few aspects of American life have been so thoroughly treated in historical and imaginative literature as has Puritanism. Yet, despite the extensive research which has been focused on the subject, no attempt to study the disciplinary action of the Congregational churches of Massachusetts has been made hitherto. Charles Francis Adams called attention to the wealth of information on this subject available in the church records,[1] but to date the sources have not been systematically exploited. Local histories, particularly those of churches, almost invariably allude to this aspect of Puritan life, but usually are content with a few passing references. In a recent provocative study, Ola E. Winslow has devoted a chapter to this problem,[2] but since her book dealt with a broader subject, she was unable to present an exhaustive treatment.

This study examines the disciplinary action of the Congregational churches in Massachusetts, from the earliest known instances down to about 1830. Except for some fragmentary information available in contemporaneous writings, no records of church discipline have been found for the first decade of Plymouth history, and few records of the period 1630-80 have survived in Plymouth or Massachusetts. Some of the old church records appear to be irretrievably lost. In some instances they are known to have been destroyed by fire. Others, while not known to have been destroyed, have not been found during the last hundred years. Still others, known or presumed to be in existence, have not been consulted, either because they were not available for examination, or because they were inaccessible.

With rare exceptions, no records of churches founded after 1765 have been consulted, and since this study deals with Puritanism, the records of Congregational and Unitarian churches only have been used; the records of the few Congregational churches founded before 1765 which later turned Universalist were not available. Some of the records suggest that the enforcement of church discipline ceased abruptly, usually between 1790 and 1810, while other records indicate that discipline was administered well into the nineteenth century. Any study of church discipline in Plymouth and Massachusetts must therefore be suggestive rather than conclusive.

In all but four counties it has been possible to obtain a fair sample of the records. The older records of the churches in Dukes and Nantucket counties appear to be lost. In Bristol County, the records of four churches are either lost or not available; eight churches in the county became extinct before 1750, and their records could not be traced. The only records found in that county, those of the Norton church, are incomplete and not very informative. In Worcester County the only really useful information was found in the records of the First Church of Sutton, which are unusually complete and informative. Only a few fragments of the records of the First Church of Worcester, disclosing but four cases, were available.

Printed or otherwise transcribed copies of the original records have been freely used whenever they appeared to be accurate and complete. The original records are not always complete and accurate, however. A number of entries, for instance, mention collateral papers in statements like "for particulars see files." [3] These files were probably destroyed a century or more ago. Names and, in some cases, entire entries have been obliterated.[4] Descendants of censured church members have unblushingly removed entire pages from the books.[5] In some churches, the members deliberately expunged unsavory items from the records.[6] Still other volumes have suffered unintentioned damage.[7] Some entries have become so faded that they are illegible; others cannot be deciphered.[8]

Finally, there is no guarantee that every case was faithfully recorded. The church records, in distinction to the parish records, were the quasi-private property of the minister. In the matter of record-keeping the minister was responsible to no one; he could enter what he pleased.[9] History-in-actuality has been described as the "unrecoverable totality of the past," [10] and only a fraction of the recoverable part is here presented.

Because of the greatly varying scope of the records, certain statistics based on all the available information would be misleading. In some instances it was therefore necessary to use only those records which were complete for several decades and which covered the same periods of time. Other comparisons, such as those involving the offender's sex or the disposition of the case, were based on all available sources. Except in tables I-V, VII, and VIII, which are based on all records which have been consulted, the records used in compiling statistical data in the tables have been clearly identified.[11] A full discussion of the records is found in the bibliography.

A word must be said concerning some terms which, if not explained, are capable of ambiguity. The much abused word *Puritan* and its derivatives, no less than the word *Catholic* (whose real meaning has become obscured by the popular identification of the Catholic Church with the *Roman* Catholic Church), has acquired a wide variety of meanings. Illegitimately used, *Puritan* frequently serves as a term of opprobrium to denote certain persons who often have no connection with Puritanism. Thus members of the following groups, among others, may find themselves branded as Puritans: Methodists, especially in the North, who believe that ministers must not smoke; certain fundamentalists, often in the South, who consider dancing sinful; Mormons, who dance but do not drink tea or coffee; persons found in all denominations who, although not prohibitionists, are teetotalers; Christians of all denominations, who reject "free love"; certain Protestants in Toronto, who oppose their mayor's attempts to make Sunday a happier and livelier day; and Roman Catholics in Quebec, who demand, among other things, provincial censorship of television programs. But even when legitimately used, *Puritan* may imply different things. The term *Puritan* was first used, probably derisively, during the first decade of Elizabeth I's reign, at which time it denoted a person who opposed some or all of the liturgical practices of the Church of England. Before long, the word was applied indiscriminately to anybody who deviated from the Anglican norm, regardless of whether the deviation was of a liturgical, doctrinal, or moral nature. Thus, in English church history, a Puritan may be a Separatist or Independent, as well as an Anglican bishop like Hooper.[12] Considering that there is no general agreement on what constitutes a Puritan, the term must be more clearly defined.

It is almost impossible to define Puritanism accurately. We can, however, make some generalizations about the nature of the Puritan. Preeminently he was God-centered. He was a biblicist who scrupulously adhered to the letter of the Scriptures. Somewhere or other in the Book he could find the rule for any given situation, and this rule he followed meticulously. Theology was not unimportant to him; he took the Fall and the Atonement seriously, but theology was not allowed to stand in the way of morality, for he was a strict moralist who, although he accepted the doctrine of salvation by faith alone, could not help looking for good works as evidence of his faith. Since prosperity was a sign of election, he was thrifty. His life was austere, and his worship was marked by simplicity. Above all, he was austere in the use of time, for time has been entrusted to his stewardship by God and must be redeemed. But for all his austerity he was no ascetic. He could properly enjoy the good things of this world, but his enjoyment of worldly pleasures was subject to his love of God, to which all else was subordinate: the lesser good must not stand in the way of the attainment of the ultimate good.

The Puritan used his head to systematize his theology, but this, too, was subordinate to his faith, and for the Puritan faith was not the acceptance of a system of doctrine (*fides*), as in Roman Catholicism, but trust in God (*fiducia*), as in Luther. His relationship with God was direct and personal, unencumbered by intermediaries. But while he stood in a direct relationship with God, he was a clericalist. The clergy led the way, but the layman was not without responsibility, and no clergyman could relieve him of it. He was zealous in his faith. Zealously he loved God, zealously he pursued his calling, and zealously he hated evil. Secularism and popery both were evil in his sight, and so was the multitude of offenses for which he placed his fellow Puritan on trial. And finally, the Puritan, as we shall presently see, was eminently censorious.

Obviously we need a narrower definition of *Puritan* for our present purpose. Hence we shall use the word to refer to the religious tradition of the Congregationalists of New England, including those of Plymouth as well as those of the Bay Colony. The word *Congregational* is used to include orthodox Congregationalism and its offshoot, Unitarianism, which is also congregational in polity.

Church, congregation, and *parish* were not used interchangeably by the Puritans; each had a distinct meaning. The church was the body of professed Christians who had been accepted into membership upon owning the covenant. The congregation was the larger group of persons who attended services and contributed to the support of the church, whether or not they were members. The parish was a temporal institution. In today's legal parlance it would be called a religious society. In colonial Massachusetts it was usually coterminous with the town, and all men qualified to vote in the town meeting might vote at the parish meeting; the two were in effect identical. The distinction between church and parish became extremely important after the adoption of the Halfway Covenant. Persons whose membership derived from the Halfway Covenant were accorded the civil liberties held by church members and, as voters, were entitled to participate in parish meetings. Since they were not communicants of the church, however, they had no part in the deliberations and votes of the church. Except in isolated instances, church and parish records were distinct books; the commonplace remark, that the old church records were also the town records, is incorrect. The *parish* records were the town records; the church records were a distinct set of minutes and other entries, usually kept by the minister, not the clerk.[13]

Another expression which requires clarification is *civil law*. For the legal historian, civil law usually means Roman law. More often, the term is used in contrast to criminal law. In the early records of the Massachusetts churches, civil law is used to refer to the law of the colony or state, including statutory, common, and customary law. Hence a *civil court* was a colonial or state court, regardless of whether it had jurisdiction in civil or criminal cases. It is in that sense that terms such as *civil law, civil courts,* and *civil authority* are used here. It need hardly be said that *record* or *records,* unless otherwise specified, refers to the records of the churches.

Confusion may also arise from the fact that not all religious groups in the Judaeo-Christian tradition accept the same arrangement of the Decalogue. In the usage of the Roman Catholic Church, the first three commandments form the first table of the law; the last seven, the second table. Luther followed this arrangement, but Calvin, together with the vast majority of Protestants, returned to the older custom of the Jews, who divided the Decalogue into tables of four and six commandments, respectively. The Puritans adhered to the traditional arrangement used by the Hebrews and by Calvin. Thus the First Commandment prohibited the worship of idols, while the Second forbade the manufacture and worship of certain images. The Third forbade the vain use of the Lord's Name, and the Fourth, the last of the first table, enjoined the people to observe the Sabbath. The Fifth, beginning the second table, required due respect to parents, while the Sixth, Seventh, and Eighth respectively prohibited murder, adultery, and theft. Perjury was forbidden by the Ninth, and the Tenth prohibited covetousness.[14]

The Authorized, or King James, Version of the Bible was normally used by the Puritans during the period here studied. For that reason, rather than from any sentimental attachment to antiquity, the Authorized Version has been used in citing texts mentioned in the records, except in one case, in which it seemed a pity not to use the poetry of the Revised Standard Version. In all other cases, except a quotation from the Apocrypha, which has not yet been issued in that version, the Revised Standard Version has been used.

A brief explanation of Congregational polity is necessary for the understanding of the administration of church discipline. "We do not know any visible Church of the New Testament properly so called, but onely [*sic*] a particular congregation," Richard Mather wrote in 1643.[15] No good Congregationalist ever speaks of a "Congregational Church in the United States," as a Methodist or Episcopalian can properly speak of his denomination. Except on the local level, there is no such thing as the "Congregational Church." Good Congregationalists, therefore, invariably speak of the totality of their groups as "Congregational Churches" in the plural.[16] There may be a Congregational church in one town, others in neighboring towns, but together they form a plurality of churches, each one of which is autonomous. A council, conference, synod, or association, which may include a number of churches, is superior to the several churches in a quantitative sense only, never in a qualitative sense.[17] From a doctrinal standpoint it is, of course, absurd to say that any church, congregational, presbyterian, or episcopal, is ultimately autonomous. No such claim was ever made by the Puritan divines, who emphasized that the power of the churches was derived from Christ.[18] What congregational autonomy therefore means is that no temporal authority is superior to the local church.[19] There are as many visible churches as there are congregations, all of which partake of the name and nature of the Catholic Church.[20]

The autonomy of the local churches did not prevent a measure of intercommunion and fellowship among the churches. John Cotton listed seven ways in which a church could enjoy communion with others.[21] Only six are listed in the Cambridge Platform, but these embody the seven mentioned by Cotton. The churches could exercise fellowship through the mutual care for one another's welfare, or through consultation and, if necessary, admonition. By admitting visitors to the Lord's Supper, churches could exercise communion by participation and, if a member moved to another town, by recommendation. Finally, in case of need, churches could assist each other with officers and financial support.[22] The second and third ways of intercommunion are the most important for our purposes. Neighboring churches could be asked to lend their assistance in deciding issues, but their advice could not be binding. If a church failed to heed the advice of a council, however, the offending church might find its fellowship with other churches withdrawn.[23]

Because there was no single "Congregational Church" in Massachusetts, it is not precisely accurate to speak of "church and state" in this connection. Instead we must speak of "churches and state" or, perhaps better still, of "churches and towns," for it is on the local level that the interaction of the ecclesiastical and civil institutions is best seen. The two cannot be identified: Massachusetts was not a church-state, and the churches were not, properly speaking, state churches.[24] The leaders of the quasi-"theocracy" had no distinct legal status and formed no special part of the body politic. They did exercise a great deal of authority, but such power as they had was exercised by means of their prestige and influence. Immediately upon arrival the churchmen took control of the government and, by excluding non-members from the elective franchise, kept the civil authority in their hands.[25] In this way, rather than by constitutional enactment, there arose an intimate coalition of civil rule and ecclesiastical power.[26]

Throughout the seventeenth century the government continued to support the Congregational churches, and down to the Second Charter church members enjoyed a privileged position. Stunned by 110 applications for freeman status, the General Court in 1631 decided to admit none save church members.[27] To guard against the acquisition of the rights of freemen by members of other religious groups, the court in 1636 defined a church member as a person who had been admitted to church licensed by the colony, which was tantamount to restricting the status to Puritans.[28] With rare and relatively insignificant exceptions, only freemen, and hence only church members, were accorded the elective franchise in colonial elections. On the other hand, all residents were taxed for the support of the ministry and churches.[29] The sole exception to this rule was the city of Boston, whose residents were permitted a choice of churches, and whose churches were supported by voluntary contributions.[30]

A generation after the arrival of the first settlers in Massachusetts, the colonial leaders were confronted with the problem of the decreasing number of persons eligible for freeman status. The oncoming third generation brought the problem to a head. The right of communicants to have their children baptized was undisputed. The latter were baptized persons, presumptive but not proven saints, subject to the watch and care of the churches. Upon attaining the age of discretion they were expected to make a confession of their conversion and to be admitted to the Lord's Table. But the second generation already showed a decline in piety; many prospective-presumptive saints failed to qualify as communicants. Nevertheless, these persons sought to have their children baptized. This presented a dilemma: if these persons were admitted, the Puritan ideal of regenerate churches would be destroyed; if they were excluded, the church membership would become an ineffective minority, and the churches would be prevented from exercising disciplinary jurisdiction over them.[31]

The Halfway Covenant was designed to solve this problem. Proposed by the clergy in 1657 and adopted by a synod in 1662, the Halfway Covenant permitted baptized persons who had not qualified for communicant status to present their children for baptism. Upon attaining majority, the children, being church members, were entitled to the civil rights of members, but not being communicants, they were excluded from a voice or vote in church meetings. In essence, the Halfway Covenant was a religious, not a political, device. The statutory requirements for admission to the suffrage were left unaltered, but the basis of eligibility was broadened by the churches.[32] Although the Halfway Covenant had no direct influence on the exercise of church discipline, it reduced the value of full membership until, by 1800, formal religious obligations became a downright burden.[33]

The statutory changes, the first of which were passed in 1660 and 1664, to be supplemented soon thereafter by others enacted at the insistence of Edward Randolph, were little more than legal subterfuges, providing no significant extension of the franchise. In the eighteenth century, however, an increasing measure of relief from colonial taxes for the support of the churches was accorded to dissenters.[34] Not until the state constitution of 1780 went into effect was the equality of all Christians recognized. Even then the Congregational establishment remained. In 1820 a proposed amendment, providing for disestablishment, was defeated at the polls by a ratio of almost two to one. During the next thirteen years public opinion underwent a radical change, and finally, in 1833, disestablishment was approved by an overwhelming majority of the voters.[35]

Notwithstanding the close cooperation between the churches and the state, ecclesiastical and civil functions were distinctly separated. In 1636, John Cotton wrote:

> It is very suitable to God's all-sufficient wisdome . . . to avoide both the churches usurpation upon civill institutions . . . and the commonwealth invasion upon ecclesiastical administrations. Gods institutions (such as the government of church and commonwealth be) may be close and compact, and co-ordinate one to another, and yet not confounded.[36]

Cotton's principle was given official sanction by the Cambridge Synod of 1649 [37] and was rigorously applied in disciplinary matters. The civil government had plenary authority to punish the wrongdoer, be his crime of a secular or religious nature, but it could never excommunicate a person.[38] The churches, on the other hand, had plenary power to excommunicate members for whatever actions they considered offensive,[39] but they could not trespass on the civil authorities' function of imposing temporal punishments.[40] This system of dual jurisdiction is implied in Nathaniel Ward's code of 1641.[41] The injunction against double jeopardy, which is found in the Body of Liberties, carefully provided that no person should be tried twice for the same crime "by Civill Justice," [42] and by implication permitted the churches to try persons previously acquitted by the courts. Officials of the state and of the churches enjoyed no immunity from prosecution by either authority. Thus churches could excommunicate a magistrate, but such censure did not necessarily lead to the official's removal from office, for that was a temporal matter. No such cases have, however, been located. A civil court, in turn, could punish ministers for crimes, but could no inflict spiritual censures on them.[43] These principles, first expressed in the Body of Liberties, were reenacted in 1660,[44] and still hold true today.

Under this system of dual jurisdiction, the state could inflict temporal punishments on persons who had been convicted of offenses which, from today's point of view, might be purely religious, but such penalties were not acts of church discipline. The alleged witches of Salem were sent to the gallows not by the churches but by the judicial branch of the civil government. Although clergymen aided the colonial authorities in their persecutions, in the final analysis the judicial murders of Salem are the responsibility of the civil courts. Because such punishments were not acts of church discipline, they do not come within the scope of this study. The functions of the tithingman are likewise beyond its scope. This official was appointed by the parish, not by the church, and in his official capacity he had no part in the enforcement of church discipline.[45] As herein used, *church discipline* refers exclusively to the actions of the churches towards their members. Any parallel or collateral actions by the civil government or any civil act which was influenced by the churches, is therefore excluded from this discussion, except to furnish background information.

1. The Covenant Owned

One of the most distinctive features of the theology of the Puritans was the covenant. By "owning the covenant," the Puritan became a full-fledged church member, and all of the disciplinary action of the churches was based on the covenant relationship. It is, therefore, necessary to examine the basic features of Puritan theology. Such a discussion must logically begin with a review of Calvin's theology. Puritanism was not Calvinism, if by Calvinism we mean the theology of the Geneva reformer himself, but until relatively recently the two traditions were so closely identified that few writers, including theologians, distinguished Puritanism from Calvinism.[1]

Calvin's position in the history of the Reformation is unique. Of the four major movements in sixteenth-century Protestantism (Lutheranism, Calvinism, Anglicanism, and Sectarianism), only Calvinism can claim a leader who was both a systematic theologian and an original reformer. Luther will always head the list of reformers, but his intensely active involvement in the affairs of his time left him no time to formulate a coherent and complete system of theology. Perhaps he left that task to Melanchthon, but whatever Luther may have expected of him, Melanchthon produced the theology, not of Lutheranism, but of Melanchthonianism.[2] Sectarianism and, to a lesser degree, Anglicanism never had a definitive theology, much less a definitive theologian.[3]

Calvin's assertion that Adam's sin had corrupted all mankind merely reaffirmed orthodox Christian teaching. Even his emphasis on predestination was but a restatement of a doctrine expounded more than ten centuries before by Augustine. One of the features of Calvin's system was the doctrine of *double* predestination. In Augustine's theology, God elected to eternal life whomsoever he would, but Calvin went beyond Augustine in his assertion that those whom God did not elect to life, he damned to hell. In Calvin's system, election to reprobation was as much a deliberate act of choice on God's part as election to life. The elect, Calvin held, were generally known by their church membership. They were the saints of God, the chosen ones, who were to enjoy eternal bliss. Christ, through the Holy Ghost, had led them to faith which, through repentance, justified them before God, who would accept them in spite of their sinfulness. Their justification opened a new life of righteousness and sanctification, but never, in this life, of complete perfection.[4] That God should be so arbitrary as to elect some to life and others to reprobation, without giving man a chance to participate in the decision, was an unpleasant thought to some Protestants in the Calvinist tradition. On the other hand, any rejection of Calvin's emphasis on the sovereignty of God was equally objectionable. What they needed was a *via media*. Being good biblicists, they had little difficulty finding a scriptural basis for their doctrine.[5]

One of the dominant themes in the Old Testament is the idea of the covenant. God had made covenants with Adam, Noah, and Abraham.[6] In each case God had entered into an agreement with a representative of mankind. The covenant was one of works and had been violated on the part of man, who had thus made his salvation impossible. Hence God made a new covenant with Christ, also a Representative of the human race.[7] This covenant differed from the old one, however, for Christ, being both God and man, was able, in legal terminology, to offer God the requisite valuable consideration to secure a settlement of God's suit against the world.[8] To acquire the benefits of the covenant between God and the Representative Man, each individual man must enter into a subsidiary covenant with God. Those called to this relationship, the saints, must form a "Visible-Political-Union" by entering into covenant with each other and with God.[9] The covenant, therefore, was in effect a tripartite agreement between God, the covenanting member who was about to enter the church, and the already covenanted members within the church.[10]

The history of the church covenant in Protestantism is obscure. Neither Luther nor Calvin mentioned it, though both may have implied it.[11] Zwingli and Bullinger show traces of a covenant theology; [12] Rudolph Walther or Gualter of Zurich (1519-86) was influenced by it; [13] and the covenant appears in the theology of the Anabaptists.[14] Its principal exponent was Cocceius, whose *Summa Doctrinae de Foedure et Testamento Dei* appeared in 1648.[15] More than a half century before Cocceius's work appeared in print, however, the covenant had been introduced into British theological thought. Robert Browne introduced the covenant into his Separatist church at Norwich in 1581-82, and in his *Booke Which Sheweth the Life and Manners of All True Christians* (1585) Browne held that a Christian owed his status to his covenant with God.[16] In Scotland the covenant appeared in Robert Rollock's *Treatise on Effectual Calling* (1597), which had been anticipated by Robert Bruce.[17] In the history of Puritanism, however, it was William Perkins who popularized this concept most extensively, while his student William Ames spread the doctrine among the Puritan divines both in England and New England, largely through his own students, John Preston and Richard Sibbes.[18]

A full discussion of the covenant is found in Richard Baxter's *Christian Directory* (1673), wherein the covenant is defined as

> a Contract between God and man, through the Mediation of Jesus Christ, for the return and reconciliation of sinners unto God, and their Justification, Adoption, Sanctification and Glorification by him, to his Glory.[19]

On God's part, the matter of the contract was that he would be God, because

1 . . . on the title of *Creation* and *Redemption* he is our *Owner,* so he doth take us as his *own peculiar people;*

2 . . . he hath title to be our *Absolute King and Governour,* so he doth take us as his *subjects;* 3 . . . he will be our *Grand Benefactor* and *Felicity,* or our *Most Loving Father* (which comprizeth all the rest).[20]

On man's part, the covenant was shorter and less definite. Man promised to accept the Lord as God, and to "forsake the *Flesh,* the *World,* and the *Devil,* as they are adverse to our *Relations* and *Duties* to God." [21] To enter into a valid covenant, the covenanting person must understand its meaning and own it in person, while *compos mentis,* sober, and rational. He must have the right intention, give absolute and unreserved consent, and intend that the covenant go into effect immediately. Unless all the essential aspects were present, the covenant was not valid.[22]

Why should man enter into covenant with God? Baxter provided an answer. God needed nothing; he could get along without the covenant. It was man who needed it. By owning and remaining faithful to the covenant, man reaped the fruits of God's forgiveness and grace, his eternal protection and preservation, his pardon, justification, and adoption, and ultimately his glory in heaven.[23]

By providing a remedy for a serious defect in Calvin's system, the Covenant Theology deviated considerably from Calvinism. The covenant theologians wanted a God whose ways were intelligible to human reason, a God whose ways were not merely arbitrary. Arminianism provided an answer but went too far: it stripped God of too much sovereignty and left too much to man. The Covenant Theology, however, provided a solution which compromised the demands of the heart with those of the head. God's sovereignty was unimpaired; he could damn whomsoever he pleased. But by definition God could not be untrue to himself. Once he had voluntarily entered into covenant with man, he could not break his promise.[24] Whether the Covenant Theology abrogated Calvinism depends on one's definition of Calvinism, and scholars are far from unanimous in their conclusions.[25] For all practical purposes, however, the doctrine of predestination was severely modified.

Real Calvinism was unknown among the Massachusetts Puritans until Jonathan Edwards, by affirming God's sovereignty, introduced a theology similar to that of Calvin.[26] Under the influence of the Halfway Covenant the Covenant Theology had declined in importance until, under the leadership of Solomon Stoddard, churches began to admit baptized but unregenerate persons to the Eucharist, which to Stoddard was not so much an ordinance to be observed by the converted as an ordinance which in itself converted the unregenerate.[27] Although Stoddard did not consider open sinners to be in covenant relationship with God, his emphasis on the Lord's Supper as a converting ordinance made it difficult to judge who had been properly converted.[28] Edwards rebelled against this loose system of admission and its Arminian implications.[29] Seeking to refute Arminianism, he stressed God's sovereignty, man's total depravity, and in an effective but ultimately illogical argument, man's free will.[30] The Covenant Theology is distinguished in Edwards's works by its absence. Thus Edwards, far from reverting to the Federal Theology of the early Puritans, in effect proclaimed Calvinism.[31]

The century of Jonathan Edwards is the most important for students of American Puritan theology. By 1700 Puritanism had deviated radically from the Covenant Theology; twenty years later Arminianism was widespread, and Semi-Arianism, Pelagianism, and even Arianism were in the offing. Religious fervor had waned until it had reached its lowest point in colonial New England. The Great Awakening was the response to the crisis, but it in turn accentuated theological differences and created new crises. Although the Covenant Theology survived, one group of Congregationalists, headed for Arianism and Unitarianism, tended towards heresy, while the followers of Edwards superimposed the New Calvinism on the Covenant Theology.[32]

While the "Old Calvinists," following in the tradition of the Covenant Theology, were more interested in the practical application of theological principles, the Edwardeans, who were given to theological speculation, were far from static in their thought and soon deviated from the theology of Edwards.[33] Their preaching inevitably tended towards Arminianism, and their acceptance of Grotius's governmental doctrine of the Atonement, which reduced the meaning of the Passion to a demonstration of God's hatred of sin and proof that he would punish sinners, further intensified this trend.[34] Joseph Bellamy accepted Edwards's views of sin and virtue, but held that the Atonement was for all men.[35] The theology of Samuel Hopkins was a curious hybrid of Calvinism and Arminianism, combining the Calvinistic doctrines of man's total depravity and of unregenerate man's inability to do good in God's eyes with an Arminian soteriology.[36] Distinctly Arminian was the theology of Nathaniel Emmons, who saw in the covenant God's offer of salvation to anyone who would offer faith in Christ as the consideration.[37] The "New Calvinism," with moralism substituted for Edwards's piety, was bewildering to churchmen who had been brought up in the theological chaos which followed the decline of the old Covenant Theology; to its opponents it was simply ridiculous.[38] Before long the new theological currents came into conflict with the spirit of the Enlightenment. The combination of Sunday Calvinism with weekday rationalism was incongruous, and where Arminian moralism superseded Calvinism, men sought to find God's goodness in men and hence were blinded to the glory of God.[39]

Western Massachusetts and Connecticut provided fertile ground for the Edwardean theology. Starting with Edwards in Northampton, the new current of religious thought spread into the Berkshires and down the Connecticut River Valley, mingling with the surviving Covenant Theology. In the seaboard counties the prevailing influence was that of Jonathan Mayhew and Charles Chaunchy, two stanch liberals who paved the way for Unitarianism. While an evolution of doctrinal thought from the Covenant Theology to Edwardeanism and then to moralism was taking place in the west, the dominant theology of eastern Massachusetts was transformed from the Puritan Christianity of the Covenant Theology to Unitarian liberalism, which, meeting with stern opposition from the Old Calvinist leaders, Lyman Beecher and Nathaniel Taylor of Connecticut, was confined to the Boston area.[40]

Although the theology of New England Puritanism underwent a radical change in the east and a somewhat milder change in the west, it was not a system of theology or a creed, but the covenant, which formed the basis of a Congregational church. As in the case of the early Church, polity was the chief concern. Doctrine was taken for granted until, in the face of heretical attacks, it had to be defended. In the rare instances where creeds were used in early Congregationalism, they were but footnotes to statements of polity, until the onslaught of liberalism forced the Trinitarians to state their beliefs explicitly.[41] Thus the covenant of the Palmer church, adopted in 1811, opens with a doctrinal affirmation:

> You do now in the presence of this assembly, in the presence of angels, and of God, avouch the Lord Jehovah to be your God, Christ to be your redeemer, and the Holy Ghost to be your sanctifier.[42]

Such a statement was unnecessary in 1629, when the First Church of Salem was founded by a covenant. Short and concise, its covenant implied much more than it expressed:

> We Covenant with the Lord, and one with another and doe bynd ourselves in the presence of God to walke together in all his waies, according as he is pleased to reveale himself unto us in his Blessed word of truth.[43]

This covenant is typical of the early period of Massachusetts history. Gradually the covenants were expanded in length, until they came to resemble modern leases, in which the tenants covenant for several pages but the landlords only for one brief paragraph: [44] the obligations on man's part were stated in detail, those on God's part were indicated in broad terms and largely implied.[45] This development of the form of the covenants is well illustrated by a comparison of the Salem covenant of 1629 with the Salem covenant of 1660. The first contains forty-one words; the second, ten paragraphs.[46] The covenant of 1660 remained in effect until 1817, at which time a new one, in line with the church's Unitarian position, was adopted.[47]

"Owning the covenant" entitled a person to membership in a church. No doctrinal affirmation, no subscription to a creed, but submission to the terms of the covenant was the basic requirement.[48] In this respect American Puritanism relied not on the English Puritan tradition, which considered all Englishmen who were not excommunicate to be church members,[49] but on the restrictive policy of the Puritan churches on the Continent. In the church which Whittingham established in Frankfurt during the Marian exile, no person of tainted morals was admitted to membership unless he made a special acknowledgment of his sin,[50] and the first confession of the London-Amsterdam Church, adopted in 1589, stated the restrictive policy in graphic terms:

> Into this Temple entreth no uncleane thing, neither whatsoever worketh abhominations or lyes, but they which are written in the Lambes Book of life . . . .
>
> But without this CHURCH shalbe [*sic*] dogs and Enchaunters, and Whoremongers, and Murderers, and Idolatours, and whosoever loveth and maketh lyes.[51]

This principle was embodied in the Cambridge Platform of 1649. Therein it was held that the "*Saints* by calling" and their children constituted the visible church.[52] These persons must be "free from gross and open scandals . . . so that in charitable discretion they may be accounted saints by calling," although some might be hypocrites.[53] To keep the membership pure, a rigid examination was originally required of all applicants. A private interview with the pastor was the first step. The pastor then propounded the name to the members, along with a résumé of his conversation with the applicant. The final decision on the application was reached by the entire church; the function could not be delegated. When the church had voted to accept the applicant, he was formally admitted to own the covenant and to join the brotherhood of the saints.[54] Once he had been admitted as a member, he could have his children baptized, but these were expected to make a confession of faith when they reached the age of discretion. Their confessions, as well as those of adult applicants, must be supported by outward manifestations of repentance and holiness of life.[55] Some cases presented no problem, but the majority of applicants were neither notorious sinners nor shining examples of holiness and purity. Every decision on an application for admission to membership involved an element of subjective judgment.[56]

By the end of the seventeenth century the tradition of requiring a confession of faith from a propounded member was challenged. In 1697 the Cambridge church voted that an applicant might make a confession if he so desired, but that this should not be required of prospective members,[57] and in 1714 the pastor of Medford refused to reject prospective communicants who would not make confessions.[58] Twenty years later the church in Hull violated a basic principle of Calvinism when, by voting that public confessions of faith and repentance should be "left as an indifferent thing," it admitted the possibility of adiaphora in polity or doctrine.[59] Public confessions of faith were discontinued by the Natick church in 1730,[60] and on the eve of the Revolution the North Church of Salem voted to discontinue not only this practice but also the custom of publicly propounding prospective members.[61] This liberal trend was strongly opposed by Jonathan Edwards and other ministers who, partly from their reaction to the increasing disregard of the traditional tests of fitness for church membership, espoused the Great Awakening. Edwards, holding that a public confession was an indispensable prerequisite to membership unless the applicant was hindered by a physical handicap,[62] clearly indicated his disapproval of the reduced standards of admission.

Closely related to the confession of faith and repentance was the confession of particular sins which, according to tradition, was expected of an applicant who had committed a notorious sin before he was propounded. Such confessions were generally required in the seventeenth and eighteenth centuries, and in 1699 the Danvers church expressly resolved to continue the requirement.[63] Anticipating the liberal trend of the latter part of the eighteenth century, the Walpole church in 1729 voted to place such confessions on an optional basis, but the records fail to indicate whether the option was on the part of the church or of the applicant.[64] In the early nineteenth century, however, two churches voted that the option was at their discretion.[65] By this time, however, public confessions of particular sins committed prior to the admission to church membership were in disfavor. During the decade following the Revolution the tendency was toward the abolition of the practice, and to admit persons to the church covenant without special confessions of past offenses.[66]

Once a person had owned the covenant he was subject to the watch and care of the church. The ecclesiastical jurisdiction invariably extended to all covenanted members, whether or not they were in full communion, and frequently to the baptized children of covenanted members.[67] Children of members, unless themselves excommunicated, were held to be members by the First Church of Salem, which asserted its disciplinary authority over them,[68] and the Sutton church voted that the status of adopted children was identical with that of others.[69] Indian members of the Stockbridge church were considered amenable to the same discipline as whites, save that the private steps were to be taken before the charge was made public, even in the event of public offenses.[70] Neither political nor parochial boundaries could diminish a church's jurisdiction. A member who left his parish without a dismission, or who, having received a dismission, failed to enter into covenant with another church, remained under the watch and care of the church with which he had joined in covenant. Conversely, a member of one church who lived within the parochial limits of another was not amenable to the church in his town.[71] A notable exception to the latter principle is found in the Northampton records for 1714. In a resolution, which was at variance with true Congregationalism, the church held that every baptized person was a member of the holy Catholic Church and, by his baptismal vows (or the vows made for him, in case of an infant), had bound himself to subjection to the government of Christ. This authority, the church voted, was to be exercised "in the Place in which he lives." [72]

Church membership was in the local church, the ecclesiastical unit which, in Congregational thought, best embodied the Church. Several churches might be in fellowship, but membership in one church did not *ipso facto* entitle a person to fellowship with another. A member who desired to change his domicile was required to apply for a dismission. If he could not continue in his church without sinfulness, if he was subject to persecution, or if there was a real, "and not only pretended, *want* of competent subsistence" where he lived and he had a good chance of earning a livelihood elsewhere, he was entitled to a dismission. A member who merely intended to visit in another place might have a recommendation, which would entitle him to occasional communion as a guest, but which would not permit him to join the church in the other town. In no event was a dismission to be granted to a person under discipline.[73]

The rules governing admissions and dismissions were clearly stated in the Cambridge Platform, but their application was left to the churches, which had to decide whether a dismission was justified in a particular case. Ordinarily a member in good standing received a dismission without difficulty; hundreds of dismissions are listed in the records, usually without comment. It was inevitable, however, that difficulties should arise from time to time. The most frequent cause was the dismissed member's failure to join the church in his new domicle. In such a case, the church which had dismissed the negligent member could properly claim jurisdiction.

In Roxbury the church took notice of the fact that one of its members had violated his covenant obligations by not joining the church in Hartford, his new domicile,[74] and Roger Jud, of the Third Church of Boston, found himself excommunicated because he had left his church without a dismission:

> The matter of Offense [the minister noted], is not his going off from this Church; for wee acknowledge there is a lawfulness to do so, provided it bee orderly; but the manner of it. I know none of any persuasion, but who reckon that there is a Discipline appointed by Christ in his Churches: and a person who is orderly become a member of one Church, is lyable to be proceeded with in way of Discipline in that church till he orderly removed his immediate relation to another.[75]

Later in the seventeenth century the churches of Plymouth and Barnstable withdrew their watch and care from four members, including an elder, who left their parishes without dismissions.[76] No similar cases in the eighteenth century have been found, but in the nineteenth century the problem arose again. A member of the Lanesborough church who, after moving to Vermont, had failed to join the church in Rutland was excommunicated by the church of which he had been a member, but a forgetful woman of Plymouth was dismissed after she apologized for her negligence in not obtaining a dismission before she had left the town.[77] Because a dismission presupposed the existence of a church in the town where a member desired to reside, several members of the Deerfield church were refused dismissions until a church had been gathered in South Deerfield, where they intended to settle.[78] Indicative of the liberal trend of the nineteenth century is a case in the records of the Palmer church, which had remained Trinitarian. A couple who left Palmer to settle in Michigan failed to obtain a dismission before they joined the church there, but upon entering into covenant at Michigan were dismissed.[79]

Until a person had been formally admitted to full communion with the church, he had no ecclesiastical rights as a church member, and if he attempted to usurp the rights of communicants, he was liable to censure. A covenanted member who was not a communicant and intruded on a church meeting to cast a vote for the new pastor had his vote removed and was evicted and rebuked by the elder.[80] When Perez Rice, a noncommunicant member, walked into a meeting of the Sutton church, he was told that the meeting was private. For replying that "he hoped his being with the church was not an Intrusion," Rice was forcibly ejected from the meeting house.[81] On the other hand, the First Church of Salem overlooked the offense of a woman who, while her application for admission to communicant status was pending, negligently partook of the Lord's Supper.[82]

II. The Covenant Broken

That covenanted saints should stray from the narrow path marked out for them by Puritan moral theology was inevitable. John Cotton knew this only too well when he observed that what church members "ought to be *de jure* was far from what they are, or are want to be *de facto*." [1] The problem of the sinner among the saints, or perhaps more accurately, of the saint in sin, has been with the Church from its beginning, and the Puritan churches were no exception. Like Israel, the Puritans alternately kept and broke the covenant, and like the prophets of Israel and Judah, the New England divines kept reminding them: "You are not fulfilling your covenant obligations." [2] The covenant might be brief and vague, but its implications were extensive. The observation of a judge that "every contract executory imports in itself an assumpsit" [3] could equally well be applied to the church covenant, because whenever a person entered into covenant with a church, he undertook to do (and, what is more important for our purposes, not to do) a great many more things than were expressed in the covenant. Moreover, the church covenant was always executory, never executed, as long as the covenanting member lived. Only God knew whether he had the grace to fulfill his obligations. Thus God's sovereignty was protected, but the rigor of predestination was mitigated, for God had voluntarily entered into a covenant and could not break it. Any breach must be on the part of man. Both parties had obligations, but only one was capable of failing in his duties.[4]

In contrast to traditional Calvinism, which was primarily

oriented along doctrinal lines, Puritanism was predominantly an ethically oriented religious movement.[5] Its moral theology was demanding and severe. The glory of God was the Puritan's supreme aim, and to the attainment of that end he subjected all lesser goods, although he knew that the goal was beyond his reach.[6] As Ralph Barton Perry put it, these "moral athletes"[7] were ever striving to attain the goal, trying to be more Christian than the Christians.[8] While no Puritan would have used that metaphor to describe himself, the idea of the moral athlete is implicit in the Puritans' favorite theme of moral teaching, the allegorical "pilgrimage of life." The pilgrimage began when Christ, through the Holy Spirit, called the sinful man out of the city of destruction. Journeying through the terror of the Law, the pilgrim became aware of his moral inadequacy and of the futility of any attempt at self-redemption. Afar off he saw the beacon light: Christ, shining in his righteousness. Proceeding toward the light, he entered through the gate of repentance, experienced the assurance of forgiveness, and continued on the road to the holy city.[9]

This pilgrimage represented the ideal. The practice was often quite different, and many a covenanted saint went astray. The devil was always at work and his ways were subtle.[10] He might put an inattentive person to sleep in church, so that the ministry of the Word could not reach him.[11] Or he might take advantage of an idle person and enter into the vacuum created by the careless churchman's inactivity.[12] If he succeeded in his strategems, it was a sign that his victim was likely to go to hell unless he repented. Although rarely the subject of a sermon, there was no lack of allusions to hell in Puritan preaching, and for the Puritan hell was a place as well as a condition. Liberally combining medieval tradition with biblical theology, the Puritan's idea of hell was not lacking in vividness: "Little was said about the location of the place, but much was written concerning the nature of the state." And if the materialistic conception of hell eventually disappeared, the imagery remained.[13]

When the saint had gone astray, whatever may have caused his error, the church stepped in and exercised its disciplinary authority, which in theory was always intended to reconcile the sinner and to restore him to the fellowship of the church.[14] The "parts of dicipline," Ames wrote,

> are brotherly correction, and excommunication. For it does not either only or chiefly consist in the thunderclaps of Excommunication and *Anathemais* [*sic*], but chiefly in Christian correction.[15]

Ames's "brotherly [or 'Christian'] correction" may be equated with the lesser censures, such as admonition and suspension. For the most part the recorded cases, except those resulting in acquittals, resulted either in formal confessions or in censures.

The Bible and patristic authorities provided the basis for the disciplinary action. Cotton Mather showed that the practice of public confession was akin to the exomologesis described by Tertullian,[16] but rejected the patristic requirement of sackcloth, ashes, fasting, and groaning. Not these, but *"Humility, Modesty, Patience, Petition, Tears,* with *Reformation"* were required. The sincerity of the penitent must be outwardly manifest. Every offender must have an opportunity to repent before the church could excommunicate him.[17] A truly penitent person must be restored, no matter how grievous his sin and even if excommunicate at the time of his repentance. So that none might be denied the chance of restoration, the pastor and some of the brethren might, without prior approval of the church, accept a confession *in extremis,*[18] but ordinarily the repentance was to be judged by the church as a whole, and the restoration to be by the majority of the members.[19] Finally, no commutation was possible, for as Ames proclaimed in typical seventeenth-century language: "Indulgences, Commutations, and humane transactions in those things unto which Christ hath ordained the *Discipline* of the Church, are wages of the great Whore."[20]

A careful distinction was made between public and private offenses. The former were acts committed in the presence of more than one or two witnesses and invariably required public action. A private offense was to be dealt with privately and, unless the offender failed to give satisfaction, was not to be made public.[21] In such cases the aggrieved party or a witness to the act was to admonish the offender and to secure his repentance. If the sinner proved obstinate, he was to be visited again by the witness and two or three others. If this visit produced no results a complaint was to be presented to the church. Only in this manner was a private offense to be brought to the attention of the church. Lest members press unjustified charges, Hooker warned that no complaint should be presented unless the complainant could "plainly and peremptorily lay in his accusation of another, touching such speeches and carriages of which upon thorough search, he is well assured." [22] No code defined the scope of public offenses. Sometimes the question arose in the course of litigation, but not until the church had decided the question on the merits of the particular case could a member know whether an offense was public or private. Cotton Mather, however, had a list of offenses which he considered to be public and censurable, but this list had no official standing. Swearing, cursing, Sabbath-breaking, drunkenness, fighting, defamation, fornication, unchastity, cheating, stealing, idleness, lying, and "such *Heresies* as manifestly overturn the Foundations of the *Christian Religion* and of all PIETY," Mather held, deserved public attention.[23]

Since the Puritans had no ecclesiastical courts but, in contrast to Calvin's Geneva system,[24] rejected such tribunals, each church functioned as a court when the occasion arose. Unless some exceptionally weighty matter, such as the election of a new minister, was before the church, disciplinary cases were the staples on the church's agenda, and an accused brother who dared to defy the church's summons immediately incurred the additional guilt of treating his church with contempt. If by any chance there were no cases on the calendar, it was a fact worth noting.[25]

Thomas Lechford has left for us the following account of church procedure in the early history of Massachusetts:

Also all matters of publique offence are heard and determined in publique, before all the Church, (and strangers too in *Boston,* not so in other places). The party is called forth, and the matter declared and testified to by two witnesses; then he is put to answer: Which finished, one of the ruling Elders asketh the congregation if they are satisfied with the parties expressions? If they are, he requireth them to use their *liberty,* and declare their satisfiednesse; If not, and that they hold the party worthy of admonition or excommunication, that they witnesse their assent thereto by their silence. If they be silent, the sentence is denounced. If it be for defaults in erroneous opinion onely, the Teacher, they say, is to denounce the sentence; If for matter of ill manners, the Pastor denounceth it; the ruling Elders doe not usually denounce any sentence: But I have heard, a Captaine delivered one to Satan, in the Church at *Dorchester,* in the absence of their Minister.

Ordinarily matter of offence is to be brought to the Elders in private, they may not otherwise *tell the Church* in ordinary matters, and so it hath been declared in publique, by the Pastors of *Boston.*

The admonished must, in good manners, abstain from the Communion, and must goe on to satisfie the Church, else Excommunication follows.

The excommunicate is held *as an Heathen and Publican:* Yet it hath been declared at *Boston* in divers cases, that children may eat with their parents excommunicate; that an elected Magistrate excommunicate may hold his place, but better another were chosen; that an hereditary Magistrate, though excommunicate, is to be obeyed still in civill things; that the excommunicate person may come and heare the Word, and be present at Prayer, so that he give not publique offence, by taking up an eminent place in the Assembly. . . .

There hath been some difference about jurisdictions, or cognizance of causes: Some have held, that in causes between brethren of the Church, the matter should be first told the Church, before they goe to the civill Magistrate, because all causes in difference doe amount, one way or other, to a matter of offence; and that all criminal matters concerning Church members, should first be heard by the Church. But these opinionists are held, by the wiser sort, not to know the dangerous issues and consequences of such tenets. The Magistrates, and Church-leaders, labour for a just and equall correspondence in jurisdictions, not to intrench one on the other, neither the civill Magistrates to be exempt from Ecclesiasticall censure, nor the Ministers from Civill: and whether Ecclesiasticall, or Civill power first begin to lay hold of a man, the same to proceed, not barring the other to intermeddle.[26]

The eldership, which Lechford mentioned, fell into desuetude at an early date, and its functions were assumed by the church. In Thomas Hooker's scheme, the elders loomed large; unless the people could convince them of error, they must accept their judgment.[27] Cotton, too, maintained that the elders held the keys of authority: they had the "authority"; the people had the "privilege and power," and both must concur in a vote before the church could act.[28] In 1748 the Chelsea church debated whether an individual elder could veto a church vote and concluded that the elders must act collectively,[29] but by this time few churches had elders and debates concerning their authority was largely academic. With the passing of this office, trials were conducted not only before, but by, the churches.[30]

Church trials were quasi-judicial in nature[31] and, although not generally marked by formalities of pleading and practice, were conducted with due solemnity. Because each church was autonomous, and in the absence of a code of procedure, the rules varied from church to church; sometimes questions of procedure were litigated in the course of a trial.[32] In the eighteenth and nineteenth centuries, the accused was often accorded safeguards comparable to those which he would have received at law. In some instances, however, particularly in the seventeenth century, the hearing before the church bore little resemblance to a judicial trial. The burden of proof was sometimes placed on the accused; in other cases the churchmen who were to judge an accused brother were obviously biased, and sometimes the functions of judge and prosecutor were not distinguished. On the whole, however, the churches considered the administration of discipline as judicial in nature. Expressions such as "this judicature," [33] "Trial and Judgment of Causes," [34] and "the affair ought to be examined in a judicial manner," [35] are found in the records; other terms likewise indicate that the churches considered their disciplinary functions to be of a quasi-legal nature,[36] and in the nineteenth century references to counsel are found. In three cases ministers acted as counsel for one party; [37] in one of these a brother of the church was appointed counsel by the accused after the church had voted to permit "some minister of the Gospel or some brother in communion with this Church not an attorney" to represent him.[38]

In the eighteenth century several churches enacted rules to affirm or supplement those in common usage. In South Hadley the church decided that it would not receive complaints immediately before the Holy Communion, and later ruled that all complaints must be stated in writing.[39] The Lenox church permitted complaints to vote unless they were "personally and singularly interested," and in Millbury the church decided that the pastor was to caution all witnesses "to speak the Truth, the whole Truth and nothing but the Truth." [40]

Hearing witnesses and discoursing with offenders could be a tedious task. To relieve the entire membership of these duties, some churches appointed standing committees to assist in the enforcement of discipline. In 1731 the First Church of Haverhill instructed a committee of ten brethren to

> make it their business to inquire into scandalous reports; and meet together with the pastor at certain times, to receive informations and to examine cases and judge of them; and if it may be prevent the trouble of laying them before the whole Brotherhood; and if they cant be healed with such a private hearing, to ripen the matter for a more public hearing.[41]

A committee created by the Medford church in 1818 to distribute the surplus of the communion offering was further charged with "the increased duty of aiding the pastors in matters pertaining to order and discipline." [42] The added function is noteworthy because of the almost total absence of disciplinary cases in the Medford records. Equally significant is the Northampton church's appointment of a committee to assist the minister in the trial of "causes" and "to determine and finish all matters that come before them, unless they are carried to a Council." [43] This extreme delegation of authority, unparalleled in the Congregational churches of Massachusetts, was tantamount to the creation of a parochial court.

Because each church was autonomous, no appellate tribunal could actually reverse the decision of a church. An aggrieved litigant could, however, request that his church join in a mutual council and, if the church denied the request, could call an ex-parte council. The council, patterned on biblical precedents, consisted of delegates from neighboring churches. Once a moderator had been elected, the delegates heard the parties in public and then retired for private deliberations and to draw up the "result," in which the members stated their findings of fact and law and gave their advice, often heavily supported by judiciously selected texts. No church had to accept a council's advice, but if the result ran counter to the church's wishes, and if the church failed to accept the advice, the council could recommend that neighboring churches withdraw from fellowship with the offending church. If the injured appellant was not restored in accordance with the council's advice, he could be admitted to another church in the vicinity without a dismission.[44] On rare occasions, when the circumstances justified it, councils did not hesitate recommend such action.

Church officers were subject to the same disciplinary procedure as lay members, with such modifications as arose from their status. The right of a church to censure its elders was expressly affirmed in the Cambridge Platform, but since in the early period the elders administered the censures, no church could censure all the elders at one time.[45] With the desuetude of the office, however, this problem became obsolete. A pastor was to be proceeded against as though he were a layman, "only with such *special Terms* of *Respect* (and Repetition of *Address*) as the Relation of a *Father* may call for." If, however, the censure was to extend to the dissolution of the pastoral relationship or to deposition from the ministry, a council must first be convened and must assent to the judgment. Should a pastor's excommunication be necessary, a "Grave Pastor" of a neighboring church was to administer the censure.[46]

No general rule defined the offender's status from the time of the accusation or conviction to the time of the restoration or excommunication. In some churches a member accused in a complaint was automatically suspended from the communion.[47] More frequently, however, suspensions were voted in particular cases, and if they failed to bring the sinner to repentance were followed by one or more admonitions.[48] If the offender lived in a remote place, the admonition might be sent by letter; normally it was read in his presence. A person who failed to appear before a church which had duly cited him was to be excommunicated.[49]

The offender's restoration, which was one of the aims of every censure, was almost invariably accompanied by a confession, which traditionally was read before the entire congregation on Sunday. Towards the end of the seventeenth century, the Plymouth church questioned the wisdom of the practice but after considerable discussion voted to continue public confessions.[50] First to modify the requirement was the church in Beverly, which in 1704 voted that confessions might be made before the members only if the penitent person so desired.[51] A similar provision was enacted in Groton in 1741, and in 1826 the Lenox church decided to accept confessions before the members only, if the acknowledgment was otherwise satisfactory.[52] The brethren of the West Church of Granville reluctantly permitted private confessions, but asserted that the practice of public confession was "a good one, and preferable where the offence is generally known," and the Windsor church decided in 1813 that no private offense should be made public by the requirement of a public confession.[53] During and after the Revolution the relative merits of public or private confession were much debated. The churches in Falmouth, North Andover, and Weston followed the earlier example of the Chelsea church and abolished all public confessions, followed, in 1838, by the Amherst church.[54] On the other hand, the churches in Charlemont, Mattapoisett, and Pittsfield reaffirmed their support of public confessions, followed, in the nineteenth century, by those in Danvers, Great Barrington, and Sutton.[55]

Neither public nor private confessions were pleasant experiences in the lives of those who made them. Obstinate members who refused to acknowledge their guilt exposed themselves to the greatest censure which a church could impose: excommunication. Citing the Church Fathers, Cotton Mather defined excommunication as "A driving away from the church," "An abjection and a Depulsion from the Church," and "A Separation from the Church and an Ejection out of it." [56] The power to eject, as well as the power to restore, lay in the local church, which had succeeded to the Petrine power of loosing and binding sins,[57] and even in the days when elders ruled the churches, this power was restricted to the entire church, which could not delegate it to any body of officers.[58] Only after the brethren, by majority vote, had decided on the sentence, could the pastor proclaim the excommunication. The announcement was to be preceded by an address to the offender, followed by an exposition of his evils and impenitence. The meaning of excommunication was to be explained to the people, and then, at the end, the sentence was to be pronounced.[59] The suggestion that excommunication was the peculiar penalty for "exceptionally serious offenses such as heresy or blasphemy" [60] is not entirely accurate. In such cases, excommunication might be pronounced immediately, once the accused's guilt was established,[61] but heresy and blasphemy were not the only offenses for which summary excommunications were imposed. Most often the excommunication was not pronounced immediately, but only after patient waiting by the church, and then not so much for the primary offense as for the offender's refusal to repent and make satisfaction. Impenitent sinners of all sorts, including drunkards, fornicators, liars, and slanderers, as well as blasphemers and heretics, were excommunicated for impenitence and obstinacy, and in 1699 the Bradford church voted that *any* offender who remained obstinate after a censure was to be excommunicated.[62]

The rationale of an excommunication was that this grave sentence might eventually bring the sinner to repentance or, if that proved impossible, that the sinner's soul might ultimately be saved. Even an excommunicate person might be pardoned by God, and to the end of securing repentance at some stage, in this life or the next, the sentence was imposed.[63] In the case of a woman excommunicated for failing to repent of her thefts, the pastor commented: "May the great Head of the church make use of this solemn act, as a means of bringing her to sincere and humble repentance, Amen." [64] In another case, the hope that "God [may] move his heart yet, to effectual and saving repentance" was expressed.[65]

Because an excommunicate person was always potentially penitent and might again become a church member in good standing, he was not to be treated as an enemy but as a brother in need of admonition, never as a "common Sinner" who had always been outside the Church.[66] To the end that he might be restored, an excommunicate was not only permitted, but required, to attend the services of his church, because by attending the preaching of the Word he might come to a fuller understanding of his sin and repent.[67] If he repented and offered an acceptable confession, the excommunicate was restored to church fellowship, rather than admitted *de novo,* for he had never ceased to be a member, although he had temporarily forfeited the privileges of membership.[68] Until he repented, however, he was to be avoided as much as possible. As far as the church was concerned, his rights as a member of the body politic were unimpaired. Whatever temporal disabilities he incurred were imposed by the civil government;

Massachusetts knew nothing analogous to the writ *de excommunicate capiendo.*[69] In social matters, on the other hand, he was to be treated as a fallen saint. According to the Cambridge Platform, he was to de deprived of "all familiar communion . . . farther than the necessity of natural, of domestical, or civil relations do require," and was not to eat at the same table with members in good standing,[70] and Cotton Mather suggested that such a person be treated humanely but without familiarity.[71] If a member violated the quarentine of an excommunicate, he was himself subject to discipline, but no such censure has been found.[72]

One of the most fully recorded cases which terminated in an excommunication is that of Sarah Wescott, a Marblehead rogue of the early eighteenth century. The first reference to the case is found in an entry dated August 24, 1720, at which time the indignant church voted that "the vindication of the Name of God, the Honour of Jesus Christ, the great Head of the Church, and the Holiness of the Church, and the purity of its Institutions" required the excommunication of Sarah Wescott, "for the mortifying of her flesh, that her Soul may be Saved in the day of the Lord Jesus," and as an example to others.[73]

The background of the case narrated in the formal statement of excommunication, which was read to the congregation on September 11. More than two years had elapsed since Sarah had been first accused. In March, 1718, her mother had entered a complaint, charging Sarah with violations of five commandments: the Second, by saying "you wished *you had Dyed that Day when you Joined yourself to the Church";* the Third, by the use of abusive language and profanation of her mother's name; the Fourth, by absence from worship; the Fifth, by rebelling against her parents to the extent of endangering her mother's life; the Sixth, by attempted suicide. Because Sarah would not answer the charges and refused to appear before the church, she was suspended.[74]

The case against Sarah Wescott was reopened in August,

1720, after the church had learned that Sarah had given birth to her third illegitimate child. The church had been willing to overlook the first bastard because he had been born before Sarah's admission to the church. Nothing is said of the second, but report of the birth of the third moved the church to bear witness against "such vile polluters of the House and Ordinances of God." On the seventeenth Sarah was cited to appear before the church, but the committee appointed to summon her brought the "melancholy Tydings" that Sarah had no intention of subjecting herself to further discipline. The same day, and on the next, the pastor vainly attempted to see Sarah at her house. On the nineteenth she appeared to tell the church that she was "hunted like a partridge upon the mountains, as David was by Soul [*sic*]." Six days later, in response to another citation, Sarah met with the pastor. Told that she must submit to the discipline of Christ, Sarah amazed the minister with her "atheism and unbelief," declaring that the institution was not of Christ, but of Paul, "a man of passions with us." When the pastor attempted to explain the meaning of the excommunication, voted by the church two days before, Sarah listened to his exposition of a Pauline text[75] and concluded that the Scripture contradicted itself. Sarah had come to the conference in an obstinate frame of mind; as she had come, so she went home, unmoved by the pastor's entreaties.

By this time the congregation must have been hanging on to every word as the pastor recounted the steps which he and the church had taken to reclaim the sinner. He was preparing his people for the climax: the announcement of the highest censure which the church could impose. At this point, the record reads like a melodrama, complete with stage directions. Not only does it read like a play; it was a life drama, and Sarah was its star performer:

The Pastor: . . . and at the same time you has the confidence to tell me that the Scripture was contradictory to itself; which you had said to one of the Brethren before; and no longer than the last Evening persisted in—

Hard about, Sarah Wescott turns to go out of the assembly.
Pastor: Sarah Wescott, I command you to stay.
Shee kept on, going out.
Pastor: Sarah Wescott, I command you in the Name of Jesus Christ to Stay.
Somebody attempted to step her way, but she would go, notwithstanding all. She goes out.
Pastor. Let her go; no doubt She is not of us, for if she were of us, she would not go out from us.

Sarah had indeed stolen the show from the minister, who ad libbed:

Brethren, you have seen her obstinacy and Contempt of the Authority of Jesus Christ in the Church, and we doubt not but this whole Assembly, as well as the Church, looks upon such a person as very unfitt to be a member of the Church of Christ.

Then the pastor returned to his prepared script:

"You see the united Sense of the Church of Christ of which Sarah Wescott is a Member in particular, calls for her being cutt off from Our Holy Communion.

"And it is now the part of the Ministers of the Lord Jesus Christ whom He hath made the Stewards of this House and committed the keys thereof unto giving them special Charge to the faithfull in Opening and Shutting and in dealing to every one their portion in due Season, as of Counsells, Instructions, Comforts, and priviledges, so also of Admonitions and Censures proportionable to the Deserts of these, whose Souls He hath putt under their watch; and as representing the person of Christ Himself, in His Name and by His authority, to pronounce the dreadful Sentence: a Sentence more terrible than that of Death itself pronounced by the Civill Judge upon the Convicted Malefactors. . . .

"Therefore in the Name of the Lord Jesus Christ and with His power, we do pronounce and declare Sarah Wescott to be Excommunicated, and cutt off from the Communion of the faithfull and debarr'd from all the Holy and Special priviledges of the Church of Christ, and we Deliver her unto Satan, for the Destruction of the flesh, that the Spirit may be saved in the day of the Lord Jesus.

"And we Exhort and Charge all the Brethren and Sisters of this

Church expecting the same from all others, to hold her as one Excommunicated, and as such to have no unnecessary friendship, Communion, or Society with her; but to turn away from her as a Leprous person, that they may not be defiled with her abominations.

"This Sentence of Excommunication thus done on Earth with such Justice and Equity and according to the Rules of the Gospel, you are to look upon as this day ratifyed and Confirmed in Heaven, leaving her to the dreadfull Judgments of God if she repenteth not; according to what Christ has said, (Math. 18.18) *whatsoever ye shall bind on Earth shall be bound in Heaven.*

"Let us again commend the poor Creature unto God, that a Blessing may attend His own Institutions."

After prayer, part of a psalm was sung, and then the assembly Dismissed.

Soli Deo Gloria in Ecclesius [*sic*].[76]

Not all cases terminated as unhappily as that of Sarah Wescott. Some excommunicates made confessions and were restored. The majority of convicted members valued their salvation or their church membership sufficiently to go through the embarrassing ordeal of making a confession before the church invoked final censure. Some members who stood accused were acquitted after trial, and a number of complaints were dismissed before the respondents were called to answer. Although the procedure usually followed the broad steps outlined by Cotton Mather, it varied widely in details. In the following chapters, we shall see how the churches dealt with saints who turned out to be, or were mistaken as, sinners.

III. The First Table of the Law: Sins of Omission

In six days God made the world. The seventh day, on which he rested, he blessed.[1] Ever since, in the Judaeo-Christian tradition, one day in seven has been kept as a day of rest. For Calvin the Sabbath was predominantly a day of worship, but not of marked austerity.[2] For Anglicans it was a feast day marked by worship, but with ample time for harmless recreation between services.[3] The Puritan Sabbath differed from both. Jasper Danckaert's observation of the Puritans, made in 1680, that "all their religion consists in observing Sunday, by not working or going into the taverns on the day,"[4] was perhaps as unfair as some of his other astringent comments. For the Puritans, however, as for the Hebrews whom they imitated, the Sabbath was a day not of gloom, but of joyful reverence.

The enforcement of church attendance was aided by the civil law, which, alongside the churches, punished persons who failed to attend services. In the seventeenth century, the Plymouth statutes were rather more severe than those of the Bay Colony. By an act of 1651 a person who absented himself from a church meeting on the Sabbath was subject to a fine of ten shillings, with an additional fine of ten shillings against the master of an absent child or servant.[5] The penalty against the master was repealed in 1659, but the fine assessed against the absentee was reenacted.[6] In Massachusetts, on the other hand, the fine was only five shillings,[7] and before the Revolution greater latitude was permitted, for the fine, though raised to ten shillings, applied only when persons had been absent for an entire month.[8]

It is impossible to say how well these laws were enforced by the civil government or to what extent they assisted the churches in the enforcement of attendance. Church resolutions, applicable to members only, suggest that civil punishments were inadequate to maintain regular attendance at worship. In 1661, the year of its founding, the church in Northampton adopted a resolution which noted with alarm that a large number of members was absent and that numerous churchmen had settled in the Connecticut River Valley without bringing dismissions and recommendations. In an effort to bring these persons under its discipline the church voted that persons who intended to settle in Northampton could not claim the privileges of Baptism for their children and of the Lord's Supper for themselves by virtue of their membership in another church. Occasional communion was for transients, not for residents who, from sentimental attachment to another church or from a desire to evade the discipline of the local church, failed to transfer their membership.[9] In a similar effort to place every church member under some effective discipline, the Second Church of Boston instructed its elders to speak to those members who habitually attended other churches and to urge them to apply for a dismission to the church of their choice.[10] A psychologically effective, although legally questionable, device was employed by the Chelsea church, which decided that the votes of persons who attended parish meetings but would not worship on the Sabbath should not be counted.[11]

Whether absence from services was a censurable offense was questioned only once. In the case of Job and Lydia Spalding, who were charged with absence from services except when the Lord's Supper was administered, the record states that "the accused acknowledged the truth of the charge in general, but were not convinced of its being erroneous and disorderly conduct. They declared their conviction of its being their duty so to do." The church rejected this demurrer but allowed the disorderly members to state their reasons. The couple much preferred the sermons by the pastor in Concord and reluctantly explained that they had gone there on the Lord's Day. The pastor reminded them that they were not accused of disliking him, but of violating their covenant obligations: the Spaldings owned the covenant in Chelmsford, not in Concord. In spite of the apologies offered by the couple, the church found them guilty of contempt and admonished them. Sixteen years later they offered a confession and were restored.[12] A third absentee, whose case was tried together with that of the Spaldings, was Mary Stedman, who had developed a liking for Whitefield and Tennant, the leaders of the New Lights, and who "enjoyed such immediate revelations and communications from above as raised [her] to the privilege of exemption from all ecclesiastical authority and rule on earth." Admonished by the church, Mary behaved indecorously and was suspended until she made a confession some eighteen years later.[13]

Although in the colonial period a single absence rendered a church member subject to discipline, greater leniency was allowed after the Revolution. For the clearer definition of what constituted a censurable absence, one church decided to take in action in cases where a member had missed more than one Communion service or preparatory lecture, while another ruled that continuous absence from the Lord's Supper for a year effected an automatic removal from the membership lists.[14] But no amount of ecclesiastical or civil legislation could secure the desired ends. A badly mutilated fragment of a minute of 1694 in the Bradford records indicates that church's concern regarding absentees. Similar comments on the large number of persons who failed to attend services is expressed in the records of other churches.[15]

In a majority of the proceedings against alleged absentees, the churches discontinued the prosecution before it had reached one of the customary conclusions: confession and restoration, excommunication, or dismission. Disregarding withdrawals to churches not in the Puritan tradition or to none at all and absences arising from schisms, the records disclose a total of 395 cases in which absence was the primary charge and twenty-one others in which it was secondary to another accusation.[16] In about half of all cases the result is not indicated, nor is it always clear that formal action was taken. The case may have been considered closed when an investigating committee reported its findings to the church. A person absent one Sunday may quietly have slipped back into his pew on the next, and the offense, although noted in the record, may have been disregarded.

In these cases the use of committees was especially common. Other offenders were dealt with as occasion arose; absentees were often cited in groups, and from time to time, when the laxity in attendance had reached a particularly low point, systematic prosecutions were undertaken. Thus the First Church of Salem charged four men and two women with absence in 1661 and "to avoid the tediousness" of a meeting appointed a committee to discourse with the erring members. Three of the absentees were excommunicated shortly after the committee reported its findings. The others were admonished in a sermon but, remaining obstinate, were also cast out of the church.[17]

A committee appointed to study the absentee problem in Merrimac returned a report analogous to a grand jury presentment. The committee observed that a number of persons had been admitted to the communion although they had no credentials. A woman was charged with offensive talk, and six persons, several of whom had been previously accused, were charged with absence. Noting the decay of morality in "Dayes [*sic*] of great Temptation," the committee recommended that the church solemnly renew its covenant.[18] Of the accused persons, a man was excused because of ill health, while a woman avoided prosecution because she found herself "not in so good a frame of Spirit as She thought to be to attend." [19] Three persons were suspended; the result in the sixth case remains in doubt.[20] Similar investigations, followed by multiple informations against absentees, occurred during the eighteenth century in Millbury, Northampton, Plymouth, Worthington, and Kingston.[21]

The first purge of absentees in the nineteenth century began on the initiative of the pastor of Dalton who, in a report to his church, accused nine members of habitual withdrawal from the Communion or of absence from worship. On the recommendation of a committee, three men were excommunicated; two were later restored.[22] This investigation was followed by one in Chelmsford, which resulted in the excommunication of seven men and four women.[23] In Wilbraham five brethren were charged with absence and, in one case, with nonsupport of the church. After a futile effort to convince the men of their guilt, the church concurred in a request for a council after both parties had pledged to accept the result. Unfortunately the church records, which indicate that the church followed the council's advice, do not mention that body's decision.[24] Three of the members evidently complied with it, for their names are not mentioned in the aftermath. The others presumably remained obstinate and were censured. One was restored late in 1824, on the condition that he resume his obligations. Three weeks later the only member remaining under this censure sought to be restored, citing his brother's case as a precedent. This petition, as well as requests for dismissions to Baptist and Methodist churches, was refused at the time, but three years later the church voted to restore him to its fellowship.[25]

Traces of disciplinary action for absence are found into the second half of the nineteenth century. In 1825, the Falmouth church instituted proceedings against fourteen persons who had been long absent. Of the nine who were excommunicated, only one was restored by 1833.[26] A decade later the Lenox church brought charges against an unspecified number of absentees.[27] The last such purges are found in Pittsfield. In

1837 three persons were accused of absence. Twelve others were similarly charged in 1840, and four more absentees were accused in 1853. The record in these cases is vague and incomplete; it is impossible to tell what action was taken.[28]

Although the incompleteness of the records makes accurate statistics impossible, some trends are clearly apparent.[29] Thus we find three periods in which there was either great laxity in attendance or particularly intensive discipline. These are the years 1740-59, 1780-89, and 1820-29. The first of these periods coincides with the Great Awakening. The second came at the time of the rise of scepticism and deism, during the decade in which Paine's *Reason the Only Oracle of Man,* anticipating the publication of the deistic writings of Volney and Palmer, appeared. The last of these periods was that of the revivals of the early nineteenth century.

The final disposition of these cases shows a distinct trend. Omitting the cases in which the result is indeterminate, we find only a handful of persons who did not return to the church after censures for absence until after 1750. After 1800 the number of offenders who left the church increased steadily, until it reached a peak in the 1820's. A comparison of the incidence of absenteeism among men with that among women shows that men were more often censured. Furthermore, we find that until 1810 the men who were not restored far outnumbered the women.[30]

An analysis of the statistics by counties fails to reveal a regional pattern, since the years included in the records are disparate. The one inference which can be drawn is this disciplinary action for absence not only continued in the western counties, but was considerably intensified, at a time when the churches in the seaboard area became increasingly lax in disciplinary matters.

Absence from church was frequently combined with, or the by-product of, some other offense. Thus Edward Mills, a Boston adulterer and gambler, was also convicted of contemptuous absence from services before he was excommunicated.[31] Intemperance was sometimes combined with absence, especially among men in western Massachusetts,[32] while fornication was the offense most commonly combined with absence among women,[33] and three absentees were also accused of theft.[34] Other offenses combined with absence were the abuse of one's wife,[35] slandering or otherwise abusing the pastor,[36] both theft and adultery,[37] a triple combination of intoxication, profanity, and dueling,[38] and, as might be expected, Sabbath-breaking.[39] More unusual, if less illuminating, is the record of a confession of "long distemper," neglect of worship, and "moping." [40] In 1729 the North Andover church ordered a member to make a confession of his continued absence "and for the idle lazy life he has lived these many years." Three years after the offender made his confession he was again admonished for neglect of worship.[41] More surprising are two excommunications in the nineteenth century. For absence and "disorderly conduct in everything" a man was cast out of the church in 1807, and as late as 1824 a church member was excommunicated for absence and "vain amusements." [42]

Grievances, real or imaginary, against the church, its pastor, or one or more of its brethren, frequently gave rise to withdrawals from the Holy Communion and, in some cases, from all services of worship. On rare occasions a church might permit a member to withdraw until the issue had been determined. William Wheeler, for instance, having been charged by another member with breach of contract, was allowed to withdraw until the issue was decided, and one complainant was permitted to absent himself from the Lord's Supper until the offender had made a satisfactory confession.[43] These cases were exceptions to the rule. The Cambridge Platform clearly provided that the admission of an unworthy person to the Supper was no cause for withdrawal. No member could neglect his duty, for should a person refrain from partaking of the ordinances because of a grievance, he would incur the punishment due to another.[44]

The question of the propriety of withdrawing from the communion table was first raised by a member of the First Church of Salem. Brother Humphrey had withdrawn from the Lord's Supper on two occasions, the first time because he allegedly did not want to offend the church at a time when there was a difference of opinion between him and another member, the second time because he considered himself offended by the church. The issue before the church was: may a brother withdraw from the Eucharist because he is offended by another? By finding Humphrey guilty of a censurable offense, the church answered the question in the negative.[45] Focusing their attention on the underlying causes of the absence, rather than on the immediate offense, the churches were sometimes able to promote a settlement of the dispute and incidentally to resolve the offense given by the withdrawal.[46]

Aversion to the pastor lay at the root of a number of withdrawals. A brother of the Kingston church sought to justify his absence on the ground that he disliked the pastor's performance.[47] A more specific record is found in the case of Samuel Buck, of Millbury. At the hearing, the following dialogue took place:

> Buck: You flung bane in my way.
> Pastor: You treat me with indecency laying a very big Charge against me before the Church.
> Buck: You have never been to see me or say anything about it.
> Pastor: You will have to answer for that another day.

In neither case did the church take further action against the absentee. Unless the Millbury pastor intended his last retort to be eschatological, he was wrong, for the church voted to drop the proceedings.[48] Some years afterward a man made a confession of absence caused by a grievance he bore against the pastor of the church in Hatfield,[49] and as late as 1812 we find a case in which a person refused to partake of the Lord's Supper because a collector of church taxes had made a distraint on some relatives who refused to pay their contributions. The aggrieved communicant was suspended until, seven years later, he made a confession.[50]

An entire church could occasion a withdrawal. Edward Tuttle, absent from the Lord's Supper on three consecutive occasions, explained that he had been offended by the church's refusal to baptize his grandchild. After Tuttle made his acknowledgment, the Chelsea church willingly dismissed him to Lynn, where he had formerly been a member. Tuttle had not been happy in Chelsea, and the brethren were relieved by his request for a dismission.[51] In another case the offender pleaded that he had been offended by the church's refusal to admit his friend to membership. Impenitent and obstinate, this brother was excommunicated.[52] Abner Chase, however, who had withdrawn from the Lord's Supper because his church had allegedly abused his brother Francis, offered a statement:

> In as much Frinds as you do not look upon the Reason Sufficient laid before the Church by what hase been carrid in already I must Acknoledg humbly that the Lord in all his wise Providence has inabld me to imbrace the Gospil in the Pour [power?] of it which I compare the Scripter and my one con-chance [conscience] to geather which I esteem my prieilidg [privilege] this from yor frind.
>
> ABNER CHES

Upon receipt of this misspelled but penitent note, the church voted to discontinue its proceedings against Abner Chase without requirement of a formal confession.[53]

In the case of Edward Tuttle the church had offended the withdrawing member by refusing to baptize his grandchild. Twenty-five years later, another Tuttle, Elisha, felt that he was himself slighted by the church. His brethren, Elisha maintained, "did not show that Regard to him which they did to Other Brethren." Perhaps he was one of those unfortunate persons, found in every church, who are not socially acceptable and are therefore snubbed by the "proper" people. The brethren went on record to declare that they had no prejudice against him and would be glad if he returned to communion with them. Tuttle owned his error, and the conflict came to a happy conclusion.[54]

The furors created today by changes and innovations in church music had their counterparts in the early centuries of Massachusetts history. Scarcely twenty years after the founding of the Bay Colony, the First Church of Boston excommunicated a person who had withdrawn from the church because he objected to the singing of the Psalms. The brother who considered this practice a modern human invention overlooked the fact that the ancient Hebrews sang the Psalms.[55] Not until 1775, when a Plymouth deacon was accused of attributing Watts's hymns to the devil, did church music again give rise to a disciplinary case. Splitting hairs, the church acquitted the deacon on this charge, but found him guilty of having said that Watts's settings of the Psalms were composed under satanic influence.[56] Three years later, while the Revolution was still raging, the church in Barre was the scene of an intense dispute, which began when three men refused to worship with a church which used Watts's hymnal. The church voted to refer the question to the ministerial association, which unanimously voted that the reasons were insufficient, but that disciplinary proceedings against those brethren who pleaded reasons of conscience rather than of taste should be suspended.[57] As late as 1803 a churchman in Groton objected on scriptural grounds to the use of musical instruments, presumably organs, but the disposition of the case is not indicated.[58]

Excuses for absences or withdrawals on grounds other than grievances are rarely indicated in the records. About two-thirds of the explanations offered were rejected as insufficient; the remaining eleven of the thirty-four excuses offered were accepted.

Some members charged with absence did not care to justify their offenses. A doctor in Brewster told a committee "that it was none of their business" whether he went to church or not, and later answered a committee which had been sent to summon him to a meeting "that it was his pleasure not to comply." The doctor was admonished but no final result is mentioned.[59] Equally sure of her convictions, but not quite so rude, was a Danvers widow who had been committed to the county house of correction as a disorderly person and disturber of the peace. Called upon to explain her absence, the widow plainly told the committee that she was not inclined to return to the church. Accordingly, she was excommunicated.[60]

Qualms of conscience explained some absences. Observing that Mrs. Hannah Kelley, who had been absent for some time, was "Apprehensive that she is in a Disordered State thro' Distraction in Some Degree," the Merrimac church instructed the pastor and a deacon to exercise their discretion in admitting her to, or rejecting her from, the Lord's Supper, and the pastor told Mrs. Kelley that if she felt herself to be "in a composed and quiet frame of Mind" she might partake.[61] In Ipswich, a woman sought to justify her absence on the ground that she was not qualified to make her communion. She was willing to make an acknowledgment, but hesitated lest a lack of true repentance made the confession itself sinful. At her request the church appointed a committee to converse with her. If the committee called on her during the next six years the records fail to show it. In 1788 she was again visited, and two years later made a confession.[62] In dealing with a man who was reluctant to partake of the Supper because of his irregular conduct, the Rochester church was less successful. It interpreted the self-conscious brother's statement as a hint that he should be charged with another crime and, after a year's interval, excommunicated him.[63]

Among the more unusual situations which arose from absences was a vote empowering the pastor to admit or reject, at his discretion, a penitent member who had withdrawn from the Lord's Supper.[64] One minister did not wait for such delegated authority but freely admitted three repentant absentees to the Supper, waiving the requirement of a public confession: "Their return was evidence enough of their Repentance." [65] Another instance of a pastor who sought to reclaim a fallen member by gentle persuation instead of threats is found in the Medford records. In September, 1798, the pastor wrote a lengthy letter, a masterpiece of gentleness and kindness, to Ebenezer Hall, who had been missed at meetings. After a year had elapsed the minister wrote again, pleading that Hall resume his obligations lest the case be made public and, more important, lest Hall suffer for his neglect of the church in the life to come. On October 17, 1799, the pastor recorded that a committee had been unable to see Hall. The next entry mentions Hall's death, with this added comment:

> As this case of our late Brother Ebenezer Hall Senior has been a most melancholy one, it may not be amiss to record it more fully. Through his whole life he has been esteemed for his integrity and his dealings and the benevolence of his disposition; and formerly for his exemplary piety.

In spite of his former piety, Hall had become a sceptic, and the most ardent efforts of the minister could not secure his return to the church.[66]

A variation on the theme of withdrawing from the Lord's Supper appears in the Amherst records. For pretending to partake when he did not actually receive, a brother was excommunicated after he had ignored several warnings and offers of council.[67] Equally unusual is the case of Barnabas Adams of Becket, who was charged with absence, nonpayment of church dues, and forbidding orphans in his charge to attend church services. An additional accusation was that Adams had discouraged church members from joining a society to raise a fund for the support of the pastorate. Evidently the person who had instigated the complaint and had sought to have Adams investigated underwent a change of mind. At a later meeting the complainant moved to table the resolution for an inquiry on the ground that such an investigation "implies or appears to imply" Adams's guilt.[68]

Church attendance was a solemn religious duty, but it was not the only duty towards the church. Members were expected to contribute towards the expenses of the Lord's Supper.[69] Disciplinary action for nonpayment of such dues were rare, except in Amesbury, where two men and a woman were convicted by the church in 1736. Of the eight persons found guilty of failing to support the expenses of the Supper, six were restored after confessions or payments of arrears.[70]

The offering of children in baptism was more important than the offering of money. As early as 1639, the father of a child was admonished for failing to have it christened, as well as for "distraction," absence, and neglect of family prayers and blessings at meals.[71] An applicant for church membership was rejected in 1642 because he had overlooked his child's baptism.[72] The next such case did not occur until more than a century later. In 1762 a widow sought full communion with the church in Chelsea. Formerly a member of the Cambridge church, she had neglected worship for years and had failed to offer her children in baptism. As long as she merely resided in Chelsea, the church felt that it could not require her to present her children. The application for admission enabled the church to demand, as a prerequisite to her admission, that the children be baptized.[73] In Barre, a schism led to three prosecutions for neglect of baptism. In two cases the result is not clear, while in the third case the investigating committee found that the alleged offender had died on the day the investigation was begun.[74] One failure to present children for baptism was tolerantly overlooked when the respondent pleaded conscientious scruples.[75] The last such case terminated in the excommunication of the offender, who had not only failed to present his children for christening, but who had himself left the church.[76]

That baptism must be administered by a clergyman was implied in the Sutton church's decision that two children whom their father had "pretended" to baptize were not to be regarded as baptized persons and were therefore to be christened by the minister. The father's presumption was viewed as an act of "High Prophanation." [77] Perhaps the church was right in rebuking the father, but its rejection of the validity of a lay baptism and the consequent rebaptism of the children were radical departures from Christian tradition.

Throughout the colonial period and well into the nineteenth century the churches enforced the demand that their members attend Sabbath services. Man's chief duty on that day was to join in the organized worship of God in the church of which he was a member. Complaints against absentees were frequent, and when absenteeism reached the stage of an epidemic, mass prosecutions were undertaken. As late as 1853 members were formally accused of failing to attend services, although after 1800 these cases appear rather sporadically. Personality factors were prominent causes of absences and withdrawals from communion. Dislike of the pastor, innovations in church music, and grievances against fellow members constantly threatened to interfere with man's duty to God. Coinciding with the decline of church prosecutions for absence was a change in the members' response to the complaints. After the turn of the century, confessions were fewer, as more and more members preferred to ignore the complaints and to withdraw from organized worship altogether. By 1800 the impact of the Enlightenment and the rise of individualism had indubitably affected the churches.

IV. THE FIRST TABLE OF THE LAW: SINS OF COMMISSION

The Puritan Sabbath was indeed a day of worship. Moreover, it was a day on which all work and such recreations as were otherwise permissible ceased. The most faithful churchgoer of today, were he transported back to seventeenth-century Massachusetts, would find the Puritan Sabbath a gloomy day.[1] Nothing in the New World today compares with it; not even a Sunday in Sabbatarian Ontario or in the Canadian Prairie Provinces is truly comparable with the Sabbath observance in colonial Massachusetts.

In the Puritan Sabbath two traditions merged. One was the English Sabbatarianism which antedated the Reformation and the rise of Puritanism, a tradition which went back to Ine of Wessex and Withraed of Kent, who issued Sabbath laws in the late seventh century. The other tradition was that of the later Calvinistic writers: Lancelot Andrewes, once a stanch Puritan, Richard Greenham, and above all, Nicholas Bownde, whose *The True Doctrine of the Sabbath* appeared in 1595.[2] To these influences may be added the Puritans' inherent rejection of anything tainted by Anglicanism, notably the Book of Sports, first issued by James I in 1618 and later reissued by Charles I in 1633.[3]

In the Puritan tradition, all work was strictly forbidden on the Sabbath, which began not on Sunday morning but, overlapping Jewish practice, on Saturday evening. In 1691 the First Church of Boston instructed its members to close their shops before sundown on Saturday lest the Sabbath be polluted, and another church ruled that no evidence in church trials must be taken on Saturday or Sunday.[4] Blue laws, providing for fines ranging from five to forty shillings, whipping, or imprisonment in the stocks for persons who defiled the Lord's Day by work or play, or by travel beyond the limits of the township without a good reason, aided the ecclesiastical enforcement of the sanctity of the day, and in Plymouth smoking within two miles of the meetinghouse was illegal on the Sabbath.[5] The court records of Essex and Suffolk counties clearly demonstrate that these laws were enforced in the seventeenth century.[6] When a man was trapped in a well on a Sabbath, the Christians of Yarmouth held a debate to determine whether it was lawful to dig him out on that day, or whether they must wait until Monday.[7] And some ministers reputedly questioned whether a child born on the Sabbath could be baptized.[8]

Ecclesiastical censures for violations of the Sabbath are found throughout the colonial period and into the nineteenth century. The majority of Sabbath-breakers, all but two of whom were men, quickly made confessions and were restored. In 1691, and again in 1817, church members who had been censured for needless travel on the Sabbath were restored after their confessions had been heard,[9] but Samuel Thacher, who in 1762 was found riding on the Lord's Day, was acquitted when he proved that he had a valid excuse.[10] An Essex County farmer who drove his cart, ten oxen, and two horses on the Sabbath, and a Cape Cod sea captain who was found marking fish "in holy time" were required to make confessions.[11] Similarly censured was an Amherst farmer who drove his team into the center of the town during the hours of worship and then aggravated his offense by associating with "trifling men" and "treating sacred things with unbecoming lightness," while a resident of Stockbridge, already under censure for profanity and speaking lightly of Christianity, aggravated his guilt by working in his garden one Sunday morning when he should have been in church.[12] For working on the Lord's Day or for unspecified violations of its sanctity four others made confessions, and two were excommunicated,[13] while Asa Davis of Bradford, who was caught conveying some goods to Newburyport at midnight on Saturday, was excommunicated for his violation of the Sabbath, although a charge of theft is also mentioned.[14]

If an act in itself sinful was committed on the Sabbath, that fact was sure to be recorded and most likely was considered as aggravating the offender's guilt. Sunday drunkenness was not uncommon,[15] and in Lanesborough a colonel was charged with tarrying at the public house until late one Sunday night. The officer attempted to justify himself by explaining that he was engaged in an important conversation. Had the subject of the conversation been religious he might have escaped censure. Because the subject was purely secular, the colonel was required to make a confession before he was restored.[16] For assaulting a child on the Sabbath, a brother was required to confess his violation of the Sabbath as well as his injury to the child.[17]

The most unusual Sabbath violations are found in the Northampton records. In 1698 John Taylor, temporarily committed to the Springfield jail, was released on his promise that he would attend church. For profaning the Lord's Day by absenting himself from public worship in order to elude the authorities, the fugitive was excommunicated.[18] George, an indentured servant, was publicly admonished in 1734 for excessive drinking and running away, but primarily for breaking the Sabbath by choosing that day "for so wicked a Purpose." [19]

The two women censured for violations of the Fourth Commandment present a striking contrast to the large number of men convicted of breaking the Sabbath. One woman confessed her breach of the day and, quite incidentally, acknowledged that she had been fighting.[20] The other had stayed home to pick strawberries on the wrong day.[21]

Feasts and fasts, days of thanksgiving and of humiliation were also to be observed as holy days, on which no work was to be done. For playing quoits on a fast day, a sin compounded by the fact that he played the game in bad company, John

Webb of Boston was admonished, but was restored after a public confession.[22] A feast day was violated when a Plymouth whaler engaged in his occupation. Like Webb, this brother was required to make a confession in order to be restored.[23]

For the further protection of the sanctity of the Sabbath, the colonial government and the churches took action against persons who slept or played games during the service. A Plymouth statute of 1669 required the constable to record and publish the names of persons found sleeping or playing games during the long meetings.[24] No censures for sleeping or gaming have been found in the records, but apparently some members of the Bradford congregation were prone to sleep during services. To express its disapproval of such inattention, the church voted that sleeping at worship, "and especially the Laying down of the head to sleep," were indecent and irreverent, and warned that offenders would be admonished if they did not reform.[25] The church in Weston was annoyed not only by sleepers, "extraordinary cases excepted," but also by members who turned their backs on the minister in order to gaze about.[26]

The earliest instances of misconduct at meetings are found in the Westfield records for 1732 and 1735, recording two public confessions of "unwarrantable anger" displayed in the meeting house on the Sabbath.[27] Five men and a woman were dealt with for disorderly conduct during the sermon, which in one case was held to constitute a breach of the Second, Fourth, and Fifth Commandments.[28] Three of the men were restored after confessions to the church; the fourth was deprived of the privilege of occasional communion.[29] The sole woman in the group was denied admission to full communion until she had made a confession.[30] The fifth man was restored upon his confession, made fifteen years after the censure was imposed. His restoration so annoyed a couple that they withdrew from the church and were suspended.[31]

Pushing one's neighbor out of the pew evidently was not a censurable offense. Rachel Gray had ejected her sister Miriam, but escaped censure on this count. Another charge against Rachel, to the effect that she had pushed her sister Lydia out of the pew, was dismissed for lack of evidence. Although Rachel was able to avoid censure for misconduct, she was severely rebuked for perjury arising from the incident.[32]

Congregational singing was an ideal occasion for the creation of a disturbance. It was difficult to distinguish beween a well-intentioned but unsuccessful effort to sing on pitch and a deliberate disturbance. One man, however, was convicted of deliberately singing off pitch in order to interfere with orderly worship, and was eventually excommunicated for impenitence.[33] A church on Cape Cod requested the civil authorities to detect certainly disorderly persons who had interrupted the service with a "confused noise" during the singing of a metrical Psalm.[34]

The demand that church members show their respect for God, the Church, and the clergy was not a mere Sunday obligation, but was equally effective during the week. The slightest reflection on the church, or an ill-advised comment on the pastor's sermon or his personality was likely to involve the critic in unpleasant consequences.

A girl's deranged mind and an unmarried minister in his early thirties, with whom the girl may have been in love, provide the background of a unique case in the Massachusetts church records. Prudence Parker, a communicant of the Reverend Samuel Palmer's church in Falmouth, had "walked disorderly." We are not told what her offense was, save that she manifested a "strange Carriage in Speech and Behaviour." To justify her conduct Prudence, rather than to admit her guilt, resorted to some hopelessly perverted biblical exegesis. Because of her disordered mind, no formal censure was inflicted, but the pastor quietly asked her to withdraw from the Lord's Supper. Perhaps Prudence was infatuated with the young parson, for all went well until the minister told her of his intention to marry Mercy Parker. At the receipt of this news Prudence broke out in reviling language. If the minister married Mercy, she declared, he was no better than the devil, who would surely have him and "the hottest place in Hell would be his portion." The minister could do no more. Gently he tried to convince Prudence of her error; the harder he tried the worse Prudence became. Reluctantly Palmer laid the case before the church.

In June, 1731, the church heard the minister's narrative of his dealings with Prudence. Recognizing that she was not a normal person, the church went no further than to exhort Prudence not to partake of the Lord's Supper. But Prudence, unaware of any guilt, firmly told the church that she would join them at the next celebration. At a hastily convened meeting the church formally voted that Prudence was to be excluded from the Supper and asked the minister to warn the girl. For the time being, the warning was effective.

On an August Sunday in 1637 the church was preparing to observe the Lord's Supper. Prudence had been warned not to come. If the church had any delusion concerning her obedience, it was quickly disspelled. Prudence entered the church and calmly seated herself with the communicants. In vain the pastor admonished her. If she were not a welcome participant, Prudence declared, she would be an unwelcome intruder. Forcibly she attempted to partake, and forcibly she was ejected. Accused of open contempt, Prudence remained mute at the hearing. To a committee sent to discourse with her, she had nothing to say save that "the Kingdom of Heaven suffers violence and the Violent take it by Force." Her identification of the kingdom with the church in Falmouth did not perturb the brethren; indeed, it may have delighted them. But that she should identify *herself* with the kingdom went too far. That such conduct was censurable was not disputed, but was Prudence a proper subject of an admonition or suspension? The church thought not: obviously this girl was *non compos mentis.* For the time being the church confined itself to an informal exhortation.

After a year's interval the church made a routine inquiry into Prudence's state of mind. She had nothing to say to the church; the church had no new grievances against her. The brethren would not censure her but, lest their recognition of Prudence's unstable mental condition set a bad example, they adopted a carefully worded resolution:

Voted That the formal admonishing and suspending of her (which tis judged, she is worthy of, if Compos mentis) be still deferred; (Her Frame and conduct appearing so strange and unaccountable that the Church could not tell what to do with her).

All might have gone well had Prudence remained in Falmouth. A trip to Martha's Vineyard proved too great a temptation. There was a church in Tisbury, where she was unknown. On a pretext she was admitted to occasional communion. Word of this reached the brethren in Falmouth. Alarmed lest the Tisbury church fall into sin, the Falmouth church promptly instructed its minister to notify the minister in Tisbury of Prudence's case. Another letter was sent to Prudence, urging her to repent and to withdraw from the Lord's Supper until she had manifested her repentance.

For twenty years Prudence was forgotten by the church. Then, suddenly, one day in May, 1759, she appeared before the church and congregation and publicly confessed her disorderly conduct. At long last she was permitted to join the saints at the Lord's Table.[35]

Not all church members who reviled their ministers could seek refuge from censure by claiming insanity.[36] In Barnstable, a man remained suspended seven years because he had accused his pastor of hypocrisy and prejudice, and had intimated that the minister treated him "like a dog." [37] Near the other end of the Cape, a pastor who had suffered an unspecified "Scandalous Insult" was unable to take action against the unknown offender, but asked his parishioners for a vote of confidence: "It is expected you may manifest your disapprobation of the base action, as well for the Vindication of your own Honour as a Church of Christ, as in Justice to mine and my Wifes injured Characters." The church promptly complied with the request, and the pastor expressed his gratitude by announcing that he would celebrate the Lord's Supper at the first opportunity, adding, however, that by administering it he waived no right to obtain satisfaction from the guilty party.[38]

A woman whose feelings had been hurt by the minister avenged herself by not attending the services, later acknowledging that she had been offended by the pastor's failure to attend the funeral of her child. Although she was censured for absence, her criticism of the pastor undoubtedly had its effect on the church. Repeatedly admonished, she made a confession after eight years.[39] More straightforward was the man who bluntly told the church that he had never liked the pastor and had opposed his call. This remark was considered offensive, and the pastor's opponent was ordered to make a confession.[40] In a contrasting case, a church granted a request for a dismission to a neighboring church because the petitioner, who disagreed with the pastor on some matter of opinion, was uncomfortable in her church.[41] Five other cases of this nature are found in the records, but save for the man who expressed his regret that he had not pulled the minister out of the pulpit, the details are missing.[42]

When Elizabeth Hart boasted that "all the witt the church had could not keep hir [*sic*] out," and that she had burned the summons to appear before the church "to teach old fooles more wit," the entire church was offended. For her contemptuous remark Elizabeth was promptly suspended and admonished.[43] Equally offensive was the statement that the church was *"a parcel of Devils,"* for which a brother was ordered to make a confession. Evidently the offender offered some sort of confession, for the record closes with this laconic remark: "What Brother Pitcher offered to the Church as Satisfaction, the Church voted to accept as such." [44] More blasphemous was a remark allegedly made by a winebibber in a pub. Sipping from the glass, James Mitchell was reported to have said: "This tastes better than it does in the Church or meeting house." Mitchell denied the charge, which was dismissed for want of evidence, but was convicted of slandering another member. A month later the church voted to withdraw from communion with Mitchell.[45]

A member who permitted himself the luxury of an unfavorable critique of the previous Sunday's sermon was likely to suffer for it. Sermons are still criticized at the reviewer's risk, but in colonial Massachusetts the risk was considerable.[46] A man who accused his pastor of preaching heresy was on the verge of excommunication when a council then in session urged the church to proceed with caution.[47] In Bradford, the church was wary of admitting to membership a person who confessed that he had unjustly charged his former church's minister with false doctrine. Accepted on a probationary basis for a year, he later made another confession and was admitted to full communion.[48] A few years later a brother of the Kingston church was accused of having said that the minister preached "prophane Trash" which rendered God's Word ineffective, for which he was suspended until he made his confession three years later.[49]

A day in jail as well as an admonition was the price which Elhanan Lyon paid for charging his pastor with encouraging fornication from the pulpit. A justice of the peace fined the slanderer twenty shillings. Lyon's first inclination was to take an appeal, but being penniless he thought better of it and borrowed the money to pay the fine and costs from his son. In spite of the conviction in court, Lyon, who had previously made confessions of absence, fornication, barratry, theft, lying, and rumormongering, persisted in maintaining his innocence until he was excommunicated.[50] Nine months later he died. A man like Lyon deserved more than a mere entry in the burial record. The pastor wrote:

Oct. 31.—This day was buried *Elhanan Lyon Senr.*—It was but a Year ago, this Month, since I took him into the Law for reviling and slandering me and cast him [*sic*]; and for which the Church sometime after excommunicated him. He always justified himself; and though I voluntarily, and without sending for [i.e., without being sent for] visited him, he never said one word to me about the matter. He is now gone and his Doom pronounced. While he lived he was the great *Troubler* of this church but he will trouble us no more. *Prov. 11.10.*—I think he dies as little lamented as any one in this place would have done.—God's dealings with us are worthy to be observed. There have but three Men died as yet, out of the place (though several women) and these three were such as were of the Church; (except *Lyon,* who was cast out) and were in times past the great troublers of the peace of this Church; and yet I would be far from supposing them greater Sinners than others.—*The Lord is known by the Judgments he executeth.*—Higgaion, Selah.[51]

A couple were involved in a serious case in Haverhill. Mrs. Hannah Webster, rumor had it, had said that the minister was not a Christian. Vehemently denying this charge, Mrs. Webster did admit that she had accused him of not always preaching "gospel sermons," her term for sermons on topics she liked. Accepting her acknowledgment, the church voted to drop the proceedings against Mrs. Webster and turned to examine her husband's conduct.[52]

David Webster had written several letters criticizing the church. The brethren were interested in these notes and ordered Webster to produce them at the hearing. Webster, however, had no intention of complying with what amounted to a subpoena *duces tecum.* Suspended for contempt, he was excommunicated when he sought to participate in the Lord's Supper while under censure. When the church rejected his request for a mutual council, Webster called one ex-parte, but agreed to abide by its decision. Presumably the council agreed with the judgment of the church, for Webster would not accept its decision. Under the ruthless questioning of the brethren he gradually broke down. Had he not written a damaging letter last March? Webster first denied the charge, but later admitted that although his wife and sister had written it, he had instigated it. The church continued to probe into his activities. They asked him about a rumor that he had said that he had only begun to make trouble for the church, and that if they would not have him as a member, he would join another church. Webster had no reply. The church had no alternative save to reaffirm its earlier sentence of excommunication.

As soon as the vote was passed, Webster called another ex-parte council, which advised the church to restore Webster if he showed evidence of repentance and meekness. But Webster manifested neither of these qualities, and once more the church reaffirmed the sentence.[53] Executing his threat, Webster applied for admission to the North Church, which rejected him without further inquiry. For the third time he convened a council. The advisory body disapproved of the North Church's peremptory refusal to admit Webster, but also expressed its disapproval of Webster's conduct and urged him to make a confession.[54] Whether Webster ever became a member of the North Church or was restored to fellowship with his former church is not stated in the records.

Members who because of a complaint or conviction reviled the pastor, elder, teacher, deacon, or church, aggravated their guilt. Nearly a third of the members charged with violating the honor and respect due to the church and pastor had already been charged with other offenses when they failed to restrain themselves and cast aspersions on the church. It was bad enough that Goodwife Shelley had slandered two women, but for her to say that the minister, rather than she, should be cast out of the church was the last straw. "Wee had long patience towards her and used all courteous intreaties and persuasions, but the longer wee waited the worse shee was," commented the minister when the church voted that not he, but the presumptuous woman, should be excommunicated.[55]

Many offenders might have been dealt with less severely had they not compounded their prior offenses by reviling the minister. Thus a man who, when charged with an unspecified offense, treated the church with scorn and rudely told the members that he would have no dealings with them, was summarily excommunicated for his remark.[56] A woman who, when charged with drunkenness, flew into a rage and accused the teacher of lying, was treated more leniently. Although convicted of intoxication only, she repeatedly absented herself from meetings and was excommunicated.[57] In Plymouth, however, the church overlooked the passionate conduct of the husband of a woman who had been charged with domestic mismanagement, but went on record to declare that his words had been "highly offensive." [58]

Even a contemptuous remark by the respondent himself was occasionally overlooked if he confessed the principal offense and incidentally mentioned his misconduct before the church,[59] but if he persisted in his contempt he could be sure of a censure. Thus Robert Felton, only suspended for profane cursing, was publicly admonished when he aggravated his offense by saying that "he hoped he should appear in another place where his three great Enemies (not, saith he, the witnesses) but *envy, spite,* and *partiality,* shall not come," [60] and Barzillai Hammond, originally charged with abusing his wife, was excommunicated not only for his impenitence in that matter, but also for villifying and reproaching the church and minister and for "openly casting Contempt on the Authority of the Lord Jesus . . . by turning into Ridicule the Discipline thereof." [61]

Because neglect of religious duties, Sabbath-breaking, and contempt of the church were indicative of a lack of respect for God, these offenses were viewed in a serious light. Far more serious, however, was the sin of consorting with the devil. Although the connection between Satan and witchcraft was foreign to the Bible, the Puritan theories were those traditionally held in Church history,[62] and a recent student of the role of Satan in New England thought observed: "In no respect of the devil's activity have fear and fancy, fable and folklore, delusion and superstition played so prominent a role as in witchcraft." [63]

It was not the mere belief in witchcraft, which was common in the seventeenth century, but the hysteria created by the alleged witches of Salem, which made the trials of 1692 to stand out. It must be remembered, however, that an occasional witchcraft trial had taken place before the Salem hysteria. In Cambridge, Charlestown, and Dorchester women were executed as witches in 1648. Eight years later, a woman who allegedly overheard another talking about her was held to have supernatural powers and was hung as a witch, but many incredulous Bostonians attributed the conviction to slander.[64] These convictions were but forerunners to the real epidemic, which began in 1688, when Martha Goodwin accused her laundress of stealing some linen. As the maid's Irish temper flared up, she cursed her indignant employer, who had a fit. Martha's children enjoyed the scene and prankfully imitated their mother's behavior. Their mischievous acts were promptly attributed to the unfortunate laundress's diabolical powers, for which the maid was hung. Cotton Mather visited the woman in jail and recorded her confession, in which she admitted a conspiracy with Satan. The confession implicated other persons, but whatever personal information was divulged to the parson was withheld by him in the published account of the confession.[65]

From Boston the epidemic spread to Salem Village, now Danvers, where Samuel Parris was the settled minister. Parris had a grudge against his parishioners: they had given him the use of the parsonage; he wanted a fee simple. Known for his arrogance and stern discipline, Parris was unpopular. His church, already split into factions, provided an ideal setting for intrigue and mischief. Parris's colored servants, John and his concubine Tituba, taught the parson's children and their friends how to enact fits. In December, 1691, the children, of whom Ann Putnam, twelve, and Mercy Lewis, seventeen, were particularly mischievous, performed the tricks which they had learned from John and Tituba. When their horrified elders threatened to whip this behavior out of them, the children understandably sought to lay the blame elsewhere and accused the servants of supernatural powers. Tituba and two obscure women, Sarah Good and Sarah Osburn, were soon in custody, charged with witchcraft.[66]

The details of the trials which followed are so well known that there is little need to linger on them. The three women, two of whom had no previous connection with the hysteria, and the third of whom was guilty of no more than mischief, were taken to Boston for trial. Tituba's conscience left something to be desired when, in the hope of saving her neck, she turned King's evidence. Before long, the epidemic turned into hysteria. Unscrupulous persons with wagging tongues turned against Rebeccah Nurse, who was already in disgrace with the church because of an unrelated quarrel, and against Martha Corey. Before the end of the summer, 126 persons were confined in jail pending their trial.[67]

The trials were a tragic blot on the history of Anglo-Saxon jurisprudence. The clergy's warning against rash convictions not only went unheeded but was itself marred by the suggestion that the court need not be too careful in judging defendants of tarnished reputations. At the arraignment the judges must have presupposed the defendants' guilt, for they asked them why they had afflicted their victims. The alleged witches were instructed to look at their victims, who repeated their fits as soon as they had exchanged glances with the accused. When the defendants touched the victims, the fits ceased.[68] The hearings were a farce, serving no other purpose than to stir up public indignation to a still higher pitch, far enough to guarantee that the trials would result in convictions.

Procedure in the trial court was no better. Although at variance with standard English criminal practice, it was in accord with the special procedure sanctioned for use in witchcraft cases. Popular bias ran high, but the venue was not changed. Alleged victims, sworn as witnesses, were barely able to identify the defendants. Confessed witches implicated as many others as possible in order to reduce their own guilt. The jurors themselves freely introduced evidence. Trial by ordeal was used, the defendants being required to recite the Lord's Prayer. When the judges thought that a woman had said "Hollowed be thy Name," they were sure of her guilt. But nothing at the trial was quite as fantastic as the use of "spectral evidence," testimony concerning apparitions which claimed to be the ghosts of the witches' victims; [69] the admission of such evidence was, however, permissible according to the old law books on witchcraft. The jury impanelled to determine Rebeccah Nurse's fate at first appeared to be more conscientious than the prosecutor-judge, but when it returned a verdict of "Not guilty," bedlam ensued in the courtroom. The judge, not content with the verdict, charged the jury to deliberate further and read some damaging parts of the testimony out of context. The jury then asked Rebeccah to explain some point and, finding her mute, convicted the woman.[70] A contemporary observer expressed his condemnation of the trials in no uncertain terms:

> Liberty was evermore accounted the great priviledge of an Englishman; but certainly, if the Devill will be heard against us, and his testimony taken, to the seizing and apprehending of us, our liberty vanishes, and we are fools if we boast of our liberty.[71]

Among those to go to the gallows were Rebeccah Nurse and Martha Corey. Martha's husband, Giles, himself a victim of the hysteria, refused to plead and suffered the agony of *peine forte et dure,* perhaps to atone for his lack of loyalty to Martha at the beginning of the trial, or possibly to prevent his estate from being attainted. No less than nineteen persons were judicially murdered in Salem Village in one year; the twentieth became the first victim in New England to die at the hands of an antiquated judicial device.[72]

As suddenly as it had arisen, the hysteria ended. Considerable revulsion had been aroused by the mass slaughters. Perhaps it is some malicious girls who deserve the world's gratitude for ending the terror, for by accusing the pastor of the Old South Church of Boston and the wife of a minister in Beverly they made the case ludicrous. The outburst was a sociological phenomenon which will long crave the attention of psychologists and sociologists. One explanation, suggested by a recent writer on the subject, is that the people, whose impulses had been repressed and whose security had been undercut by anxiety and terror, required some catharsis. Unable to punish the daemonic powers, they sought a scapegoat and turned themselves into a lynching mob.[73]

Before the hysteria ended, however, the churches had to deal with the alleged witches who were church members. Only three of the persons executed by judicial processes, if the procedure can be thus dignified, are mentioned in the church records. First to be excommunicated was Rebeccah Nurse. The minute is brief and to the point:

> After the Sacrament the Elders propounded to the Church, and it was by an unanimous vote consented to, that our Sister Nurse being a convicted witch by the Court and condemned to dy, should be Excommunicated, which was accordingly done in the Afternoon, she being present.[74]

There is no indication of a trial or even the slightest chance for a defense. The woman had been condemned by the court, and the church accepted the verdict without question.[75] Giles Corey, who had been admitted to church membership only in April, 1691, after repenting for his scandalous conduct in previous years, was excommunicated in September, 1692. Since he had not been convicted of witchcraft, the church had to find another justification for its sentence. On the ground that should he perchance have been innocent of witchcraft, he was guilty of suicide, the church could see no reason why he, too, should not be excommunicated. To justify this vote for posterity, a legally illiterate pastor wrote:

> He [Corey] being accused and indicted for the sin of witchcraft he refused to plead, and so incurred the sentence and penalty of pain

lost due [*sic*] being undoubtedly either guilty of the sin of witchcraft or of throwing himselfe upon sudden and certain death, if he were otherwise innocent.[76]

Martha Cory, a member of the church in Salem Village, was dealt with in that town. Like her husband, she had been admitted to membership only in April. On September 10 she was by unanimous vote excommunicated. Four days later a church committee which visited her in prison found Martha uncommunicative, "for her imperiousness would not suffer much." Martha refused prayers, and the committee left after a few minutes, first pronouncing the sentence.[77]

One of the principal, though unintentional, culprits in the hysteria had been Mary Sibly. When the disturbances in the Parris household first began nobody suspected witchcraft. Only after John had used an allegedly diabolical recipe in Mary's collection, calling for several disgusting ingredients, and had fed the product to the dog, was Satan's hand believed to be at work. Until that time no apparitions had been seen; now there were plenty. "By this means (it seems) the Devil hath been raised amongst us," the minister wrote, "and his rage is vehement and terrible, and when he shall be silenced the Lord only knows." Not John, but Mary Sibly, who had given him the recipe for the daemonic cake, was to blame. Parris had no doubt that the devil was at work in Salem Village, but was convinced that Mary had ignorantly given John the instructions which she had received from some other ignorant person. The recipe, Parris held, was not of the devil, but was certain to lead to him:

We are in duty bound, to protect [ourselves] against such actions, as being indeed a going to the Devil, for help against the Devil; we having such directions from Nature, or Gods Word, it must therefore be, and is, accounted by godly Protestants, who write or speak of such matters as Diabolical. . . .

Therefore, as we in duty, as a church of Christ are deeply bound, to protest against it, as more directly contrary to the Gosple, yet in as much, as this our sister did it in ignorance as she professeth, and we believe, we can convince her in our holy fellowship, upon her serious promise of future better advisedness and caution, and acknowledging that she is indeed sorrowful for her rashness herein.

With tearful eyes, Mary Sibly sorrowfully assented to the statement which was read to the church and accepted by the brethren in satisfaction of her sin.[78]

The witchcraft persecution haunted the memories of the residents of Salem for a long time. Five members of the church withdrew in protest against Parris's part in the trials. Finally, two years after the dissatisfied brethren had been brought to trial for their withdrawals, Parris extended to them an olive branch. "I do humbly own this day before the Lord and his people," the minister agreed to confess, "that God has been righteously spitting in my face,"[79] and in 1696 Judge Sewall, in a public confession, conceded that he might have been wrong.[80] Finally, twelve years after Parris's confession, Anne Putnam, now a young lady of twenty-seven, sought admission to full communion. This was a time when people cleared their consciences, and Anne remembered her mischievous pranks which had sent innocent persons to the gallows. Her confession, recorded by the pastor, is attested by her signature:

I desire to be humbled before God for that sad and humbling providence that befell my fathers family in the year about 92; I then being in my childhood should by such a providence of God be made an instrument for that accuseing of severall persons of a greivous crime whereby their lives were taken away from them, when now I have just grounds and good reasons to believe they were innocent persons, and that it was a great delusion of Satan that deceived me in that sad time, whereby I justly fear I have been instrumental with others though ignorantly and unwittingly to bring upon myself and this land the guilt of innocent blood. Though what was said as done by me against any person I can truly and uprightly say before God and man I did it not out of any anger malice or ill will to any person for I had no such thing against any of them; but what I did was ignorantly being deluded by Satan. And particularly as I was the chief instrument of accuseing Goodwife Nurse and her two Sisters I desire to lye in the dust and to be humbled for it in that I was a cause with others of so sad a calamity to them and this their familys, for which cause I desire to lye in the dust and earnestly begg forgiveness of God and from all those unto whom I have given just cause of sorrow and offence, whose relations were taken away or accused.

ANN PUTNAM [81]

Salem Village led the way in repairing some of the evil done by the churches. In 1703 the church voted that Martha Cory's excommunion "was not according to the mind of God." [82] The First Church of Salem waited until the General Court had repealed the attainder before it withdrew Sister Nurse's excommunication. While the Danvers church freely admitted its error, the Salem church was more wary. The testimony on which Sister Nurse had been convicted in court appeared "not now so Satisfactory" as before. Unable to resist the pressure of Rebeccah's son, the church voted to remove the blot from the record and prayed that "the mercifull God would pardon whatso act, Sin, Error, or Mistake" had been committed, but failed to say whose error was meant.[83] The case of Giles Cory was more difficult, for in the eyes of the church he had committed suicide. But as the church had found a basis of excommunication, it now found a basis for the repeal of the vote: shortly before his death, Giles had bitterly repented of his refusal to plead. He had, therefore, repented of his attempted suicide, and could be restored.[84]

Traces of belief in witchcraft were not eradicated at once. In 1718 a man in Milton accused his mother of witchcraft. The charge boomeranged, and the complainant was found guilty of violations of the Fifth, Sixth, and Ninth Commandments, for which he later made a confession.[85]

Witchcraft was a serious enough offense, but from the Puritan point of view, fortunetelling and spiritualism were even worse.[86] Two Boston women who patronized the services of a fortuneteller publicly confessed their fault in 1694, and the Danvers church, anxious to avoid a resurgence of allegedly diabolical intrigues, severely warned that Christians must not do business with witches, diviners, or fortunetellers. With relief the church noted, however, that none of its members had been among the superstitious who still walked the streets of Danvers.[87]

In the last chapter, we saw how the Puritans enforced the commands which were explicit or implicit in the first table of the Decalogue. The requirement of church attendance was rigidly enforced, but closely related to the demand that Christians participate in the worship of the Church were the prohibitions which were expressed or implied in the first four Commandments. That the Sabbatarianism of the Puritans survived the Revolution, especially in the western counties, is clearly shown in the censures which were imposed on church members who, whether or not they attended services, engaged in activities which were felt to be inconsistent with the sanctity of the Lord's Day. Considering that the Fourth Commandment was stretched to forbid even harmless diversions which did not interfere with the regular worship of the churches, we may well question whether the Puritans practiced Jesus's teaching that the Sabbath was made for man, rather than man for the Sabbath.

The sanctity of the Church, the dignity of the pastor, and, particularly, the almost sacramental importance which was attached to the sermon tended to suppress all criticism of the churches and their ministers. Fortunately for the churches, however, censures for criticism of the church were rare in the nineteenth century, the case of David Webster being a signal exception. How the most interesting critic of early Massachusetts theology was treated will be discussed in the next chapter.

The history of witchcraft in colonial New England was fantastic. Scattered cases appeared from the middle of the seventeenth century, but the Salem hysteria of 1692 was truly phenomenal in the number of persons which it affected. Even if we recognize that witchcraft was a very real thing to the people of the seventeenth century, the procedure and judgments of the courts and churches defy any attempted justifications. When the terror had run its course, the hysteria collapsed and, save for a few isolated instances of no very great importance, witchcraft delusions died with the scapegoats of Salem.

V. "FALSE DOCTRINE, HERESY, AND SCHISM"

Heresy, the one sin which only a Christian could commit, was intolerable to the Puritan mind. Anyone might get drunk, be the parent of an illegitimate child, steal, lie, or even murder, but heresy could be committed only within the Church. Hence Jews, Muslims, and other non-Christians might be tolerated.[1] For the heretic there was but one freedom: he could leave the colony. "All Familists, Antinomians, Anabaptists, and other enthusiasts shall have free liberty to keep away from us," wrote Nathaniel Ward.[2] Like the Roman Catholics, whom they hated with twice the fervor which they displayed against the Anglicans,[3] the Puritans were certain of the righteousness of their cause and believed it to be important enough to warrant ruthless action against such as would neither conform nor leave the country. If Anglican intolerance was expressed in its insistence on uniformity of worship, Puritanism was noted for its demand of uniformity of belief. The demand of homogeneity was absolute and would brook no dissention.[4] For so mild a remark as the observation that the Roman Church was *a* (not *the)* true church, an elder of Watertown was admonished.[5] In Dorchester, the church was horrified by the prospect of the Anglican parochial system when Martha Minott presented her father for admission to the church, for he was not a Congregationalist, "but a Corruption Creepinge in as an harbenger to old england practice viz. to make all members: which god prevent in mercye." [6] Thirty years later, however, a man was admitted, "notwithstanding his opinion for Prelacy." [7]

A clear distinction must always be made between religious persecution by the colonial government and heresy trials by the churches. The civil law had its penalties for heresy, but the medieval practice, by which the state executed relapsed heretics who had been convicted by the Church, was unknown in Massachusetts, although until 1677 English statutory law permitted the state to punish heretics without reviewing the judgment of the Church. Because the Massachusetts churches could go no farther than excommunication, and since there was nothing analogous to the writ *de haeretico comburendo* in New England, temporal penalties could be inflicted only upon conviction in a civil court.[8]

Civil penalties were designed to cover almost every conceivable heresy likely to arise, except Arminiamism. Idolatry, witchcraft, and blasphemy were capital crimes; for the denial of eternal life, of the resurrection of the body, of the efficacy of the Atonement, of the morality of the Fourth Commandment, and of the validity of infant baptism, and even for withdrawal from the Lord's Supper a person might be sentenced to banishment. The observance of Christmas by merely abstaining from work, not to mention participation in organized worship, subjected the offender to a fine of five shillings. A person who denied the canon of Scripture once could be fined fifty pounds or be subjected to corporal punishment, while a second offender was to be banished.[9]

In the light of the standards then prevalent in New England, the persecution of Anne Hutchinson is understandable. Whether this episode had a religious or political basis is still debated; [10] she was tried by the state for sedition and by the churches for heresy. No doubt the two aspects were closely interwoven, the churches and the colony acting in full cooperation. Save for the political agitation of the times, however, the affair might well have remained a family quarrel within the First Church of Boston.

It was there that it began, in 1634, when Anne Hutchinson

led a group which met at her home to discuss the minister's sermons. The clergy were outraged: who was Mrs. Hutchinson to go about with that "holier than thou" attitude? Soon the church was divided. Pastor John Wilson, Deputy Winthrop, and a few other members were arrayed against "This American Jesabel" (as Winthrop referred to her in his *Short Story*), who had the support of Governor Vane, a recent arrival who had been elected to succeed Winthrop as governor, of John Cotton, the church's associate pastor, of the Reverend John Wheelwright of Braintree, and of a majority of the members.[11]

By November, 1636, Vane had accepted Anne Hutchinson's idea of a "personal union" of the Holy Spirit and the believer. Cotton was more moderate: he believed in the "indwelling of the person of the Holy Ghost." Winthrop would have neither. He agreed that the Spirit *did* indwell, but denied that the Scripture offered a clue as to *how* he indwelled. Aware of the fact that the church by itself could do nothing, the aroused clergy induced the government to bring Mrs. Hutchinson before a committee of magistrates and clergy for a theological disputation. On January 29, 1637, a month after the men had matched wits with Mrs. Hutchinson, Wheelwright preached a fast day sermon which was not to the clergy's liking. The preacher was summoned to appear before the court, which, after a partly secret examination, asked the clergy's advice. All the ministers save Cotton were against Wheelwright, who was convicted not of heresy, for that was no crime at the time, but of sedition and contempt.[12]

Two events which occurred during the summer helped to bring about Anne Hutchinson's doom. In May the General Court elected Winthrop governor, and later that summer Vane sailed for England. In September a synod, meeting in Cambridge, condemned eighty-two errors. Among these were the teachings that covenants expressed in words were covenants of works, which separated man from Christ, and that a minister might not preach against erroneous doctrine without naming the alleged heretics. The teachings that a church must not inquire into evidence of holiness in the life of an applicant for membership, and that a member who was dissatisfied with his church's teaching might depart were likewise condemned, as was Anne Hutchinson's claim that an immediate revelation of her salvation, without respect to the Bible, was as clear to her "as the voyce of God from Heaven to *Paul.*" Cotton, formerly Anne Hutchinson's ally, changed sides, leaving Wheelwright alone among the clergy in his support of Mrs. Hutchinson.[13]

Having secured its position among the clergy, the court determined to attack the root of the difficulty. Because Boston was too unfriendly a place for the trial, the court changed the venue to Cambridge. This freed the court from the pressures of the Bostonians who sympathized with the prospective victim, and the court, still hampered by certain members who were expected to take Mrs. Hutchinson's side, purged itself of two hostile members. A third minority member could not be removed: Coddington, a friend of Vane, enjoyed too much prestige and respect to be summarily discarded. Then Wheelwright was banished, leaving his sister without her chief supporter. The trial, if it can be thus dignified, finally began. Neither indictment nor information was presented against the defendant, who, as the record implies but does not state, was convicted of sedition. Little evidence was offered by the prosecution, and defense witnesses were intimidated. Mrs. Hutchinson tried her own case brilliantly and came close to shattering the prosecution's case. But she made one fatal error: she opened a discussion on special revelation, which she claimed to have received. A lengthy and involved theological discussion followed. In the end the defendant was found guilty and sentenced to banishment. Asked of what crime she was convicted, the court replied: "Say no more, the court knows wherefore and is satisfied." The trial, according to modern standards, had been a farce. There was no distinction between the functions of judge and prosecutor. The entire proceeding was devoid of the least semblance of judicial procedure.[14]

The trial and sentence had been acts of the civil government. The church had acted only indirectly, through pressure on the colonial authorities. Now, after Mrs. Hutchinson had spent the winter in confinement at Roxbury, the church itself proceeded to act against the alleged heretic. Brought before the now thoroughly hostile body on March 15, 1638, Anne Hutchinson was charged with sixteen doctrinal errors. The alleged errors, improperly defined as "Antinomianism," defy classification. The issues involved intricate and, to modern theological minds, trivial problems of Christology, soteriology, and eschatology. The respondent's first reaction was a plea in abatement. The church, she held, could not try the case because the private steps had not been taken. Cotton overruled this objection on the ground that the church had no power to inquire into the sufficiency of the private steps unless there was "a manifest Breach." [15] Instead of inquiring into this question the church proceeded to an inquisition into the merits. The ensuing disputation had none of the marks of a judicial trial, but rather of a coercive attempt to convince the alleged heretic of her errors. Ample texts were cited by both sides and a generous amount of epithets was hurled at the respondent. Asked, "what doe we mene by the Cominge of C[hrist] J[esus]," Anne Hutchinson replied, ". . . he meanes, *his cominge to us in Union." "I looke at this Opinion to be dayngerous and damnable, and to be no lesse than Sadducisme and Athiisme,"* replied the inquisitor.[16] Some idea of the theological jargon in which the church indulged may be gleaned from this excerpt from the record:

Mr. Damphord: The Spirit is not a Third Substance, but the Bent and Inclination of the soule and all the faculties theareof. now this is not a substance differinge from the soule, and *that Spirit in Ecclesiastes is ment of the Soule,* the Spirit returns to God that gave it, that is, the Soule or substance thereof.

Mrs. Hutchinson: I doe not differ from Mr. Damphord, as he expresseth himselfe

Damphord: The Sp[irit] thear is in Thess[alonians] is as the Bias to the Soule.

Mr. Wilson: But the Quest[ion] is *whether that Spirit in Thessa-[lonians] is Immortal or* not.

Damphord: *That Word Spirit* in Ecclesiastes *is ment the Soule,* and *That* Spirit *in Thessa*[lonians] *is not the substance of the soule, but a* Qualitie of it. That soule w[hi]ch: Ch:[rist] speakes of in Mathew, He casts both soule and Body *into Hell, thear Soule is not ment spirit but soule.*[17]

This sort of talk continued for some time. Only occasionally was Anne Hutchinson the protagonist; more often the clergy indulged in the theological disputation among themselves. When the disputants had exhausted their resources, Wilson demanded a vote. But before the members could express their views, Mrs. Hutchinson's son-in-law interrupted to ask a question:

I desire to know by what Rule I am to express myselfe in my Assent or Dissent whan yet *my Mother* is not convinced. for I hope she will not shut her Eyes agaynst any light.[18]

Wilson admonished him:

Brother, you may as well make Question whether God will confesse yow before his Father w[hi]ch is in Heaven, whan yow now deny to confesse his Truth befor Men tho agaynst your owne Mother.[19]

An admonition was at last voted, not only for Anne Hutchinson, but for those who objected to this censure. John Cotton had the dubious honor of delivering the rebuke. A little beyond the halfway point the respondent interrupted to say that she had held none of the errors alleged against her before her imprisonment. Cotton continued the admonition and finally dismissed the victim with an order to return on the next lecture day.[20]

When the ordeal resumed, the allegations not previously disposed of, confusingly scrambled and altered in sequence, were read again. This time Mrs. Hutchinson was more conciliatory. She acknowledged six errors and modified her opinion on three other points. *"I confess now the Law is a*

Rule of Life," she firmly proclaimed. Anticipating such a move, the church was ready with four additional charges, including the allegation that Anne Hutchinson had denied that sanctification could be evidence of justification. "I never held any such Thing," was the respondent's collective reply to the four charges.[21]

The inquisition concluded, the church entered into a general discussion of Mrs. Hutchinson's position. They did not like it. Dudley, more outspoken than the others, held that her repentance was on paper only: it was "not in her Countenance," he observed. Shepard considered her worse than an ordinary heretic: she "never had any trew Grace in her heart," and had proved herself to be "a Notorious Impostor." Wilson thought she was the very instrument of the devil. One last interruption delayed the final vote. A "stranger" wanted to know whether the offense for which Mrs. Hutchinson was to be excommunicated was heresy or lying. If it was for the latter, he would support the motion; if it was for heresy, which she had renounced, he would need more evidence. Without a moment's hesitation Wilson ruled that the censure was for heresy. If the "stranger" was consistent, he did not raise his hand when the others voted to cast Anne Hutchinson out of the church.[22]

Precisely what particular beliefs led to the excommunication cannot be determined from the record. The various allegations were confused after the recess, and the church did not reach distinct findings on each charge. It has been suggested that the decisive factor in the civil court's judgment was the defendant's assertion that individual revelation was as definitive as Scripture (since both were indited by the Holy Spirit), because such a belief was incompatible with the safety and peace of a commonwealth as biblically oriented as Massachusetts.[23] Perhaps the safest conclusion would be to say that church and state worked in close association, without much respect for legal procedure, to safeguard the colony from the influence of a dissenter. Since the outcome of the case was decided before the trials began, it was hardly necessary to specify the exact grounds of the sentences. Hence the civil authorities, unable to try persons for heresy, convicted her of sedition. The church, which could properly censure members for doctrinal errors, followed suit and gave its blessing to the banishment by excommunicating Mrs. Hutchinson for heresy.

So far as the church was concerned, Anne Hutchinson's doom was sealed, but her influence lingered on. A Boston widow was excommunicated in 1639 for saying that Anne Hutchinson had deserved neither her banishment nor her excommunication.[24] Earlier, even before Anne Hutchinson herself was censured, two men of Roxbury were excommunicated for alleged Familism.[25] A former associate of Wheelwright, Thomas Wilson, was cast out of the church for undefined errors, but was restored in 1642.[26] The year after Wilson's restoration a Roxbury resident sought refuge in Rhode Island and was excommunicated for alleged Antinomianism, to be followed three years later by Sarah Keanye, who was cast out of the church for "irregular prophesying in mixt assemblies." [27]

The "Antinomian" trials were merely a prelude to the numerous heresy trials which took place throughout the colonial period. One of the earliest heretics other than the "Antinomians" was Francis Hutchinson, of Boston, who was excommunicated in 1641 for denying the reality of "particular congregates [congregational?] churches since the Apostacy of Ante [*sic*] Christ." Since the Boston church claimed to be a very real church and was congregational, it was to Hutchinson "a Whore, a Strumpett." [28] In the same decade, John Smith, of Barnstable, was cast out of the church for denying the validity of the church. After his return from New Netherland, whence he had gone following the sentence, he was restored.[29]

The principal theological currents of New England furnished the ground for a large number of heresy prosecutions. The entire church in Orleans fell under censure when its pastor, the Reverend Samuel Osborn, an Arminian, freely admitted excommunicate persons to full communion with his church.

Rebuked by the church in Brewster for maintaining so heretical a minister, the Orleans church sent a written confession to the neighboring church. Two weeks later Osborn was dismissed and began a teaching career in a Boston grammar school.[30] The Mattapoisett church succeeded in convincing a member of his errors, involving a combination of Arminianism and Pelagianism,[31] but the Haverhill church was less successful in dealing with Nathaniel Balch, who entertained a mixture of Arminian, Socinian, and Pelagian views. Balch was refused baptism for his child after a lengthy hearing. Two depositions, alleging that he had denied the doctrines of original sin, predestination, and regeneration, and that he had said that "Christ was not really God," were read. Were these errors important enough to justify the rejection of Balch, which would automatically preclude his child from baptism? The mere denial of original sin, the church held, was insufficient to bar his admission. The Christological question was tabled. Balch's refusal to receive portions of Scripture as divinely inspired was also held to be no bar. The real issue was Balch's denial of eternal punishment. He had denied that the unregenerate suffered eternal torment. Such a position, the church felt, might endanger the social structure and hence justified their refusal to admit him to membership.[32]

Some heresy cases were clearly related to the Great Awakening. In Reading, John and Rebecca Damon were suspended in 1749 because they "had fallen into the Depths of Enthusiasm" and had identified the Reading church with Antichrist. John had accused the churches throughout the colony of worshipping Baal and had described their ministers as "dragons." An attempt to prove that the Damons were demented was temporarily successful, but eventually the couple were suspended. After John's death in 1761, Rebecca made a confession and was restored.[33]

From the standpoint of the non-evangelical churches, the havoc which the Great Awakening created in the organized ministry was one of its most obnoxious features. The problem created by itinerant evangelists provided one of the seven issues discussed in the *Testimony* of 1743, in which the more traditional clergy denounced the revival. While an itinerant preacher was not subject to censure by any church save his own, a self-appointed evangelist within his own church was a proper subject of discipline of his church.

Take the case of George Weeks, who had started to preach to the Indians before the Great Awakening began. In 1731 the pastor of his church rebuked him privately. Later the church took notice that Weeks had "no more, if so much as barely common education," and pondered whether he ought to be censured, mentioning II Kings 17:32 as a possible text.[34] For nine years Weeks restrained himself, but in 1740, influenced by the Great Awakening, he told the pastor of his intention to resume his preaching to the Indians. Perhaps the pastor had himself been affected by the revivals. Instead of warning Weeks not to preach at all, he advised him only not to presume to preach to an English-speaking congregation, and left the decision on the Indian preaching to him, with a reminder of the sin of Uzziah.[35] Whether or not Weeks preached to the Indians is not told in the records. In 1748 or 1749[36] Weeks was gently reminded that a prostitute lived in his house and that he had been seen traveling with her and treating her and her illegitimate child with unusual tenderness. On the face of the record, there is not the slightest suggestion that Weeks was accused of any sexual immorality. Nothing more is said of Weeks.[37]

Similar vexation with a self-made preacher was shown by the anti-revivalist church in Concord. Ebenezer Townsend, one of its members, claimed that the Holy Spirit had inspired him to preach the Gospel. Townsend, however, had not been ordained and, what was more serious in the church's eyes, he had not been properly educated. His academic insufficiency was aggravated by the fact that he had had every opportunity to obtain an education. Townsend offered to go to Newbury, where he had some friends who would tutor him, and asked for a recommendation. However, once he had the document, instead of turning to studies, he continued to preach.[38]

Later in the century, an anti-Stoddardean church accused Jonathan Hinsdale, in doctrine a Stoddardean, of failing to have his child baptized, of neglecting the Lord's Supper, and of renouncing the covenant. Hinsdale would not attend the Eucharist until the church looked upon it as a converting ordinance. Persons not found guilty of a notorious crime, he held, must be admitted to the Supper, without further inquiry on the part of the church. Unless the church admitted him to full communion without asking any questions, Hinsdale would not offer his child in baptism. The church was not impressed by Hinsdale's argument and urged that he withdraw from fellowship, which Hinsdale refused to do. The church finally took the decisive step and voted that it could no longer walk in Christian fellowship with him.[39]

In contrast with the disciplinary action arising from issues created by the Great Awakening of the eighteenth century, the Great Revival of the nineteenth century claimed only one victim. In Danvers, John Osgood was excommunicated for "unchristian conduct." His only fault was that he had been an ardent revivalist.[40]

The other heretics, save some innovators in biblical interpretation, defy classification. One man was excommunicated for persisting in his denials that Baptism and the Lord's Supper should be externally observed.[41] On the eve of the Revolution a churchman of Great Barrington was restored when he confessed his sin of saying that the local church was not a true church,[42] and forty-five years afterwards a Hatfield member was admonished for claiming that God had created the devil to be his servant.[43] Properly described by his church as a "strange character" was Abraham Reed, of Kingston, who attempted to become a minister. Finding no support in the church, Reed professed to be a Baptist and delivered extemporaneous sermons which invariably failed to impress the listeners. Frustrated and defeated, Reed publicly confessed that he not only was still unregenerate, but that he had never been converted and that his past conduct had been the result of evil motives.[44] In the case of five others who were censured for heresy, the records offer no description whatsoever of the errors involved.[45]

Of all the Massachusetts heretics, save only Anne Hutchinson, none achieved such notoriety as George Bethune English, a former minister and a member of the church in Cambridge. In spite of his Harvard education, English was a miserable failure as a preacher. Frustrated in his profession, but versatile as an Orientalist, English took to the study of Torah and Talmud. Writing with a chip on his shoulder, daring anyone to defy his conclusions, and liberally plagiarizing from other works, he produced in 1813 *The Grounds of Christianity Examined by Comparing the New Testament with the Old.* English argued that Christianity was founded on Judaism and that the New Testament was founded on the Old.[46] So far he was on safe ground. But by maintaining that such Hebraic laws as could be observed without the Temple, such as the law of circumcision and the dietary regulations, were binding on Christians,[47] he reverted to a tradition discarded in the Apostolic age. Even more heretical was his argument that a dualism pervaded the New Testament, which, he contended, was dominated by the concept of two angels, the one of light, the other of darkness, created by God. By contrast, he maintained, the Old Testament was not marred by such a dualism. Satan was an angel sent by God for the punishment of evildoers.[48] The Zoroastrianism which English so blithely read into the New Testament was enough to upset any Christian theologian of whatever tradition. From a practical standpoint, however, his rejection of the theological virtues, faith, hope, and charity, as expressed in the New Testament,[49] made English anathema to the Congregationalists.

The reaction was swift. In a calm but firm reply, Samuel Cary upheld the Christian tradition against English's distortions.[50] A year later Edward Everett published a volume denouncing English's wholesale plagiarism.[51] The church, too, was aroused. A committee of five, including two Harvard professors, was dispatched to inquire whether English still adhered to his eccentric views. After eight months the committee reported that English had not recanted his statements, although he had admitted that his language had in part been unjustifiably contemptuous. English himself did not appear before the church, which excommunicated him.[52] English's later career illustrates both his versatility and his instability. While stationed in Alexandria as an officer of the Marine Corps, he was converted to Islam and joined the Egyptian army. In the Adams Administration, English became a secret agent assigned to conduct negotiations in Turkey. An expert in Semitic languages, English was able to pass as a native of the Near East. Shortly before his death he asked Adams for another assignment. The President could not accede to this request because by this time English's emotional instability bordered on insanity.[53]

Two other church members were prosecuted in the early national period for entertaining unorthodox views of the Bible. Some years before English's excommunication the church in Canton inquired into Jabin Fisher's opinion of the Scriptures. A committee reported that Fisher denied any intentional blasphemy of the Bible, but acknowledged that he might have spoken irreverently in the course of casual conversation. The explanation was accepted by the church, which voted to drop the case against the brother.[54] Four years after English incurred the wrath of his church, the churchmen of Granville took Mary Stow to task for allegedly denying that certain portions of Scripture had been inspired by God. Without much discussion the church voted to admonish the respondent and then proceeded to discuss the weightier matter of the new stove for the meetinghouse. Six months later, having obtained no satisfaction from Mary Stow, the church, after asking God's blessings on its deliberations, voted to excommunicate her.[55]

Greater in number than the heretics within the churches were the Congregationalists who left their communion to affiliate themselves with other religious groups, notably the Baptists. The records mention no less than seventy-five persons who were censured for becoming Baptists. In 1643 Lady Deborah Moody, who had denied the validity of infant baptism, was excommunicated when she left for Rhode Island.[56] Three persons who had joined the Baptists were excommunicated from the church in Plymouth in 1651;[57] another followed nineteen years later.[58]

The most important cases of this nature occurred in Charlestown. In 1658 Thomas Gould was asked why he had not been to church. He explained that another church was more agreeable to him. Had he not joined in covenant with the Charlestown church? This he could not deny, but, Gould maintained, they had cut him off from their communion at a time when he was only under admonition, and thus had placed him on a level with the Indians. Moreover, Gould asserted, the church was wrong in allowing infant baptism. The church asked how he, who denied infant baptism, could venture to partake of the Lord's Supper, since he had himself been baptized as an infant. Special grace from God took care of that discrepancy, he held. The discourse reached its climax when the pastor admonished the errant brother. Gould, however, was not swayed. He continued in his Baptist views, held secret meetings, and finally gathered a Baptist church.

In the meanwhile another Baptist, Thomas Osburn, had attracted the church's attention. In November, 1633, Osburn and his wife were admonished. Another admonition was delivered in February, 1664, at which time Gould was also rebuked. In July, 1665, the church made a last effort to reclaim the heretics, but Gould told the church that he had no intention of coming to the meeting. Osburn complained that the church erred in its acceptance of infant baptism, in its restriction of the ministry to men learned in the humanities, and in its severe discipline of dissenters. As if to prove the last point, the church excommunicated the two men on July 30. Gould eventually recanted his Anabaptist views and, in 1670, made a confession.[59]

In the year of Gould's and Osburn's excommunication, John Farnam, one of the pillars of the Second Church of Boston, was accused by his church. The records do not specify the charges, but obviously Farnam entertained Baptist opinions. He had criticized the Charlestown church for its excommunication of Gould and, by attending another church one Sunday, had offended the brethren of the Second Church. The first two meetings between Farnam and the church were unsuccessful. At the third session, Farnam abruptly turned his back on the pastor and walked out of the meetinghouse. At a later meeting, when the pastor discoursed on infant baptism, Farnam repeated his performance. Finally, at the seventh meeting, Farnam, still refusing to confess his guilt of turning his back on the church, stated the conditions on which he would join in the Lord's Supper. The church, Farnam demanded, must create the ordinance of prophecy and must remove the teacher as an officer. It must abolish infant baptism and must rebaptize all persons who had not been christened since infancy. These conditions were not acceptable to the church, and Farnam was severely warned that if he did not repent, he would be excommunicated.

On the day of the excommunication Farnam was present and reportedly enjoyed the ritual immensely. Sitting in the balcony, he smiled or laughed while the pastor read the sentence and then, exclaiming "This place is too hot for me," walked out. After eighteen years Farnam became convinced of his error. Receiving his humble confession, which was read publicly, the church restored him to its communion.[60]

No conversions to Baptist groups during the first half of the eighteenth century are found in the records. By 1751, however, people began to change denominations with startling frequency. Nowhere was this so prevalent as in the south-eastern part of the colony. Middleborough, Mattapoisett, Bridgewater, and Raynham were veritable centers of Baptist activity.[61] In the North Church of Middleborough utter confusion prevailed. Persons who had been faithful communicants for years rebaptized each other by immersion, and at least one sister of the church rebaptized another by immersion, which contrasts distinctly with the Puritan objection against baptism by women found in the Millenary Petition. In November, 1751, two men were suspended and admonished because they would not accept a pastor who rejected infant baptism, and four men and a woman were ordered to state their reasons for withdrawing from the church. They had left the fellowship not because they were Baptists, but because they disagreed with the pastor's objection to infant baptism. In the spring of 1752 Samuel and Solomon Alden, Robert Washburn, and Lydia Easton, who had been called upon to explain their withdrawal, said that they could not remain in fellowship with a church which had accepted Baptist principles. A mutual council found the objectors guilty of contempt but questioned the propriety of an admonition. The council's attempt to solve the embarrassing problem by having both sides join in a renewal of the covenant failed, and the pastor was rebuked by the council for not taking drastic disciplinary action against the anti-Baptist faction. In June the pastor's confession was accepted; in September Samuel Alden and Robert Washburn were excommunicated. Within a year, however, the church became convinced that in cases of members who had withdrawn from conscientious scruples, it "ought not to confuse them, but rather exercise forebearance towards them," and the excommunications imposed in 1751 were repealed, with an express statement that this vote was not to be construed as a repudiation of Baptist principles.[62]

The last Baptist defections in the eighteenth century occurred in Kingston, where the church appointed a committee to call on eleven habitual absentees. Several of the offending members, the committee found, had become Baptists. Seven, perhaps the Baptists, were suspended; the others returned to communion with the church. One of the suspended members was restored after ten years.[63]

In the nineteenth century, instances of conversion from the Congregational churches to the Baptists were more sporadic. The twenty-three persons, including four couples, who turned Baptist left the Congregational churches at widely different times and in scattered parts of the state.[64] Only three of these converts were formally excommunicated, in one case not so much for turning Baptist as for obnoxious conduct connected with the conversion. Samuel M. Dewey, at a public meeting, bitterly attacked the local church and urged its members to humble themselves before him and the Baptist minister.[65] The only other excommunication took place in 1831, at which time such censures were rare.[66]

Most of the churches reluctantly turned the converts over to the churches of their choice. The Reading church told James Dix that if "he could produce from the word of God, in support of his present sentiments, *command, example,* or *fair inference,* his reason would appear well-grounded, otherwise not." Dix failed to convince the church, but no further action was taken.[67] When, in 1817, David Mills asked the church in Needham to dismiss him to the Baptist church, he was refused on the grounds that no Baptist church would dismiss a member to a Congregational church and that such a dismission would imply that Mills was right and the church wrong. The significant matter, however, is that Mills was not censured: "If our brother is determined to leave us, it is well known that we have no power to restrain him. Nor would we wish to exercise such a power, if we possessed it." [68] Ten years later, the church in Windsor, confronted with a convert to a Baptist church, voted that "while we are grieved with some part of her conduct, we do not proceed against her by way of discipline, but withdraw our watch and care over her." [69]

Indicative of the rising recognition of religious liberty is a resolution adopted by the Dalton church in 1815:

When a church member leaves our Church to join any denomination of Christians not in fellowship with us and cannot be persuaded from such a step by the friendly counsels of the church,

Voted, we will not excommunicate such persons as tho immoral; but as soon as the Ch[urc]h shall obtain knowledge of such person's actual joining such Denomination, i.e. Joining their church—our ch[urc]h will then *publically* announce, that we do withdraw our covenant fellowship, and no longer consider such person or persons under our care and watch.[70]

A more extreme position was taken by the Barnstable church, which would not even withdraw from fellowship with a woman who had turned Baptist. Upon receipt of her notice that she had become a Baptist, the church voted that the convert had not forfeited her membership by misconduct and hence was entitled to partake of the Communion, should she wish to do so.[71] More logical was the policy of the church in Rochester, which, to keep members from joining the Baptists, voted to administer baptism by immersion when desired.[72]

The Quakers, against whom so much legislation was enacted, are rarely mentioned in the church records. The first Quakers came to Massachusetts as missionaries and hence, not being church members, were not subject to church discipline. In 1657, the year after the first Quaker missionaries arrived, Plymouth enacted severe statutes aimed at their exclusion. All Quaker literature was ordered to be seized by a statute of 1659, and in 1661 Quakers "and such like vagabonds" were to receive fifteen stripes for illegal entry into the colony.[73] The Massachusetts laws were even more severe. A resident who entertained a Quaker was to pay a fine of forty pounds per hour of entertainment, while the importer of a Quaker was to be fined a hundred pounds and to be held liable for his free return. The mere possession of Quaker literature entailed a fine.[74] Between 1653 and 1661, six Quakers went to the gallows for their refusal to stay away from the colony, and when Charles II, in 1662, ordered all Quaker trials removed to England, the colony substituted the whip for the gallows. In spite of an order to cease the infliction of corporal punishment, Quakers were subjected to such torture until 1677.[75] Not until 1724 was the last remaining anti-Quaker legislation disallowed by the Privy Council.[76]

In the light of the anti-Quaker hysteria, it is surprising that any Puritan turned to the Quaker faith. With one exception [77] the conversions occurred in Salem, where seven church members joined the Quaker faith between 1662 and 1703. Four men were excommunicated; in the other cases no further record is found.[78]

The Church of England, despised for political as well as religious reasons, had little chance to win converts from Congregationalism. The classic case of John Lyford did not involve a conversion. Lyford arrived in Plymouth early in 1623 and became a respected preacher. Before long he conspired with John Oldham to introduce Anglican practices and openly rebelled against the colonial government. Severely rebuked, Lyford made a convincing and moving confession and resumed his preaching in Plymouth, Hull, Gloucester, and Salem. But Lyford had deceived both government and church. In a letter to England he bitterly denounced the Plymouth churches. Banished from the colony, he went to Nantucket and, when in turn banished from the island, to Virginia, where he could practice his Anglicanism without fear of censure.[79]

The first recorded conversion from Puritanism to Anglicanism took place in Sutton, where the church had difficulties with Samuel Dudley, a justice of the peace, who failed to present letters of dismission and recommendation from the church in Littleton. To save the church trouble, Dudley promised not to join in the Lord's Supper, but when the Eucharist was administered he presented himself. Investigating Dudley's past, the church found that he had been convicted by a court of profanity. Was he censurable? An intricate problem of jurisdiction was before the church, Dudley's membership being in doubt. Dudley saved the church the trouble of deciding the issue by joining the Anglican communion.[80]

A decade after Dudley's conversion, David Tilden, of Canton, absented himself from the Puritan church in order to worship with the Anglicans. The Congregational minister naively informed the Anglican clergyman that Tilden had not been dismissed, but the priest cared little whether Tilden had the Congregationalists' permission to become an Episcopalian; he had already become one. Recording the vote of excommunication, the pastor logically commented: "So that as he went out from us, we have shut him out." When Mrs. Tilden turned Anglican in 1751, the pastor asked the church what it wished him to do. The church could not have cared less and would not even discuss the subject. Six years later, when Mrs. Tilden asked for the privilege of occasional communion, the church, anticipating the ecumenical movement, readily concurred.[81]

The growing tolerance of the Puritans is best shown in their treatment of converts to Methodism, which became an independent movement only after the Revolution. Only six of the twenty-four converts to Methodism were formally excommunicated. Three of them were censured by the same church which excommunicated a couple for becoming Baptists eighty years after any other church in Massachusetts imposed a censure for such a cause. But possibly Emiline O'Brien and Betsey Miller asked for this sentence when they demanded their dismissions in an arrogant letter to the pastor.[82] Two men, excommunicated by the Otis church, subsequently made confessions and were restored.[83] Four others found that Methodism was not what they had expected and returned to the Congregational churches whence they had gone out to the Methodists.[84]

Votes that the church's watch and care over the convert was withdrawn or outright dismissions were the rule in the majority of cases. In Barnstable, the East Church, having summoned Mrs. Clarissa Matthews to answer for some offense, found that she had joined the Methodist society before the commission of the act and had, by her conversion, given up her membership in the East Church.[85] Eight converts received dismissions. The only case worth noting is that of Joshua Bartlett, of Otis. In addition to charges of unchristian conduct towards one man, unbecoming language toward another, and profane expression in the presence of a third, Bartlett was accused of first deriding the local Methodist society and later joining the denomination. On the following Sunday, the pastor publicly read a protest against the dismissal of the charges, and the church, fearful that more members might become Methodists, voted that its action should not be construed as a precedent.[86]

Universalism, like Methodism, was a late development. Unlike the latter, however, it did not spring from the hated Anglican tradition, but from that of English dissent. In the colonies, Universalism received a strong Unitarian bent, with the result that at the time of the Unitarian "departure" some orthodox Congregational churches became Universalist. The most striking fact about the converts from Congregationalism to Universalism is that eleven of the twelve persons dealt with for joining the new denomination were men. Rather belatedly a single woman was excommunicated for embracing Universalist doctrines.[87]

One of the converts who was excommunicated claimed that he had received special revelations, but no such assertions were made by the others who were cast out of the churches for Universalism.[88] One convert recanted before the excommunication was voted, while another prosecution was discontinued by the vote of the church.[89] A member of the church in Reading who attempted to introduce a Universalist preacher at a celebration of the Lord's Supper was severely rebuked by his church. The respondent tried in vain to convince the church that it had been a coincidence that he had brought the preacher to the church on a Sunday at which the Eucharist was administered, and was finally excommunicated.[90] A curious twist on an old theme was the basis of James Foster's excommunication from the First Church of Rochester. Absence from the Lord's Supper, but not from other services, was a common offense. Foster varied this by absenting himself from all services except when the Supper was celebrated. Why this convert to Universalism insisted on receiving the ordinance in the First Church is not stated.[91] In another town, a minister who had requested a professed Universalist to withdraw from the Supper received a vote of confidence from his church, but no action against the offender is indicated.[92]

The only case involving a Unitarian found in the records of a church which remained Trinitarian occurred in South Hadley, where a man of "avowed Unitarian sentiments" was excommunicated.[93] The reverse situation occurred in Billerica, where two women remained Trinitarian in a Unitarian church. More liberal than the orthodox church in South Hadley, the Billerica Unitarians dismissed the women to a Trinitarian church.[94]

At least one disciplinary case concerning a Shaker is found in the Massachusetts church records. Only a decade after Mother Ann Lee's arrival in the colonies, a member of the Peru church was charged with disorderly conduct on the Lord's Day: she had attended a Shaker meeting. Called before the church to account for his conduct, the offender made a confession which was rejected in view of a report of sexual immorality. After three years he was formally admonished, but further action was obviated when he moved to New York State.[95]

Five women and three men were excommunicated in South Hadley for joining an unspecified sect. In one case, the church, through its minister, sent a lengthy letter to admonish the offending sisters:

Instead of walking with its [the church's] members in christian love, you have withdrawn from them, reviling them as children of darkness, and of the devil. In addition to all this you have formally joined yourselves to a sect that have fellowship with no church—a sect which like Israel in the days of its worst idolatry "are without the true God and without a teaching Priest and without law" . . . and rely with the utmost confidence upon the teaching of a man, who has no authority to preach, who can show no credentials of a religious or moral character, but who if report is true has been convicted of the breach of the Seventh Commandment and who has for years been living in a voluntary separation from his wife and children, and who gives no evidence of repentance or reformation.[96]

If the pastor thought that he could induce the sisters to repent, he was mistaken. Instead of the desired confession, the letter brought forth this vituperative reply:

I must confess I was astonished that you should make so many incorrect statements as I find in your letter. . . . I do entreat you for your own good to be careful (it will never hurt me) but I see the awful danger you are in—touch not mine anointed and do my Prophets no harm—I tell you the truth before God and lie not. . . . What you have stated about the family is false. . . .

I would ask you where you are and how much of the spirit of God you have whether you have anything more than the form of godliness. When I turn my eyes toward you it looks like midnight darkness while the candle of the Lord shines upon us many a time when thinking over and seeing your situation. I have been led . . . to adopt our Saviour's language would you had known even now the things that belong to your peace, but dreadful as it is they will soon be hid from the eyes that will not humble themselves and come out and separate themselves and touch not the unclean things.

You have . . . the mark of the beast upon you—none but those that are truly honest before God will be delivered. . . . I will say I have obeyed God, he commanded me to come out and be ye separate and touch not the unclean thing and I will receive you and he has received owned and blessed me beyond anything I ever experienced before and has restored unto me the joys of his salvation and upholds me with his free spirit. . . . Yes I feel the Spirit of my dear Jesus resting upon me He has permitted me to sit at his feet and learn of him—as to my brother Jacob he takes no notice of your false accusations of him but says poor man he has got to meet me before Jesus, as for us we know the Lord is on our side and if the Lord be for us who can be against us,

ABIGAIL ALVORD

We may be sure that with their newly gained self-assurance, the sisters were not especially worried about the excommunication which they incurred.[97]

While we have no clue as to the sect to which the Alvord sisters joined themselves, we know of two women in Framingham who became members of the New Jerusalem Church. Claiming that they had received "sacred oracles," Anne and Chloe Haven asked their church for a dismission. The Framingham church was more liberal than that in South Hadley. Because "every persons [*sic*] ought to be indulged with liberty of conscience," the sisters were dismissed with the warning that their views were "extremely novel and erroneous," and that the New Jerusalem Church existed "only in the imagination of that great enthusiast—Sweden boxing [*sic!*] and that of his deluded followers." [98]

The records of the other conversions to sects and cults fail to indicate the nature of the group involved. The attitude of the churches from which the converts withdrew varied considerably. In 1659 the Lincoln church voted that although Benjamin Brown's withdrawal was unjustified, they would welcome him at the Lord's Supper, should he present himself,[99] and in 1772 the Reading church gave three women liberty to join another religious body.[100] The church in Rochester matter-of-factly voted that two sisters were no longer members because they had joined another communion. The sisters had left the church voluntarily and could hardly be members of two churches. The former church therefore did nothing but to change their *de facto* condition into a *de jure* status, without placing the converts under the opprobrium of an excommunication.[101] The Plymouth church, "having respect to the rights of conscience, and disposed to treat with tenderness those whom they considered under the influence of error, prepossession, and prejudice," allowed two women to join a sect.[102] On the other hand, as late as 1833 the Westminister church excommunicated two converts to sectarian bodies.[103]

Cases of persons who professed to be atheists are rarely encountered in the records. The earliest such case resulted in the excommunication of a man who had denounced the churches as idolatrous synagogues of Satan.[104] Between 1750 and 1755 fifteen persons left the church in Westfield without joining another group or stating a reason. Three were ultimately restored; six were excommunicated, and of the other six there is no further record.[105]

"Atheism" was still considered a quasi-heresy after the Revolution. A lieutenant who had been exposed to French deistic influences was suspended because he was reported to have said: "No, nor I never [*sic*] intend to have any more concern with the church than with the devil." The officer, a rugged individualist, asserted that he would answer for his own deeds; if he went to hell, it was none of the church's business. If he had said anything of which the church disapproved, it was likewise none of their business: he had a right to say what he pleased, and he would exercise that right.[106] The Danvers church excommunicated a man in 1808, for "principles bordering upon atheism." [107] An individualist, who refused to attend services but allowed that private prayer was an important duty, was excommunicated in 1805.[108] On the other hand, a Peru couple who withdrew from the church without advising it of their intention to leave were reprimanded in 1810, but there is no record of any formal censure.[109]

While heresy is a belief which is not in accordance with orthodox doctrine, schism undermines church order and polity. Although a schism need not involve an issue of faith, it is, from a practical standpoint, as great a threat to the prosperity of a church as is heresy. The Puritan churches were constantly in danger of division and hence were on guard against factions and divisive influences.

In the fall of 1667 a group of communicants of the First Church of Boston met to organize the Old South, or Third, Church. The immediate cause of the dissention was the issuance, by the First Church, of a call to the Reverend John Davenport, of New Haven. The dissenters opposed the call on the ground that it might divide the New Haven church. Moreover, they argued that Davenport had not given another candidate, who had also been called, a chance to reply. There was considerable truth in the contention that Davenport's dismission had been irregular. On October 8, Davenport had expressed an inclination to accept the call, but seeing the impending schism in Boston, he modified his position and stated that he doubted whether a majority of the Boston church had approved the call. He would visit Boston and find out for himself.[110]

In Boston, meanwhile, the dissenters were severely rebuked, although the elders refused to accede to the demand for an admonition. After a peaceful interim, the dissenters, on May 2, 1668, asked for a council, and six weeks later Davenport observed in a prayer that "Satan hath a great hand" in the opposition. The council, which convened on August 6, urged that love should always prevail. If the dissenters would not concur in Davenport's call, they should be dismissed to another church. Twenty-nine of the aggrieved brethren asked for dismissals, but two months elapsed before the church, on October 1, turned down the request, informing the petitioners that this was no time to seek a dismission.[111]

While the dissenters were awaiting the answer to their request, messengers of the Boston church went to New Haven to obtain a formal dismission for Davenport. The agents returned with a report that the New Haven church had refused to dismiss him. Later, however a letter from the Connecticut body was read to the First Church, ostensibly removing all bars to Davenport's ordination at Boston, which was to take place on December 9. This required the participation of delegates from neighboring churches, but when the ordination day arrived, the elder announced that he had overlooked one detail: no representatives from other churches had been invited. The elder's memory had not been faulty; it was a part of a carefully devised scheme. By postponing the vote to request churches to send delegates, the leaders of the Davenport faction were assured that the dissenters could not object in time. Invitations were hurriedly dispatched and brought delegates from friendly churches, who joined in ordaining Davenport to the Boston pastorate.[112]

On January 6, the dissenters announced that they were willing to overlook the incident, provided they were given dismissions. In reply the First Church accused two of the opponents of fomenting strife. Some weeks later, when Davenport invited all, including the dissenters, to participate in the Lord's Supper, the militant minority was quick to see the snare. If they partook of the Supper, they signified their agreement to Davenport's call and forfeited their claims to dismissions. Cautious and wary of such a subterfuge, they wrote a letter to the church, explaining that they would not partake. When the Supper was held, however, the dissenters participated in the ordinance. Once more they asked the church for dismissions, their claim weakened by their participation in the Supper. The request was refused. Other requests were made: that the church call a meeting, that they promise dismissions as soon as the dissenters could erect a meetinghouse, and that the church join in a mutual council. All petitions were denied, without a word of explanation.[113]

Seeing that it was futile to deal further with the church, the dissenters turned elsewhere. To the governor and council went a petition asking for an order that they be dismissed, and for permission to gather a new church. To the churches of Lynn, Salem, and Ipswich went requests for an ex-parte council. Davenport, infuriated by these devolopments, forsook his conciliatory attitude and quickly called a meeting at which he preferred charges against the dissenters, some of whom had less than twenty-four hours' warning.[114]

The ex-parte council met on April 13, 1669. Because church and council were not on speaking terms, all communications were in writing. Four letters were carried back and forth that day. In the first, the council expressed its desire to meet with the church. The church intimated that the desire was not mutual. Again the council asked to meet with the church. "I doe not see that you are an orderly Councill," replied the church.[115]

On the fourteenth, councils of war were held by both groups. The church, assembled in the Town Hall behind locked doors, wanted to remain undisturbed while it deliberated the fate of the dissenters. The men were therefore understandably annoyed when they heard a knock on the door, and sent a man to see who wanted entry. It was Richard Mather and three others, with a letter from the council. "Tell them we desire to be in private and not disturbed," Davenport instructed. The door was locked again, and the messengers stood outside until a kindly member went to fetch some chairs. Church members, late arrivals at the meeting, found the doors locked and said: "let us go home againe." After a long wait the door was opened far enough to enable the messengers outside to hand the letter to a messenger inside. After first voting not to read the communication, the church reversed itself. Having read the message, which reiterated the earlier requests for a joint meeting, the church voted to disregard the letter. By this time the air in the Town Hall was getting stale. The weary members finally voted to censure the opposition for hindering the ordination of Mr. Davenport. Moreover, the dissenters were also convicted of receiving the Lord's Supper after having absented themselves from an earlier administration of the ordinance.[116]

The council sided with the minority of the church. Reaffirming the decision of the first council, it ruled that the dissenters might unite with another church, the First Church's refusal to dismiss them notwithstanding. One of the councillors, the Reverend John Allin of Dedham, wrote a protest in Thomistic fashion, complete with questions, answers, objections, and answers to the objections. And the dissenters proclaimed: "We shall remain steadfast."[117] The church took ample time to act on the result of the council, Allin's scholastic paper, and the dissenters' proclamation. On May 4 the dissenters were declared to be "under great guilt." Undaunted, the latter produced a document, signed by seven magistrates, permitting them to gather a separate church. A week later, however, Governor Bellingham and five other magistrates issued a statement opposing such a move.[118]

The denouement came on June 17. Some of the brethren of the First Church declared that portions of the letter allegedly clearing the way for Davenport's ordination in Boston had been suppressed. The omitted parts left considerable doubt concerning the New Haven Church's willingness to part with its pastor. The minister himself was cleared of guilt, but later confessed that he had known of the suppressed part. No action was taken by the church, but a group of ministers bore testimony against the fraud and expressed their disapproval of the action of the three elders who had conspired to suppress the embarrassing part of the letter. By this time, the dissenters had embodied themselves into the Third Church. The magistrates added their blessing; the deputies nonconcurred. But for the dissenters the case had a happy ending, for the civil barriers, raised by the deputies, were finally removed.[119]

Salem's major schism broke out in 1734, when the church dismissed the Reverend John Fiske, its pastor since 1718. Fiske and a few followers organized a separatist church. When the remnant of the First Church proceeded to the ordination of a new minister, the Fiske group, considering themselves the First Church, protested. The First Church retaliated by excommunicating the schismatics. A council called by the schismatic body decided that the First Church should lose its fellowship with the other churches for its obstinacy. A deacon of the Fiske faction initiated a slow return of some schismatics to the First Church, and a settlement was eventually reached. Under its terms, the First Church retained its name; the schismatics were to be known as the Tabernacle Church. The plate was to be equally divided. At the last minute, the secessionists demanded five acres of improved land and the equivalent of a deacon's marsh, which the First Church reluctantly agreed to transfer to the Tabernacle Church.[120]

The first of several schisms resulting from the Great Awakening began when the Concord church decided to dismiss its minister, John Whiting, who had been in office since 1712. Dismissed in 1737, Whiting was also suspended from the communion in 1739. Three of the brethren who had a strong dislike for Whiting's successor, the Reverend Daniel Bliss, absented themselves from the church and were charged with violations of covenant obligations. In the summer of 1741 the issue was referred to a mutual council. A fifteen-count information was presented by the Whiting faction. In addition to accusing Bliss of misconduct towards several members, they charged that Bliss had acted as an itinerant preacher, had encouraged laymen to preach, was of the New Lights, and held questionable doctrinal beliefs. The complainants asserted that Bliss had denied that the sacraments were seals of covenanted grace. An Edwardean, he had said that elect persons would go to heaven, however wicked their conduct might have been, while good persons who were not of the elect would go to hell. And Bliss had come close to communism by allegedly saying "that it was as great a sin for a Man to get an Estate by honest Labour if he had not a single Aim at the Glory of God, as to get it by gaming at Cards and Dice." One error was by nc means Calvinistic: Bliss allegedly had said that Christ was a deceiver.[121]

In reply to the charge of abuse, Bliss asked for a bill of particulars and asserted that the doctrinal charges were false: "I am so far from denying the Covenant of Grace, that all my Hopes for Eternal Life are founded on it." Sacraments were signs of God's purpose, but not to particular persons. He categorically denied ever having made the remark concerning gambling. The very suggestion that he encouraged people to think of Christ as a deceiver was slanderous. He had never preached in another man's church except by invitation. The one count in the information which Bliss did not deny concerned the matter of predestination and election. To this he only demurred. He had said it and would say it again. He had only spoken the truth.[122]

The council, after taking testimony and hearing arguments on both sides, acquitted Bliss on seven of the fifteen counts. The record ends abruptly, but we may assume that Bliss was acquitted on the remaining eight counts as well, for the aggrieved brethren, joined by some others, demanded another council. With remarkable patience, Bliss and his church consented to join in another council, which met in June, 1743, only to adjourn until September, when it met on four consecutive days. The result, issued on September 20, was a masterpiece of ambiguity. Bliss's theology, the council held, was in agreement with Scripture, but his utterances were so indistinct that they might well have given rise to doubt. The statement on predestination, however, was condemned as unsuitable, and that on wealth was "unwarrantable and of dangerous Tendency," but the council was satisfied that Bliss had not meant what he had said. His homily on election was very bad, but this, too, could be overlooked in view of the fact that it had been clarified on the following Sunday. His exegesis was unusual but not untenable. He had been injudicious in accepting preaching engagements but had done no wrong. The one unambiguous conclusion was that Bliss had not said that Christ was a deceiver. The dissenters were advised to return to their duty; those who had been suspended should be restored. Bliss was advised to make a confession and, above all else, to devote more time to the study of Scripture and doctrine, and not to attempt perplexing discourses on matters which he did not understand.[123]

The Concord schism was only one of several which vexed the Massachusetts churches in the 1740's. In 1741, thirty-two members of the Second Church of Boston asked to be dismissed to form a new church, and their request was granted.[124] Two years later the churches in Chelmsford and Hull were torn by schism.[125] In Chelmsford it was a Connecticut lawyer and lay preacher who atagonized the church. The hostility of the church was increased when other New Light evangelists, one of them illiterate, snared the members away from the church to their own meetings. Four women and two men eventually were restored, but three others, who decided that the pastor in Concord was more enlightening and edifying, were suspended. One repented a year later; the others remained suspended until 1772, when they submitted confessions.[126] Later in the decade the First Church of Sutton was torn by a schism whose influence continued until 1791. Twenty-four men and fourteen women withdrew to form a separatist church. The two religious groups exchanged sentences of excommunication, but six men and five women were eventually restored, in some cases twenty-five years after their withdrawal. Little was done to censure the others until a new pastor arrived in 1791. Under the influence of the new minister the church became impressed "with a sense of the importance of regularity in its members, and the absolute necessity of Gospel discipline," and voted that the last step in discipline had become "indispensably necessary."[127] The final schism of the decade took place in Westfield, where Jedediah Dewey was excommunicated for forming a separatist society of which he was the self-appointed pastor.[128]

A willful and obstinate pastor could easily divide his church. In Barre, the Reverend Thomas Frink, installed in 1753, made himself thoroughly unpopular in the eyes of his parishoners. He arbitrarily told two members to withdraw from the communion and organized an inquisition into the private affairs of a third. In his conversation, Frink indulged in abusive language and spoke contemptuously of his colleagues. At meetings he was overbearing and arbitrary, refusing the floor to members whom he did not like and failing to obey the rules of procedure. Such a minister invariably will find himself at odds with his people, and Frink was no exception. Unable to tolerate Frink's abuses, the members appealed to a council which convicted Frink on nine of the ten counts preferred against him; the one count on which he was acquitted had alleged negligence in catechizing. Although dismissed and without a church, Frink was not without followers. Continuing to style himself as the duly settled minister of Barre, Frink haughtily rejected a protest sent by the church. Soon his adherents found that life was pleasanter without Frink's meddling and returned to the church, which welcomed them back. Soon thereafter, and to the rejoicing of the church, Frink left Barre.[129]

The last schism of the colonial period again involved the First Church of Salem. In 1772 the church dismissed the Reverend Thomas Barnard and called Asa Dunbar to its pastorate. Although the vote had been fifteen to eight in favor of Dunbar, some fifty-two members disagreed with the choice. In a letter to the church, the dissatisfied brethren asked to be dismissed to form a new church. After weighing the possibility of disciplining the would-be secessionists, the church reluctantly consented and turned five-twelfths of its property over to the new group, which named Barnard as its first minister. If there were hard feelings, the records do not show it.[130]

Feelings were less cordial in Pittsfield, where the First Church, in 1808, was confronted with a movement to create a competing religious society, the Union Parish. The very act of signing a petition for the creation of that body was held to be offensive. In February, 1810, ten separatists were admonished to repent lest they be excommunicated. Thirteen excommunications were voted in September. The success of this move was phenomenal. By April, 1811, all thirteen excommunicates had made confessions and were restored, although the church wished that the acknowledgments had been more precise. Twenty-one others, all women, who apparently had withdrawn from the First Church, but who evidently had not been formally censured, made confessions. Only one man could not be swayed. Asked, after his excommunication, whether he considered himself in any relation to the church, or had any regrets, this brother, cocksure of his position, replied: "By no means." [131]

VI. Domestic and Marital Relations

God did not think it good for Adam to be alone. He therefore gave him Eve, according to biblical tradition, and together they formed the first family, an institution which has existed ever since. Marriage, the basis of family life, has always been recognized by the Church as not only a tolerable and necessary institution, but as one endowed with special sanctity. An occasional heretic, such as Marcion, might object to it, but the Puritans were not Marcionites. Nor did they accept the double standard of Roman Catholicism, according to which marriage was good but celibacy better. The suggestion that Puritanism was sexually ascetic, differing from monasticism in degree only,[1] is not supported by the evidence. Calvin encouraged marriage not only as the means to beget offspring, but as a morally proper and good remedy for incontinence. A good biblicist, he had no difficulty reconciling marriage with Scripture, but found it more difficult to support his inclination toward monogamy with the Old Testament, to which Calvin turned so often in search of guidance. He finally fell back on the story that God had given Adam only one wife.[2] The New England Puritans, influenced by Dutch practices, by Hebraic tradition, and by Calvin, considered marriage a civil matter endowed with a sacred character.[3] Implied in the contract was the divinely imposed obligation to love one's spouse. It was a love commanded by will and based on reason, more often the effect of the marriage than its cause. Moreover, marital love was inferior to the love of God and hence affections must be controlled even in love letters. But the Puritans "knew how to laugh and . . . knew how to love." [4]

Although common law did not require parental consent to the marriage of a boy of fourteen or a girl of twelve, the Puritans required such consent, but the governor could override the parents' refusal to grant it.[5] However important parental control, sometimes supported by the invocation of the Fifth Commandment, might be, it was not absolute, for no good Puritan could neglect the proper wishes of his children,[6] and the consent of the parties was as essential as parental agreement.[7] The actual marriage consisted of two parts, spousals and the solemnization. Spousals, analogous to our betrothals, might be *de futuro* or *de praesenti;* in the former case they could be broken for cause.[8] In England even clandestine spousals *de praesenti* were valid,[9] and Robert Browne considered the spousals to be covenants. Cartwright and Perkins advocated open betrothals *de praesenti,* witnessed by a minister and two elders. These were to be followed by the publication of the banns, after which the marriage, already covenanted in the spousals, was to be solemnized in church.[10]

The fact that three prominent English Puritans considered spousals to be valid marriages failed to deter the church in Framingham from ruling to the contrary. In 1795 Mary Palmer was suspected of premarital sexual relations. In a letter she claimed that she was validly married, but admitted that she had disregarded the required "formalities of law" and could not disclose the identity of the official who had solemnized the marriage without exposing him to punishment, which she would not do. The explanation was rejected. The church held that Mary Palmer could not be considered a married woman unless she was able to produce a certificate. Until that time she was suspended.[11] A dubious marriage is also found in the Charlemont records, but unfortunately there is little information as to its nature. A couple, propounded for admission, confessed fornication. The marriage itself was then questioned on biblical grounds. Unwilling to condemn it, but evidently equally unwilling to condone it, the church voted that it was not "satisfied that such marriages are allowable by scripture." Final decision was deferred until a council could offer advice. The result is not available, but two years afterward the church voted that the nature of the marriage was no bar to their admission to full communion.[12]

Incest appears only rarely in church and court records. Six civil cases, none of which are paralleled in the church records, have been found.[13] The earliest church case involving incest is that of Josiah Owen, of Quincy. In 1690 a group of soldiers were en route to Canada when smallpox appeared on board ship. Six died, four of whom, including Josiah's brother Ebenezer, were thrown overboard off Cape Ann. Josiah then proceeded to marry the deceased's widow. Having violated the law,[14] he fled the jurisdiction, only to be surprised one day when the pastor and two lay members called at his cottage. Refusing to appear before the church, Owen was excommunicated as an "impenitent, scandalous, wicked, incestuous sinner."[15] A man publicly confessed incest in 1716,[16] and two women made similar confessions in the 1780's.[17] In 1798 Job Northrop, of Lenox, was found guilty of incest with his daughter and was excommunicated because he had refused to give satisfaction *before* the trial but after the complaint was filed.[18] One woman may have had a child by her deceased sister's husband in 1740 but, because of insufficient evidence concerning the child's paternity, was restored on a confession of fornication only.[19] The Plymouth church refused to rule on the validity of a marriage with a deceased niece's husband,[20] and by 1794 there was some doubt concerning the illegality of a marriage with a deceased brother's spouse, for the Charlemont church was unable to rule on the propriety of such a marriage. The church concluded that such marriages were inexpedient and held that persons so married could not *thereafter* be admitted to membership.[21]

A church member who married a person not acceptable to the church might become subject to its discipline. The law might permit the marriage; the church would not. In 1658

Christopher Winter was charged in two counts. Previously warned against marrying the scandalous Mrs. Cooper, a woman who was "vaine, light, proud . . . and much given to scoffing," he had married her in spite of all. The second count alleged that he had married secretly and had pretended that there had been no marriage. Convicted by the church on both counts, Winter was excommunicated.[22] More than a century later the church in Great Barrington heard a man confess that he had married a woman of "unchristian character." [23]

The *cause célèbre* of this nature was that of Livinia Deane, of Stockbridge. Youthful, attractive, widowed, and rather wealthy, Livinia had fallen in love with Stockbridge's well-mannered and pleasant schoolteacher, John Fisk. Fisk had been a commissioned officer in the Revolution and had displayed bravery in action. Unfortunately his vocabulary included some expressions which were not countenanced by the church. He had been overheard saying "I swear" and "damn it" in the wrong context. When he learned of the church's objection to the intended marriage, Fisk, according to the sources, may even have considered shooting the pastor and a deacon or two, but whatever ideas he may have entertained, he committed no overt act. In January, 1777, the church opposed the intended union, holding that it was intolerable that church members should marry "profane or immoral persons." A committee was sent to inform Livinia of the decision; another group was instructed to investigate her beau's morals. The latter body reported that Fisk conceded that he had sometimes used unsuitable language. Again the church voted against the marriage. On the last day of February, however, the church noted with alarm that the marriage had taken place. Livinia was suspended and, as if to stress the point, the church voted once more that its members might not marry "immoral or profane" persons. Ten days later the unrepentant Livinia was excommunicated.[24]

After a delay of two years Livinia Fisk took the issue to a council, which convened on May 10, 1779. Three questions were before the advisory body. Was it lawful for members to marry "profane and immoral" persons? Was John Fisk such a person? Had the church proceeded regularly in excommunicating Mrs. Fisk? The Reverend Doctor Joseph Huntington, of Coventry, who thought that Mrs. Fisk had been shamefully abused, pleaded eloquently for the excommunicate woman. He readily conceded that Fisk's profanity was censurable, but argued that no law of God forbade a Christian to marry a person outside the church.[25]

> If the members of this church may not marry, until they find partners that have nothing in their hearts, or lives, that grace disapproves of, I apprehend marriages will not be very frequent among them. . . .
>
> But we hear, that the affections of a gracious and wicked person, if married together, cannot unite in any common interest: And is it indeed so! Cannot they unite, in loving their children and friends? Cannot such unite, in one common interest, in all things of a temporal kind?—They may, indeed, in every thing that pertains to this world; and marriage, like all other blessings of common Providence, is for this world only,—Marriage has nothing of a spiritual nature in it, but is merely a civil, social connection and relation.[26]

The Connecticut divine held that saving grace was not essential to the marriage relationship: heathen had married heathen for centuries. The gravamen of the argument, however, was the utter absurdity of requiring Mrs. Fisk to make a confession and then permitting her to remain in the offensive relationship. Marriage was a continuing state, and if it was sinful to marry a heathen or a profane person, then surely it must be sinful to remain married to such a spouse.[27]

In his plea Huntington preached a parable. Once there was man, Sophron, who had fallen in love with Clarissa. Because the woman did not meet the church's standards, Sophron was advised to marry the eminently saintly Cornicula, of whose piety there could be no doubt. That Cornicula was devoid of all feminine charm did not matter, the church told Sophron, for "Marriage is all holy and spiritual; grace marries grace, holiness weds holiness, and the less there is in either party to allure natural passions and carnal desires, so much the better." Sophron called on Cornicula: "He entered the door; she nodded; he started back! she looked at him, and grinned horribly a ghastly smile!" Making a determined effort to concentrate on Cornicula's spiritual graces, Sophron "fell into a swoon." Then and there he put Cornicula out of his mind and returned to his beloved Clarissa. Unable to marry her, he merely lived with her in her house, in an intimate friendship, until their predicament was such that "they both knew that the word of GOD expressly commanded them to marry each other." Even then the church would not see the light and excommunicated Sophron, who was treated with contempt and disdain, although the people of the town unanimously agreed that Sophron might still be their leading citizen, renowned for his piety and virtue—had it not been for Clarissa.[28]

Stephen West, the noted pastor of Stockbridge, presented the church's argument. In the early Church, he contended, intermarriage was illegal. Briefly mentioning Cain's murder of Abel, and quickly passing over it, West argued that there had been no violence in the world until Cain and Seth chose the wrong mates. Marriage was a civil matter, he agreed, but it concerned Christian character. In answer to Huntington's point concerning the nature of the marriage relationship, West urged that the continuance of the marriage would not prolong the sin. The interests of religion forbade the union in the first place, but the same interests demanded the continuance of the marriage, once it was entered into, for its dissolution would be sinful.[29]

The council reached an absurd decision. It held that members could not marry immoral or profane persons, but declined to say whether "gracious persons may lawfully join in marriage with graceless persons, not only immoral and profane." In October the council reconvened to examine the evidence. Fisk was held to be immoral and profane; the church and its pastor were complimented for their "admirable Christian spirit." But again the council evaded the real issue. The cause was remanded to the church with the suggestion that another hearing be held on the merits.[30] The church waited for Mrs. Fisk to take the initiative in November. After a long hearing, a motion to remove the censure was defeated by a large majority.[31]

Although Huntington lost his case, the civil status of marriage was generally accepted. Marriage being a civil contract, it could also be dissolved by the civil authorities, and between 1639 and 1692 no less than forty petitions for divorce were entertained by the courts, chiefly on the ground of desertion with adultery or remarriage.[32] Puritan thought on divorce was the most liberal of the time. Milton, considering divorce "a law of moral equity," added indisposition, incompatability, and contrariety of mind to desertion, cruelty, long absence, and adultery, which Perkins recognized as grounds for divorce.[33] Unless a question of possible bigamy was involved, the churches appear to have taken no interest in divorce.

With the exception of a case in 1727,[34] all such cases occurred in the nineteenth century. In 1801 Doctor Brown, of Sandisfield, was suspended until he gave satisfaction for separating from his second wife and marrying a third while the second was still living.[35] The church in Palmer cautiously sought the advice of the ministerial association in the case of Achsa Olds who, in February, 1804, had separated from Nathan Rice. Ten years later she married Enoch Olds, only to learn that Rice was still living. Advice was sought on two points: was the written agreement of separation the equivalent of a divorce, and could Achsa Rice remarry as long as she did not know for sure that Nathan was living? Considering the uncontested statement of facts, the association held that there had been no divorce; hence Achsa Olds should not have remarried.[36] In a worse predicament was Mrs. Williams, of Worthington, who had two former husbands. At the time of her second marriage, she presumed that the first spouse, who had left her, was dead. The second husband also left and learning of his remarriage, Mrs. Williams considered herself free to contract a third marriage. The church disapproved of such marital adventures and suspended her pending a further investigation.[37]

The best Enoch Arden case found in the records occurred in Pittsfield shortly before the Civil War. John Barnard must have experienced some surprise when Cynthia Holmes's husband unexpectedly turned up after sixteen years, for Barnard, a widower, had married Mrs. Cynthia Holmes in 1842, five years after her husband had left her. The evidence indicated that Holmes had remarried. Barnard cautiously asked some church members whether he must obtain a divorce before he could marry Cynthia and was told that this was unnecessary. He had lived with Cynthia sixteen years before Mr. Holmes suddenly appeared, presumably still Cynthia's husband. The Holmes who had remarried, it developed, was another person. Barnard, a gentleman, turned Cynthia over to Holmes. In Barnard's own words, the record states:

> On thus claiming his wife, with deep regret, but as a matter of duty, and with sincere respect on both sides, Mrs. Holmes and myself ceased to live together as husband and wife, and she returned to said Holmes, the only man to whom it appears she was ever legally married.

Barnard then acknowledged his error in not asking Cynthia to obtain a divorce and asked forgiveness of the church. The members voted their gratitude for the "frankness and christian spirit" shown by Barnard and expressed their satisfaction that he had been the victim of circumstances.[38]

Their passive attitude on divorce notwithstanding, the churches took an active interest in the sanctity of family life. As long as a couple were lawfully married they were required to live together even if in disagreement with one another.[39] Five cases are found in which wives forsook their husbands and were censured by the churches. One woman made a confession nine years after her conviction; [40] two offenders, applicants for church membership, were rejected; [41] and in two cases the record is inconclusive.[42] A man who lived apart from his wife was suspended in 1800; [43] twenty years later a brother who had been convicted of forsaking his wife, committing adultery, and attempted prostitution, as well as theft, was excommunicated after the church rejected his confession as inadequate.[44]

Attempts to settle family quarrels which had not reached the stage of separation were not much more successful. The husband was the head of the household, but the wife was not his slave,[45] and a man who beat his wife might well find himself in court [46] or before the church.

In 1757 Anne Hammond brought a complaint against her husband Barzillai, accusing him of nonsupport of the church, perpetual quarreling, slander, neglect of family prayers, and such ill-treatment that she was compelled to leave her home. After some discourse, Barzillai made a confession. "The differences," the minister optimistically observed, "were peacably adjusted." A year later the quarrel broke out anew. Committee after committee conversed with Hammond, without effect, until an admonition was sent in 1760. This, too, made no impact on Hammond. After a lapse of two years, Hammond's offenses being aggravated by his absence from meetings, the church decided to give him one last chance. Unmoved and unrepentant, Hammond finally was cast out of the church.[47] The Hammond case is the only one found in which the offended spouse brought the complaint before the church. In other cases the complaint came from outsiders, possibly from persons sincerely interested in helping to effect a reconciliation, possibly from those concerned about the church, but probably, in most cases, from snoopers who may have borne a grudge against the respondent.

An early case against a husband brought on the complaint of a person outside the family involved a man who had forcibly ejected his wife from his home and had caused her to bleed at the mouth. The Dorchester church required the brother to make a confession, but permitted him to own it before the church only.[48] In Merrimac, the church sought to reconcile Samuel Jewel and his wife in 1729 and at first was able to effect a truce. In 1730, and again in 1734, however, Jewel, who had again abused his wife, was required to make a public confession. Another two years elapsed before Jewel was suspended for adultery. What finally became of him the record fails to disclose.[49]

On the brighter side are the records of two family quarrels, one of which involved a daughter as well, which were amicably settled among the parties, without recourse to a hearing before the church.[50] Also satisfactorily concluded, for a while at least, was the dispute between Lemuel Phelps and his wife. In this case, a committee sent by the church accomplished its mission, for in the spring of 1770 Mr. and Mrs. Phelps confessed their sins before the church. Mrs. Phelps's confession was read first:

I acknowledge that I have transgressed the Rules and Duties of a Wife towards her Husband in some of my past conduct in assuming too much Authority over him and controuling him in Civil and religious matters and that I am sorry for it and ask Forgiveness and that I will in my future Conduct whilst I live with him behave as a dutiful and obedient wife.[51]

The confession was accepted. Next Mr. Phelps confessed to Mrs. Phelps:

I acknowledge that I have abused and treated you unbecoming a kind and tender husband in beating you in an unmerciful manner in various Instances; in speaking unadvisedly concerning your Death and the Birth of your last child and in not Discovering that affection I ought to bear towards you by acts of kindness and love; and in telling that I thought you had committed the unpardonable sin, for which I am heartily sorry and ask the Forgiveness of God and your Forgiveness and promise to behave towards you for the future as a kind and tender husband.[52]

And finally Mr. Phelps made his confession to the church:

I acknowledge to this Church that I have broken a Christian Rule and thereby dishonoured God and brought a scandal upon the holy Religion which I profess by my unchristian treatment of my wife in beating her and in speaking to others of her as having committed the unpardonable sin, in speaking unadvisedly concerning her Death and the Birth of her last child, and in not having that love and affection towards her I engaged by my Marriage Covenant, for which I am heartily sorry and ask the Forgiveness and restoration to your Church and ask your Prayers for me.[53]

This, too, was accepted. Things seemed to go smoothly in the Phelps household for some three years, when Phelps once more confessed that he had been quarreling with his wife: once more he had charged that she had committed the unpardonable sin.[54]

A deacon of the First Church of Marblehead was suspended in spite of his public confession of "scandalizing" his wife, so that the church might test the sincerity of his repentance. A year later the offender was found unfit for the office of deacon.[55] Another husband, who had abused his wife while intoxicated, was excommunicated when the church rejected his proposed "trifling" confession.[56] Likewise influenced by liquor was Ebenezer Parker, of Cambridge, who in 1733 had attempted to stab his wife, who was providentially saved by a book which she carried in her bosom. Because Parker willingly made a public confession, he was restored.[57] Because Eleazer Tiffany, of Lanesborough, "failed to show the least symptom of januine [*sic*] repentance, nor any disposition to reform," he was excommunicated after the church had found him guilty of abusing his wife, although there is no indication that he, unlike Ebenezer Parker, had homicidal inclinations.[58]

As might have been expected, women appear to have been censured for abusing their husbands at an earlier date than were men for mistreating their wives. Three women were excommunicated from churches in the Boston area for offenses against their husbands, and a sister of the Salem church was publicly admonished for neglecting her husband.[59] When Dorothy Clark publicly confessed that she had committed "some breach of the Rule in her management of the differences betwixt her and her now Husband," the Plymouth church thought it proper to instruct its elder to give her some wholesome advice. Resenting this rebuke, Clarke lost his temper as he accused the church of acquitting the guilty and condemning the innocent, and declared that his salvation might be furthered if he left the church. Although the church plainly told Clarke that his remarks were offensive, no disciplinary action was taken, and Mrs. Clarke was restored.[60] A woman who called her husband a dog and said that he was under daemonic influence was suspended in 1762, and one who lived in discord with her husband was required to make a public confession in 1780.[61] Rather cryptic is the record in the case of a woman who, presumably having been suspended, was restored because it appeared that she was the victim of her husband's abuse and that civil court had justified her conduct.[62] Did the church reverse its original judgment and, by implication, concede a miscarriage of justice?

The case of Bethia Hinkley of Barnstable is *sui generis* and defies specific classification. The only extant information is contained in the record of the second admonition, voted by the church on November 10, 1683. Either Bethia Hinkley was insane, or else even a twentieth-century reader of the record must accept the seventeenth-century observation that she was "So furr left of God into the temptations of Satan and the corruptions of her own heart, as greatly to dishonour God, and to give matter of just offence." The fifteen counts alleged against her compare in circumstantial detail with a modern indictment. Four of these involved transgressions of the Eighth Commandment: (1) giving away her husband's property without his consent, (2) destroying God-given goods by burning her clothes, (3) wasting God-given time in idleness and unnecessary visiting, and (4) wasting more God-given goods in burning more clothes after the first admonition. Furthermore, she had violated the

Sixth Commandment, "Thou shalt do no murder, i.e., thou Shalt do nothing to injure the Life or comfort of Life of thy Selfe or neighbour," by (5) not being her husband's helpmeet, (6) not providing necessities and conveniences for him, and (7) giving away parts of his estate to others.[63] She had also broken the Fifth Commandment, here construed to require persons to reverence and respect their superiors, including husbands, because (8) she had not been lovingly and humbly reverent towards her husband[64] by refusing to explain her frequent absences from home, (9) she had accused him of wickedness and railing, thus showing "great Pride of heart," and (10) she had opposed his Christian will in violation of Scripture.[65] At the hearing before the church she had (11) treated the Lord's people with contempt, violating the Third Commandment. Finally, she had violated her covenant obligations because she had promised (12) to obey the commands of God, but had broken them, and (13) to subject herself to the discipline of the church, but had treated it with contempt. She had (14) lied to the church and had (15) added obstinacy to her other sins. Bethia had earlier pleaded guilty to the first ten counts. The eleventh required no proof; it had been committed in the presence of the church. The last four, it appears, were thrown in for good measure after the proceedings had begun. With this second admonition Bethia Hinkley was excommunicated.[66]

Conflicts between parents and children existed long before the child psychologist made his appearance on the American scene. In the absence of psychologists and psychiatrists, the church took cognizance of violations of the Fifth Commandment, supplementing the statutes which made a child's cursing of a parent and a son's rebellious behavior capital crimes.[67] Thus a married couple, already charged with fornication, were also accused of disobedience to their respective parents because the marriage had taken place without their consent.[68] Disobedience to parents was added to other offenses in the case of a Boston drunkard who, incidentally, also resisted the authority of the local constable, and in the case of a Negro thief.[69] Five others were dealt with for unspecified forms of abuse of parents,[70] and four children who slandered their parents were censured. Abigail Bush, accused of having offered to pay a piece of eight, which was all she had, if her father left the land, and of having said that his recent marriage was not for love, the woman being "as hot as a bitch," limited her confession to the first point. For lack of proof on the second charge, the confession was accepted and read in public. Abigail was restored with an exhortation "to be very tender of Parentall honour." Fifteen years later Abigail was placed on a two months' trial period before she was forgiven for more bad language to her father.[71] A man who reviled his father was excommunicated, while a woman who had accused her mother of witchcraft was found guilty of violations of the Fifth, Sixth, and Ninth Commandments, but was restored on her confession.[72] For slandering a parent and sibling rivalry a woman was required to make a confession, while two quarreling brothers, were persuaded to make mutual confessions.[73] A quarrel between two brothers, a lieutenant, and a captain was similarly settled, and the brothers asked each other's forgiveness.[74]

The obligations of children to parents had their counterpart in parental duties towards their children. Some time before December, 1635, Robert Parker was excommunicated for "scandalous oppression of his wives [*sic*] children." If, as the record implies, the children were the issue of a former marriage of Mrs. Parker, Robert Parker becomes an example of the legendary harsh stepfather who deprives his stepchildren of their inheritance, which is precisely what Parker did. Presumably Parker made satisfaction, for the excommunication was withdrawn.[75] Three years later the church which had censured Parker excommunicated a woman who had been convicted of cruelty to her children, in addition to intoxication, lasciviousness, and lying.[76] For neglect of their daughter, dangerously ill in childbed, and of their infant grandson, whose life was allegedly shortened by their neglect, Captain William Ellis and his wife Deborah were repeatedly admonished. Deborah, unrepentant, was excommunicated. Her husband must have been restored, for the record of his death shortly thereafter mentions him as a church member in communion at that time.[77]

An unusual version of in-law difficulties appears in the Falmouth records. "Common report and public talk" led the church to inquire into the relationship between Lacheus and Mercy Hatch and their son-in-law, Ezekiel Eldred. Ezekiel's wife Susanna (née Hatch) then offered a confession stating that she had refused to have sexual intercourse with her husband. The church bypassed consideration of the confession to investigate the rumor that Susanna's parents had encouraged her misconduct. After further deliberation the church voted to suspend Lacheus and Mercy Hatch until they made a confession.[78]

Disobedience of a slave or servant to his master was also construed as a violation of the Fifth Commandment. A servant made a confession of such disobedience in 1720, and Flora, a Negro woman, publicly acknowledged that she had disobeyed her mistress, besides drinking, swearing, and absenting herself from church.[79]

In the colonial churches the functions of pastor, marital relations consultant, child psychologist, and domestic relations court merged.[80] In spite of the civil nature of marriage and divorce, the churches concerned themselves with situations directly connected with these and other aspects of family life. From the cases which have been uncovered, we have no clear idea of the churches' attitude on marriage with a deceased spouse's brother or sister; "that annual blister, marriage with deceased wife's sister," appears into the early national period, at which time the question was still unresolved. On the other hand, there can be no doubt that the churches did not countenance the remarriage of a person whose spouse was still alive unless there had been a proper divorce. Where such a marriage had been consummated in good faith, however, notably in the case of John Barnard, the churches were more interested in resolving the difficulty than in censuring offenders.

The threat or application of ecclesiastical sanctions failed to deter married couples from separation, which was not permitted by the churches. Family quarrels which had not reached this stage also came under the cognizance of the churches, which endeavored, with varying degrees of success, to settle the issues and to restore harmony to the home. Wives and husbands could look to the churches for protection against an unjust spouse, and citing the precepts of the Fifth Commandment, the churches, on the one hand, assisted in disciplining misbehaved children, while on the other hand they protected children against delinquent or negligent parents.

In dealing with domestic problems the churches were generally less effective than they were in other areas which came under their jurisdiction. Perhaps the best explanation for the relatively large number of failures in the churches' attempts to restore harmony in discordant homes is that the churches resorted to quasi-judicial techniques in cases which called for pastoral services. The coldness of the law, unmitigated by its modern sociological adjuncts, prevailed over the empathetic understanding which the churches should have shown for those members whose family lives were in danger of disintegration.

VII. Extramarital Relations

The prohibition of adultery furnished the basis of more ecclesiastical prosecutions than any other provision in the Decalogue. Like all the other commandments, the Seventh was broadly construed. Together with the express sanction of marriage, this commandment was held to preclude all sexual relations out of wedlock.[1] A majority of all sexual offenders and a plurality of all church members dealt with for violations of their religious obligations were charged with fornication. The records, however, are not always distinct. The expression "violation of the Seventh Commandment" might mean any sexual offense, but in the absence of a more explicit term may be assumed to mean a sexual act involving unmarried or widowed persons. In the absence of more definite information, all cases in which this or similar expressions appear have been thus classified. Whenever the relationship was clearly adulterous, involving at least one married person, the case has been classified as one of adultery.[2]

Aside from difficulties of classification, a problem arises from the often inadequate information concerning the termination of the case. A record which merely indicates that an application for a dismission was refused unless the applicant made a confession of fornication and which is followed by neither a record of such a confession nor by a censure, offers no clue to the termination of the case, unless we assume that the matter was dropped.[3] No more enlightening is the record of a conviction not followed by a record of either a restoration or an excommunication.[4] A common factor does exist, however: in of these cases we may assume that the persons involved were guilty in the eyes of the church. Still another difficulty arises from the incompleteness of the records. It is therefore impossible to compute, with any degree of accuracy, the incidence of fornication in the churches of colonial Massachusetts, much less in the entire colony or state. Statistics derived from the records of any one church whose records are complete over a fairly long period of time are, however, useful guides to the trends in the morality and discipline within that one church. Even the total number of cases may be used for limited purposes, such as to distinguish between confessions made by couples and those made by men or women separately, or to compare the results with the statistics based on civil court records.

With these limitations in mind, the records disclose a total of 1,242 cases of fornication between 1620 and 1839. A chronological analysis would be misleading because of the scarcity of records in the early period, but the evidence clearly indicates the prevalence of premarital relations in the early decades of Massachusetts history. In 1665 the General Court noted with alarm the increase in fornication. Three years later it commented on the large number of bastards in the colony,[5] and in 1676 the church in Dorchester adopted a "Covenant for Reformation" in which "lasciviousness" and "uncleanness" were expressly included in a list of "gineral [*sic*] growing evill[s] of this time." [6] Somewhat more accurate for purposes of comparison are the separate figures for couples, for women, and for men.[7] Married couples and single or married women were involved in 480 cases each, single or married men in 151 cases, and in 133 cases the sex of the offender cannot be ascertained from the records. Cases involving couples constitute a majority in two counties, a plurality in two others, and a possible plurality in one.[8] In the remaining counties, except Bristol, where the records are too incomplete to permit any conclusion,[9] and Dukes and Nantucket, where they are entirely lost, cases involving women constitute a majority. The predominance of women over men is scarcely surprising:

motherhood is hard to conceal and is readily ascertained; fatherhood is difficult to prove.

A comparison of these statistics with those based on court records suggests that the courts handled proportionately fewer couples charged with fornication than did the churches. During the years 1726-80, the Middlesex Court of General Sessions sentenced 523 single women for fornication, but only 160 couples.[10] During the same period, the church records of Middlesex County mention thirty-four couples, thirty-four women, and eleven men who presumably were guilty of fornication. In the decade 1671-80, the Suffolk County Court dealt with fifty-three couples, forty-three women, and fifty-six men guilty of the same offense.[11] The extremely partial church records for that period and county mention five women and two men. But however incomplete these records may be, the large proportion of men sentenced by the courts contrasts with the comparatively small proportion of men censured by the churches. Unmarried men particularly were inclined to confess their offense in court or to plead guilty when arraigned.[12]

Much more meaningful are the statistics of cases in churches whose records are complete for some years.[13] On the assumption that these churches were representative of the churches in the county, an impression of the trends in these counties may be had. No inferences can be drawn from the records of the seventeenth century. Some churches show a distinct drop in the number of cases after 1690, while others show a marked increase.[14] It is therefore impossible to ascertain what influence, if any, the constitutional changes of the time exerted on church discipline.

More definite inferences may be drawn from the records of cases in the early eighteenth century. Taking the records of eight churches with reasonably complete records for the period 1700-1769,[15] we find in each case a distinct increase during a particular decade. In those eight churches we find only six cases in the first decade of the century, but fifty-five cases between 1730 and 1739. During the next ten-year period, the figure drops to forty, but then, for the decade 1750-59, rises to forty-nine.[16] The records of the individual churches show even greater variations. In Plymouth, no cases are recorded in the 1720's or 1740's, but ten in the thirties. In Quincy, only three cases are mentioned in the 1720's, but thirteen in the following decade, and only one in the forties. The largest number of cases found in the records of any one church during any one decade is Westfield, where the church dealt with twenty-five persons accused of fornication between 1750 and 1759.

Of the sixteen churches listed in Table VI of the appendix, twelve have records going back to 1720 and extending to 1769 or beyond. In five of these twelve churches the peak was reached between 1730 and 1739, in three in the fifties, and in two in both the twenties and forties.[17] Two factors may have influenced these fluctuations. One is the Great Awakening, a subject which must be reserved for a more extended discussion at a later point.[18] The other factor which must be considered is the decline of civil action. The last known instance in which a person was sentenced for fornication by a civil court in Suffolk County occured in 1704. After the 1730's no sentences were imposed for premarital relations by any court in eastern Massachusetts.[19] It may well be that one reason for the rise of cases in the churches in the early eighteenth century was the decline of civil prosecutions.

The birth of a child within less than seven months after the marriage of its parents was prima facie evidence of fornication.[20] The shortest period of time which has been found in the church records between the marriage of the parents and the birth of the child was six weeks.[21] Other intervals mentioned are four months, "about 5 months and 17 days," six months and six days, twenty-six weeks, and six months and three weeks.[22] In all save the last case the offenders were dealt with by the churches. In one instance a father voluntarily made a confession of fornication, although, had he taken a chance on a trial, he might well have received the benefit of the doubt, as the child had been born only six or seven weeks before the normal period of gestation.[23] In the case of Mrs. Shaw, of Haverhill, the church first voted that the child might be baptized although it was born "in seven weekly months" (i.e., about two weeks less than seven full months) after the marriage. Mrs. Shaw failed to appear at the hearing, and the meeting was adjourned. The vote to admit the child to baptism was later held to be "an imperfect vote, or none at all," so that the baptism was not administered.[24] Two years later the same church refused to admit a woman to membership because her child had been born seven months and a day after the marriage, and there was some other damaging evidence: the applicant had evasively alleged that "she had nothing to do with her husband before he was her husband." [25]

Because the child born of William Hersey's wife "had a full-grown body Ripe for the birth and long hair and hard nails, and Cryd and fed well when it was first born," a council vindicated the Dorchester church, which had refused to allow the christening of the child unless the parents made a confession. The council acted largely on the basis of the testimony of witnesses who had appeared before a justice of the peace. The judge had held that "no Child ever attained such ripeness and perfections at 5 months and nine days from its Conception." [26] The First Church of Haverhill rejected the plea of James Mitchell and his wife that their child had been prematurely born, because the child had survived although allegedly born six months and three weeks after conception.[27] The Pittsfield church, on the other hand, dropped a case against a couple when the father insisted on his innocence, in spite of the evidence that the child at its birth "was full grown and of the usual size, but without nails on the fingers." [28]

A late prosecution for fornication, the record of which is unusually complete, took place in Sheffield in 1838. In April of that year Sophia S. West was charged with fornication and lying. She pleaded guilty to the first charge but denied the second. No action was taken during the summer, but in October the church appointed a committee to inquire into the evidence on the charge of falsehood. Asked whether she still denied the charges, Sophia admitted that she had evaded questions concerning the child, but insisted that "she was not conscious of having positively denied it." The committee reported that it had located a witness who could testify that shortly before her confinement Sophia West had told her "that no man, except her father, knew what its sex was," while another witness found by the committee was prepared to swear that Sophia had told her: "God knows that I am innocent." The church, unanimous except for one member, convicted Sophia on the charge of lying and required her to make a confession. In January, 1839, Sophia offered an acknowledgment, but it, as well as a second proposal, was rejected as inadequate. Obviously unable to obtain an acceptable statement from the offender, the church requested the pastor to draw up an acceptable confession, to which Sophia assented in public.[29]

Recognizing that some children might be born within seven months, the churches permitted suspected parents to make a "declaration of innocence" on oath, but Cotton Mather left a loophole open to the churches when he wrote that some births might be so premature that no declaration was admissable.[30] He did not define "so Premature" and presumably left the definition to the churches. A woman who availed herself of the "declaration of innocence" but was subsequently found guilty of fornication would thus compound her offense with perjury. Such declarations were accepted in cases of children born six days less than seven months, and five months and six days, after the marriage of the parents.[31] One declaration, in the case of a child born "about 7 months and 10 days after marriage," which was accepted, should have been unnecessary had the seven months rule been properly observed.[32] In two instances the declaration was rejected.[33] A couple who refused to declare their innocence were suspended after the midwife testified that the child at birth did not appear to be premature.[34] Mrs. Elizabeth Craig, however, who gave birth to a child five months and two weeks after her marriage, was acquitted on the strength of the testimony of a midwife, a nurse, and a physician, who, as expert witnesses, testified that an illness had hastened the birth.[35] In one case the church decided that the evidence was insufficient to bar the baptism of a child allegedly conceived out of wedlock.[36]

Three of the cases involving premarital relations may give us some idea how the churches used evidence (other than the dates of the marriage and the birth) to determine the accused's guilt or innocence. In Milton a woman evidently pleaded that her child was born later than alleged. The child actually born during the night in which hers was allegedly born was that of another woman, the respondent insisted. The church relied principally on previous testimony given in court, but nevertheless conducted its own investigation. A witness was asked whether other children had been born during the night in question. The witness's answer is not recorded, but the alleged mother was convicted by the church.[37] A two-man committee was appointed by the First Church in Haverhill to investigate rumors that Hannah Middleton's children had been conceived before her marriage. One of the men reported that he had discussed the case with William Townshend and his wife, both of whom claimed to have seen a letter by Hannah to Middleton. The letter, antedating the marriage, stated that she was with child by him. Hannah denied the authorship of the letter, and rather than rely on the investigator's report, the church asked Townshend to testify. The witness repeated his earlier testimony, adding that Hannah, before her marriage, had told him that she was pregnant with Middleton's child. After two adjournments the church voted not to admit the children to baptism.[38] Similar evidence was introduced in a case in which a putative father and applicant for membership pleaded not guilty. A witness, however, recalled that the applicant had earlier admitted his paternity. On this flimsy evidence the church voted to reject the application for membership.[39]

Some persons aggravated their initial offense of fornication by adding other sins. A namesake of his church's former pastor, John Cotton, made a confession of lascivious relations with three women and of lying about the affair, and a woman of Westfield, four years after she confessed her fornication, acknowledged her perjury in the matter.[40] William and Lydia Harlow, previously mentioned in connection with their marriage, aggravated their guilt by denying it, as did a servant girl who had sought to conceal her child.[41]

That the concealment of the father's identity was no bar to a restoration is implied in a Barnstable case, in which only five members voted against the acceptance of a confession which omitted the father's name.[42] Two women charged with wrongfully accusing a man of being the father of their children were acquitted on that count.[43] Two men aggravated their guilt by absconding from the parish and were excommunicated,[44] and in Deerfield the church abetted Amos Allen's braggartism by requiring him to confess that he had aggravated his sin of fornication by boasting about it.[45] Amos Allen ardently desired publicity and got his full share. Jacob Dwinal shunned publicity, but without success. When the Millbury church assembled to discuss the case, the meeting was adjourned because of the poor attendance, but not until the church, for educational reasons, had voted to invite all baptized persons "of years of Discretion" to attend the adjourned meeting. When the church reconvened a month later the house was packed to capacity. The pastor availed himself of the opportunity to lecture to the assembly on church discipline, citing the Scriptures, Church Fathers, colonial synods, and the Cambridge Platform. The Dwinal case was then referred to a committee, whose report, the contents of which are not mentioned, was accepted.[46] One of the last persons censured for fornication aggravated her guilt to indulging in "improper company at improper hours of the night" in her boardinghouse room.[47]

A unique case occurred in 1678, when Robert Cox was accused of intoxication, lasciviousness with a Negro woman, and lying by saying that he had contracted a veneral disease in an accidental injury. The church excommunicated Cox, but voted to suspend the effect of the censure indefinitely. By going abroad Cox aggravated his guilt, and when he at last appeared, was ordered to show cause why he should not be excommunicated. Cox confessed that he had been drunk but denied the rest, for which he was cast out of the church. Two years later, standing propounded for readmission, he broke the Sabbath while his case was still pending. Upon a confession of his latest offense, Cox was admitted to membership; the charges of fornication and lying were overlooked.[48]

Since the end of all disciplinary action was the offender's restoration, the churches always aimed at obtaining a satisfactory confession. The majority of fornicators made their confessions willingly; in one case, however, not until thirty-eight years after the commission of the offense.[49] Only a few of the actual confessions have been preserved. Lengthy, formal in style, and self-abasing in content, confessions of sexual transgressions rarely mentioned the offense which had been committed; at best the offender acknowledged that he had committed "a very Scandalous breach of the Seventh Command." [50] Distinctly exceptional is the record of the confession of Maria Parker, made before the Groton church in 1707. Recorded in mediocre Latin, the acknowledgement contains the customary outpouring of guilt feelings, a note of intense and sincere repentance, a prayer for forgiveness, and a request for the prayers of the church. Directly following the heading, and preceding the confession proper, the word *fornication* appears in Greek.[51] Although an occasional Latin phrase has been found in the records of other churches, this is the only confession in Greek and Latin which has been uncovered.

Cotton Mather held that a "Public Acknowledgment before the whole Church" was adequate in such cases, unless the offender was hardened, in which case an admonition was in order.[52] By "Public Acknowledgment before the whole

Church," a contradiction in terms, Mather probably meant a confession before the church and the congregation, read by the pastor at the Sunday service and acknowledged by the offender. That this was the usual practice appears evident from the debates in the churches over the desirability of continuing the practice. The Groton church discussed this problem in 1740 and voted

> that this Custom, has (on the one hand) Proved (with some of the less Conscientious) a Prevailing Temptation to belye their Consciences, adding Sin to Sin: and being *thought by some* an Hardship (on the other hand) upon the more Consciencious (and Doubted at least whither it be Right) to Compel *them* Publickly to acknowledge, what is, (if not absolutely yet) next to Impossible to Convict them of: Therefore tis desired that for the future (till further Light be afforded) in such Cases; the Pastor of this Church, admitt them to desired Priviledges: without Compelling them to *Either*.[53]

Observing that the requirement of a public confession of fornication kept many potential communicants from the Lord's Supper, and their children from Baptism, the First Church of Salem voted in 1779 to discontinue public confessions in these cases.[54] A committee of the Milton church advised in 1789 that public confessions of fornication were both unnecessary and inexpedient, and recommended their abolition. In Milton, as in other churches, such confessions were abolished.[55] An exception to the prevailing trend was the Billerica church, which insisted on public confessions by married persons whose children had been conceived before the marriage. But when the pastor recorded these confessions some members objected. A number of persons whose confessions were recorded demanded an attested copy for use as evidence in proposed tort actions for defamation. The person who copied the original records observed that the pastor then erased these entries, "pleading, that what he had put in, of his own, he had a right to put out. This is told as a Fact, by one who had it from the

Pastor's own mouth. As to the Expediency of it, They that come after will judge." [56]

Not every confession resulted in the immediate restoration of the offender. When Benjamin Balsh and his wife confessed their sin, they were admonished and placed on an indeterminate period of probation, during which they were suspended from the communion.[57] A deacon who had made his confession willingly submitted to a continued suspension, "hoping it would for ever be a Monitor to him and to all others In exciting to A diligent heed and watchfulness." [58] A second offender, Elizabeth Van Ness, of Lenox, in the most recent case of fornication found in the records, was excommunicated with the proviso that she might be restored "when by an after life of penitence and purity she shall furnish evidence that she is forgiven and accepted of God." [59]

If some churches dealt severely with second offenders, we can imagine what they thought of even greater recidivists. For a fourth offender we may turn to Lydia Foster, of Haverhill. Suspended in 1732 for having her second bastard, she proceeded to have a third, for which she offered "a very penitent" confession in 1734. Because her outward behavior hardly conformed to the intentions expressed in her confession, the suspension was continued while the church waited for a manifestation of her repentance. The birth of the fourth bastard child exhausted the church's patience. The exasperated minister recapitulated Lydia's previous record and observed: "And after all this, Having this winter, again been delivered of *another* Bastard Child; Upon which twas voted unanimously that She is worthy of a *Solemn Censure of Excommunication.*" A year later Lydia offered still another confession, which was read twice. While no objection was offered, it was evidently rejected, for the pastor proposed that Lydia be excommunicated. At the offender's request, the church deferred action on the proposal. In 1743 the confession of "Lydia Dowe (lately Foster)" was finally accepted.[60]

Pressure from relatives deterred some otherwise willing persons from making confessions. When Mrs. Negus positively refused to permit her daughter to make a confession, the church voted that "the matter being soe fowle and haynous, we doe declare her to be none of us," but failed to specify for the record whether the daughter was excommunicated for failing to make a confession, or the mother for her refusal to let the daughter make it.[61] More commonly the pressure was exerted by the husband. One woman simply made her own confession, leaving her spouse at home.[62] Another did the same, but by acknowledging her sin encouraged her husband to follow suit.[63] A woman in Salem waited until her husband was dead and she herself close to it. On her deathbed she bargained that should God save her life, she would make her confession. Beyond the comment that this decision was communicated to the church, the record fails to tell whether she recovered and, if so, whether she kept her part of the agreement.[64] In Canton, a conscience-stricken woman went to see her pastor after she had withdrawn a proposed confession because her husband objected to it. "The woman [was] penitent and sorrowful," the pastor noted. "Thus nobly did she *hate* her Husband for the sake of a good conscience, the Law of God and the love of Christ according to that recorded in Luke, XIV. 26." [65] At the close of the century, when the churches were more lenient, a woman, whose husband objected to her making a public confession, was permitted to present her acknowledgment before the church only.[66]

In one case the husband, but not the wife, made a confession. Having acknowledged his error, John Pattin was admitted to full communion. His wife, however, was afflicted with "such a distemper of body and mind, that any thing that is surprizing to her causes her to swound away." Mrs. Pattin never became a full-fledged member.[67] Another hopeless case was that of Hannah Mackentire, a morally weak and mentally debilitated person, who was so ignorant of the meaning of a confession that the church expected none from her and permitted her to join in the Lord's Supper in spite of her offense. Six years later Hannah surprised the church with a public confession, only to be excommunicated the following year. A new pastor had arrived shortly after her confession had been received. His first project was to investigate the morals of his flock. A new charge of lasciviousness was pressed against Hannah, and the church responded with unusual promptness and vigor. "The patience of the Ch[urc]h is clearly worn out—Her weakness of understanding has pleaded for her in the view of the Ch[urc]h untill it can plead no more," the newly installed disciplinarian wrote.[68]

A principal cause of confessions of fornication was the parents' desire to have the child baptized.[69] The records disclose numerous instances in which the confession was shortly followed by the baptism of a child. If the child was a bastard, that, too, would be recorded. Thus Hannah Howard, of Beverly, after making a confession jointly with Samuel Hoskins, whom she evidently did not marry, had her "base-born" child christened.[70] As late as 1773 a man was denied baptism because his child had been illegitimately begotten and later made a public confession.[71]

The statistical evidence supports the conclusion that many confessions were prompted by the desire to obtain baptism for the children. In Plymouth County, the Hanover records for 1730-60 disclose thirteen confessions by parents prior to their children's baptisms.[72] In West Roxbury, five of the eight couples who made confessions between 1734 and 1760 had children christened shortly thereafter.[73] Somewhat different proportions prevailed in the First Church of Salem, where between 1670 and 1740 thirteen of the thirty-one women who made confessions had children baptized, but for the period 1730-40 we find seven confessions followed by a baptism, but only one where there was no corresponding christening.[74]

Like other public confessions, pre-baptismal confessions became unpopular during the course of the eighteenth century. In 1702 a pastor could still record in the minutes that a confession restored a member "to the priviledge of transmitting baptism to his child, which by his fall he had cutt himselfe off from [*sic*]." [75] Just how a parent could "transmit" baptism was not explained. Ten years later a Plymouth parson took a more charitable stand and baptized the unlawfully begotten daughter of a physician. There were objections, to be sure, but the pastor rejected them as unscriptural. To punish a child by denying it baptism because of the parents' sins, the minister held, was unjust and unchristian.[76] But this charitable parson was ahead of his time. In Scituate, pre-baptismal parental confessions continued until 1769, and in Brewster until 1772, while in Plymouth at least three women confessed fornication prior to their children's baptisms in 1780.[77] In these late cases, however, an additional factor was involved: the admission of the parent to church membership. Concerted moves to abolish these confessions resulted in 1788 in a vote by the Cambridge church, permitting the baptism of all children *born* in wedlock, provided one parent was in communion, without any requirement of confession.[78] The last such resolution pertaining particularly to the baptism of children was uncovered in Truro for the year 1814.[79]

Perhaps as important a factor as the desire for the baptism of one's offspring in motivating confessions of fornication was the offender's wish to be admitted to covenant relationship or full communion. Somewhat more than a third of all confessions of fornication made in Plymouth between 1683 and 1788 involved the penitent's own admission to some form of church membership.[80] In Sharon, every single confession of fornication made between 1747 and 1766 was accompanied by the admission of the penitent person to the covenant, and fourteen of the sixty-four persons who owned the covenant in these years made such confessions.[81] An unusual variation of the theme of pre-admission confessions is found in the Deerfield records, which disclose a number of antenuptial confessions. Forty-one couples acknowledged their transgressions between 1732 and 1780, in seventeen instances shortly before their marriage, and sometimes as little as a day before.[82]

In some churches confessions for premarital relations run

well into the nineteenth century. In Danvers, of the 164 persons admitted to full communion between 1773 and 1800, thirty made confessions. No admissions are recorded for 1801 and 1802; seven were admitted in 1803, and ten in 1804. One of the ten made a confession. No later confessions in connection with admissions have been found in Danvers, but in 1834 one woman made a confession to the church before her child was baptized.[83] The last confession of fornication found in the records was made privately, before the church in Wilbraham, in 1849.[84] The last excommunication for the same offense occurred in 1842, when the Hatfield church censured an absconding member.[85]

"Bundling," prevalent in New England from an early date, was especially common on Cape Cod,[86] but the one mention of it in the records, and that by implication only, is found in Canton. In the church trial of Joseph Tucker, the depositions of two witnesses alleged that they had seen Tucker and one Susannah Pelton "early in the morning in bed together, covered with Bedding." Because this was "a thing of no good report," Tucker was required to make a confession. Instead, he produced evidence on the strength of which he was acquitted.[87] At first a respectable practice, devised to permit strangers to share a scarce bed, bundling soon led to obvious abuses which brought forth attacks from the clergy.[88] In 1730 the pastor of Brewster lamented the increase in illicit relations, attributing it in part to "a wicked practice of young people in their courtships," which he had previously opposed in his preaching.[89]

Amorous behavior between unmarried persons was sometimes sufficient cause of censure, even in the absence of any suggestion that there had been illicit sexual relations. Thus Simon Bird, of Boston, was excommunicated in 1646 for his dalliances with a servant, but was restored after a public confession, and in Dorchester a father was admonished because he entertained his daughter's beau too frequently.[90] More than a century later, in 1800, a deacon in Worthington was acquitted on a charge of improper conduct with the complainant's sister, but was told that he had been at the girl's house too often for the church to rest in peace.[91] In the same year a complaint against a man of Charlemont, alleging "indecent familiarity" with a girl, aggravated by the fact that it had taken place on the Sabbath, was dismissed for want of evidence,[92] but in 1813 Lemuel Sturtevant, of Rochester, was suspended until he made a confession because of his "unbecoming familiarities with Molly David, a woman of colour." He had given her a half pint of rum, had been seen "talking freely" with her, "requesting her to stay" until the people were gone, and had been caught walking up the street with her.[93] In Stockbridge the church found a member guilty of "very mysterious, equivocal" conduct in the company of a woman at Lee, but acquitted him on the charge that the conduct had also been "highly indecorous." [94] By far the quaintest conviction in this category is that of Joshua Bartlett, who was found in another man's house, sitting in the lap of his girl friend, Alice Whitney.[95]

If fornication was common, prostitution was exceedingly rare in the colonial period. Such prostitution as existed was largely ignored by the clergy.[96] A twelve-year-old lad of Boston was admonished in 1653 for keeping evil company and patronizing a house of prostitution, and towards the end of the century a woman was excommunicated for bawdery.[97] No other cases of prostitution have been found in the church records, save for a manuscript copy of a complaint dated January 4, 1872, alleging that Catherine Phelps had "attracted to her house persons of such repute and with such frequency as to cause . . . the strong belief that they were there for no proper purpose but on the contrary for an improper and licentious one." [98]

The crime for which Hawthorne's heroine was condemned to wear the scarlet letter appears only rarely in the court records of colonial Massachusetts.[99] But while the colonial adulterer might well calculate his chances of evading punishment by the civil authorities, he could be fairly certain of summary excommunication once the church found him out.[100] The earliest adultery case found in the records concerns James Mattock, a Boston cooper, who was excommunicated in the spring of 1640. Before coming to America, Mattock had denied conjugal fellowship to his wife on the ground that he had abused her before his marriage and was now punishing himself. He had failed to support his children, but had given two shillings a week to one Mrs. Whittacker, whose company he frequented until he was sent to Newgate Prison for ten days. While drunk in England, he had engaged in "uncleane dallyance and filthy Carriage" with the barmaid of the public house. After his arrival in Boston, Mattock displayed no change in his behavior. He was found drunk twice and continued his friendship with Mrs. Whittacker by mail. In an attempt to convince the church of the harmless nature of his correspondence, he exhibited two harmless letters from his mistress, but concealed two others which were distinctly damaging. The church was not deceived and promptly excommunicated Mattock. A year later he made a public confession and was restored.[101]

A fortnight after Mattock's excommunication, the same church similarly censured Captain John Underhill, who had previously been involved in the Anne Hutchinson case. The captain was accused of adultery with Joseph Tabar's wife and of attempted adultery with another woman. A proposed confession was rejected because it lacked humility and allegedly contained lies intended to justify the captain's conduct.[102] In this case as well, the excommunication was imposed as soon as the offender was found guilty and before he had an opportunity to offer a confession.

Later in the century, John Eli of the Second Church of Boston was charged with adultery, allegedly committed on board a ship bound for Barbados. Eli denied the accusation but said that neither of his two witnesses was in the country at the time. Before the witnesses returned, another charge was added: that he had committed adultery with his wife's sister, whom he had taken along to the island. The church put the burden of proof on Eli, who found it impossible to vindicate himself and was suspended.[103] Ten years later a Salem sea captain was admonished for adultery after a civil conviction, but was restored upon his confession.[104] Shortly before the turn of the century the Second Church of Boston excommunicated Edward Mills and an unnamed woman, probably his mistress. Mills's difficulties began when his landlady, known for her chastity, first turned adulteress and then repented. In her confession she accused Mills of debauching her. On the grounds that Mills neither denied the charges nor made a confession, and in spite of the fact that the only evidence against him was the uncorroborated testimony of his presumed mistress, the church found him guilty. In addition, Mills was convicted of playing illegal games, of boasting of his adulteries in intercepted letters, of slander, and of absence from worship. For good measure, a sixth offense was thrown in: Mills had manifested no symptoms of repentance.[105]

Summary excommunications for adultery were less common in the eighteenth century. Two Indians, a white man, a white woman, and a Negro man were excommunicated, but, except in the last instance, only after they had refused to confess their sins.[106] The Negro, Primus, was first discharged for want of evidence. Then a committee decided that Primus was not worth the time of a trial and recommended his excommunication, which the church voted. Eleven years later Primus died. The pastor, in recording the burial, observed that the Negro had intended to make a confession but was prevented from executing it by death.[107] A total of eight people including an Indian, two women, and a person whose name has been obliterated, made confessions of adultery during the century. Three others, a man and two women, were suspended and nothing more is known about them.[108]

One woman was disciplined in two churches. In December, 1730, the First Church of Haverhill decided that the Widow Bradley should be investigated. A deacon reported that she was indeed living with a man, Stephen Badger, but that she claimed to be his wife, although she refused to say when or where she had married him. From the facts it would appear that the widow's offense was fornication, but she was suspended for "the Sin of Adultery," until she could prove that Badger was her husband.[109] Six months later the church in North Andover sent two deacons to Haverhill to collect evidence against the widow, charged with having committed fornication with Badger. How the unfortunate widow could have been a member of two churches and subject to the discipline of both is not explained. In North Andover, too, Mrs. Bradley was suspended, but finally made a confession.[110] One woman was convicted of adultery because she had asked to be vindicated. In 1772 Mehetable Goof(*sic*), of Pittsfield, learning that she was the subject of rumors of adultery, asked the church to investigate her in order to put an end to the rumors. The church accepted the offer, inquired into the evidence, and found Mehetable guilty.[111]

Some suspects were acquitted. When Josiah Loomis applied for membership in the Egremont church, some of the brethren objected to his admission, alleging that he had committed adultery; a second objection, charging that he was an Anglican, was dismissed. Loomis, the church noted, had made a confession of fornication to the Egremont congregation before it was gathered as a church. Only a formality stood between Loomis and his admission to membership. Late in July, 1770, Loomis repeated his confession and was about to be admitted to membership, when a new complaint was made, alleging that ten years ago he had, under an alias, rented a room at the house of Elias Reed and had lived there with a woman, presumably the wife of one Benjamin Franklin. At the trial, Reed and his wife severally identified Loomis as the man who ten years earlier had taken the room. Mrs. Reed testified that Loomis had called himself Johnson, but her more cautious husband would not corroborate this testimony. The church convicted Loomis and required that he make a confession. Until he acknowledged his error, Loomis was not to be admitted. The case remained suspended for five months. Then, early in May, 1771, the church voted to refer the issue to a committee. Two months later this body reported that the charge was not sustained by the evidence. Following the committee's recommendation, the church voted to receive Loomis into its fellowship; the record discloses no reason for this curious *volte-face*.[112]

During the Revolution, when more pressing business sometimes interfered with the swift administration of ecclesiastical discipline, Colonel Easton was accused of adultery and was subjected to an investigation by the Pittsfield church. A formal complaint was entered in September, 1781. Late in November, the church, apparently uneasy, referred the issue to a council which convened in February, 1782, and advised a further adjournment. Finally, in July, 1783, the church voted on the merits of the case. Nine members were for conviction, ten for acquittal. The minority asked for, and was joined in, a council. More than a year later, in September, 1784, the church voted to give Easton four months in which to obtain evidence in his favor, and appointed a three-man committee, including the complainant, to review the evidence already before it. Evidently Easton was censured at some time, for on November 30, the church voted to reconsider the unrecorded censure and acquitted Easton.[113] Shortly after the turn of the century, a member of the Groton church was acquitted of adultery, but later made a confession of a lesser sexual offense.[114]

After 1800 adulterers rarely made confessions. Evidently indifferent to church membership, people began to prefer excommunication. Six impenitent adulterers, two men and four women, were excommunicated when persuasion failed.[115] Two of the excommunicates went into voluntary exile, leaving for "parts unknown" in order to avoid notoriety.[116] Another woman was excommunicated when the church learned that after she had expressed her intention to make a confession, she had continued in her adulterous ways.[117]

The last excommunication for adultery found in the records

occurred in 1854. It is of interest not only because of its late date, but because of the exceptionally complete record. The case began on June 27, 1851, when Martha Baldwin asked to be dismissed from the Pittsfield church. Because of some ugly rumors the church would not immediately comply and appointed an investigating committee.[118] On December 20, the committee charged Mrs. Baldwin with adultery, and brought the following complaint:

> You stand charged with having received the visits of the said Dodge in your chamber, sometimes two or three times a day . . . when your husband was away, and that one evening, when he was out of town, and Mr. Dodge was with you in the chamber your door was found locked, and it was nearly an hour after that, before he came downstairs and left the house.
>
> . . . It is testified that Mr Dodge was seen repeatedly climbing the high stockade fence in the rear of your house on Fenn St. and entering the house from that quarter instead of in front as was most convenient and natural. And your domestics, having their suspicions excited by his repeated visits testify that they had noticed during that time what they believed to be signals from certain windows to Mr Dodge, that Mr Baldwin had gone out, and that very soon Mr Dodge would appear and enter the house.[119]

The church had apparently constituted itself a grand jury and had launched an investigation before any charges were preferred. A confession offered in March, 1854, was rejected because it was not sufficiently specific, particularly in its failure to mention a love letter to Martha's "husband and only love" from his "most devoted wife." The church felt that "the confession is carefully worded, and while we may not assume to judge the motions of the heart, it carried under all the circumstances the appearances of disingenuousness and insincerity." [120] At this point in the proceedings the damaging love letter, somehow obtained by the church, was read and copied into the records. Martha had written to Dodge:

> Did I not know you would be disappointed should you receive no note I should not write you dearest; for really my minutes are

every one needed for my children; but with double diligence will I work for them and give you my only love a few brief moments. Do you know dearest I have not one word of yours to comfort me? Before going out this morning I threw the last note in the fire and now I fear I am about to be interrupted as my peaches have come and I have promised to assist Mr. McKay by paring them. Darling, what a school of self-control will our journey be to us! how necessary and yet how next to impossible!

5½ o'clock P.M. Could you see me now dearest, I know you would say, dear wife don't write, you really seem too weary. I am indeed weary, still I may not see you alone this evening, and I would not have you leave with a sad heart, after I have been loving you with all my soul, as I have this day.

The peaches demand my instant attention and now I have a backache, head ache, all sorts of aches except an aching heart. Thank God *that* I have not. He went down to see Mrs. Dodge after dinner and learned you had gone to Lenox. Oh darling in these absences, do you love me as I love you? Are you in very deed all truthful to me? Do you know how little I know of you these past few days? Do you know how I am hungering and thirsting for the manna of your daily allowance of affection, such as I used to receive in no stinted measure? Oh darling, you are very dear to me and ever do I pray that you may be all my living, idolizing heart would ask for the object of its intensest affection. I have been thinking whether it would not be more to her, for us to leave you at Anapolis, and we return to Baltimore and wait for you. . . . He [my husband] has returned with the children from a drive and I can no longer write, but that I am with all my powers your most devoted wife.

M.T.

P.S. All night long will I be true to you and love you only as your own. M.T.[121]

Until now the church had been willing to accept a thorough confession. But when Martha Baldwin denied having written the above letter, although she conceded the authorship of others, she was treated as a person who had "so far destroyed all evidence of Christian character that she ought to be, and hereby is, excommunicated from this church of Christ." A protest and a request for council were denied.[122]

A marginal case remains to be mentioned. In 1696 the Second Church of Boston dealt with Hannah Bishop, the wife of a seaman who, although he had not been gone to sea for a full year, had not been heard from. Hannah had promised to marry another man, "which if they [*sic*] had been consummated, her offence had by the law of this province been capital." What the church probably meant was that the marriage had not been solemnized, for Hannah was also charged with sexual relations with this same man. By the time the case was called to the attention of the church, Hannah was in Rhode Island. Sworn witnesses testified in the presence of the governor of that colony; the church read their depositions. Warned to make a confession or face excommunication, Hannah was suspended. Three months later she appeared in person, making a great impression on the church, which voted to restore her, although there is no mention of a confession in the records.[123]

Rape is rarely mentioned in the church records. In Reading a man joined the church after confessing an attempted rape. Shortly thereafter, he was accused of romancing with his maidservant and pleaded guilty.[124] In 1821 a member of the Montague church confessed that he had made several attacks on women, but there is no definite indication that rape was involved.[125] Another marginal case, and one of unusual interest, is that of George Bates of Boston, who was excommunicated in 1666. If the "unchast carridges" with a girl, for which Bates was censured, involved a sexual act, he was, by modern standards, guilty of statutory rape: the girl was only "nine or ten years old." [126]

Only one case of bestiality has been uncovered in the church records, and in all of New England only four such cases have been found in the records of the civil courts during the entire colonial period.[127] Benjamin Good, of Roxbury, was excommunicated for this crime in 1674, and was executed two weeks later.[128] Samuel Danforth, the local pastor, was quick to exploit the crime to deliver a homiletical harangue. Preaching on the text, Genesis 18:20-21, Danforth stressed that God's judgment on Good, a youth who probably was mentally deranged, was a warning to all:

Such judgments as these have a voice, a loud voice, a clamorous voice, a dreadful voice, calling to all *Israel, to Hear and Fear, and do no more so wickedly.*

God had "cutt off this rotten and putrid Member, that he might prevent spreading the Infection." In conclusion, Danforth observed: " 'Tis an Angelic Service to pluck poor sinners out of the Snare of Lasciviousness." [129]

An analysis of the ecclesiastical prosecutions for sexual offenses clearly shows that although the churches strove to limit sexual relations to married couples, they were less successful in controlling the sexual relations of their members than they were in regulating their members' morals in other areas. The fact that the vast majority of confessions of fornication were recorded in a matter-of-fact manner, without further comment than the date, name of the offender, and the fact that the acknowledgment had been made, indicates that such confessions were almost a part of the churches' routine. To be sure, the average number of fornication cases found in the records for the period from 1620 to 1839 was only 5.64 per year, but it must be remembered that the records consulted, especially in the case of the early period and of the post-Revolutionary decades, do not represent the entire picture. For the years from 1730 to 1769, for which the records are particularly complete, the average number of cases is almost seventeen per year, and it was at this time that the practice of public confession in fornication cases began to be challenged. That these confessions were more embarrassing to offenders than acknowledgments of certain other offenses, particularly in the eighteenth and early nineteenth centuries, is obvious. Although a majority of offenders was eventually restored, the confessions were not as readily forthcoming as in some other cases. No doubt the desires to have children baptized and to be admitted to full communion served as strong incentives.

The incompleteness of the records makes any correlation with present-day morality extremely hazardous. The Kinsey Reports' findings state that almost three-fourths of all American males have premarital sexual relations by the age of twenty-one,[130] while among women married by the time they were twenty, nearly half have had premarital relations.[131] Interestingly enough, however, the reports also show that the incidence among persons who are actively affiliated with a religious body is distinctly less than in the case of the total population.[132]

As in the case of domestic relations, the churches of Massachusetts erred in giving publicity to matters which should have been handled privately. On the other hand, however faulty their methods may have been, the churches, by enforcing their standards, seriously attempted to uphold the sacredness of the body.

VIII. "The Affected Bottle" and Its Consequences

Alcoholism, an ubiquitous and perennial problem of society, was well known to the Puritans. Like Calvin before them, they had no objection to the use of spirituous liquor in the colonial period. The "Puritan" who shuddered at the very sight (or thought) of a glass of beer or wine, not to mention hard liquor, did not live in colonial Massachusetts; almost two centuries elapsed between the arrival of the *Mayflower* and the founding of the Massachusetts Society for the Supression of Intemperance in 1813, while the Maine Law was not enacted until 1851.

Not the moderate use of alcoholic beverages, but their abuse, was objectionable to the Puritans. While prohibition was unknown in the colonial period, laws against drunkenness were enacted at an early date.[1] In the Plymouth Colony fines or other punishments for intoxication were enacted in 1636, and a statute of 1646 provided that a person who lisped, faultered in speech, staggered, vomited, or was unable to follow his profession was to be considered intoxicated.[2] In Massachusetts a half pint was the maximum any patron could obtain at a time in a tavern, and his tippling was restricted to a half hour; if he stayed longer, he risked a fine of a half crown, and in 1696 the selectmen were instructed to post lists of notorious drinkers.[3]

Intoxication was generally considered a public offense. Persons convicted of drunkenness were expected to make public confessions, and in two instances proposed private confessions were rejected,[4] but in another case the church decided that only if the offense was generally known was a public confession required, thus suggesting that intoxication might be a private offense.[5]

Considering the incompleteness of the extant records, the figures on alcoholism show no significant trends, either by counties or by periods.[6] The one exception is the rise of cases after 1810. During the forty years from 1770 to 1809, a total of ninety-four cases are found, but for the following thirty years the total is 104. The increase in Hampden and Berkshire counties is largely the result of the continuing disciplinary action in the west at a time when church discipline elsewhere went into desuetude. There is no evidence to suggest that alcoholism was especially prominent in the west, and the increase may well be explained by a growing awareness on the part of the churches of the problem of alcoholism. No "grape juice Protestants" could be found among the Congregationalists of seventeenth-century Massachusetts. In the nineteenth century, however, references to the use of unfermented grape juice at the Lord's Supper are more frequent.[7]

This change reflected a trend in the churches' attitude towards the use of alcoholic liquor. In 1676, and again in 1684, the elders of the Plymouth church observed that churchmen were reported to have been seen drunk, and exhorted the members to deal with their intoxicated friends.[8] Increase Mather, struck by the coincidence of a smallpox epidemic and the multiplication of alehouses,[9] sorrowfully observed that the days when people did not waste entire nights or Sabbaths at taverns were gone, and expressed his position by proclaiming *Wo to Drunkards*.[10] Cotton Mather, too, was disturbed. "The Consequences of the affected Bottel [*sic*] . . . are beyond all Imagination," he wrote in 1710.[11] His own communicants included "several wicked people" given to too much liquor,[12] and some time later, concerned about a minister who had taken to the bottle, he resolved to write a solemn letter of rebuke.[13] Other ministers joined the Mathers' denunciation of drunkenness.[14] The minister of Brewster complained that the noise made by the people during the intermission between Sabbath services was unparalleled even in populous Boston, and exhorted them to temperance in the use of liquor, especially on the Sabbath. They must elect responsible selectmen, he told his flock, so that the laws against intoxication and intemperance might be enforced. The pastor, better at exhortation than in theology, justified his remark:

and that I should not have said w[ha]t I did were it not that an Infinite Person whome I knew to be then present had commanded me to warn my p[eo]p[le], and to doe it whether they would heir [hear] or whether they would forbear, yea tho they should be rebellious; and that if I did not warn them it should be on this penalty that he would require their blood and the blood of their children at my hand.[15]

But never did a minister or church require abstinence: temperance was the aim.

The churches' temperance crusade lingered on into the nineteenth century. In Sheffield, the church appropriated funds for the purchase of eight copies of Dr. Beecher's sermons on intemperance, and the Becket church voted to consider its covenant a "bond of temperance." [16] But three churches voted that the use of spirits, except for medicinal purposes, was contrary to the Christian profession, and one church launched an investigation into its members' drinking habits.[17] Temperance was giving way to abstinence.

Army life during the intercolonial wars was conducive to intemperance. A soldier returning from King William's War was admonished for cursing, swearing, and intoxication, "both abroad among the soldiers, and here since he came home." The implication here was that he was temperate before he enlisted.[18] The assistant minister of the Brattle Street Church in Boston made a public confession of intemperance, a habit which he had acquired while serving as a chaplain in Queen Anne's War.[19] If he was the only chaplain thus disciplined, there were some ministers untainted by army life who also were given to excessive drinking. A Topsfield pastor was dismissed in 1671 because of intemperance,[20] and in 1706 and 1815 pastoral relationships were dissolved because the ministers were intemperate.[21] Another minister saved himself from dismissal by making a confession. The Reverend Samuel Palmer, of Falmouth, kept unusually legible records, but two of his entries are almost illegible. In the smallest possible writing Samuel Palmer recorded the fact that he had himself made a public confession of intemperance.[22] That such behavior on the pastor's part should be a cause of concern to the church is understandable. More surprising is the record of a confession by a brother who, as the record carefully points out, was drunk while gathering wood for the pastor.[23]

Some confessions, such as that of Stephen Kellogg, of Westfield, were spontaneous, anticipating censures. Lounging near his barn on a warm spring day, Kellogg was soon joined by Joseph Pixlie. Together they drank some cider. There was no proof that Kellogg was actually drunk, but sensing public dissatisfaction with his conduct, Kellogg confessed that he was "a very sinful creature." Evidently Kellogg stayed sober for two years and then suffered a relapse. This time it was a warm autumn day, and Kellogg had gone to buy cattle. As he stopped to examine John Shephard's oxen, he paused to drink two or three pots of liquor with his friend. Going on to view Samuel Ashly's oxen, he consumed another pot or two. By this time Kellogg staggered and reeled, but firmly insisted that he had merely a queasy stomach. Convicted by the church on the evidence of witnesses, Kellogg offered a confession which was rejected. Another confession, submitted six years later, restored him to fellowship.[24]

Excuses, frequently offered by persons charged with drunkenness, rarely fooled the churches. Lydia Cushman attributed her state to bodily infirmity, but the church would not accept the explanation. Neither was the evidence sufficient to convict her. Since there was no proof of her guilt, she was restored with a warning that "the Lord is a Jealous God, whose Eyes are as a Flaming Fire, who searcheth the Rains [*sic,* reins?] and the Heart and will give to every man according to his work." The exhortation was effective: after two years Lydia voluntarily appeared before the church and confessed that she had indeed been drunk.[25] A deacon who ascribed his unusual behavior to an injury sustained in a fall from a horse was found guilty and lost his office, although his confession was accepted.[26] One man who made a public confession of drunkenness defended his conduct on the ground that he had been oblivious of his actions because of a blow received some years earlier.[27] Anticipating a social evil of increasing prominence today was the excuse offered by Elias Hayden, who alleged that his condition was caused not by liquor but by opium. The explanation was rejected as unsatisfactory: if he did indeed use opium, which the church doubted, his frequent use of it would render him unfit as a member of the church.[28]

Several alcoholics were dealt with by the churches after the courts had convicted them.[29] When the pastor of Salem learned that Samuel Archer had been convicted by the county court, he presented the record of the court to the church. This included the testimony of a witness who deposed that the defendant had staggered along and fallen down before returning his greeting with a "Hogh," after which he had fallen to the ground. On the basis of the evidence before the court, the church convicted Archer and, for his failure to give satisfaction, excommunicated him.[30] Similarly censured was John Archer, perhaps Samuel's brother, after his conviction of drunkenness by a court.[31] Somewhat different was the treatment given to Lieutenant Stockwell, who had been arrested for intoxication. The church voted to take no notice of the case unless a formal complaint were made. Anticipating this, Stockwell appeared to apologize for his misconduct. The church would not censure Stockwell for this offense, but later charged him with intoxication on two other occasions, neither of which had resulted in the arrest. Because Stockwell left the town, the proceedings were discontinued. Two years later, when he and his wife publicly confessed their fornication, the intoxication charge was overlooked.[32]

Of the persons dealt with for alcoholism, 46 women and 186 men were restored and presumably remained sober, while 22 women and 72 men were eventually excommunicated, sometimes as recidivists. In the remaining cases the result is in doubt. On the whole, recidivists were not treated more severely than first offenders. Of the twenty-six men and two women who were twice charged with intoxication or intemperance, thirteen were restored to the fellowship.[33] Seven were excommunicated, one died before the church could take final action, and in the remaining cases the conclusion is not indicated, or the case was dropped.[34] Only one of the six members charged three times with drunkenness was excommunicated.[35] The others, four men and a woman, were restored,[36] in one instance with a warning that another conviction would result in excommunication.[37]

A sincere concern for the welfare of alcoholics was shown by the churches.[38] Sometimes the restoration was preceded by a period of probation, a practice which appears already in the last quarter of the seventeenth century. Thus Samuel Rigby, who gave some satisfaction for his intemperance, was suspended and placed on his good behavior. Had his behavior met the church's standards he would have been restored, but like so many alcoholics Rigby relapsed into drunkenness and was excommunicated.[39] Probation was the standard practice of the First Church of Marblehead during the third decade of the nineteenth century. Of the six persons charged with drunkenness in the 1820's, all of whom were women, four were placed on probation. The general practice was to suspend the alcoholic for periods ranging from two to four months, and to continue the suspension on a monthly, bimonthly, or even quarterly basis, until the evidence was sufficient to convince the church that the woman had reformed. Of the four women thus treated, two were restored, one after nine months, the other after two years.[40] That this method was not generally effective in attaining the desired end is shown by the fact that of the sixteen alcoholics placed on probation by the churches, seven were eventually excommunicated.[41] In five cases the result cannot be ascertained.[42] Except for the two women in Marblehead, only one drunkard was definitely restored after a probationary period,[43] but the last entry in one case states that the alcoholic woman's behavior had improved.[44]

Evidence of reformation, unaccompanied by a confession, was a sufficient basis of restoration in some cases. In the case of a woman convicted of intemperance, the church refused to accept a proposed confession because it was not matched by the offender's conduct. Six months later the woman was forgiven and restored without a confession, either because the church observed her repentance, or else the confession originally submitted was accepted in lieu of one at the time of the restoration.[45] In Plymouth, a brother, suspended eighteen years earlier, was able to convince the church of his reformation and exemplary behavior, and was restored without a confession.[46] A similar restoration is found in the Ipswich records, but the forgiven woman relapsed into drunkenness and was again suspended.[47] More interesting from a legal standpoint is the case of a Marblehead woman who, after a six months' suspension for intemperance, was restored without demand of confession. Her plea that she drank to excess only when mentally disordered was accepted by the church, which took judicial notice of the fact that "she had been notoriously heretofore in a State of Delirum." [48]

Acquittals in cases of alcoholism were comparatively rare. In one case the church, without hearing any testimony, voted to dismiss a complaint as unsupported, while two other complaints were dismissed after a hearing.[49] A conviction, followed by a suspension, was revoked two weeks later when, upon reconsideration of the evidence, the church voted to acquit the respondent.[50] One man, charged with excessive drinking and lying, was convicted of the latter but was acquitted on the charge of intemperance.[51]

Illegal liquor sales troubled the Truro church, which in 1728 voted to discipline members who engaged in the liquor trade without a license.[52] The only case involving such sales, however, was found in Plymouth, where a member was admonished in 1681 for selling liquor to Indians.[53]

Closely related to intoxication was profanity. God's Name, the Third Commandment admonished, was not to be taken in vain. As jealous protectors of God's majesty, the Puritans were understandably intolerant of any abuse of his name, or of any light talk on a sacred subject. In his "Farewell Exhortation" of 1657, Richard Mather observed with alarm that profanity, swearing, and scoffing at religion were becoming increasingly common in Massachusetts,[54] and more than a generation later Cotton Mather placed swearing and cursing at the head of the list of sins for which, he insisted, his church should make a confession.[55]

In nearly a third of the sixty-one cases of profanity, including one acquittal, the offenders were simultaneously charged with drunkenness.[56] In contrast to cases involving intemperance, which required reformation as well as repentance, or to confessions of fornication, which involved a social stigma, members convicted of profanity made their confessions quickly, unless the profanity was a by-product of drunkenness or of some offense. An exception was Melita Newport, who not only refused to make a confession, but threatened a church member, saying that she would "knock his damned brains out." The church, as much shocked by the profanity as by the threat, excommunicated Melita.[57]

The exact words with which God's Name was abused were never recorded. A typical entry reads: "Confessed publicly the Sin of taking Gods Name in vain." [58] Hebraists may take comfort in the fact that one man made profane use of "the Lord's name of Jahveh," rather than of the less accurate but more popular "Jehovah." [59]

Certain language might be objectionable even if not profane. Thus persons were censured for the use of expressions which ran the gamut from "lascivious," [60] "vain, Impure, and scornful," [61] "reviling," [62] "unguarded," [63] and "filthy and obscene," [64] to "unchristian" [65] or simply "offensive," [66] and in Reading a man's "passionate" speech in town meeting rendered him subject to censure.[67] Of the persons accused of improper (but not profane) language only one was excommunicated, for impenitence.[68] In one instance the church refused to censure a convicted member; another conviction, unaccompanied by any censure, was subsequently vacated.[69] A pastor who in discussing the Seventh Commandment allegedly had used "language grossly indelicate," causing "disagreeable sensations in the minds of the pious and bluch [*sic*] on the cheek of modesty, and exciting the laughter and ridicule of the less serious part of the congregation," was acquitted. Later, however, he was dismissed from office, but for other reasons.[70]

Passionate or contentious persons, many of whom were also charged with indecent language, were subject to censure by the church. The record often leaves considerable doubt whether the action was for assault, breach of the peace, or lesser varieties of disorderly conduct. At common law, a trespass *vi et armis* might or might not involve a breach of the peace; conversely, not every breach of the peace involved an assault.[71] For the sake of clarity we may distinguish between cases in which a church member was accused of fighting, contentiousness, or passionate conduct in itself, even if a specific assault is mentioned, and those in which a person was charged with a specific and isolated assault.

Quarrelsome behavior was censurable even in the absence of any assault. Thus John Pemmerton in 1639 publicly acknowledged his contentiousness and the use of reviling language.[72]

At later dates three men confessed their "unchristian passion," while a fourth conviction for this offense was disregarded when the respondent applied for a dismission to the Methodist Church.[73] Two men jointly confessed that they had quarreled, and a third acknowledged that he had a "contentious and quarrelsome disposition," but no overt act is mentioned in these cases.[74] Other confessions mention such vague concepts as an "improper disposition," [75] ill-temperedness,[76] and, in an acknowledgment made jointly by two women, "unfriendly feelings." [77] An officer was excommunicated for impenitence following a conviction for "overbearing and abusive treatment of his fellow men" and with obscene language,[78] and early in the history of the First Church of Salem a man was cast out for "unnaturalness to his wife," who had recently been executed for the murder of her child.[79] In Canton, Mary Billing was suspended for her *"abusive* and *unchristian"* conduct towards an aged woman. Fifteen years later, when Mary declared her innocence and apologized for absence from the trial, the complaint was dismissed.[80] Also dismissed was a complaint alleging "oppression," the respondent agreeing to submit the issue informally to a group of the brethren.[81] A man who obviously was at odds with his brethren and drank toasts "to the damnation of those who did not love him" was admonished to repent lest he be excommunicated, but the record fails to show whether he made the desired confession.[82]

Turning to the cases which mention or imply physical violence, we come to the margin between assault and breach of the peace. For breaches of the Sixth and Eighth commandments by fighting and wasting their substance, Samuel Smeed, of Deerfield, and Joseph Younglove, his father or father-in-law, were severely rebuked by the minister. The cause of the contention is not known, but an assault is mentioned in the record. In the hope that Smeed would repent, the church deferred action. In the meanwhile, Younglove was accused of kicking his or Smeed's wife (the record is not clear), whereupon Smeed struck Younglove. Thus both men incurred the censure of the church and were required to make confessions for fighting.[83] That the Smeed-Younglove case was not unusual, except in its particulars, is shown by the other confessions for "fighting," sometimes combined with drunkenness or abusive language, which appear in the records,[84] while in two instances men were required to make satisfaction for conduct distinctly described as breaches of the peace.[85]

Not only the use of physical violence, but the mere threat of it rendered a church member subject to discipline.[86] The Weston church accepted the confession of a man who had threatened to take his father's life, while a churchman of Cambridge was suspended for threatening to kill his mother.[87] As late as 1815 a church heard the confession of John Forbes who, while drunk, had threatened to break Royal Cooper's ribs if his adversary consented to a fight. Another charge, that Forbes had said that he was the only honest man in town and that the others used liquor too freely, was dismissed for lack of a second witness.[88] A council which sat in Lanesborough held that it was "contrary to Christian wisdom and prudence" for an officer engaged in executing a warrant to point a pistol at a fellow townsman. Stephen Jewett, charged with conduct "unbecoming his Christian character," being passionate, and using improper language, had appealed his conviction by the church. The council upheld the church, which accepted the council's advice and excommunicated the unrepentant Jewett.[89]

A partial acquittal is found in the case of Mrs. McNitt, of Palmer, who had been charged in three counts with falsehood, beginning a contention with her son, and beginning another quarrel in a matter which is not described. After a trial, the church acquitted Mrs. McNitt on the first and second counts, and divided the third count into two parts, alleging that she had begun a quarrel with Mrs. Grover and then had behaved in "an unchristlike manner." On the first part, alleging that she had begun the contention, Mrs. McNitt was acquitted, but paradoxically the church found her guilty on the second part of the count, alleging unchristian conduct, because "it does appear that Mrs. Ruth McNitt began the contention." Mrs. McNitt, doubtless happy about the church's inconsistency, made a confession of her guilt as charged in the latter part of the third count, thus leaving us as mystified as before.[90]

That drunkenness was not uncommon in colonial Massachusetts is clearly apparent from the records. Although the early statutes placed no prohibition on alcoholic beverages, they provided rigid standards, drawing the line between sobriety and drunkenness. The churches, free from statutory definitions, followed their own judgment rather than rely on the legal definitions, which were perhaps a bit too rigid. Constantly on the alert for intoxicated or intemperate persons, the churches doubtless supplemented the civil authorities' suppression of drunkenness. Recognizing the fact that intemperance is a condition rather than an act, the churches displayed their resourcefulness in placing alcoholics on probation before restoring them. Clearly associated with alcoholism were the use of profane language and fighting. Going beyond the strict limits of the law, the churches censured not only those who actually participated in brawls, but also those who quarreled orally or who threatened to commit an assault. Although some churches advocated abstinence in the nineteenth century, moderation was the sin throughout the colonial period. The consumption of alcoholic liquor was in itself unobjectionable, but the church member who overstepped the line between temperate drinking and intoxication was sure to find himself arraigned before the church.[91]

IX. The Sixth Commandment: Offenses against the Person

Life was God's gift, and no man had the right to take it upon himself to deprive another or himself of it. The Sixth Commandment clearly forbade murder, but like the others it was broadly construed to encompass any trespass on another person's body, or any other act which might endanger a person's safety.[1] While murder cases are rare in the church records, we find a fairly steady stream of cases involving street brawls, vaguely defined acts of "fighting," accusations of quarrelsomeness, as well as clearly specified acts of assault, twenty in all, well distributed in the period down to 1820.

The earliest such case, and the cruelest short of those involving murder, is that of Nathaniel Eaton, who, equipped with the Ph.D. and M.D. degrees from Padua, arrived in America in 1637 and soon became headmaster of what was to become Harvard College. His career as an educator was cut short in 1639, when he was punished by a court for inflicting two hundred stripes on Nathaniel Briscoe, his companion, with whom he had an argument. As soon as the colony had closed its case against Eaton the church exercised its own authority. Not satisfied with the evidence before the court, the church asked the governor whether it might call additional witnesses. The official could see no need for this, but told the church that if it wanted to conduct a separate trial it might do so. Before the church was able to proceed, however, Eaton fled, was arrested, and escaped again by a ruse in which the gubernatorial agent was nearly drowned. When Eaton's creditors learned of his escape, they immediately acted to attach his property, for the fugitive owed them a hundred pounds. By the time the church had excommunicated Eaton, he was safe in Virginia, whence he returned to England. After an undistinguished clerical career, Eaton died in debtor's prison. Whatever other charges might have been laid to Eaton, the excommunication was based on his assault of Briscoe.[2]

Later in the century John Lowden found himself at odds with a Boston constable who attempted to deal with him for drunkenness. For striking the unfortunate officer Lowden was required to make a public confession, whereupon he was restored. Six years later, however, Lowden, an incorrigible alcoholic, was first admonished and then excommunicated.[3] Except for a man who in 1707 was admonished for rebelling against the authority of the constable,[4] the records mention no other officials who were assaulted between 1667 and 1814. In the latter year, a collector in Peru learned the hard way that men in his position were not popular. Obadiah Abbe, who like so many others did not like to pay taxes, heaped abuse on the innocent collector and assaulted him. At first Abbe consented to make a confession. Then he changed his mind and absented himself from church meetings for seven years. In 1821 he appeared before the church to announce that he would acknowledge the offense. The church voted to hear it in a week, but when the members reassembled Abbe was absent, "through forgetfulness," as he later told the church. Abbe was repeatedly admonished and, seven years after his initial offense, was excommunicated. A month later, however, the censure was rescinded and a suspension voted in its place. Whether Abbe ever made a confession is not stated.[5]

The typical ecclesiastical prosecution for assault was of a quasi-criminal nature. In most cases the action was begun by a complaint presented by some member not directly involved in the trespass, or by the church's taking cognizance of a member's conviction by a court. Thus Lieutenant Amos Stanley, who was not directly affected by the incident, brought a complaint against Lieutenant Lemuel Collens for striking Dan Welles and John Adams with an ox whip. The church found that Collens had struck both men, but concluded that the assault on Adams was not censurable. Evenly divided as to whether the attack on Welles should subject Collens to censure, the church referred the issue to a council, which advised that Collens had transgressed the rule in both instances and should make a public confession. After first accepting the council's advice, the church reconsidered its vote and rejected the finding that Collens had wronged Adams. However, Collens was required to confess his assault on Welles, which he did.[6]

Similar doubts on the part of the churches held up the final determination in the cases of Ephraim Robards and Henry Badger. Robards had been suspended for striking an Irish neighbor, but the church was undecided whether the confession should be public. Eighteen months later a proposed confession was tabled, pending a decision on the undecided matter. Another year elapsed, during which Robards resisted unofficial pressure on the part of church members who attempted to induce him to make a public confession. Finally the church retracted the original suspension. Noting that the assault had been provoked by the Irishman, who had beaten Robards's son, the church voted to restore Robards without a confession.[7] In Badger's case the church first voted to dismiss the complaint, alleging that he had whipped Miss Keeny with his stick, because the complainant had not exhausted the private steps. Then the church held a hearing on the merits and, by a vote of twelve to nine, acquitted Badger.[8]

An assault on a child was sure to incur the church's wrath on the offender, particularly when the victim was the pastor's son. Josiah Cotton, the son of John Cotton, Jr., pastor of Plymouth, enjoyed climbing trees. Seeing the boy in her tree, Mrs. Dorothy Clarke, who might not have objected had Josiah confined his climbing to his father's trees, was enraged. Instead of calling Mrs. Cotton, the infuriated tree owner, unable to reach any higher, pulled Josiah's leg until he fell to the ground bleeding. Called before the church, Mrs. Clarke, described as a woman with "an evill frame of spirit," argued that she had taken Josiah from the tree gently and had placed him on his feet. The bleeding, she insisted, had been deliberately provoked by Mrs. Cotton, who had afterwards cut Josiah with a key which she placed in his mouth. The church accepted Mrs. Cotton's version of the incident and required Mrs. Clarke to make a confession. Her first reaction was to tell the church committee that she would have nothing to do with them, but on second thought she decided to make a public confession in order to be restored.[9]

Nearly a century later a Mattapoisett churchman was convicted of cruelty to a boy who lived in his house, aggravated by the fact that the scourging had taken place on the Sabbath. The offender finally repented and made a confession to the church.[10] In another church, a complaint against a man, charging that he had struck a boy not in his charge and had failed to heal the injury, was merged in a later complaint alleging prevarication and was decided on the merits of the latter charge.[11]

Although the majority of prosecutions for assault were of a quasi-criminal nature, two cases analogous to tort actions, instituted by the aggrieved party, are found in the records. In Canton, John Wentworth, previously convicted by his church of several real estate frauds and of fornication, was accused by Joseph Estis of assaulting him. When the church met to try the case both parties were absent. Estis was in jail, awaiting arraignment on a criminal charge brought by Wentworth; Wentworth had simply decided not to come. Nevertheless the church proceeded to discuss the case and voted that Estis had ample cause to bring the complaint before the church, rather than to pursue private steps. Two weeks later Wentworth submitted an acknowledgment to Estis, which was accepted by the complainant with the consent of the church.[12] Some years later, Mary Jones accused John Scudder of assaulting her with a stick. Scudder pleaded guilty before the church but refused to sign a confession which was to be read publicly, and was suspended.[13]

A large majority of persons convicted of assault made confessions and were restored. Alone to be excommunicated, apart from the insolvent schoolmaster of Cambridge, was a man who while under the influence of liquor had struck his father and refused to make a confession.[14] Another, who had struck his father on the Sabbath was restored when he made a confession,[15] as were two men who had assaulted their brother and cousin, respectively.[16] Except for three cases in which the outcome is not indicated and the three excommunications, all persons charged with assault were restored.[17]

Disciplinary cases arising from cruelty to slaves or servants are rarely found in the church records. In 1643 William Franklin or Frankling, of Roxbury, was excommunicated for cruelty to a servant boy, which resulted in the lad's death. Shortly thereafter, the church record states, Franklin was executed.[18] If Franklin was indeed executed, it must have been another William Franklin (this time spelled Francklyn) who, in 1645, was excommunicated in Boston for cruelty to a servant. Seven months later he was restored, only to be excommunicated late in 1646 for extortion.[19] The only other case of this nature is found in the Barnstable records, which mention a woman who was reproved for joining her landlady in beating a maid.[20]

The most interesting confession concerning slaves or servants, however, was made for a somewhat different reason. In 1830 Deacon Asa Marble, of Worthington, made a confession which is unique in the records of the Massachusetts churches:

Brethren, I know that he who spake as never man speaks has said It is impossible but that offenses must come, but not to him through whom they come. With some faint view of this awful denunciation I would beseech him not to lay this sin to my charge.

Since I have been a member of this church, as often as I have heard an offending brother confess to it and the world his faults I have said in my heart at least—He has a pleasure the stranger intermeddleth not with. Brethren, I ask it as a privilege of which I am not worthy to stand before you this day and in the public manner to acknowledge I have been a backslider all my days and particularly to acknowledge all the sin I feel to have been guilty of buying, keeping, offering, and selling a creature of which I need not further speak. I think I can say for all the occasion I have given the world to speak reproachfully for all the dishonor done to the cause of Christ by thus doing I am sorry from my heart. For every wound a brother feels or has felt in this case, brethren, I am sorry, and ask you to forgive me and to pray to God to forgive me and keep me that I sin no more against him nor my brethren. Brethren, I would and think that I do acknowledge, with all the honest of my heart all that I feel in this case. If I do not see and feel so much sin in this as do my brethren I would not ask for more than did Naaman: "The Lord pardon thy servant in this thing." [21]

Although several murderers are incidentally mentioned in the church records, only two, Franklin and a woman, Dorothy Talbye, were subjected to ecclesiastical censures. A victim of melancholia and delusions, Dorothy Talbye murdered her three-year-old daughter, who had been given the curious name of "Difficulty." In the interval between her conviction in 1639 and her execution, Dorothy Talbye was repeatedly admonished by her church. When all efforts to secure a confession failed, the church excommunicated her. The murderess received the announcement of the censure with contempt and had to be forcefully stopped from walking out on the pastor.[22] The reason for the atrocity is not known, but we know that in their eagerness to punish fornication, the magistrates and ministers were oblivious to the danger that mothers might kill their illegitimate children. A number of executions for such murders are found in the records and diaries of ministers, but no records of corresponding ecclesiastical censures have been uncovered,[23] although the records of the First Church of Boston mention a woman's confession for the attempted drowning of her child. There is no indication, however, that the child was illegitimate.[24]

Although not herself a murderess, Sarah Cleaves was censured for her actions which indirectly led to the death of a child. Sarah, who was given to lavish entertaining, was known to have corrupted the morals of her neighbors' children and servants. Under her influence a woman slave had become so debased that one night she set fire to her mistress's house. In the ensuing holocaust a girl was burned to death and the other members of the family barely escaped with their lives. Presumably the slave was not a church member; there is no indication that she was censured. Sarah Cleaves, however, who had instigated the arson, was publicly admonished. Over two years elapsed before she made a confession and was restored.[25]

The commandment against murder was stretched to apply to a woman who had failed to accommodate travelers who were in danger of their lives. For this offense Elizabeth Hart, of Reading, was required to submit a confession. The proposed acknowledgment was accepted although it was "far short of what they judged needful," and Elizabeth was restored.[26]

Because dueling might cause death, John Fenno was brought before the church for agreeing to engage in a duel. Fenno admitted the fact, but challenged the church's belief that dueling or challenging a person to a duel was a censurable offense. This argument was rejected when the church required a public confession of Fenno, which he made a week later.[27] A confession before the congregation was also required of a brother of the Lanesborough church who had accepted a challenge.[28]

With its terrible threat of the possibility of everlasting doom, and with the constant uncertainty as to whether one was of the elect or not, Puritanism was ideally suited to induce persons of unstable emotions to commit suicide. Even the Covenant Theology's modification of Calvinism could not wholly remove this threat. A person who had become convinced that he had not been called to eternal life and had made a mistake in owning the covenant might justifiably feel that, if he was destined to eternal reprobation, he might as well reach the predetermined end without first going through the anguish which awaited him in this life.[29] So frequent were suicides in the early period of Massachusetts history that a statute was enacted to prohibit Christian burial for suicides. As a deterrent to potential suicides, persons who had taken their own lives were to be buried in a highway; the grave was to be covered with a cartload of stones.[30]

In their disciplinary action the churches were necessarily limited to the censure of persons who had unsuccessfully attempted to take their lives. The earliest such case, which is found in the Roxbury records for 1682, gives us no information other than the fact that Isack Heath was restored to church fellowship after his confession of attempted suicide.[31] In Salem, a woman swallowed one and a half spoons full of pounded glass but survived. After a prolonged convalescence, during which she also suffered from pangs of conscience, she made a confession and was restored.[32] No more successful was Samuel Bliss, of Longmeadow, who attempted to drown himself, but "God restrained him—and Suffered not Satan to have power over him." The Longmeadow records cannot be found, but the pastor's diary mentions a prayer that God might remove Bliss's malady.[33] The last case, found in Falmouth, concerns Joseph Bourne, who acknowledged in writing that he had attempted suicide while mentally deranged. Because of the "solemnity" of the crime, Bourne was required to read the confession himself.[34]

X. Bearers of False Witness

The Ninth Commandment, which Calvin construed broadly,[1] together with the history of the law of slander, gave the Puritans a firm basis on which to discipline members who hurled calumnies at others or who committed perjury. In its early days the English law left defamation to the ecclesiastical courts. With the decline of canon law and the rise of common law, slander became a species of trespass on the case, while libel, a crime, was punishable in the king's court. The current distinction between defamation by the spoken word and defamation in print was a later innovation.[2] If tradition is a guide, it was therefore entirely appropriate for the churches to take cognizance of such cases, although the civil (i.e., nonecclesiastical) law provided penalties for slander. In Plymouth, a willful lie told with an intent to deceive or abuse persons rendered the offender liable to a fine of ten shillings or confinement in the stocks.[3] In Massachusetts, similar laws were in effect. There an act of 1645 provided for a fine of ten shillings or two hours' confinement in the stocks for the publication of a lie detrimental to the public welfare or injurious to a person, if told with a malicious intent. Recidivists were subject to a fine of twenty shillings or ten lashes, while children were to be corrected by their parents or masters in the presence of an officer appointed by the court.[4] Moreover, slander was a tort and rendered the offender liable for damages. In tort actions for slander, as distinguished from criminal prosecutions for libel, truth was always a defense, and a criminal action was no bar to a tort action.[5]

In twenty-one of the eighty-seven cases of slander found in the records, the proceedings were of a quasi-criminal nature, the church taking the initiative and treating the matter as a public case from the beginning. More often the case came before the church when the complainant had failed to obtain satisfaction and had vainly taken the prescribed private steps. In the field of defamation, therefore, the churches acted primarily as civil court, seeking to redress the wrong done to the injured party, rather than as criminal tribunals.

The most common ground of complaint was a false accusation of lying.[6] An early case of this nature occurred on Cape Cod in 1649, when a woman was excommunicated for obstinately refusing to give satisfaction for slandering two women.[7] In Boston, a man who had been accused of calling the complainant a "base fellow, lying fellow, rogue," refused to plead and was suspended, while in neighboring Dorchester a sister confessed that she had slandered a brother of the church by charging him with lies and perjury.[8] For saying that a brother would gladly trade a lie "for a bit of bread and cheese and a pot of syder," a Salisbury churchman was found guilty of slander, but the outcome of the case is not recorded.[9] One church accepted a confession from a man who had referred to a deacon as "an old *One-Eyed Hypocrite* and a lying *Old Sinner*," while another was able to settle a case which had begun when one member called another "a Rascal-Hypocrete [*sic*]." [10]

Four aggrieved brethren alleged that they had been accused not only of lying, but of perjuring themselves under oath. One case was satisfactorily settled with the aid of a committee; in another the slanderer made a public confession, while in the third the record is incomplete.[11] The fourth case resulted from Brother Hazzan's objection against Thomas Haynes's admission to the church. Hazzan alleged that Haynes had charged him with perjury and demanded satisfaction. Maintaining that the quarrel had previously been settled, with an understanding that it should not be raised anew, Haynes refused to comply with the church's ruling that he make a confession. But

Haynes had broken the agreement not to mention the incident and had thus opened the way to a church trial. After hearing the witnesses, the church acquitted Haynes on the charge of breaking the agreement and held that any satisfaction he might have given Hazzan estopped Hazzan from seeking further redress. Rather illogically, however, the church ruled that Haynes must make a public confession for his slander. At this point, if the sequence of events is properly recorded, Haynes produced "six or seven" witnesses to prove that Hazzan had committed perjury. The verdict was ambiguous. The church concluded that "Haynes's charge against Hazzan is true . . . nevertheless it appears so dark and doubtful whether true or false that we chuse to leave it to the Decision of our Great Judge whenever He shall please to reveal it," and rescinded the decision that Haynes make a confession.[12]

Cases arising from allegedly false accusations of theft and fraud were only slightly less common than actions for statements implying that the complainant was a liar. A tax collector in Worthington, who was apparently honest, considered himself slandered by three citizens. One had accused him of a fraud in collecting taxes but, after two meetings with the church, made a public confession. The others, Messrs. Benjamin and Parish, had charged the collector with a dishonest transaction involving some bricks which the collector had attached. At the first hearing Benjamin was absent, but Parish and the collector presented their cases. There was truth on both sides, and the church, feeling that both litigants had acted sincerely, accepted Parish's acknowledgment that "instead of saying positively that things were so he should have said he understood so." At a somewhat later date Benjamin issued a public statement apologizing for having innocently given rise to a misunderstanding.[13]

A similar defense was offered by Major John Bradford, of Plymouth, who had been accused of slandering a member by saying that he had cut wood on Bradford's property. Unable to decide whether Bradford "had positively charged him thus, or only had said that he believed he had Cutt so much," the church took refuse in a technicality. The parties had violated an agreement to attempt a settlement and were required to make a confession. Bradford made his immediately; his adversary tarried a while, but was finally convinced of his fault.[14]

Among the other cases arising from false accusations of theft [15] or fraud [16] is that of Anne Hibbon, of Boston, who was excommunicated for slanderously accusing some brethren of charging extortionate rates.[17] In Groton, Prudence Parker complained that her brother, John Cummings, had falsely accused her of stealing a fifty-pound note and twenty pounds worth of rye. Furthermore, Prudence alleged that Cummings had said that she thirsted after his estate "as bad as Pirrotts [*sic*] do after Blood," and that he would surely recover, from her or her heirs, the property of which she had wronged him. After hearing the parties and their witnesses, the church found both persons guilty of "imprudent, unchristian, and unguarded treatment of each other." Both parties had intimated that they would not accept an unfavorable decision and that if they could not win their cases before the church, they would go to law. The church was in a dilemma. If it gave judgment for one side or the other, it might find itself reversed by the court. Hence it attempted to settle the dispute, urging mutual forgiveness and warning both sides that should they go to law, they would be suspended until the case was decided. After two adjournments the parties complied with the church's suggestion, settling the issue out of church.[18]

Unjustified statements attributing sexual immorality to persons were held to be slanderous. Edward Mills, Boston's notorious adulterer, was charged, among other things, with slandering a woman by accusing her of prostitution,[19] and a man who engaged in the following dialogue,

> Blackman: How doth she do?
> Rhodes: What *She?*
> Blackman: Your wife and my whore. . . .

Rhodes: What do you mean my wife to be your whore?
Blackman: Yes, and I can prove it. . . .

was summoned before the church. Blackman, pleading that he said it in jest, was convicted of slander and obscenity, the words being "morally evil in themselves." He conceded that his choice of words was "unadvised," but refused to make a confession and was suspended. A year later he publicly confessed his slander.[20] Also considered slanderous were charges that a member's wife was the mother of the respondent's child,[21] that an almshousekeeper had attempted to have sexual relations with an inmate,[22] and that a woman was "as bad as Mrs. Tyler," a person of notorious lewdness.[23]

Unique among the confessions found in the records is that of the Bradford church, which had falsely convicted Brother Kimball of fornication with a Negro woman. An apparently honest and sincere witness had testified that Kimball had committed the act. Later the witness asserted that it had been another man. The church apologized and asked Kimball's forgiveness:

We acknowledging ourselves obliged to Shew our Selves as forward to vindicate P. Kimbal['s] Reputation So far as we can See any reason as we were to accuse Him: We do now declare that though we really thot in the time of it, that it was P. Kimbal: Yet we are Satisfyd that we could not know it was He, *as the case was circumstanced* and do not know it was He: and yet we are heartily sorry that we did not go out of said Room where we were to have prevented the Wickedness we saw: and also that we are Sensible we were very Rash and are Sorry we were so rash as to affirm to make oath in the case without taking more Effectual Method, that we did to discover fulle the Truth in the Matter: And if P. Kimball be as we hope he is innocent and wish he may appear So in the case: we are heartily sorry and ask his forgiveness for what we have done to take away his good name: And also for all that we have done amiss in this and in any other case when we have given offence to any we beg forgiveness of God and Man: . . . [end of quotation missing] [24]

Perhaps even more interesting is the confession of Susannah Curtis, made while she lay dying of injuries sustained in resisting an attempted rape. Susannah had previously accused David Parker of rape, and on this evidence Parker had been convicted by the church. On the day preceding her death, Susannah confided to a friend that she had falsely accused Parker, and then repeated her confession to the pastor.[25]

For falsely accusing a sister of drunkenness Mrs. Patee was charged with slander and was summoned to appear before the First Church of Haverhill. Worse than the slander itself was the fact that Mrs. Patee had previously prepared and dispatched a confession to the complainant, but had later retracted it. Mrs. Patee denied having made such an acknowledgment and insisted that if one existed, it had been illegally extorted. A deacon, however, testified that he had written the confession for Mrs. Patee and rejected the contention that it had been procured by duress. When Mrs. Patee saw that her case was hopeless, she offered a confession, which was rejected as inadequate. Four months later Mrs. Patee offered an acceptable confession and was restored.[26] A person who called a man a drunkard because he had been drunk once was considered guilty of slander, and Anna Torrey, of Pittsfield, was convicted of slander because she had accused an ordinarily temperate man of intemperance, but was acquitted on another count, which alleged that she had falsely accused a man of picking her geese.[27]

A false charge of trespass was the basis of a complaint by Robert Parker, who had accused Moses Hatch of unjustly charging him with pulling down his fence. After a trial, Hatch was acquitted. In the meanwhile, however, Parker had repeatedly withdrawn from the Lord's Supper, justifying his behavior on the ground that Hatch had offended him. The church tabled this matter until Hatch was acquitted and then admonished Parker for withdrawal and barratry. The incident closed when the two litigants mutually expressed their forgiveness and charity.[28]

The alleged removal of a landmark led to a prolonged trial for slander, held before the Canton church between 1729 and 1731. John Wentworth had accused his neighbor, David Tilden, of removing the mark, for which remark Tilden promptly charged Wentworth with slander. Wentworth, a man of "incorrigible and obstinate spirit," was suspended, and a request for a council was denied. He finally offered a confession and was restored, only to be suspended again when some of the brethren felt that the confession was inadequate. Tilden challenged Wentworth: "Brother Wentworth, do you think Brother Tilden to be an honest, truth speaking man in this solemn appeal to God?" Wentworth evaded the question: "I have no business with Tilden—I have no ways wronged him. If he be wronged it is the Court that has done it; and he may go to the Civil Law for his recompense." In calling for a vote, the pastor displayed his bias: "If it be your minds to admit John Wentworth to your Communion, notwithstanding his obstinacy against the Church and his uncharitableness against our Brother Tilden, I desire you would manifest it." Not one hand was raised. Wentworth, undaunted by the continued suspension, appealed the case to the Hull association of ministers, which recommended that the church restore him after a confession. The church accepted the advice over the objection of several brethren, one of whom "somewhat violently opposed it." [29]

Bringing a false complaint before the church or attempting to stop a member from partaking of the Lord's Supper could have unpleasant consequences. For "wittingly, and designedly, with intention to slander the good name, blast the reputation, and render the said Benjamin odious" by saying in open church that he should not be allowed to partake of the ordinance, Philip Smith was charged with slander by Benjamin Tremaine. Such an attempt to prevent a brother from participating in the Eucharist, the church held, was slanderous unless the facts justified it. Smith was unable to justify his interruption of the service and was suspended until he made a confession.[30] In

Granville, a couple who sought admission to church membership complained that a deacon had injured their reputation by charging them with crimes which he could not prove. The church conceded that the couple had not been convicted of any offense, but justified the deacon on the ground that he *believed* that he had evidence to debar the couple. After an investigation, the couple were admitted; six months later the deacon belatedly acknowledged that he "might have been mistaken." [31]

In the remaining slander cases the records are not clear concerning the nature of the alleged defamation. One complaint was dismissed because the private steps had not been taken.[32] Two persons were acquitted, while a third was acquitted on a slander charge included along with two others.[33] The Reading church referred one complaint to a committee, which refused "to have anything to do with the business." The church then heard the parties and decided that although the respondent had been imprudent, he could not be convicted because of a want of evidence. Since the charge was not fully proved, the church recommended that the issue be forgotten.[34] Four cases were amicably settled by the church or a committee.[35]

In a plurality of cases, one of which involved a published libel, the offenders were restored after a confession.[36] Five slanderers were excommunicated, one summarily and the others for impenitence; three others were excommunicated for a variety of offenses which included slander.[37] In seven cases the final disposition is not stated in the records.[38]

The punishment of perjury was an area in which canon law traditionally reinforced the administration of civil justice. In medieval England the civil law required ecclesiastical penance of perjurers, of which there were many. The civil law assisted the church in enforcing penances by means of sanctions, while the Church inflicted its punishments on those who evaded the secular penalties.[39] Not until 1540 did Parliament provide a temporal punishment for perjury.[40] In Plymouth, perjury intended to deprive a person of life was a capital crime, and through the exercise of power of excommunication the churches acted as an additional deterrent to would-be perjurers.[41]

Early in the history of Massachusetts the Roxbury church admonished Hugh Clark, who had testified in court that his son-in-law "was committed for murder." [42] "It doth appear that Hugh Clark therein told a notorious lie against the light of his conscience," remarked the pastor. Clark's "soul was sick and needed medicine," and so the church "dispensed" an admonition, after which Clark repented and was forgiven.[43] In the following decade a churchman of Beverly, who had perjured himself by testifying that his daughter's child had been begotten in wedlock, was admonished. Three years elapsed before the perjurer manifested repentance and was restored.[44] A man who was charged with perjury on two counts was acquitted on one and convicted on the other. The acquittal was by one vote and the respondent was admonished, with respect to this count, to be more cautious about speaking the truth.[45] Church and state were at odds in the case of a woman who was excommunicated for perjury, although the grand jury had repeatedly refused to return a true bill against her.[46]

An incomplete record of a perjury trial concerns a case in which two women, relatives of the complainant, deposed at the church trial that Thomas Parker had testified at a previous civil trial that the complainant had stolen posts from the land of the parsonage in Malden. Although the complaint was for slander, the testimony concerned Parker's alleged perjury.[47] In Billerica, John Hill was accused of perjury and of conspiring with others to commit the same crime. After reading the depositions of six witnesses and hearing oral testimony, the church concluded that Hill was guilty in part, but that the complaint was not fully supported by the evidence. A proposed confession was rejected, but after a ten months' suspension Hill offered an acceptable acknowledgment and was restored.[48]

The ratio of acquittals to convictions and pleas of guilty in perjury cases is surprisingly large. Eight persons accused of perjury were found guilty, but an equal number were acquitted or otherwise discharged. In six cases the church either acquitted the respondents or held that the complaints were not supported,[49] but one, William Dun, was later charged with the same offense in a new complaint, thus placing him in double jeopardy. At the second trial, it was urged that Dun, who is described as "a member of the Church of Scotland," was not a church member and hence not subject to censure. Others, presupposing that he was a member, demanded that he be required to make a public confession. After a two-hour debate the church concluded that Dun was in full communion, but that the alleged offense was a private matter. Since the private steps had not been taken, the complaint was held premature and was dismissed.[50] In one case the church decided that the respondent's defense was sufficient to reconcile apparent contradictions in the testimony which he had given in court; [51] another conviction was reversed by a council.[52] One complaint was dismissed because the complainant and the respondent had been together at the Lord's Supper after the complaint had been submitted, which was held to estop the complainant from pressing his case.[53]

The strangest perjury case found in the church records never was fully resolved. According to the evidence, Rachel Gray, of Harwich, who was in a playful mood, pushed her sisters out of the family pew one Sunday morning. Apparently Rachel was arraigned in court, for we know that her sister Miriam testified under oath that one Thomas Gray, who had previously given evidence against Rachel, had not been in the pew at the time of the incident. Rachel, too, testified, presumably denying her guilt. Miriam then brought a complaint before the church, accusing Rachel of perjury. In another complaint Miriam charged Ebenezer Bangs, who had accused her of perjury, with slander. It took the church four hours to disentangle the charges and the countercharges. Finally the church concluded that the evidence did not warrant Rachel's conviction on the charge of hunching Miriam and that her eviction of her other sister, Lydia, from the pew, was not worth the trouble of a censure. There remained the question of perjury. Witnesses were called to show that Miriam had been under oath when she said that Gray had not been in the pew. Both sisters were convicted, Miriam of denying Gray's presence in the pew, and Rachel of denying her guilt in court. Miriam speedily confessed her guilt and was restored. Rachel tarried seven years and then requested a council, which was refused because the church did not consider her sincere. Whether Rachel ever made the required confession is not known. Miriam recanted her acknowledgment and absented herself from the church. On a reconsideration of the perjury charge against her, the church decided that she had testified conscientiously and had not intended to commit perjury, and invited her to return to the fellowship of the church.[54]

Perjury resulting from a denial of guilt before the church was as sinful as perjury by a witness, and an offense which might otherwise be treated in a routine manner could become serious if the offender denied his guilt and was then convicted.[55] Such a denial of guilt must not be confused with a refusal to make a confession. A convicted member who would not own his guilt in public or, in some instances, before the church, was merely impenitent, but if he continued to assert his innocence he was guilty of perjury as well. By denying their guilt, persons convicted of various offenses, or those who denied the existence of an agreement, aggravated their guilt and were expected to confess their falsehoods along with the other sins.[56]

For impenitence after convictions for theft, for lying about it, and for changing his name, presumably to avoid detection, a Quincy churchman was excommunicated.[57] In Charlemont, a man was convicted of deceit and "indecent familiarity," but was acquitted on a charge of prevarication concerning his other offenses, while the Westfield church convicted a Negro of lying about an act of adultery which the church found inadequately supported to warrant a conviction.[58] In the case of Robert Cox, who was excommunicated for intoxication, lasciviousness, and lying concerning the source of his venereal disease, the allegation of falsehood forms a separate and distinct charge,[59] and although the record of the trial of Anne Hutchinson clearly suggests that she was excommunicated for heresy, the only minute in the church records refers to her excommunication for telling a lie.[60]

In cases of falsehoods or lies told when the offender was not under oath, the proportion of acquittals is considerably smaller than in the cases of perjury under oath. Only six persons thus charged were unambiguously acquitted, in one case three years after the accusation was made.[61] One woman was acquitted, but only because witnesses repudiated their depositions. Fifteen years later she was again charged with lying and was suspended; an acknowledgment that she had been guilty of "foolish talking" was rejected. The reasons given for her acquittal at the first trial clearly indicate that the church had considerable doubts about her innocence.[62] Another church was equally doubtful of the innocence of Don Taylor when it ruled that the complaint was not sufficiently supported "to render said Taylor censurably guilty."[63]

In contrast to the nine cases which did not result in censures are thirteen convictions or admissions of guilt on charges of lying (other than perjury). Five offenders made confessions and were restored; one, an applicant for membership, was rejected; one prosecution was overlooked in the light of a later charge; and four were excommunicated for impenitence.[64] In the remaining cases the final determination is not recorded.[65]

Unfortunately we know little about these liars, except in three cases. One of the confessions was made by a bogus physician, who acknowledged that he had no medical training.[66] The case of Ruth Lane, who had been convicted of falsehood, was referred to a council, which considered the complaint supported on the evidence of her published *Essay to Vindicate the Cause of Truth* and advised the church to continue its efforts to reclaim her and obtain satisfaction.[67]

The most brazen liar to be censured was John Budd Pitkin,

of Great Barrington. A confirmed braggart, Pitkin, who had no cause to boast of anything in his personal life, went about telling tall tales concerning his ancestors. According to Pitkin, one of his uncles, the late Henry Pitkin, had once saved a beautiful heiress from drowning in the River Thames. Her father, a fabulously wealthy Englishman, had now come to America to bestow a handsome reward on Uncle Henry's heir, John Budd Pitkin. So romantic a story, together with other, similar tales, none of which have been preserved for posterity, was bound to cause some raised eyebrows. The pastor, informed of the tale, decided to take the private steps with Pitkin. Anticipating this move, the liar fled to Canada. Two days after Pitkin's sudden departure the precentor of Lenox Academy testified before the church concerning some more tales, which Pitkin had told at the school. Pitkin's chronic lying now needed no further proof. Without much discussion, the church excommunicated the liar.[68]

From this point on the available record in Pitkin's case is vague and incomplete. A half year later Pitkin appeared before the church and submitted a confession which was accepted. Restored in October, 1821, he was again excommunicated in the winter of 1825, possibly for telling still more tales.[69]

The protection of the interests of innocent parties was the churches' primary aim in dealing with accused slanderers. Most often these prosecutions were based on the complaint of the person who had been defamed; only a fourth of the cases were of a quasi-criminal nature. Accusations to the effect that the respondent had falsely accused a person of committing some offense were particularly frequent. A plurality of alleged slanderers made confessions and were restored; only five of the eighty-seven members so charged were definitely cast out of the church. Unique among the confessions of slander, and greatly to the credit of the church concerned, is the public acknowledgment by the members of the Bradford church, who had unjustly convicted a brother of fornication.

Perjury charges resulted in relatively few convictions; half of the respondents were acquitted. In contrast, thirteen of the twenty-two members charged with lying (other than perjury) pleaded guilty or were convicted; only six acquittals have been found. A possible reason for the inconsistency is that a charge of perjury was naturally more serious. Hence the churches would be more cautious in convicting an alleged perjurer.

XI. Business Ethics and Property Rights

"Be stedfast in thy covenant, and be conversant therein, And wax old in thy work," [1] an ancient Jewish writer told his reader. The same advice might have been given by a Puritan minister to his flock. Although the Puritan's aim was set in the next world, he lived in this world; more particularly, the Puritan with whom we are concerned lived in Massachusetts, in a particular community. As long as he lived in this world as a member of society and of his community, he had no reason to avoid it.

The ideal community of the first American Puritans was the compact agricultural town or village, with the meetinghouse as its center. This was to be a Christian community, in which the church and the town were closely related and conterminous in the geographical extent of their jurisdictions. This society, however, soon was forced to give way to new influences. The promise of land had been a strong inducement to the first emigrants, and the later settlers, too, were attracted in no small measure by the availability of land. As more and more settlers reached Massachusetts during the Great Migration, the outlying common land of the towns was assigned to the new arrivals. Thus the compact unity of the Christian community was destroyed. Towns were divided into parishes, each with its own church, and although new towns were set off from the old ones, the division of the church generally preceded that of the political unit.[2]

Another development must be noted, however. The overwhelming importance of farming could not survive in an age of expanding commerce and trade. Before long, artisans and tradesmen grew more numerous, and Boston became the hub of New England commerce. To the older clergy the rise of a commercial class was far from welcome. Here was a threat to the *de facto* supremacy of the clergy, for an aristocracy of merchants might become a formidable rival to the ministerial group. Furthermore, commerce was likely to bring with it social and economic evils hitherto unknown in Massachusetts. Even the stanchest advocates of the agricultural communal order, however, were compelled to accept the inevitable. Recognizing that commerce had come to stay, the clergy turned from attacks on the new influences to the denunciation of the evils incident to it.[3]

Not the least of these evils was the danger that men might strive to accumulate wealth for its own sake. Mere ownership and the enjoyment of worldly goods was unobjectionable. The Puritan had a strong sense of vocation. A merchant or an artisan might be as good a Christian as a farmer, theologian, or missionary, provided he conceived of his occupation as a divinely ordained calling to be followed with a sense of responsibility. Whatever his place in society, he must work diligently at his worldly task in order to glorify God. The more grace he had, the better he would work; the better he worked, the greater the reward would be. Hence worldly riches, although useless as means of obtaining grace, were evidence of grace already received.[4]

Since wealth was not an end in itself, it could not be an ultimate good. If it was acquired unjustly it was evil; material gain was not the sole evidence of virtue. Only salvation was free, a gift of God; everything else had to be earned.[5] Furthermore, the interests of the individual must be balanced against the interests of the social order. Hence the Puritans advocated that the accumulation of wealth be limited, but left a wide margin of doubt in failing to define the limits.[6]

The churches' demand that money be acquired honestly and justly exceeded the strictly legal requirements. Calvin had lifted the ban on usury in its strict sense (i.e., any interest at all), but firmly opposed usury in its modern sense (i.e., excessive interest). While some English Puritans denounced all interest, the prevailing opinion opposed it only in its excessive form. Ames, who opposed the Italian banking practices of his time, held that it was entirely lawful and morally proper to earn the fruits of invested money.[7]

By English statute law, the maximum interest permitted in 1545 was 10 percent, but the statute was largely a dead letter.[8] Beginning in 1623 Parliament reduced the rate progressively, but in 1854 all regulation of interest was repealed.[9] In Massachusetts the statutory limit was somewhat higher than in England, but money was scarcer in the colonies. In 1660, when Parliament put into effect the Commonwealth limit of 6 percent, the colony placed an 8 percent limit on interest.[10]

In Massachusetts, where labor was scarce, the government also experimented with wage ceilings. An attempt to prescribe maximum wages was made in 1630, but the legislation then enacted was repealed in the following year. In 1633 a ceiling was placed on commodities, excepting only a few perishable imported goods, and wage regulation was delegated to the municipalities. In spite of the numerous local regulations, few violators were prosecuted. Not until 1675, when the General Court passed a statute to reform "Provoking Evils," were wages again controlled on a colonial basis.[11]

Church censures for breach of contract, trespass, and fraud are found from an early date and extend into the nineteenth century, but only in the earliest years did the churches deal with members whose commercial offenses were not of a strictly legal nature. The notorious case of Robert Keayne is one of several such incidents. Considering the fact that Keayne was a communicant of the church, an eminent man, wealthy and with only one child to support, and that he had come to America to escape religious persecution, his case was indeed "very evil." For making a profit of more than six pence on the shilling (by today's standards an enormous excess profit, but at that time the customary limit), Keayne was fined two hundred pounds by the courts. The magistrates later commuted half of the fine because Keayne had violated no statute and was by no means the only offender.

The church had an interest in the case, for the Eighth Commandment, "Thou shalt not steal," was broadly construed. Keayne's tearful confession inspired John Cotton to preach a vigorous sermon, in which the divine outlined four principles of business ethics. The current market price was the norm, Cotton held, and no tradesman must charge more than the proper price. A loss sustained from a lack of skill must be absorbed by the trader; it must not be passed to another, and a loss due to a providential act must likewise be absorbed by the injured tradesman.[12] Cotton wanted the church to excommunicate Keayne, but the church, not convinced that Keayne had acted from covetous motives, limited the censure to an admonition. Six months later, after he had made a public confession, Keayne was restored.[13]

No other cases of this nature during the early period of Massachusetts history have been found, but we know of two women who were censured for cheating on weights and measures.[14] A tanner who had spoiled too many hides given to him for treatment, and then covered up his poor workmanship with forgeries and lies, was suspended,[15] and two Boston tradesmen, one of whom foolishly promised his customers more than he was able to perform, made confessions of unethical business practices.[16] Only one case which involves a violation of an ethical rather than a legal standard has been found for the period after 1700. In 1752 the Reading church convicted a man of a number of offenses, including "harsh and oppressive dealing," for which he made a confession.[17]

With the decline of church discipline in certain areas of business ethics came a steady rise of cases involving outright fraud. In the first part of the eighteenth century two men were charged with frauds of an unspecified nature. In one case, the offender was admonished; in the other the church deferred decision pending a judgment by the courts.[18] At the close of the Revolution a man was convicted of altering a receipt and made a public confession, and a miller, convicted of fraud in packing flour, was excommunicated for impenitence.[19] Another miller made a confession in the nineteenth century, acknowledging that he had used a farmer's grain, given to him for milling, to clean his mill,[20] and a farmer owned that he had mixed hay of an inferior quality with high-priced hay without reducing his price.[21]

Frauds connected with negotiable instruments are mentioned in four cases. With the exception of a case in 1774, concerning a man who had wrongfully received a discharge of two notes which had not been paid,[22] these cases are of relatively late dates. A man who had obtained endorsements of his worthless notes by giving his endorsers to understand that the notes would not be cashed, but who then deposited them in the Northampton bank, was required to make a public confession, whereupon he was restored.[23] Twenty years later the Peru church rejected the confessions of two men who had altered a note. A motion to restore one of the men was defeated, and a mutual council was called. Its result, which is lost, was accepted by the church. Either the council recommended the restoration of the men on the basis of the earlier confessions, or the men submitted new and acceptable acknowledgments, for both were restored to communion with the church.[24]

For passing two counterfeit Rhode Island five-pound bills a member of the North Andover church was required to make a confession in 1734, and an unspecified forgery was confessed in Lenox in 1809, at which time the Charlemont church dealt with a slanderer who had accused the complainant of dealing in counterfeit currency.[25] Daniel Foot, of Pittsfield, who had been accused of passing a counterfeit ten-dollar bill, forging a receipt, and stealing a bag of flour, was acquitted on these charges, but an investigating committee regretfully reported that it was unable to exonerate him on a charge of fraud arising from a transaction with Lemuel Pomeroy. Three weeks later, however, it was not Pomeroy, but Josiah Bissell, who brought a complaint against Foot. The information given in the record is too incomplete to permit a reconstruction of the events. At a preliminary hearing the church concluded that either a deliberate fraud or an error in bookkeeping had taken place and decided to hold a trial a fortnight later. After it had examined the documents and heard the witnesses, the church, by a vote of thirty-two to seventeen, convicted Foot of fraud. The judgment was upheld by a council, but Foot, remaining obstinate, was excommunicated.[26]

The public officials of colonial Massachusetts were on the whole honest. But there were exceptions, and if the dishonest official happened to be a church member, he was subject to discipline by two authorities. One of these officials was Brother Sunderland, the clerk of a training company in Boston. In conspiracy with Robert Cannon, Sunderland made up a fraudulent account, assigning a balance of thirty-five shillings to the company, which was the rightful owner of twelve pounds. We may assume that Sunderland kept the balance of ten pounds five shillings for himself. When the fraud was discovered, the church took the initiative in censuring the wayward clerk, and only after it had suspended and admonished him did the civil authorities prosecute him. The court fined Sunderland five pounds, disqualified him from training for three years, and disfranchised him. Learning of the civil sentence, the church took sterner measures. Sunderland, already convicted by the church of embezzlement, was found guilty of perjury and of corrupting a non-churchman. The pastor sharply rebuked him for his misconduct. Sunderland, upon some reflection, made a public confession and was restored.[27]

A decade after Sunderland's conviction in 1675 the frontier village of Westfield was shocked by the embezzlement of funds from the county treasury. The culprit was Joseph Pomeroy, the local constable, who publicly confessed that he had tampered with the tax money which was in his possession.[28] According to the available records, only one corrupt official was disciplined by a church in the eighteenth century. In Sutton, a clerk acknowledged that he had defrauded the colonial government by making false entries in his muster roll.[29]

Not all embezzlers, however, were public officials. In 1698 a Boston woman who collected donations, supposedly for the relief of the poor, was publicly admonished when the church learned that she had kept the bulk of the receipts for herself.[30] Nearly a century later Eli Metcalf undertook to collect donations of articles and money for the relief of Seth Willis, who had lost his house and belongings in a fire in 1789. But Metcalf's motive was far from charitable. Here was an unusual opportunity to exploit the good faith of the generous residents of Worthington, and Metcalf made the most of it. Collecting gifts of a "considerable value," Metcalf, instead of relieving Willis's plight, raised his own standard of living. Called before the church, he attempted to lie his way out and failing that walked out of the church. Twice admonished but still impenitent, the embezzler was excommunicated. After six years, Metcalf repented and was restored, only to be excommunicated in 1811 for his neglect of church ordinances.[31]

The total absence of any censures of church officials for fraud testifies to their honesty. The only such officer accused of embezzlement was acquitted. Investigating a complaint against a deacon of the church in Becket, the church found that the amount in question was so small, and the evidence of an intent to commit fraud so entirely lacking, that it attributed the discrepancy to an error in bookkeeping.[32] More serious than an accounting error was the loss of church records. The Danvers church must share the responsibility for the damage which Sally Nourse did to its records. By carelessly lending a volume to Sally, whose confessions for slander had been repeatedly rejected, the church nearly lost the priceless volume in which the witchcraft cases were recorded. The members' intention had been good: by lending the books to Sally the church hoped to procure a confession. When Sally kept the books for an excessive period of time, the church sent a messenger to claim them. Sally demanded that the record of her conviction be expunged as shameful and unfit for reading. The church rejected the demand and sent the sheriff to seize the book if she did not return it voluntarily. When the officer called at her home, she gave him the volume without the slightest objection, well knowing that the page with the embarrassing minutes had been removed. Once more the sheriff called on her and finally retrieved the missing leaf.[33]

As might be expected, the most common crime against property was stealing. The churches made no effort to distinguish larceny, robbery, and burglary, but, with one exception, used the comprehensive term *theft*. It is obvious, however, from those cases in which considerable information is given, that the typical theft was one of larceny.

The earliest cases, save one in Barnstable, occurred in Boston and its vicinity.[34] In 1638 Richard Wayte was excommunicated as an impenitent thief who had stolen enough leather to make three men's gloves.[35] Six years later a man was cast out of the church for the theft of several gallons of wine and for corrupting the rest with beer. In his confession, made a year later, the winebibber not only acknowledged his theft but, understandably enough, his drunkenness.[36] A man who had stolen a cheese made a confession, while a woman who had stolen her father's money when she eloped refused to repent and was excommunicated.[37]

Beyond the limits of Boston and its immediate vicinity four horse thieves attracted the attention of the churches.[38] Benjamin Morgin, sentenced by a court for the theft of two horses and several oxen, was summarily convicted, "the fact being so notorious and evident" that it required no further proof. Summoned to appear before the church, Morgin reviled the brethren and "by his irreverend Carriage and Dumbe Silence manifested himself to be a lamentable Spectacle of a Stupifyed Sinner and forsaken of God," worthy of excommunication.[39] As the Beverly church had taken judicial notice of Morgin's theft, so the First Church of Salem felt that the guilt of Joseph Williams was so notorious that it required no proof, but in contrast to the Morgin case, Williams was given a chance to repent and was finally restored.[40] A horsethief with a more charitable motive was arraigned before the Danvers church. In need of a horse for his wife, Ezekiel Cheeves helped himself to one in his neighbor's stable. Judging from the almost illegible record, it would seem that Cheeves was repeatedly asked to give satisfaction and, failing to do so, was severely admonished by the pastor.[41] In Quincy the church took to task an habitual thief, Isaac Theer, who had been convicted by a court of stealing pewter from a lady, cheese from a gentleman, and a horse from a pasture in Bridgewater. In addition to these felonies, Theer had assumed an alias and had consistently denied his guilt. Standing impudently before the church, he admitted his guilt and routinely asked the church's forgiveness, in a voice so low that it was scarcely audible. The church was not impressed by such a performance and ordered that he be admonished. As the pastor began his exhortation Theer turned toward the door. The pastor ordered him to stay; Theer, insolently but silently, walked out of the building and, shortly thereafter, was cast out of the church.[42]

A similar assortment of thieves was censured during the eighteenth century.[43] John Davis, of Haverhill, was admonished for intemperance, absence, and the theft of two birds. At the church trial Jonathan Robards testified that he had caught Davis in his father's barn; one fowl was in Davis's hand, the other lay near the bottle at Davis's feet. A criminal prosecution had been discontinued when Robards was permitted to withdraw his complaint. At the church trial Davis pleaded that the liquor had made him insensible and that he had no idea how he came to be in Robards's barn. Other witnesses impeached this evidence, proving that notwithstanding his chronic intemperance, Davis had not been drunk at that time.

In response to the charge of absence, Davis pleaded a want of shoes, an excuse which the church rejected in view of his prolonged absence. Cited to appear for an admonition, Davis pleaded a lack of clothes. The church furnished him with a coat, but Davis refused to come. Unable to reach him directly, the church admonished him *in absentia* and ordered a copy of the admonition to be sent to him.[44] Hay and spikes were the subject matter of a larceny in Kingston, where Samuel Foster was found guilty after a lengthy trial, begun on the initiative of Deacon Brewster, whose spikes Foster had stolen. Foster resented the deacon's complaint and sued him for three hundred pounds' damages. Instead of inducing the deacon to withdraw the complaint, the law suit encouraged the church to suspend Foster for his interference in the administration of ecclesiastical discipline.[45]

Of the nineteen persons convicted of larceny between 1700 and 1770, thirteen were restored. Two women made confessions but evidently were not restored. In one case the church voted to defer the restoration; in the other, involving a notorious sexual offender, the confession was rejected.[46] Three men were suspended, but no further censure is mentioned in the records, and in one case, resulting in a conviction, there is no reference to a censure.[47] Only one thief, a woman, was excommunicated.[48]

A man and a woman, tried by their churches for larceny, were acquitted. Abraham Skinner, charged with the theft of posts from the lands of the Malden parsonage, and previously convicted by a court, was acquitted by the church because the conviction had been based on the testimony of only one witness, and that one a possible perjurer.[49] A woman charged with an unspecified violation of the Eighth Commandment was acquitted by the church in Great Barrington.[50]

A minor crime wave occurred between 1735 and 1745 in the town of Deerfield. In the five-year period from June, 1735, to April, 1741, two Negroes made five confessions, each time including theft in the catalogue of their sins. Adam and Peter jointly acknowledged theft, fornication, and drunkenness in

1735, and were restored. Three years later Peter confessed the same offenses again, and a white man made a confession of theft. After an interval of three more years, Peter made his third confession of theft, followed within a few months by Adam, who had again fallen into his former sins. A woman acknowledged stealing and lying in 1745, but in 1763 the conviction of a lieutenant, who had been charged with theft, was reversed by a council, which invalidated the church's verdict because the complainants had cast votes. The last conviction for larceny in colonial Deerfield followed within a few months of the lieutenant's trial and once again involved a Negro.[51]

On the eve of the Revolution a trial for larceny was held by the Millbury church. After hearing witnesses by deposition and in person, the church voted on the three separate points on which David Buckman's conviction depended. The brethren first decided that the witnesses had proved that Buckman and his son had passed the Widow Hooker while they were en route to Worcester. Next, the allegation that Buckman's cart, carrying a load of pine, had passed a man on the street, was held proved. Finally, the church decided that the allegation that Buckman had not obtained the wood from Captain Goddard's land, as Buckman had claimed, was also proved. Hence, the church concluded, Buckman was guilty of theft. A committee, appointed to recommend an appropriate censure, urged Buckman's suspension. A written admonition was approved a year later but, for an unknown reason, was not dispatched until 1779. Whether it was effective is not stated.[52]

The Revolution and its aftermath appear to have had no effect on thievery in Massachusetts. Only three cases have been found for the period from 1774 to 1782, and only six during the rest of the century. The records in these cases are disappointingly scanty. One man was suspended on the strength of a deposition by a justice of the peace, who certified that David Morse had been convicted of the theft of some meal.[53] Four men and two women made confessions for unspecified thefts,[54] one man was excommunicated for impenitence after a conviction of theft,[55] and in the case of a man who refused to make his confession in public, the final disposition of the case is missing from the records.[56]

In the nineteenth century the churches were distinctly less successful in administering discipline on thieves. Lemuel Morse, of Sheffield, charged with unlawfully shearing another's sheep and converting their wool to his own use, and of fraudulently altering the sheep's marks, was found guilty on two of the three counts alleged against him and, remaining impenitent, was excommunicated.[57] A woman, convicted of stealing cotton, sugar, coffee, and other small articles also refused to own her guilt in public and was excommunicated, but in one case the church permitted a sister who objected to a public confession to acknowledge her theft before the church only. After two years she relapsed, stole again, and was cast out.[58] Another member to be excommunicated was Asa Davis, of Bradford, who had been convicted on four counts. Three of these alleged Sabbath-breaking by engaging in his otherwise lawful trade on the Lord's Day, absence, and theft. The fourth count also involved Sabbath-breaking, but of a different sort. At one o'clock one Sunday morning Davis was seen conveying some goods by barge to Newburyport. Although there is no express indication that he was conveying stolen goods, it seems not unlikely that a person engaged in such an operation in the dark hours of the night had a clandestine purpose. Davis declined to meet with the church and, failing to make a confession, was excommunicated.[59] In contrast to these and three other excommunications, all of which were for impenitence after conviction on charges of larceny,[60] are four confessions. One of the penitent thieves had stolen a watch and another had taken a note;[61] the thefts of the others who made confessions are not described.[62] In three cases it cannot be ascertained whether the convicted thieves made confessions or were censured for impenitence.[63]

With one exception the alleged accessories to thieves whose names are found in the records were women. The one case in which a man was involved resulted in the vindication of a couple suspected of having aided a thief. When Oliver and Elizabeth Pier applied for admission to the church in Egremont, a brother objected on the ground that they had aided a felon by concealing goods stolen from the house of Oliver's father. An investigating committee found that the applicants had been ignorant of the nature of the goods when they accepted them for safekeeping, and Oliver's father, in a letter to the church, certified that he had not accused his son or daughter-in-law of the theft or of being accessories to it. The stolen goods, he alleged, had been concealed in their house but had been returned to their rightful owner. Their reputation cleared, the Olivers became communicants of the church.[64] Two women were censured for receiving goods which they knew to have been stolen. One was summarily excommunicated in 1691, but additional offenses may have aggravated the case,[65] while the other woman, previously convicted by a court, was suspended. The aftermath of the suspension may have been recorded on a page which has been torn from the record.[66] An elderly widow of Sutton was excommunicated for impenitence after she had been found guilty of aiding a Negro thief; another woman, convicted of soliciting a clandestinely married girl to steal cotton wool and other goods from the house in which she lived, was restored after a public confession.[67]

In the sole burglary case found in the records, Joseph and Susannah Severe of Sutton, convicted in 1750, were suspended when a proposed confession was rejected. Whether Joseph made a confession is not known; Susannah's acknowledgment, sent to the church during a serious illness, was accepted on the condition that she make a public confession upon her recovery.[68]

Only two confessions of arson have been discovered in the records. The first one, in 1683, was made by a woman who had corrupted a slave to set fire to her master's house, thus burning a girl to death.[69] In the other, made in 1838, William Jacobs confessed that he had set fire to some wood belonging to two other church members, in addition to stealing a watch and denying his guilt.[70]

Property in slaves presented a curious paradox. Being chattels, slaves could be stolen. Being persons, they could run away from their masters and thus deprive them of their services. The records disclose no thefts of slaves in the usual sense of the term, but a number of runaway slaves were censured under the Eighth Commandment: "Thou shalt not steal." In effect the theory of the churches was that a runaway slave was a thief who had stolen the property in himself from his master.[71] In 1742 the Negro London, who had left his master, was censured by the Westfield church and made a public confession of his breach of the Eighth Commandment. Early in 1746 London was again apprehended and brought before the church, this time as the thief of some articles as well as a runaway slave. London admitted his larceny but interposed a demurrer on the second count, arguing that his master had no right to his services. Against this plea the complainant (not his master) argued that London had formerly made a confession for running away and had promised faithfulness to his master. A minority of the brethren, however, held that this promise was not binding, because London might have believed that he was under a moral obligation to serve his owner and had later learned otherwise. Repeatedly admonished but obstinately impenitent, London was excommunicated.[72]

In the meanwhile, Pompey, who earlier had made a confession of fornication, attempted assault on his mistress, disrespectful talk to his master, and "telling a story out of the house," was arraigned before the church as a runaway slave. Pompey's demurrer, based on that of London, was overruled, and the slave was required to make a confession. Pompey prepared one, recanted it, then recanted his recantation, and finally recanted that. By 1751 the church's patience was worn out, and the brethren decided to excommunicate him.[73]

XII. The Churches as Courts of Law

"When one of you has a grievance against a brother," Paul asked the church in Corinth, "does he dare go to law before the unrighteous instead of the saints?" [1] Paul's attitude towards Christians who had lawsuits against their brethren in the courts of pagan Rome is understandable. More difficult to understand is the objection which some of the Puritan churches raised against lawsuits between members. The churches of Massachusetts could hardly accuse the government, which their members controlled, of unrighteousness. Moreover, such objections ran counter to Calvin, who held that civil litigation was permissible, provided it was not undertaken from motives of bitterness or vengeance.[2]

In 1636 the town of Boston voted that no member of the congregation or other inhabitant should bring an action in the courts until the church had heard the dispute.[3] The rule was modified in 1649, when the First Church decided to appoint a committee to examine prospective plaintiffs and to approve or reject their petitions for leave to go to law.[4] No church censures for bringing a lawsuit have been discovered prior to 1757, however. In that year, a member of the Kingston church brought suit against a person who had accused him of theft. The church frankly expressed its disapproval of the action. Were this to become a common practice, the members observed, it would subvert the authority of the churches. The plaintiff in the civil action, already convicted by the church of theft, was also found guilty of wrongfully instituting an action at law and was suspended from the communion of the church.

A request for a mutual council was denied.[5] Three years later the Concord church decided that it was intolerable that an applicant for membership should have taken a case pending before the church into the courts and required the litigant to make a special confession of his offense prior to his admission.[6]

The opposition against civil litigation among church members was modified during the Revolution. When a member of the East Church of Barnstable accused twelve brethren of preferring charges against him, the church held that it had no right to prevent its brethren from going to law or to question the acts of the courts, and urged the complainant to return to the Lord's Supper.[7] In 1789, a charge alleging that a brother motivated by "unfriendly" feelings had procured the complainant's indictment was dismissed for want of evidence. The basic question, "Is it lawful for a member to sue a brother at law?" was not raised,[8] but fifteen years later the Charlemont church expressly permitted its members to invoke the aid of the courts against their brethren.[9] Contrasting with the Charlemont decision is a resolution adopted by the Lenox church in 1820. Although lawsuits among members were not absolutely prohibited, they were strongly discouraged. A committee of three members was designated to induce potential litigants to submit their causes to them for settlement.[10]

If the records disclose but a few cases in which the churches disciplined their members for bringing lawsuits against their fellow members, they reveal numerous instances in which causes, although actionable at law, were litigated in the churches. Thus the churches in effect exercised concurrent jurisdiction with the civil courts[11] in matters concerning property, both real and personal. The judgment of a church had no effect on the courts, but members generally accepted the decisions of their church. Cases analogous to assumpsit, case, covenant, debt, and trespass are found in the church records, but the forms are never defined. It must be remembered, however, that in civil practice as well forms of action were neglected. Case was the predominant form in the civil courts and was used in place of debt, detinue, ejectment, trover, and assumpsit.[12]

The only church case analogous to an action of debt is found in the Salisbury records for 1688. Robert Pike brought a complaint against Deacon Brown, alleging that the deacon owed Pike's son five shillings and six pence. Brown was acquitted on this count, and a settlement was reached on four others, which alleged slander.[13] Other debtors are mentioned in the records, but none save Pike was sued for debt. In Billerica, a brother who had been accused of absence explained that he could not possibly have attended church: he had spent the Lord's Day in the debtors' prison. The excuse was accepted and the debtor restored, but no church action concerning the debt is mentioned.[14] More alarming than this brother's absence was the fact that a deacon of the Dalton church had absconded. His sudden departure from town was attributed to his debts. Two weeks later, as suddenly as he had left, the deacon returned to acknowledge his error and to resign his office. After a public confession the former deacon was restored to church fellowship.[15] A businessman of Lanesborough, who had unsuccessfully requested a debtor to submit to an accounting, invoked the assistance of the church, which found the offender guilty and required him to make a confession. Whether the complainant succeeded in opening the debtor's books is not stated.[16]

In cases arising from contractual obligations, prospective plaintiffs sometimes resorted to the church instead of the court. The records fail to disclose any cases of this nature before 1735. In that year a widow was acquitted of a charge of breach of an agreement, the nature of which is not stated.[17] Three years afterward Betty Hatch, of Falmouth, accused Robert Parker of a breach of promise, possibly a promise to marry. Parker was acquitted by the church and, in turn, accused Betty of barratry. For bringing an unsupported complaint Betty Hatch was suspended until she made a confession four years later.[18] A church member who refused to negotiate a settlement in a dispute over a contract was suspended until he gave satisfaction.[19] In Amesbury, three men who had been accused of wrongfully withdrawing from the Lord's Supper justified their absence on the ground that they had been offended by a member and, to support their defense, charged Doctor Ordway with a breach of promise. With the doctor's apologies to the aggrieved brethren the issue was settled.[20] In an action by a farmhand for an unspecified breach of a contract with the employer, the church appointed five members to settle the dispute and required the employer to abide by the decision.[21]

An unusual breach of contract case was litigated in Amherst in 1770. On Elijah Flint's complaint Joseph Eastman was charged with breaking a promise, which, as two witnesses testified, was made during a conversation between Eastman and Martin Kellogg. Some months earlier Eastman and Kellogg discussed a deal concerning Broadgutter, a desirable tract of land on the outskirts of Amherst. Eastman coveted this plot, and when he heard that Kellogg intended to purchase some land, his curiosity was aroused. Where was the land, Eastman asked Kellogg. Since the deed had not been signed, Kellogg was wary of divulging the information to a potential competitor, but Eastman persisted in asking the question. He, too, intended to buy some land, Eastman told Kellogg, and he certainly did not want to compete with his friend; anything Kellogg might tell him would be held in strictest confidence. At length Kellogg gave in and told Eastman that he intended to buy Broadgutter.

Within hours the news of Kellogg's projected purchase was known to the entire populace. Two witnesses, including Kellogg's brother, testified that soon after his conversation with Kellogg, Eastman had told him about the deal. But Eastman had done more than merely break his pledge of secrecy. He had indiscreetly told his friends that he had engaged a man to purchase Broadgutter for him. Asked how he had been discharged from his promise of secrecy, Eastman illogically replied that he did not consider a promise made "five or twelve" months ago binding. Obviously Eastman had broken his agreement. The church required that he make a public confession and, upon hearing the acknowledgment, declared itself satisfied.[22]

A Falmouth widow and her brother-in-law were the litigants in a case pressed by Jabisha Dimmuck, who accused her brother-in-law Joseph of violating an agreement to sell a house and lot. In settlement of a debt, Jabisha's husband had given the title to his real estate to his brother. Jabisha, who could not reconcile herself to the loss of the property, had asked Joseph to restore the title to her. According to her complaint, Joseph had agreed to the request provided Jabisha pay a sum of money in consideration of the land and house. Unable to raise the amount immediately after her husband's death, Jabisha pinned her hope on a hundred dollars which she expected to collect from a debt owed to her husband's estate. The debtor, however, was Joseph, who had no intention of paying the debt. Unable to receive satisfaction from her brother-in-law, Jabisha took her case to the church, which found itself unable to censure either party. A motion to vote on the merits of the case was tabled, and the church adjourned.

Five months later Joseph presented his defense. When the question of the house had first been raised, Joseph pleaded, Jabisha had asked him if she could have the property in case she were destitute. He had told her that the money must be available immediately after her husband's death. Since she neither was destitute nor had paid him on time, she had forfeited whatever rights she might have had. Joseph stressed that there had been no definite agreement: at best Jabisha had an implied option on the property. Furthermore, she was under no necessity, while he needed the land for his family. Should she desire to buy the estate at some future time, Joseph condescendingly added, he might consider selling it for the value of his former debt to his brother, subject, of course, to allowances for depreciation or improvements. The case was too difficult for the church, which sought to evade the issue and advised the litigants to "endeavor to live in love, peace, and charity with each other for the future." This was more easily said than done, as was the suggestion that the matter be referred to "three judicious men to be chosen mutually between them." Scarcely a year elapsed before the case was back in church. Jabisha had been charged with withdrawal from the Lord's Supper and had justified her action on the ground that she had a grievance against Joseph, who had refused to submit the case to arbitration. A month later the contestants agreed to submit their claims to a committee, but if the issue was satisfactorily resolved during the next forty years, the records fail to indicate it.[23]

Allegations of breach of contract are found in seven other cases, but the records in these matters fail to indicate the nature of the agreement.[24] The most recent such complaint was located in the Peru records for 1823. A disappointed member charged that Sylvia Smith had broken her promise to marry the complainant. Instead of marrying her old rural beau, she had united herself with a Boston physician. Upon making the required confession, Sylvia was restored.[25]

As mediators and arbitrators of miscellaneous disputes the churches met with varying degrees of success. In such situations the churches acted either at the request of one of the parties or on their own initiative. When the First Church in Salem learned of a "scandalous contention" between two brothers of the Putnam family, it appointed a committee of four to effect a reconciliation. The committee accomplished what it thought was a settlement, only to find that one of the brothers renounced the agreement and withdrew from the Lord's table.[26] While the attempt to settle the Putnam case failed, other settlements proved more successful. Twelve cases were settled to the satisfaction of the parties concerned, but unfortunately we do not know the nature of the disputes.[27]

Every opportunity was given to contending parties to settle their quarrels, even in cases where the church had begun to exercise its disciplinary authority. In three instances the church allowed the parties a designated period of time in which to effect a reconciliation,[28] and the Barre church withdrew from a case when it learned that the contenders had agreed to "bury the matter in Oblivion." [29] Churches similarly withdrew from cases in which settlements were accomplished after a complaint had been presented, but before the issue had been joined.[30] In one dispute the parties agreed to request the church's assistance in solving the problem.[31] Two complaints were dismissed for unspecified reasons, and in one case a church rejected an applicant for membership who refused to settle a case.[32]

A touch of gaiety was added to one session, at which the pastor and ten brethren successfully resolved an issue between Captain Cook and Captain Fisher, at whose request the committee had been appointed. To cement the renewed friendship of the officers, the pastor combined solemnity with gaiety:

> We sang *Psalm 133.*[33] I [the pastor] called for a tankard of drink and drank to both of the heretofore contending, but now reconciled Brethren, wishing and praying that the "peace of God which passeth all understanding might keep their minds through Christ Jesus" and that they and all of us, for the time to come, might live and act together in love and favour, that the God of love and peace might be with us; to which Captain *Cook* said, Amen. I gave the tankard into Captain *Cook's* hand, he drank himself, and drank to Captain *Fisher.* We all drank, ut sic finitur, so the matter ended.[34]

No church trial in the early history of Westfield caused so much stir as that of John Mosely or Maundesly, a resident of that frontier village. During King Phillip's War, which had terminated a few months before, the residents of Hatfield had been driven out of their homes. When the danger had apparently passed, they returned to their houses, only to be evicted again by a roving band of Indians. To accommodate these victims of the war the town of Westfield appointed a committee, including Mosely, to reapportion the land. For every acre of land in the residential section of the town which a resident surrendered he was given two acres of common land. At this time Mosely purchased a home lot of four acres of improved land. Soon after he occupied his new house, he found the adjacent five-acre lot more to his liking and bought it. For the four acres which he relinquished to the town, he was to receive eight acres of common land. The deeds effecting the exchange already been executed when Mrs. Mosely learned of the transaction. Her husband might be satisfied with the common land; she was not. What she wanted was a choice lot which was up for sale. The amount which Mosely could have received for his old lot, had he sold it to a private person instead of relinquishing it to the town, would have been sufficient to purchase the land which she coveted.

While Mrs. Mosely suppressed her indignation, new problems arose. First the town decided to construct a lane into the woods. This would run alongside of, but not through, Mosely's property. Then Hanchet, who had received half of Mosely's old lot, wanted to move to another location. Because Mosely would not buy the old land back, Hanchet sold it to another man. Mosely objected to this conveyance and, having no claim on Hanchet, petitioned the town for compensation. He had received only half of the legal satisfaction for his old lot, Mosely contended, demanding the land which Hanchet had sold or the amount paid for it in lieu of the ten pounds allegedly due him. But above these considerations was another grievance which Mosely had against the town: he did not want that lane adjacent to his property.

In March, 1652, Mosely sent a petition for relief to the General Court, which forwarded it to the Hampshire County Court. When the church learned of the petition, it took firm action and charged Mosely with violations of the Eighth, Ninth, and Tenth commandments. By attempting to obtain a charitable gift from the town instead of by enriching himself by his labors Mosely had violated the Eighth Commandment. The

Ninth, the church alleged, had been violated in the petition: Mosely had received his satisfaction but implied that he had not. In coveting Hanchet's land and trying to keep the lane away from his estate he had broken the Tenth Commandment.

The close cooperation between the churches and the towns is clearly apparent in this case. The leaders of the one were the rulers of the other. If the town lost its case in court, it would suffer considerable loss. What could have been safer than to refer the issue to the church? Ecclesiastical litigation could, if necessary, be swift. There were no fees and no danger of an award for costs. Had Mosely pressed his claim, which appears unfounded, he would have been excommunicated. By acting as a church, the leaders of the town won their case. Mosely confessed his errors and was restored; the town retained its property.[35]

Although the churches shunned cases involving land titles,[36] they frequently decided other matters concerning real estate. Two men were required to make a public confession of altering or forging deeds,[37] and one was similarly censured for having a deed fraudulently recorded.[38] A discharged parson who tenaciously held on to the parsonage and justifiably claimed that he had a lien on it until the arrears of his salary had been paid was ordered to appear for a hearing. For seven years the case was held in abeyance, and two more years were required before a settlement was accomplished.[39]

Claims concerning easements were another source of church litigation, sometimes supplementing civil suits. Thus Perez Rice, already convicted by a court of unlawfully closing off a stream of water, was censured by the Sutton church.[40] A man who had an easement on a spring on Daniel Hutchinson's land complained that the landholder refused to permit him to draw water from the well. The church convicted Hutchinson and required that he make a public confession.[41] An unusual twist is found in a case in which David Brown accused Henry Badger, who stood propounded for admission to membership, of closing a gate to a road which Brown was legally entitled to use. Badger, who did not object to Brown's use of the road, declared that he had merely closed the gate and would pay Badger for the labor of opening and closing it. The church, however, would not admit the landholder to membership until he had made a confession. After six weeks Badger made such a confession and was admitted. Brown resented the church's action and, moving to New York State, "bid adieu" to the church, for which he was admonished. Later, repenting of his hasty withdrawal, Brown sent a confession to the church and received a dismission.[42]

As late as 1821 the Amherst church acted in a quasi-judicial capacity in a realty case. In December, 1821, Samuel Church, who had unsuccessfully taken the private steps with Samuel Smith, complained that Smith had (1) violated an agreement permitting Church to pass through his land, (2) obliterated the boundary between their properties, (3) broken an agreement to restore a fence which had been moved from its original position, (4) refused to surrender some rails which Church owned, (5) slanderously accused Church of cheating, and (6) manifested "a wrongful spirit inconsistent with the gospel." Smith conceded that he had denied Church access to his land, but maintained that Church had not given him the consideration specified in the agreement, and acknowledged the possibility of a slander: "I may have said something wrong and unadvisedly."

A committee found that the second and fourth charges were not supported. The church, upholding the committee's find ings, voted that the boundary line, though obliterated, had not been destroyed by Smith, and that although the rails in Smith's possession had been taken from Church, there was no evidence that they had been taken by Smith. This reduced the issues to three. On the first charge the church observed that Church had acquired his easement when he sold two acres to Smith, who in turn had conveyed the land to his sons. The church properly concluded that Smith had no right to deed the property to another without reserving Church's rights, although presumably Church could have asserted his rights against the present owners. With respect to the third charge, which alleged that the fence had been moved from its original position, the church was distressed to note that Smith had commenced criminal proceedings against Church. An action to try the title, the church told Smith, would have been in order. The criminal prosecution was evidence of vindictiveness.

Smith's defense on the fifth charge was a weird *non sequitur.* About the year 1790 Smith had brought fifteen acres of land from Billings. After Billings's death Church bought the remainder of the estate. Shortly thereafter Smith was vexed to find that he had been cheated: he had not received the full fifteen acres from Billings, and therefore accused *Church* of fraud. Smith, whose logic left something to be desired, demanded that Church cede to him the balance. Church, who felt no responsibility towards Smith, justifiably resented the suggestion that he had defrauded Smith. The committee, whose members were endowed with more logical powers than was Smith, immediately understood that Smith, however badly he might have been cheated by Billings, had no claim against Church. A conviction on the sixth count necessarily depended on a conviction on one or more of the other charges. The committee cautiously but logically concluded that if its findings on the other charges were correct, Smith was necessarily guilty on the sixth count as well.

Unwilling to accept these conclusions, Smith requested a council, which was the last thing the church desired. The dispute had already embarrassed the church, which feared that, whatever a council might decide, a schism would follow. Desperately trying to avert the need for a council, the church debated at some length whether Smith might not be restored on the basis of his vague acknowledgment of the possible slander. The opponents of this suggestion argued that the statement which Smith had made contained no confession at all. A compromise was finally accepted: Smith should be encouraged to offer a more complete confession. He was to be instructed that

> To say, I was wrong, always does a man honour. It is saying, I am wiser today than I was yesterday; yesterday I was unwise enough to commit the sin; today I am wise enough to be ashamed of it and confess it.[43]

In the meanwhile Smith had withdrawn from the church to attend meetings in another town. This was promptly added to his offenses, but Smith was willing to acknowledge this. In the hope that it might dispose of the land and slander issues at the same time, the church offered to restore him if he made a public confession of his withdrawal and his "want of a christian temper and spirit." But before Smith could make this confession fifteen of the members objected to the proposed restoration. The confession, they properly maintained, had no intrinsic reference to the land dispute; "want of a christian temper and spirit" might well be construed to refer to the withdrawal only. Smith replied in a counterprotest, which so annoyed the church that it withdrew the offer of restoration. A week later the church excommunicated Smith for withdrawal.[44]

Smith had only begun to fight. In the spring of 1825 he petitioned for a council. The church concurred in the request and made preliminary arrangements for the meeting. Two months later Smith told the church that he had called an ex-parte council. Having previously agreed to join in a mutual council, the church voted not to recognize the authority of an ex-parte council. Smith waited another three years and then petitioned that his excommunication be rescinded, but a committee recommended that the request be denied. Again Smith requested a mutual council, and again the church concurred. The council finally convened and held that because the protest of the fifteen had been improper in content, and the church wrong in excommunicating Smith, he should be restored on the basis of the proposed confession. On the other hand, the council stated that no error should be assigned to the church.[45] Although there is no record of a reconciliation, Smith may have been restored, for in 1833 he was excommunicated for indisposition to walk in Christian fellowship.[46]

The action which Zenas Clark brought against Mrs. Newell is one of three in which the churches assumed the functions of probate courts. Mrs. Newell had previously brought suit in the civil courts to contest Clark's title to some lands which he had brought from her deceased husband, Ezra Hall. Several conveyances had been executed by Hall before his death, but because of a technical flaw in the deeds the courts had permitted Mrs. Newall to bring actions to recover her dowry. Some of the suits had been decided in her favor; one, against Clark, was still pending. In his complaint Clark alleged that Mrs. Newell had no "moral right" to prosecute her claims. Mrs. Newell had moved to Virginia but had not been dismissed from the Lanesborough church, which was therefore able to take cognizance of the case. In reply to the complaint, which was sent to her, Mrs. Newell acknowledged her error and promised to withdraw the pending litigation. The church was satisfied with the settlement and voted to dismiss Mrs. Newell to the church in Charlotte.[47]

In Hatfield, a brother alleged that the executor of an estate had taken advantage of a legal, but unethical, technicality to deprive the complainant's father of a just claim against the estate. In denying the request for the payment of a debt, the complainant charged, the executor had lied and contradicted himself. Barred by a technicality from going to law, the aggrieved brother sought the aid of the church. Counsel appeared for both parties, but at the time when the issue was to be tried, the church found itself preoccupied with the election of a new pastor and therefore failed to act on the complaint.[48] The only other case concerning a decedent's estate is found in the Plymouth records for 1793. A creditor requested the church to instruct Mercy Bramhall, the executrix of her husband's estate, to make a settlement. The church referred the matter of a committee, instructing it to approach not Mrs. Bramhall, but her son, the executrix being ignorant in business matters and depending on her children to settle all claims on the estate. The records fail to indicate the outcome of the case; it may have been settled privately, the committee acting as a mediator.[49]

Eight complaints alleging trespass [50] were considered by the churches during the eighteenth century, but no corresponding cases have been found for the seventeenth or nineteenth centuries. An unusual case, analogous to an action of trespass on the case and resulting in a unique judgment, is found in the Needham records. When Matthias Ockinton applied for admission to church membership, several brethren objected on the ground that he had not given satisfaction for damage done by his horses to Farmer Woodcock's corn. Ockinton's confession was accepted, but the church would not admit him to membership until he had recompensed Woodcock by giving him a bushel of corn.[51] Thus the church not only demanded a confession, but awarded Woodcock an equitable remedy in a case arising from a common law tort.[52] Another church trial for an alleged trespass occurred after the Revolution, when a former lieutenant turned his cattle out of his own enclosure and into his neighbor's field. The church was unable to reach an agreement and referred the question to a council, which held that the officer's conduct was culpable and recommended that he be required to make a confession.[53] On the other hand, in an earlier case before the same church, a council held that the church had no right to demand a public confession of a member who had torn down his neighbor's fence in order to enable his team to pass through the opening.[54]

In the midst of the Revolutionary War the Lanesborough church became involved in complaints brought by Colonel Powell and Deacon Buck against each other. Buck alleged that Powell had destroyed his fence in the spring of 1775, and that he had removed a load of hay from the complainant's land and had arbitrarily ordered his men to mow Buck's grass in July, 1776. When the deacon's hands refused to leave the field, Buck had attempted to evict them, but the men overpowered him and walked off with his hay. Powell's defense was that he had only defended his interests by removing some unspecified encroachments from his land. The church firmly refused to try the title to the land, but warned that it would take notice of any violation of Christian conduct. After a full year's delay the case was reopened on Buck's complaint. Powell attempted to prove that the private steps had not been taken, but made the mistake of admitting, before the procedural question had been determined, that he had been remiss in striving with Buck over the title. The church upheld Powell's argument that the complainant had acted irregularly, but in view of Powell's voluntary admission offered to restore him if he made a public confession. After several adjournments Buck set an example by acknowledging his "unruly Passions and . . . sinfull Anger." A fortnight later Powell followed suit and publicly confessed his "wrong Biases of heart and over Attachment to an earthly Interest." [55]

In three marginal cases the records are fragmentary and offer no clue to the nature of the trespass.[56] Some information is available, however, in a case before the church in Concord, but the verdict and judgment are not recorded. In a bill of particulars requested by a respondent who had been accused of "a contentious Disposition, greatly indulging in a Spirit of Variance and Strife," the complainant alleged that John Flagg had illegally seized Colonel Minot's sheep. Flagg's own sheep had earlier been seized by legal process, perhaps incidental to a lawsuit prosecuted by Minot. One day, when the colonel's sheep had left the enclosure and walked unto the public highway, Flagg had seized them. Minot furthermore alleged that Flagg had refused to release the sheep until Minot had paid him a ransom sufficient to permit Flagg to redeem his own sheep. The bill concludes: "*Therefore, all Things whatsoever*

Ye would that Men should do to You, do Ye even so unto them. (Matt. 7:12.)"[57]

In adjudicating disputes between members the churches exercised quasi-concurrent jurisdiction with the courts. Although ecclesiastical judgments had no standing at law, the churches functioned as popular tribunals for the adjudication of issues among members and applied spiritual sanctions to enforce their decisions. Cases involving contracts, torts, and decedents' estates were tried by the churches, but in matters of real estate the churches manifested an aversion to trying titles. In one case, a church, unhindered by legal technicalities, was able to dispense justice, which the courts, subject to procedural rules, were unable to do. In another instance, a church awarded what amounts to an equitable remedy in a tort case. Since ecclesiastical actions of this nature were generally private cases, prosecuted by an aggrieved member rather than by the church, it is not surprising that their number declined as the churches' toleration of civil litigation among members increased.

XIII. The Churches and the State

In return for the support which they received from the government, the churches occasionally came to the aid of the civil authorities. Although the two were separate institutions, churches and state formed a generally harmonious coalition. Thus Anne Hutchinson was subjected to indignities at the hands of the courts and was excommunicated by a church which was under pressure from the magistrates. Roger Williams was another victim of this system; he, too, was subjected to the wrath of an intolerant civil government and was excommunicated by the ecclesiastical authorities. But whereas Anne Hutchinson was censured for beliefs whose political overtones, however distinct, were only implicit, Roger Williams was condemned for beliefs which explicity affected the political theory of the Puritans.

Roger Williams, a former Anglican, was a convinced Puritan when he arrived in America. Later in life he became a Baptist and a Seeker, but the only thing of importance here is his position from his arrival in 1631 to his banishment in 1635. In most respects Williams was perfectly orthodox. He was a biblicist and believed in the depravity of man and the need for divine grace. He had his quirks, to be sure: he would not allow that women must wear veils, and he objected to the cross of St. George in the English flag. These, however, were trivial matters in the light of some other beliefs which he entertained. Unlike the Massachusetts Puritans, Williams was a Separatist and rejected the doctrine on non-Separatist Congregationalism. Because the First Church of Boston would not repudiate the

Ames doctrine, he rejected a call to become its teacher and turned to Salem, where Separatism was accepted. When the church in that town wanted to call him to its pastorate, the civil authorities were annoyed, and Williams went on to Plymouth, only to return to Salem in 1635, at which time the church again called him as pastor.[1]

Two years earlier Williams had embarrassed the Massachusetts authorities by challenging the Crown's right to issue charters and letters patent to Indian lands. At some other time such a statement might have been disregarded as the opinion of a crank, but at the time it was made the Massachusetts charter was under attack by Mason and Gorges. The denial of its validity on the part of a resident who had no interest in the Mason and Gorges enterprises was obviously embarrassing to those who sought to defend the charter. When Williams repeated his denunciation in 1643, he was hailed before the governor and magistrates. None save the church members supported him; the magistrates, in turn, opposed the call which the church extended to Williams in 1635.[2]

This time the civil authorities were better equipped to deal with Salem church. Contemporaneously with its call, the town of Salem had petitioned the magistrates for land on Marblehead Neck. The magistrates made the most of the coincidence: they rejected the petition on the ground that the church should not have called a minister whose case was pending in court. To rebuke the magistrates for their interference, the church requested the assistance of neighboring churches, whereupon the magistrates retaliated by expelling the Salem deputies in the General Court. Having temporarily suppressed the opposition, the court returned to the Williams case. Only the sentence remained to be pronounced, and on October 9, 1635, the court ordered that Williams be banished from the colony.[3] In a brief speech Governor Winthrop summed up the charges against Williams. First he mentioned the charter question; secondly, Williams had denied that the state had authority to call on unregenerate persons to take oaths or to pray; thirdly, he had said that it was not lawful to hear an Anglican clergyman. The basic problem, however, was in the fourth charge: Williams had denied that the civil government had any authority in religious matters; its jurisdiction, he had maintained, was limited to "the bodies and goods and outward state of men." [4]

Much has been said about Williams's championship of religious liberty, and doubtless he was the first prominent American to advocate such a policy. But Williams was no forerunner of the Enlightenment of Jefferson. Neither was his religious liberalism the result of his experiences in Massachusetts. He had a profounder, more objective basis for his position. When Jefferson advocated religious liberty, he did it as a child of the Enlightenment; his motive was political and social. With Williams, the child of a theological age, the motive was wholly religious.[5]

Williams's view of the state was the inevitable result of his exegesis. In this matter he was clearly unorthodox, running counter to the bulk of Christian tradition. For him the New Testament was not the fulfillment of the Old, but its radical repudiation. The Old Testament types had no other purpose than to be rejected by those of the New. Moses had established a system of state control of religion, God had given Canaan to his elect, Israel was a nation in which the religious and the temporal were not distinguished, her people stood in a unique relationship to Yahweh. All these were Old Testament concepts; Christ had repudiated them all, and with the Incarnation the traditions of the Old Testament had vanished. The old patterns could never again be produced; Israel had been replaced by the Church, a mystical nation. On this basis Williams repudiated the New England vision of a static society in perpetual covenant with Yahweh, for only Israel had enjoyed such a relationship, and her unique status had come to an end with Christ.[6]

The state, Williams held, was wholly wordly. It had no authority in matters pertaining to the first table of the Decalogue, for the first four commandments were religious in nature, and the state, which was not a community of Christians, but of men as such, could not interfere in religious matters. Whether the magistrate was a Christian or not did not affect his functions, except that a Christian magistrate was under a religious duty to protect religious freedom in order to enable the spread of the Gospel. The state must guarantee freedom for the word of God, but it must never coerce the people to accept and follow it; the acceptance of the Gospel must not be influenced by political or social considerations. Finally, he argued, the state must not control the Church, for if it did so the Church might fall under the sway of misguided people. In religious matters the majority was not necessarily correct. Moreover, no state could impose "truth" on anybody; it could impose nothing at all but imposition. If the state interfered with a heretical group, the breach of the peace would be on the part of the state; the heretic as well as the conformist must be given equal protection as long as he behaved in an outwardly orderly manner.[7]

It was these opinions which formed the basis of Williams's difficulties with the civil authorities. The General Court's action not only removed Williams from the colony; it also crushed the Salem opposition, driving a small remnant of Williams's followers underground. To the town's residents, Marblehead Neck and representation in the General Court were more important than Williams.[8] Hence the church, which less than a year earlier had defied political interference in the choice of its pastor, felt no compunction about excommunicating Williams. Four couples and two women who continued to support the excommunicate minister were likewise cast out of the church, for contempt and schism.[9]

The Williams case was closed, but the General Court and the Salem church were still in a hostile mood. While the court proceeded to take final action against Anne Hutchinson, the church turned to consider the case of Sister Weston, who had dared to challenge two jurors in a civil action. Unfortunately the record of the case is incomplete, but we know that the respondent had challenged two veniremen without stating a reason.[10] The church demanded that she justify her temerity. Did the men indicate that they would not do her justice? Did they harbor some grudge against her? Sister Weston would not answer lest, by impeaching the prospective jurors' veracity, she be accused of slander. However the case may have terminated, it proves that a church member's manner of trying a case in court was not immune from attack by the church.[11]

During the second half of the seventeenth century two members found that an unguarded comment on a political matter could incur the displeasure of the churches as well as of the civil authorities. A Dorchester woman who had been convicted of slandering Governor Bellingham and who had remained impenitent was excommunicated in 1666, but the same church restored a man who had given satisfaction for several remarks against the militia.[12] In neighboring Roxbury the church "absolved" a woman fugitive from justice who, upon her return from Rhode Island, made a confession.[13]

Public officials whose sense of responsibility left something to be desired were also liable to ecclesiastical prosecution. In 1696 the Second Church of Boston tried a militia officer who had permitted two of the four guardsmen under his supervision to go off duty, thereby increasing the work of the others. After hearing five witnesses the church convicted the officer and ordered that he be admonished.[14] A soldier who had deserted during Queen Anne's War was similarly censured, but was restored after he made a confession.[15]

Where disciplinary matters were concerned, the churches respected neither rank nor wealth. In Framingham, Justice Joseph Haven was severely rebuked for a variety of offenses, including assault, usury, and malfeasance in office. As might be expected of a lawyer, the judge read the complaint with great care and then objected to its ambiguity and "general Nature." If the church furnished him with a bill of particulars, he said, he would "join issue." Perhaps the judge hoped to confound the church with his legal terminology. As soon as the brethren had voted to join issue, the judge changed his mind and on the one hand told the members that he would not join issue, but on the other hand said that he admitted nothing and would cross-examine the witnesses.

The first witness, Edmund Marrett Hopkinton, testified that Haven had assaulted him with a pitchfork. Hopkinton was followed by a witness who corroborated this evidence, and his brother, Gillan Denet Hopkinton, testified that Haven had taken 15 percent interest from him. By nightfall these and other witnesses had not only demonstrated the probability of the assault and usury counts, but had also implicated the judge in an extortion charge. When the church was compelled to interrupt its proceedings in order to light candles, Haven pleaded illness and started toward the door. The moderator ordered him to stay. "I shall take no further Notice of the Affair at present," replied the indignant judge, walking out.

Four days later the church reconvened and, Haven not being present, tried its brother *in absentia.* Thomas Trowbridge, the first witness of the day, testified that he had asked Haven for a loan of one hundred pounds. To be on the safe side Haven had collected four pounds as interest in advance, giving Trowbridge only ninety-six. A year later Haven demanded an additional 10 percent interest, making it a total of almost 15 percent. Nat Bigelow, who followed Trowbridge on the witness stand, swore that Haven had given him a loan of £6.13.4, but had demanded six shillings above the legal rate. Subsequent witnesses corroborated Trowbridge's and Bigelow's evidence.

The star witness was Joshua Fairbank, a onetime litigant in Justice Haven's court. In a case in which Fairbank was the defendant, Justice Haven had shown distinct partiality to the plaintiff, Colonel Taylor. Fairbank had been anxious to settle out of court, and Haven had told him that if he paid the sum he owed to Taylor, the court would not burden him with costs.

Fairbank borrowed a sum of money to settle the debt, but upon further examination the amount proved to be slightly less than what the plaintiff claimed. Haven condescendingly promised not to call the case until Fairbank had borrowed the remainder, but even before Fairbank returned to court with the money, which was only four minutes later, judgment by default and an award for costs had been entered against him.

The sole witness who followed Fairbank testified to another instance of usury. Finding that the complaint was amply supported, the church demanded that Haven make a confession. Should he appear at the Lord's Supper before he had made satisfaction, the church warned, he would increase his guilt. "For God's Sake, for his Souls Sake, the Churchs Sake, for the Sake of his Family" he should repent, the church exhorted. Not long thereafter Haven's confession was accepted after some debate.[16]

It was inevitable that the Revolution should affect and at times interfere with the life and work of the churches. Modern Congregationalists, accustomed to quarterly Communions and unfermented grape juice, will find evidence of a different era in a resolution of the Reading church, adopted in 1776:

> Voted, that in future during the Church's pleasure, The Communion shall be once in two months, Wine being obtained with Difficulty on account of our Public Troubles.[17]

Other churches faced more serious problems during the Revolutionary period. Already in 1774 the revolutionary spirit was manifest in the Becket church, some of whose members warned Aaron Bliss, who had preached a sermon allegedly advocating Loyalist principles, to leave the town by five o'clock on the following morning. On the next Sabbath, the church's pastor, Zadock Hunn, accused the members of a conspiracy to expel Bliss from Becket. The members retaliated by accusing the pastor of preferring false charges against them. The record of the case is incomplete; all we know is that late in 1775 John

Crane, a member of the church, confessed that "whatever I did or said upon God's holy sabath that was unnecessary to be done or said, I am convinced is an evident violation of the Fourth Command of the Moral Law." [18]

A more complete record is available in the case of the Reverend Samuel Dana, of Groton. Like most Congregational churches, that in Groton supported the Patriot cause. Unlike most New England ministers,[19] Dana, although not a Tory, did not support the Revolution. Until Burgoyne's surrender, Dana opposed the Revolution, not because of loyalty to the Crown, but because he thought that the war would have an adverse effect on the future of the colony. Although he acknowledged his lack of revolutionary zeal, the members would not tolerate his neutrality, rejected his confession, and dismissed him. His support of the war after Saratoga did not redeem him in the eyes of his parishioners. After a brief ministry in the Presbyterian Church, Dana went to New Hampshire, where he was successively elected register of probate, judge of probate, and state senator.[20]

A Plymouth deacon who favored passive resistance met with active opposition from his church. The case, which began on March 12, 1775, was unusually protracted. Twelve days after the first meeting had been called the church convened. Deacon Foster appeared, but no specific charges had been prepared. After two adjournments the church met again and denied the deacon's plea that the private steps had not been taken. A week later Foster asked for a bill of particulars, which was sent to him in August. On the sixteenth he began to answer the charges, but had barely finished his reply to the allegations in the first count when the meeting was adjourned for a fortnight because of darkness. From the end of August through the following January the church convened at irregular intervals, but only to adjourn again. Twice the pastor was indisposed, twice a storm kept the members at home, and twice, when the weather was clear, the brethren simply preferred to stay at home. Once the meeting coincided with the term of the court, and late in

December the accusers were absent. After the adjournment on January 17, 1776, the pastor explained the position of the church:

I know not what else to attribute it to, but to the public Distress of this Land, involved in the calamities of a Civil War which so much engrosses the Minds and Concerns of every one that they scarce know how to attend, even upon an affair of such Importance as this. However, we must acknowledge, we are guilty of a sad and criminal Neglect—as no public or private Troubles ought ever to prevent attending on those Duties, in which the Honor of Christ, of this Church, and the good of the Delinquent, are so much concerned. The Lord heal and save our Land, and give peace and prosperity to this Church.[21]

When the church met in March, the Battle of Dorchester was raging, and the meeting was adjourned until May 1, when the church finally attended to the case. The members considered the four counts severally. That of falsehood and prevarication had been settled by Foster's own admission more than a year ago. The second count alleged that Foster was guilty of "frequent violent Passions and Extravagant Expressions, and wicked Wishes, bordering upon Profaness [*sic*]." Some minor incidents in the court were quickly disposed of. Foster apologized for saying that Watts's Psalms had been composed under the influence of the devil, and for calling Mrs. Churchill "a cursed, murderous Bitch," and the church forgave him. The offense alleged in the third count, that of attending the Lord's Supper when asked not to do so, was held not censurable. The first three counts, however, were negligible in the light of the fourth. This alleged that Foster has displayed a "Willingness to have this Country enslaved" and had advocated "the Destructive Doctrines of Passive Obedience and Non Resistance." Foster's position, the members believed, tended to undercut the foundation of the churches. While they were unanimous in their condemnation of Foster's political views, they did not want to act rashly or inadvisedly. The only solution was to adjourn without a vote on the crucial count of the information.

Once more the principal issue was left unresolved as the church adjourned the case for the sixteenth time.

The church had intended to resume its deliberations on July 1, but on that day the deacon had to leave Plymouth on business. On the seventeenth the church met to decide the embarrassing case. A member reminded the Patriots in the church that, from a Loyalist standpoint, they were guilty of treason. How did Foster feel about that? He did not "think it expedient" to tell them. All that he would say was that he would not recant his opinions. Still cautious, the members voted that they "could not contentedly communicate with him" and advised Foster to consider his position. Again the church adjourned without reaching a decision. The twentieth meeting, scheduled for October, 1776, was canceled because the pastor was absent, but the church had not given up hope. A further meeting was contemplated, for the record concludes: "And thus the Affair remains to be concluded if Providence permit, at some future Meeting, to be appointed or warned anew." [22]

Providence, however, brought about a different conclusion from that which had been expected, but the result was equally satisfactory to the members. In January, 1777, Deacon Foster died of smallpox, the dread disease which had claimed the life of another deacon a few weeks earlier. The pastor saw God's hand at work in history as he wrote:

> A surprizing Providence! two Deacons of this Church have dyd within a Month, of this terrible Disease. The first, viz. Deacon Torrey, was innoculated, but twas thought he had previously taken it, the natural way. The other catched it, but had no knowledge how or when.
>
> May this Church be enabled wisely to improve such a mysterious Dispensation.[23]

Happier for all but the Loyalists was the confession of Captain Nathaniel Williams, whose zeal for the Revolution had been below the expectation of his church. The captain publicly acknowledged that his political principles and conduct had given cause of dissatisfaction and asked the forgiveness of his brethren.[24]

Shays's Rebellion, the result of the acute economic depression which followed upon the heels of the Revolution, indirectly affected the church in Barre, where several members withdrew from the communion and expressed their disapproval of four brethren who had presumably been in the mob at Petersham. Two of the rebels sent acceptable explanations; a third was out of the state. The only unrepentant participant, Richard Mills, stalled repeatedly until, in February, 1789, he asked to be restored. Looking further into the case, the church convicted him of being an accomplice in the revolt and had him admonished. Two years elapsed before either side took a step. In March, 1791, Mills's request for a mutual council was denied. After an interval of four months, during which he apologized for his failure to respond to a citation, Mills successfully confessed his excessive zeal in political affairs.[25]

Even after the establishment of the state government the churches occasionally dealt in political matters. In 1792 a woman of the Canton church, who had been charged with absence, explained that she had been offended by two members of the church, both of them state officers, who had taken her grandchild and bound him out. The sister acknowledged her failure to take the private steps, but the officials were held culpable and were required to apologize for their conduct.[26] The last such case which has been located occurred in Pittsfield, where a man who refused to open his books in connection with a pension dispute was considered unworthy of a dismission until he had given satisfaction for his lack of cooperation.[27]

XIV. THE ENJOYMENT OF TIME AND WORLDLY PLEASURES

The good things of the world, Calvin said, were given to men by God, and although he had no sympathy with the otherwise saintly ascetic who limited his material pleasures to the barest essentials, the Geneva reformer insisted that they be used with restraint. The Christian was to indulge in as little as possible. He was to live a life of frugality lest his worldly goods become an hindrance instead of a help. Every man had his divinely assigned station in life and must not usurp another's position. Calvin did not need the help of Veblen to become aware of the "conspicuous consumption" on the part of persons who merely desired to attract attention.[1]

The Massachusetts Puritans shared Calvin's repugnance to waste and conspicuous consumption. Doubtless influenced by the manpower shortage as well as by moral considerations, the colonial statutes of Massachusetts forbade idleness as well as excessive apparel, but the public authorities found it difficult to suppress all displays of worldly pride.[2] Cotton Mather observed in 1707 that "*Worldliness,* or *Covetousness*" was "eminently the Sin of my own Countrey,"[3] and five years later wrote:

> I have a Neece, in whose Conduct, there are some Vanities and Fooleries, whereof she needs to be admonished; and I would endeavour for her the most engaging and effectual Admonitions.[4]

No less sinful from the Puritans' viewpoint was "conspicuous leisure." Idleness, Calvin held, violated the Eighth Commandment, and Increase Mather emphasized that time was a gift which God had entrusted to men, who were to use it with a sense of stewardship.[5] What a conscience-striken Puritan woman thought of wasted time is shown in an anonymous writing of 1727:

I often mourn the Loss of that *Time* I have spent in reading *useless Books,* which I am sensible had been better improv'd in working out my Souls Salvation. . . . The Things that *once* appear'd innocent Amusements, *now* appear to be sinful. It amazes me to think that one so Young as I, scarce *Twenty* Years Old, should have heap'd up so much Sin and Guilt.[6]

Church censures for idleness itself were rare. In 1641 a man was excommunicated for his idle life and for being "somewhat proud,"[7] and in 1657 a woman who said that Christ had commanded her to remain idle was cast out of the church.[8] Well within the eighteenth century an idler of North Andover publicly confessed that he had led a lazy life.[9]

While the Revolution was raging in New England, Hannah Melvin, the town gossip of Concord, was charged on six counts including slander, lying, and fornication. The only count worth noting alleged that she had gone "from House to House, as an idle person and busy Body, not minding her own Business." Convicted on all counts, Hannah vainly sought permission to make her confession before the church only. Because she refused to own her idleness publicly, she was admonished and five years later received a severe warning that she would be excommunicated if she did not make a public confession. The church waited another three years before it put its final censure into effect. When the pastor prepared to read the sentence, Hannah was found sitting in the gallery. She had repeatedly stated that she would not appear; now the church expected a disturbance at the crucial moment. The pastor, however, ignored Hannah's presence and read the sentence as if she were absent.[10] Another busybody, Mehitable Whitney, of Otis, who asserted an undoubted right to supervise the activities of the Strickland family, and to inquire into its affairs, found that the best way to obtain information concerning Mr. Strickland's private affairs was to take the children out of the meetinghouse on the Sabbath, thereby "disaffecting the minds of the children and destroying the government of the family." After a lengthy trial, but before the church had reached a decision, the Stricklands and Mehitable settled their dispute and agreed not to divulge the terms of the reconciliation.[11]

The Puritan attitude towards amusements and recreation was closely related to their view of the proper use of time. The question whether Puritanism was opposed to amusements in themselves will remain a subject of debate as long as writers differ on the definition of amusements. The scholar who maintains that the Puritans opposed all amusements as temptations of the devil is challenged by the scholar who holds that only the abuse of amusements was considered sinful.[12] In certain cases, notably the theatre, the conviction that the devil was at work in it strengthened the opposition. "Let not Christian Boston goe beyond Heathen Rome in the practice of shameful vanities," warned Samuel Sewall when a play was about to be produced.[13] Other recreations, such as physical sports, if exercised in moderation, were centainly not condemned in themselves. The man who was convicted of playing quoits on a day of thanksgiving[14] was censured not because he enjoyed the game, but because he had chosen the wrong day on which to enjoy it; Calvin himself played quoits, but not on feast days.[15] Shooting, running, fencing, chess, and music were permissible recreations; the theatre and games of chance were not.[16] Weeden's statement, that for lack of other recreations and amusements, the training day and the gallows furnished the Puritans' principal entertainment,[17] is an unjustified exaggeration. Cotton Mather, rather than keep his children from games and sports, exploited their activities to remind them of "those pious Instructions, which the Circumstances of their play may lead them to think upon."[18]

For the express purpose of preventing the waste of time, a Massachusetts statute of 1660 forbade the games of shuffleboard and bowling. Gambling was also prohibited on the penalty of a fine three times the amount of money involved in the game, half of which fine could be recovered by a *qui tam* action.[19] In Plymouth the very possession, not to mention the use, of playing cards or dice was punishable by a fine, but no conviction could be had except on the testimony of two witnesses.[20] Idleness itself, apart from gambling or other amusements, was illegal in both colonies, and the Massachusetts statute instructed constables to take notice "especially of common Coasters, unprofitable Foulers, and Tobacco takers." [21] The Worcester court records disclose that as late as 1761 persons were fined for the mere possession of playing cards, and twenty years later a person caught playing a game for a stake was fined.[22]

The very acts of shuffling, cutting, and dealing cards contained the elements of a lottery, John Cotton observed in opposing such games. Man was only the accidental cause of the distribution of the cards; the determination as to who should receive any particular combination of cards was in the hands of God. Hence Cotton could not countenance card playing, for to "appeal to him [God] and his immediate providence for dispensing these ludicra, seemeth . . . a taking of God's name in vain." [23] Increase Mather also opposed games of chance, but for a different reason:

> For a Christian to use Recreation is very lawful, and in some cases a great Duty, but to waste so much Time in any Recreation, though never so innocent and laudable, as Gamesters usually do at Cards, and Dice, and Tables, is haynously sinfull.

Time must not be wasted, the Boston pastor and educator warned; it must be used to prepare for eternity.[24] Towards the end of the seventeenth century Cotton Mather followed in his father's footsteps in opposing the "scandalous Games of Lottery," [25] while as late as 1743 the Deerfield church voted that card playing, because it was "attended with so many Evil consequences," was sinful.[26]

The only specific mention of gaming found in the seventeenth-century records concerns a member of the Second Church of Boston whose adultery overshadowed his gambling.[27] Two confessions were made towards the close of the eighteenth century; a third person who had been found guilty of gambling moved to Portland and was not further disciplined.[28] Card playing was one of the five offenses included in the confession of a Pittsfield deacon in 1819, and was again confessed in that church in 1840, when a brother owned his sins of gambling and "mingling in scenes of dissipation." [29] Less clearly defined is the offense for which an impenitent brother, who had been convicted of indulging in "vain amusements," was excommunicated in 1824.[30]

If the Puritan divines were unanimous in their opposition to games of chance, they were more hesitant in condemning the dance. While Perkins, the English Congregationalist, feared that dancing encouraged idolatry, sexual misconduct, and drunkenness, John Cotton was not worried about mixed dancing: "only lascivious dancing to wanton ditties, and in amorous gestures, and wanton dalliances, especially after great feasts," were condemned as "great flabella libidinis." [31] Later in the century, however, after a Boston dancing master had been ordered by the courts to close his school, Cotton Mather denounced mixed dances from the pulpit, using as his text Isaiah 3:16-17.[32] That more obvious evidence could have been cited for the other side, and that dancing was unquestionably an activity sanctioned in the Bible, were probably suppressed. Samuel Sewall seconded Mather's denunciation: "Mr. Mather struck at the Root, speaking against mixed dances." [33]

Gradually dancing became an accepted part of social life, even in Massachusetts, and in 1723 a dancing master openly advertised his school in Boston.[34] Some churches, however, did not approve of the introduction of the dance into Puritan life and warned their members that if they engaged in such amusements, they would be censured.[35] Because she did not heed her church's warning, Sylvia Morgan, who had associated with "vain, light, and airy company" at dances, was excommunicated from the church in Stockbridge, but was subsequently restored after a confession.[36] In Great Barrington, a brother who enjoyed dancing was similarly censured and was denied recourse to council,[37] and as late as 1840 an unrepentant landlord who had rented his hall to a dancing master was cast out of the church in Danvers.[38]

Less clearly defined are the offenses of a Boston woman who made a confession of keeping disorderly company and giving her guests too much alcoholic liquor, and of a woman of Roxbury who was admonished because of her notorious reputation for "unreasonable entertaining."[39] In 1813 the Otis church investigated the conduct of Paul Larkom and Mrs. Rhoda Norton. After some discussion with the church, Rhoda confessed that she had "joined in merry companies" at late hours of the night and had engaged in "undue familiarities . . . unbecoming a married woman," which, the pastor noted, did not imply sexual relations. Larkom, who had spread the mischievous rumor concerning Rhoda Norton, confessed his imprudence in giving rise to the stories.[40]

Church censures for overt expressions of pride, vanity, and other forms of conspicuous consumption were less common than those for idleness and leisure. Two men, one of whom was "too much addicted to the world," while the other was known for his "rash carriage and speaches savouring of selfe confidence," were dealt with in Dedham in 1636, two years before the church was gathered. The "worldly" man, Joseph Kingsbury, would not be swayed by the entreaties of the brethren and flung at one of his opponents. The church concluded that it was not "the mind of God" that he should be admitted to the company of the elect who were shortly to gather themselves into a church, but that he should be left to the judgment of the church once it was organized. The self-confident Anthony Fisher, on the other hand, acknowledged his pride and was about to be admitted into the group which was to constitute the church. Additional charges were made, however, and Fisher, too, was left to the judgment of the gathered church. Kingsbury, who made a confession, was admitted to the church in 1641, followed four years later by the penitent Fisher.[41]

Three years after the men of Dedham rejected Kingsbury and Fisher, the Salem church censured a man for pride, and in 1678 a member of the Plymouth church was rebuked for "inordinate walking."[42] Later in the century two women were found guilty by their churches, the one of pride, disobedience to her parents, and fornication, the other of intemperate carriage, obscenity, and receiving stolen property, and in 1735 a brother of the Westfield church was censured for vanity.[43] For her ingratitude in criticizing the "Laudable Diet" which she received at the almshouse and, incidentally, for slandering its keeper by suggesting that he had attempted to have sexual relations with her, Abigail Day was excommunicated from the Second Church of Boston in 1697.[44]

Abigail, evidently a gourmet, was concerned with the quality of her food. More concerned with quantity was Joseph David, Jr., of Barnstable, who evidently was a gourmand. In 1792 David voluntarily read the following confession to the church:

As it becomes those who have by their irregular and immoral conduct brought a scandal upon their profession, to make all the reparation in their power for the injury they have done, not only by confessing their sins to God, but by frankly acknowledging them before their Christian Brethren-; I desire with deep humiliation and self abasement to confess that I have grossly violated the laws of sobriety and temperance in many instances, having lived for months and years under the too prevailing influence of an inordinate and depraved appetite. . . . I hope and trust that it hath pleased God in his great mercy to bring me to a true sight and sense of my iniquities. While I bless him for those chastisements which have been the means of opening my eyes to my guilt and danger, I would [illegible] implore his forgiveness and the powerful aids of his Spirit that I may be enabled to keep those good resolutions which I have solemnly formed.

Having acknowledged his gluttony, David warned his brethren against "this pernicious habit" and was restored.[45]

The churches did a thoroughgoing job in censuring members for manifestations of vanity and idleness and, stressing the value of time, regulated the Puritans' amusements. Although they never banned recreation as such, the churches' opposition to games of chance and mixed dancing diminished only gradually. Nevertheless, the liberal trend is clearly apparent; the censures for card playing and dancing imposed in 1840 were distinctly exceptional. Outward pride, too, was considered as censurable. A more vicious form of pride, however, was ever present and could not be rooted out by disciplinary action, for no amount of evidence could prove the existence of spiritual pride.[46] Jonathan Edwards considered spiritual pride the "first and worst cause of errors" attending the Great Awakening, and wrote:

Spiritual pride in its own nature is so secret, that it is not so well discerned by immediate intuition on the thing itself, as by the effects and fruits of it; . . . Spiritual pride disposes to speak of other persons' sins, their enmity against God and his people, the miserable delusion of hypocrites and their enmity against vital piety, and the deadness of some saints, with bitterness, or with laughter and levity, and an air of contempt. . . . Spiritual pride is very apt to suspect others; . . . is apt to find fault with other saints, that they are low in grace.[47]

XV. The Unattained Utopia

The morality of the people claimed the constant attention of the Puritan clergy. But whatever utopian hopes the first settlers of Plymouth or of the Bay Colony may have entertained were soon shattered. The revolt against the moral standards of the original settlers began already with the second generation, and by the middle of the seventeenth century a distinct decline in morality set it.[1] The Reform Synod of 1679 observed with distress that ungodliness, worldliness, profanity, Sabbath-breaking, intemperance, strife among church members, and laxity in family discipline were mounting.[2] Five years later Increase Mather, commenting on the morality of his times, wrote that "things look at this day with a dark and dismal face," [3] and Cotton Mather, shortly before the turn of the century, complained that swearing, cursing, intemperance, the sale of liquor to Indians, vanity, sorcery, sabbath-breaking, piracy, contention, animosity, sexual impurity (especially lewdness at harvest time), fraud, oppression, lying, and slander were widespread.[4] John Cotton, Jr., the minister of Plymouth, saw the judgment of God in the Charter of 1691: the churches had been negligent in discipline, and a goodly number of the brethren had been given to "sensuality, intemperance, long tarrying, drinking and gaming at ordinaries: Yea, and prophaning the Sabbath in needlesse drinking." [5] Almost eighty years later, when the hated Tea Tax replaced the only slightly more annoying Townshend duties, the churchmen of Plymouth attributed their misfortunes to their sin and laxity. Although the church failed to pass a formal resolution, the brethren agreed informally to be more watchful, and the minister expressed his sentiments for the record:

We have been very criminally negligent and slack in the Matter of Church Discipline. And yet, alas, how strangely backward, (as a Church) to actual and immediate reformation: The Lord give us all a heart to repent and reform in This Thing particularly, which I believe, is one aweful and provoking Cause of the mellancholly withdraw[al] of the Spirit and comforting presence of Christ.[6]

Five years later, the Revolution well under way, the conscience-stricken church in Egremont solemnly resolved to do its utmost to suppress vice.[7] Quite obviously Massachusetts had not become the desired utopia. Man was still man, and therefore sinner.

The disparity of the available church records makes any purely statistical analysis of cases useless and misleading. There are, however, seven churches of some size which have complete records for the years 1690-1809. By comparing the number of cases in these churches during three forty-year periods we can see some trends. The first period includes the years from the charter of 1691 through the decade preceding the Great Awakening. The next forty years include the Great Awakening and the two following decades, while the last period includes the Revolution and its aftermath, and the first twenty years of the Union under the Constitution.

A comparison of the total number of cases in the first and second periods reveals a striking increase in the number of persons involved in fornication cases.[8] Allowance must be made for the ninefold increase in Westfield, a rapidly growing frontier town, but even if the Westfield figures are disregarded the increase remains plainly apparent. Although the number of cases during the forty years which include the Great Awakening is far greater than during the previous forty years, the impact of the Great Awakening on church discipline can properly be seen only in the records of those churches which were directly affected by the movement and which are reasonably complete for some years before and after the revivals. The records of eight churches which meet both requirements throw some light on the relationship of the Great Awakening to church discipline.[9]

In some of these churches there was no apparent connection between the Awakening and the enforcement of moral standards. Thus the Plymouth church, which had a revival in 1740,[10] dealt with fifteen persons during the 1730's, but with only five members during the next decade, and with none at all in the year of the revival. Evidently the revival had no influence on the administration of discipline in Plymouth, or public morality improved considerably. A similar lack of any correlation appears in the Northampton records, although other reasons may account for this,[11] and the increase from two cases in 1741 to three in 1742 in Reading can hardly be taken as proof that the Reading revival of 1742 [12] had any effect on church discipline in that town. Contrasting evidence appears in the records of the churches in Roxbury, Marblehead, Sutton, Deerfield, and Westfield. Roxbury had a revival in 1740.[13] No cases are recorded for that year, but five persons were censured or made confessions in 1741, and a total of seventeen during the decade, as against two during the 1730's. In the decade before Whitefield's visit to Marblehead in September, 1740,[14] the two churches in the town dealt with only fourteen offenders. Only one person was hailed before the church in 1740, but six more followed in 1741, four in 1742, and two in 1743. During the rest of the decade, the people of Marblehead must have led lives of amazing purity or the churches must have been exceedingly lax, for no further cases are recorded until the next decade, in which thirteen persons made confessions or were censured. Equally revealing are the Sutton records, which disclose an increase of cases after the revivals of 1735 and 1740.[15] From 1730 to 1734 the church dealt with three offenders; during the rest of the decade it accepted confessions from, or imposed censures on, nine members, four of whom were disciplined in the year following the revival. More noticeable is the increase which followed the larger revival of 1740. No cases are recorded for 1738 or 1739, but twenty-seven persons were involved in disciplinary action during the forties. A similar, though less striking, trend is found in the Deerfield records. Five persons were subjected to discipline between 1732 and 1734, but six cases came before the church in the year of its revival, 1735.[16] The increase of two in the year following the revival of 1743 [17] is less revealing. Of like interest is the sudden rise in cases in Westfield, where Whitefield conducted a revival in 1740.[18] In 1738, 1739, and 1740, three persons were disciplined each year, but in 1741, the year after the revival, eight persons made confessions or were censured, while nine others are listed for the next two years.[19]

In his study of sexual morality in the colonial period, Charles Francis Adams found that the bulk of fornication cases in the records of the North Precinct Church of Braintree (i.e., Quincy) occurred between 1716 and 1744.[20] The Braintree justice of the peace records from 1716 to 1761, however, disclosed only four bastardy cases and one of fornication. Adams attributes this discrepancy to the Great Awakening. According to Adams, this "pestiferous stuff" led to morbidity and spiritual excitement. Young women, brooding over undisclosed sins, sought catharsis in public confessions. When the spiritual insanity had passed its peak and had begun to wane, persons aroused by the revival sought another outlet for their pent-up emotions and committed still more sexual violations, increasing not only the number of confessions, but the number of offenses as well.[21] This suggestion is supported by the increases in cases during the years *following* the revivals.

Allegedly refuting Adams, Henry B. Parkes maintained that the Great Awakening did not increase the rate of sexual violations but, on the contrary, that it led to a stricter observance of the moral codes.[22] In another article, however, Parkes noted the increase of fornication cases in the court records for the period after 1710 and found that the church records corroborated his conclusion that morals were strict until Queen Anne's War, degenerated between 1713 and the Great Awakening, improved somewhat during the Awakening, and declined again during the Revolutionary period. Nevertheless, Parkes maintains that morality was high.[23]

Except for Adams's assertion that sexual morality was low and Parkes's insistence that it was high (which is, after all, a matter of definition), Parkes's revised position [24] is not irreconcilable with that of Adams. It is quite possible that persons influenced by the Awakening were impressed with a sense of guilt of *prior* offenses and hence made their confessions. Others may have been converted by the revivals and may have offered confessions, in connection with their admission to church membership, of sins committed years ago. One of the most startling confessions accepted by any church during the period of the Great Awakening acknowledged an act of fornication committed thirty-eight years earlier.[25] The record implies that the confession was voluntary and spontaneous. It seems extremely unlikely that a person should suddenly repent of such an offense after thirty-eight years unless religious fervor was at its height. Neither is the increase in the number of confessions during the period of the Awakening irreconcilable with Parkes's suggestion that the moral aspect of the Awakening deterred some persons from committing offenses, for the revivals doubtless made the churches more vigilant in the enforcement of discipline. Finally, some of the confessions which were publicly read in the churches may have put ideas into the minds of the people, and, as Adams suggests, some persons of high repute may have fallen into sexual offenses because of the Awakening, for in a state of "insanity," he notes, influences may effect the opposite of what was intended.[26]

The decline of church discipline began in the decade following the Great Awakening. The Revolution and the impact of the Enlightenment inevitably disrupted the old religious traditions, and by the turn of the century religious apathy was plainly evident.[27] The practice of public confession, especially in sexual cases, became increasingly unpopular, and the number of fornication cases decreased steadily.

Before church discipline fell into desuetude, however, it had one last revival, especially in cases of alcoholism and absenteeism. For the years 1770-1809, ninety-four cases of intoxication or intemperance have been found, or an average of 2.35 a year. During the next thirty years, 104 persons were censured, or an average of 3.76 a year.[28] The reason for the increase is doubtless the changing emphasis from temperance to abstinence. More significant than the rise in liquor cases is the increase in actions arising from absences. Excluding cases of persons who were converted to other denominations and those arising from schisms, there is a distinct increase in these cases after 1810.[29] The implications of this become apparent in the light of the rise of religious liberty, culminating in the disestablishment of 1833, which must have encouraged church members of merely nominal loyalty to withdraw from the established churches if they preferred to worship elsewhere. Although such cases have not been included in these figures,[30] cases of persons who withdrew from their churches without joining any other denomination have been listed, which may in part explain the increase. But another factor must be considered: the revivals of the post-Revolutionary era.[31] If some members, influenced by the rise of religious liberty, forsook organized worship altogether, others, influenced by the revivals, doubtless took a firmer stand against those who would no longer worship with their brethren. Judging from the increasing proportion of absentees and withdrawing members who were not restored,[32] religious liberty and individualism seem to have won the race against the claims of the churches and the old patterns of behavior.

Although the desuetude of church discipline had its origins in the eighteenth century, it did not reach its fulfillment until the nineteenth. Church discipline was never abolished; no resolution was ever passed to relegate the system to the realm of antiquity. It simply disappeared from the scene, like many a tradition which has outlived its usefulness or which had come into conflict with a developing and changing culture.

For a clearer picture of the disappearance of church discipline in its traditional Puritan form, we must turn to the cases in those churches whose records, apparently complete for a considerable part of the nineteenth century, it was possible to consult.[33] Thus we find one church, that in Chelsea, which has no recorded cases whatsoever in the nineteenth century. The sole confession listed in the Chelsea records for the post-Revolutionary period was made in 1798, when a woman confessed an act of fornication, and this confession was made in connection with her admission to full communion.[34] The Plymouth records disclose only three cases, two of which were for absence, after 1799; the third case involved a drunkard, who made a confession in 1834, eighteen years after he was censured.[35] The solitary case in the records of the North Church of Middleborough involved a man who confessed fornication in 1800.[36]

Absence, intoxication, and intemperance were the most frequent causes of confessions or censures after 1800 in the eastern counties.[37] Of the twenty-one members censured in Plymouth during the 1820's, seventeen were absentees, while three were addicted to the bottle. The only unusual case involved a man who was excommunicated for failing to repent of striking his aged father.[38] A similar assortment of alcoholics and absentees, along with an occasional member of loose sexual morals, provided the bulk of nineteenth-century cases in the First Church of Haverhill, the First Church of Marblehead, and to a lesser degree, the church in Danvers,[39] which also dealt with a thief and with a crook.[40] Distinctly unusual were the excommunications by the Danvers church of William Barry, who had permitted the use of his hall for instruction in the terpsichorean art, and of a woman who had become a Universalist, and the same censure imposed by the Haverhill church on David Webster, the author of some compromising letters.[41] In Cambridge, where the church had restored a fornicator in 1809, the church proceeded in 1814 to excommunicate the Harvard alumnus who had barely begun the religious pilgrimage which was to lead him to Islam.[42] A curious case appears in the Reading records for 1829. The case is unique in that Jonathan Emerson, who had committed an unspecified "scandalous sin," was excommunicated in spite of his confession, because the church members could "in no other way *clear themselves in this matter.*" [43] This apparently summary excommunication is not only unique for this late period, but stands in sharp contrast to an earlier entry in the same records, made in 1808, which tells of Polly Putnam's confession of fornication and adds: "*Of course* she was by Vote unanimous restored." [44]

In the western counties, nineteenth-century church discipline differed little from that of the eighteenth. Except for one confession of fornication and one of intoxication, the Northampton records for the period have been obliterated, but the Amherst records mention confessions of a Sabbath-breaker in 1823 and of a thief and incendiary in 1838,[45] while the Worthington church, in addition to dealing with the more common offenders, suspended a woman who had embraked on a bigamous marriage.[46] The bulk of the late cases in the Berkshire County churches involved alcoholics and absentees; as late as 1840 a brother confessed that he had used alcoholic liquor.[47] A plurality of the Pittsfield cases arose from absences; a majority of them were not prosecuted to any logical conclusion.[48] The Lenox church indulged in a wholesale prosecution of absentees in 1835, but these cases, too, were not followed through to the offender's restoration or excommunication.[49] In the last cases found in the records of any Massachusetts church, the letter-writing adulteress of Pittsfield, Martha Baldwin, and her lover, Nathaniel Dodge, were cast out of the church, and John Barnard surrendered his sweetheart and wife presumptive to her returned husband.[50] To bring the narrative into the post-Civil War period, we may once more mention the complaint, dated 1872, which in circuitous but unmistakable language accused a member of the Stockbridge church of operating a house of ill fame.[51]

Although the application of church discipline as it was practiced in the colonial period is now rarely if ever found, the principles are still adhered to. A manual published in 1838 contains instructions not unlike those found in Cotton Mather's *Ratio Disciplinae*.[52] Later manuals [53] follow in the same line of thought but reflect changing social and legal concepts. A report dated 1846 [54] contains the old rules of procedure but emphasizes the function of witnesses. Their competence is to be judged by the church, they may be challenged and their testimony impeached, they must not hear the evidence of previous witnesses save by the consent of all parties, and they may be sworn. No conviction shall be had except on the evidence of two or more witnesses. A church member who refuses to testify may be charged with contumacy. Whenever possible, the report urges, rules of common law and equity shall be followed.[55] The two-witness rule, of biblical origin, is stressed in these manuals, and Cummings's *Dictionary of Congregational Usages and Principles* (1853) warns against convictions based on mere rumor, although rumors may justify an investigation by the church.[56] In contrast to the report of 1846, which urged the churches to follow court procedure, a manual of 1883 held that legal rules were inapplicable in ecclesiastical trials, mainly because the churches could not compel the attendance of witnesses and could not punish contempt. Hence broader rules were needed: husbands and wives could testify against their spouses, and hearsay evidence was admissible. This manual was the first to assure the churches that participants in church trials were immune from tort actions,[57] but a manual issued twenty years later held that the churches should not publicize or openly announce censures. A church member who from reasons of conscience desired to join another denomination should not be restrained, for neither the church nor the member would benefit from an enforced and nominal membership. A person could be excommunicated for the peace of the church, but not for the sake of his soul: "The old idea of excommunication as a censure and curse was not a Scriptural one." [58]

A more orthodox attitude was taken by W. E. Barton in 1916, who affirmed the right of churches to censure their members and maintained the distinction between public and private offenses. The rules of procedure, however, are amplified: the charges must be stated in writing, counsel may be had from outside the church, but the lawyer must not obstruct the administration of ecclesiastical justice by the intrusion of "court technicalities." If the respondent is in prison and pleads guilty, he may appear by counsel. If he has absconded, he may be tried *in absentia,* provided he has been cited and cannot be located. As a concession to modern business methods, Barton suggests that such a respondent be cited by registered mail.[59] The most recent manual on Congregational polity allows that churches may "withdraw fellowship," but cautions against the use of censures.[60]

The civil law has allowed considerable freedom to churches engaged in the administration of ecclesiastical discipline. In 1824 the Massachusetts courts ruled that a non-member might bring charges without risking a tort action: "accusations made to a body competent to try the offender, cannot be made the subject of an action for slander," [61] and in 1847 a plaintiff who had been excommunicated for fornication nonsuited because he had voluntarily submitted to the discipline of the church when he became a member.[62] In the enforcement of the disciplinary functions, even to the point of publicly announcing an excommunication, provided the announcement is not malicious and is limited in content to the necessary information, churches and their officers are not actionable.[63] The courts will not question the judgments of churches unless civil or proprietary rights are involved,[64] and excommunication has been held not to involve any temporal rights.[65] In an unusual case, a would-be plaintiff-in-error learned to his regret that certiorari did not lie to bring an ecclesiastical court's record up for review by a civil court.[66]

The avowed purpose of this area of the churches' activities was to secure the repentance and restoration of transgressors of the moral code, but it obviously had considerable social implications as well. The churches assumed the oversight of the morals of their members, and in a society dominated by the church members such regulation necessarily tended to set the moral standards for the entire community. Through influence in the legislature the churches could secure the enactment of statutes governing the behavior of the people in accordance with their own standards. Through the administration of censures civil sanctions could be supplemented by those of the churches, and where legislation or law enforcement did not meet the churches' demands, ecclesiastical censures could be applied to compensate for the legal loopholes as far as church members were concerned. The personal emphasis in church discipline notwithstanding, the standards of the Congregational churches inevitably influenced the general community.

The reasons for the decline of the disciplinary system were for the greater part inherent in Puritanism, although political pressures from Whitehall and the changing cultural environment helped to hasten the process. The cooperation between the churches and the civil authorities in the seventeenth century was an indispensable adjunct to the churches in their disciplinary work. In the eighteenth century, and especially after the Revolution, the standards set by the churches were at variance from those of the larger community. As the civil government was increasingly freed from clerical influence, the churches were deprived of civil support in the regulation of morals and imposed their own standards on their members. Attempting to enforce these standards by coercive measures rather than by proclaiming them from the pulpits, the word of

God became an inflexible and harsh code of laws,[67] and the churches assumed the naturally unpopular functions of a police force. With the weakening of religious faith until, by the end of the eighteenth century, it was thoroughly stale and dry, and Unitarianism had to come to the rescue, the old ethic could not fail to collapse.

For Calvin, a High Churchman (in the best sense of the word), the separation of morals from the concept of the Church was unthinkable, and the basis of church discipline was the sense of holiness.[68] No doubt the same was true of the great Puritan divines, but on the whole the New England churches eventually permitted the sect spirit to dominate the church spirit. Sectarianism, marked by exclusiveness (we might say "religious snobbery"), suspicion, and an obsession for moral and doctrinal uniformity, turned the churches into closed corporations, in which the members thought they had a vested interest. Jealous of their assumed purity, the churches were not so much interested in winning followers as in keeping people out, and in demonstrating that New England would not tolerate sin.[69] When Puritanism lost its sense of communion, when church membership came to be regarded as somewhat akin to membership in a social club for the chosen few of suitable standing, and when the religious emphasis declined, ethics became dissociated from theology, and an alien moralism, unrelated to the faith of the people, replaced what had been one aspect, however exaggerated it may have been, of a coherent system of belief.[70]

Ethics have an undoubted place in any theological system, but the biblicism of the Puritans, with its notion that Scripture furnished the definitive rule for any moral problem, prevented them from distinguishing the abiding moral law from specific laws promulgated for certain occasions and made for an outward nomism which defeated spontaneity of action and feeling.[71] Making a person's behavior the chief criterion of eligibility for membership, a common sectarian trait, was itself a mistake. If a sister was caught slandering her neighbor, or if a brother was found to be addicted to the bottle, the fact was considered prima facie evidence that the member should not have entered into covenant. Men's status in the eyes of God was judged by their outward acts; their inward thoughts, which defied the scrutiny of the most ardent moralists, were disregarded. Morbidly preoccupied with the state of their souls and wondering whether they would make the grade, the Puritans inevitably became self-centered introverts.[72] Moreover, by identifying sin with carnal desire, they were blinded to the fact that the sin underlying sins is man's inevitable inclination to exalt himself. Emphasizing sins, they overlooked sin.

Even today the combination of Puritan moralism and censoriousness manifests itself at times. A minister who had taken charge of a church in the Adirondacks was horrified by the "heart-searching session" which was the core of the weekly "prayer meeting":

> The so-called heart-searching session hit me like a physical blow. I have never heard personalties so ruthlessly exposed and discussed as they were at those early "prayer meetings" in Wadhams. "Josh Corot is hitting the bottle again—we better remember him." . . . [*sic*] "That Partin girl is up to no good with that tractor man, mark my words." . . . [*sic*]
>
> . . . Always I was called upon to close with a prayer. And each time I felt it was desecration.[73]

The minister eventually succeeded in putting an end to these sessions, which were not even tempered by the procedural safeguards usually found in colonial church trials, by stimulating some "heart-searchings" herself. "Of course," she told her people, "you all realize that, as your pastor, I am learning more each day about sin and the lost souls here in the north country," and then read some words which must have disturbed the professional searchers: "Judge not, that you be not judged. . . . You hypocrite, first take the log out of your own eye, and then you will see clearly to take the speck out of your brother's eye."[74] There were no more "searchings of heart" in Wadhams.

A secret confession can at worst fill one person with a feeling of self-satisfaction. The public confessions of the Puritans filled whole congregations with it. When Isaac Crocker, in a confession for fornication, depicted hell, saying that he was "numbered among the unclean amonst the abominable and whore-Mongers and them who shall have their part in the Lake which burneth with fire and brimstone," and desired to "fly to the atoning blood and merits of Jesus Christ for cleansing, for pardon and acceptance with God,"[75] there could hardly have been a person present who did not enjoy a comfortable feeling of smug self-satisfaction. By 1770 fire and brimstone were no longer mentioned in confessions, and that of Josiah Loomis, also for fornication, was less picturesque, though as penitent, as that of Isaac Crocker:

Whereas I have gone astray from God's holy commandments, and have in many things erred from the right way, but especially the winter before last in keeping company with bad and wicked persons, by which I have sinned against God, and also have given just occasion of suspicion to all people of the sin of uncleanness to have been by me committed, in that I was so much in company with a woman of bad character, for which conduct I am now heartily sorry, and I sincerely pray that God would pardon and remit my sin herein: and I heartily desire the forgiveness of all my fellow men who are hereby offended: I desire the prayers of all God's people for me, that I may keep a conscience void of offence towards God my Creator, and towards men my fellow creatures: and humbly desire that this Church would receive me into their charity, and not retain my faults any longer against me in love and charity continually.[76]

The colonial clergy, no less than the modern minister of Wadhams, were not unaware of the problem. As Jonathan Edwards had remarked, spiritual pride was a secret matter. It was impossible to try a member on a charge of self-righteousness. Once in a while a preacher might shatter his congregation's pride, as Jeremiah Shepard perhaps did when he told his flock that "there are many in Hell, that have had a Presumptuous Confidence that they should go to Heaven," and that "many that are Ear-mark'd among Christ's sheep here will be found to be Goats," [77] but the churches' rigidly enforced moralism could not fail to augment man's inexhaustible reservoir of self-righteousness. In 1700 the neurotic [78] Cotton Mather, who was ever ready to observe the miscarriages of his flock [79] and whose *Essays to Do Good* are an outstanding example of the Puritans' "inverted moralism," [80] recorded the confession of a Pharisee in his diary:

> On this Day, I laid before the Lord, the *Reproaches,* which I suffered, from abundance of impious people, for the sake of my Faithfulness to His Churches and Interests.
>
> I acknowledged myself to bee *viler* before Him, than any of my causeless and cruel Adversaries could make mee, when they *reviled* mee. And I gave exceeding Thanks unto Him, for his præserving mee, from the Unhappiness of being made obnoxious to their Malice, by any *real Blemish,* whereof if they could gett the least Notice, how wonderfully they would aggravate it.[81]

There is always a temptation to associate Phariseeism with hypocrisy. Nothing could be further from the truth. Cotton Mather, like the Pharisee, was a legalist who thought he had a vested interest in God, who owed him a dividend. The Pharisee of the biblical story was no hypocrite but an eminently honest man; the publican was a scoundrel, but he perceived that God for all his holiness would have mercy even upon a crooked tax collector.[82] A modern scholar has described the Pharisee as "a patriot and an upright man, and probably the chairman both of the forefathers' day society and the temple charity fund," [83] a description which fits the Puritan almost equally well. The Pharisee did more than his share of fasting and tithing; his religious practice was exemplary. But this was his tragedy: "He had too much religion. He was its servant instead of God's son." [84]

The Puritan, too, was an eminently honest man, but he shared the Pharisee's tragedy: he too was the servant of religion for whom the kerygma had become a revised version of an older code of law, full of the temptations which beset the Pharisee.[85] Salvation was attested by good works which were more or less capable of objective measurement. Since there was little or no adiaphora, every decision was of supreme importance.[86] The position that moral decisions must be made on the assumption that they *may* be wrong, in spite of the best intentions, but that God will accept men in spite of their sin, was unacceptable to the Puritan. Although, far from being Pelagians, the Puritans were keenly aware of man's fallen nature, they expected the regenerate person, the saint, to be able to live a sinless life.[87] Good legalists, they had no use for Luther's insight that regenerate man was *simul iustus et peccator,* just and sinful at the same time, nor could they go along with the view that repentance and absolution are not matters of a particular moment, but continuous processes.[88] A Puritan had to be either saint or sinner; he could not be both. The theology of Puritanism had no room for Luther's advice to Melanchthon: "Be a sinner and sin bravely, but trust and rejoice more bravely in Christ, who is the Vanquisher of sin, death, and the world." [89]

That the Puritans' hope of a holy commonwealth was not attained should hardly surprise us. Nor can we ascribe their failure to realize their ambition to adverse social or political conditions. The very idea, which never became a fact, was, as a philosopher has observed, as preposterous as Plato's Republic.[90] Because even the Puritans were human, they could not fail to bring with them the element of sin, which they had sought to leave behind,[91] and their utopia shared the common fate of all attempts to establish a perfect society on imperfect man.

Appendix: Tables I-XI

With the exception of tables VI, IX, X, and XI, the figures found below are based on all the records which have been consulted in the various counties. Those in tables VI, IX, X, and XI are based on the records of the churches mentioned.

The following symbols have been used:

C Couples (tables IV and V only)
M Men
W Women
? Sex of person unknown
F Fornication cases only (tables IX and X)
O All other cases (tables IX and X)
T Total

In all tables the present Hapden and Franklin counties are included with the figures for Hampshire County. The few Bristol County cases are included in the totals, but not in breakdowns by counties.

TABLE I

CASES INVOLVING ABSENCE OR WITHDRAWAL FROM THE LORD'S SUPPER (EXCLUDING THOSE ARISING FROM SCHISMS OR CONVERSIONS TO OTHER GROUPS, AND THOSE IN WHICH ABSENCE WAS INCIDENTAL TO ANOTHER OFFENSE), BY COUNTIES, PERIODS, AND OFFENDER'S SEX

PERIOD	NUMBER OF YEARS	PLYMOUTH			BARNSTABLE			NORFOLK		
		W	M	T	W	M	T	W	M	T
1620-1689	70	0	1	1	0	1	1	0	0	0
1690-1729	40	1	1	2	0	0	0	0	0	0
1730-1769	40	3	7	10	7	15	22	0	7	7
1770-1809	40	1	6	7	3	3	6	3	8	11
1810-1849	40	0	1	1	11	13	24	1	3	4
Total	230	5	16	21	21	32	53	4	18	22

PERIOD	NUMBER OF YEARS	SUFFOLK			ESSEX			MIDDLESEX		
		W	M	T	W	M	T	W	M	T
1620-1689	70	3	6	9	2	5	7	0	1	1
1690-1729	40	1	4	5	1	4	5	0	3	3
1730-1769	40	0	3	3	5	15	20	5	9	14
1770-1809	40	0	0	0	6	3	9	1	8	9
1810-1849	40	0	0	0	9	7	16	5	6	11
Total	230	4	13	17	23	34	57	11	27	38

PERIOD	NUMBER OF YEARS	WORCESTER			HAMPSHIRE			BERKSHIRE			
		W	M	T	W	M	T	W	M	?	T
1690-1729	40	0	0	0	0	1	1	0	0	0	0
1730-1769	40	0	2	2	6	9	15	2	1	0	3
1770-1809	40	4	12	16	7	14	21	8	30	0	38
1810-1849	40	1	2	3	7	18	25	5	37	15	57
1850–		0	0	0	0	0	0	0	0	4	4
Total	160 +	5	16	21	20	42	62	15	68	19	102

TABLE II

CASES INVOLVING ABSENCE OR WITHDRAWAL FROM THE LORD'S SUPPER (EXCLUDING THOSE ARISING FROM SCHISMS OR CONVERSION TO OTHER GROUPS, AND THOSE IN WHICH ABSENCE WAS INCIDENTAL TO ANOTHER OFFENSE), BY PERIODS AND SEX

PERIOD	NUMBER OF YEARS	WOMEN	MEN	UNKNOWN	TOTAL
1620-1689	70	5	14	0	19
1690-1729	40	3	13	0	16
1730-1769	40	28	68	0	96
1770-1809	40	33	84	0	117
1810-1849	40	39	87	15	141
1850–		0	0	4	4
Total	230 +	108	266	19	393

TABLE III

CASES INVOLVING ABSENCE OR WITHDRAWAL FROM THE LORD'S SUPPER (EXCLUDING THOSE ARISING FROM SCHISMS OR CONVERSIONS TO OTHER GROUPS, AND THOSE IN WHICH ABSENCE WAS INCIDENTAL TO ANOTHER OFFENSE), 1690-1839, BY DECADES, OFFENDER'S SEX, AND FINAL RESULT

	RETURNED [a]			LEFT CHURCH [b]			RESULT IN DOUBT [c]			TOTAL		
DECADE	W	M	T	W	M	T	W	M	T	W	M	T
1690-1699	0	1	1	0	0	0	0	2	2	0	3	3
1700-1709	0	1	1	0	0	0	2	2	4	2	3	5
1710-1719	0	1	1	0	0	0	0	0	0	0	1	1
1720-1729	1	5	6	0	1	1	0	0	0	1	6	7
1730-1739	1	7	8	0	0	0	2	8	10	3	15	18
1740-1749	3	9	12	0	2	2	5	10	15	8	21	29
1750-1759	5	7	12	1	1	2	7	9	16	13	17	30
1760-1769	1	5	6	0	3	3	3	7	10	4	15	19
1770-1779	1	7	8	0	5	5	1	5	6	2	17	19
1780-1789	7	12	19	1	2	3	4	13	17	12	27	39
1790-1799	8	9	17	1	0	1	2	9	11	11	18	29
1800-1809	3	9	12	0	4	4	5	9	14	8	22	30
1810-1819	0	3	3	5	7	12	3	4	7	8	14	22
1820-1829	3	16	19	12	15	27	14	7	21	29	38	67
1830-1839	0	2	2	0	9	9	1	19	23 [d]	1	30	34 [d]
Total	33	94	127	20	49	69	49	104	156 [d]	101	247	352 [d]

[a] Including cases in which the offender presumably resumed his church obligations, regardless of whether a confession was made, and those whose offenses were overlooked or excused.

[b] Including persons who presumably did not return to church meetings on a regular basis, including those excommunicated or declared to be beyond the church's watch and care.

[c] Including persons admonished or suspended, but neither excommunicated nor definitely restored, also cases in which no censures are mentioned but in which an investigation into the absence of withdrawal was undertaken.

[d] Includes three persons whose sex could not be ascertained.

TABLE IV

CASES OF FORNICATION, BY COUNTY, PERIOD, AND OFFENDER'S SEX

PERIOD	NUMBER OF YEARS	PLYMOUTH					BARNSTABLE				
		C	W	M	?	T	C	W	M	?	T
1620-1689	70	1	2	1	0	4	0	3	3	0	6
1690-1729	40	4	3	2	0	9	2	2	1	0	5
1730-1769	40	4	13	4	43	64	39	26	5	1	71
1770-1809	40	1	11	5	12	29	1	9	0	0	10
1810-1839	30	0	3	0	0	3	0	0	0	0	0
Total	220	10	32	12	55	109	42	40	9	1	92

PERIOD	NUMBER OF YEARS	NORFOLK					SUFFOLK				
		C	W	M	?	T	C	W	M	?	T
1620-1689	70	0	3	0	0	3	2	15	11	0	28
1690-1729	40	10	12	3	0	25	14	16	11	0	41
1730-1769	40	54	27	9	0	90	13	13	4	0	30
1770-1809	40	11	7	2	0	20	1	10	0	0	11
1810-1839	30	0	0	0	0	0	0	2	0	0	2
Total	220	75	49	14	0	138	30	56	26	0	112

PERIOD	NUMBER OF YEARS	ESSEX					MIDDLESEX				
		C	W	M	?	T	C	W	M	?	T
1620-1689	70	3	9	2	1	15	0	1	0	0	1
1690-1729	40	19	42	6	0	67	16	9	5	0	30
1730-1769	40	42	60	17	1	120	56	27	7	44[a]	134[a]
1770-1809	40	15	19	2	0	36	13	5	4	22[a]	44[a]
1810-1839	30	0	1	0	0	1	0	0	0	0	0
Total	220	79	131	27	2	239	85	42	16	66	209

PERIOD	NUMBER OF YEARS	WORCESTER					HAMPSHIRE				
		C	W	M	?	T	C	W	M	?	T
1620-1689	70	0	0	0	0	0	0	0	0	0	0
1690-1729	40	0	1	0	0	1	3	6	0	0	9
1730-1769	40	23	3	6	0	32	69	44	20	0	133
1770-1809	40	7	11	1	0	19	44	34	9	9	96
1810-1839	30	0	1	0	0	1	1	10	1	0	12
1840–		0	0	0	0	0	0	0	1	0	1
Total	220 +	30	16	7	0	53	117	94	31	9	251

TABLE IV (*Continued*)

CASES OF FORNICATION, BY COUNTY, PERIOD, AND OFFENDER'S SEX

BERKSHIRE

		C	W	M	T
1620-1729	110	0	0	0	0
1730-1769	40	3	1	1	5
1770-1809	40	8	11	6	25
1810-1839	30	1	7	2	10
1840–		0	1	0	1
Total	220 +	12	20	9	41

[a] C. F. Adams, "Some Phases of Sexual Morality and Church Discipline in Colonial New England," *Proceedings of the Massachusetts Historical Society,* 2nd Ser., VI, 494-95, mentions 66 cases between 1761 and 1775. These have been arbitrarily divided: two-thirds, or 44 cases, in the period 1730-69; the rest in the following forty-year period. Adams offers no chronological analysis for these cases.

TABLE V

FORNICATION CASES, BY PERIODS AND OFFENDER'S SEX

PERIOD	NUMBER OF YEARS	COUPLES	WOMEN	MEN	UNKNOWN	TOTAL
1620-1689	70	6	33	17	1	57
1690-1729	40	68	91	28	0	187
1730-1769	40	303	214	73	89	679
1770-1809	40	101	117	29	43	290
1810-1839	40	2	24	3	0	29
1840–		0	1	1	0	2
Total	220	480	480	151	133	1244

TABLE VI

FORNICATION CASES IN REPRESENTATIVE CHURCHES, BY DECADES (1640-1809) AND SEX OF OFFENDER, EXCLUSIVE OF ACQUITTALS

	BARNSTABLE CHURCHES				BOSTON FIRST CH.				BOSTON SECOND CH.			
	C	W	M	T	C	W	M	T	C	W	M	T
1640-1649	0	0	1	1	0	1	1	2	(Records begin			
1650-1659	0	1	0	1	0	0	2	2	1673)			
1660-1669	0	0	0	0	0	3	4	7				
1670-1679	0	0	1	1	0	1	0	1	0	0	0	0
1680-1689	0	1	0	1	0	0	1	1	0	0	0	0
1690-1699	0	0	0	0	0	0	0	0	1	0	0	1
1700-1709	0	0	0	0	0	0	0	0	0	0	1	1
1710-1719	0	0	0	0	0	1	0	1	0	2	0	2
1720-1729	0	0	0	0	0	2	1	3	0	2	1	3
1730-1739	1	1	0	2	0	3	1	4	0	1	0	1
1740-1749	0	5	0	5	0	2	0	2	0	0	1	1
1750-1759	0	0	2	2					0	0	0	0
1760-1769	0	0	0	0	(Records end				0	0	0	0
1770-1779	0	1	0	1	1745)				0	0	0	0
1780-1789	1	3	0	4					1	0	0	0
1790-1799	0	1	0	1					0	0	0	0
1800-1809	0	0	0	0					0	0	0	0
Date missing		1	1									
Total	2	14	5	21	0	13	10	23	2	5	3	10

	BRADFORD				BREWSTER				CANTON			
	C	W	M	T	C	W	M	T	C	W	M	T
1640-1649	(Records begin				(Records begin				(Records begin			
1650-1659	1682)				1726)				1721)			
1660-1669												
1670-1679												
1680-1689	1	0	0	1								
1690-1699	0	0	0	0								
1700-1709	1	0	0	1								
1710-1719	1	0	0	1								
1720-1729	1	3	0	4	1	2	3	6	0	2	1	3
1730-1739	1	1	0	2	10	2	0	12	7	6	3	16
1740-1749	5	0	1	6	3	0	3	6	6	6	1	13
1750-1759	6	1	1	8	3	1	0	4	6	3	1	10
1760-1769	5	0	0	5	7	2	0	9	9	2	0	11
1770-1779	4	1	0	5	0	1	0	1	8	7	2	17
1780-1789	0	0	0	0	0	1	0	1	6	1	0	7
1790-1799	1	0	1	2	(Records end				1	0	0	1
1800-1809	0	0	0	0	1785)				0	0	0	0
Total	26	6	3	35	24	9	6	39	43	27	8	78

TABLE VI (*Continued*)

FORNICATION CASES IN REPRESENTATIVE CHURCHES, BY DECADES (1640-1809) AND SEX OF OFFENDER, EXCLUSIVE OF ACQUITTALS

	DANVERS				DEERFIELD				DORCHESTER			
	C	W	M	T	C	W	M	T	C	W	M	T
1640-1649	(Records begin 1689)				(Records begin 1733)				(Records begin 1654)			
1650-1659									1	0	1	2
1660-1669									0	0	0	0
1670-1679									0	2	1	3
1680-1689	0	0	0	0					0	0	0	0
1690-1699	0	0	0	0					4	1	1	6
1700-1709	1	0	0	1					2	2	1	5
1710-1719	2	0	0	2					4	0	2	6
1720-1729	2	6	1	9					2	4	1	7
1730-1739	3	2	0	5	4	5	3	12				
1740-1749	3	1	3	7	11	4	5	20	(Records end 1729)			
1750-1759	5	2	0	7	7	8	1	16				
1760-1769	4	1	0	5	7	3	0	10				
1770-1779	3	0	0	3	12	1	1	14				
1780-1789	2	3	0	5	1	7	0	8				
1790-1799	1	7	0	8	2	0	0	2				
1800-1809	0	1	1	2	2	0	0	2				
Total	26	23	5	54	46	28	10	84	13	9	7	29

	FRAMINGHAM				PLYMOUTH FIRST CH.					QUINCY			
	C	W	M	T	C	W	M	?	T	C	W	M	T
1660-1669	(Records begin 1717)				(Complete records begin only 1683)					(Records begin 1673)			
1670-1679										0	0	0	0
1680-1689					1	2	1	0	4	0	1	0	1
1690-1699					1	0	1	0	2	0	0	0	0
1700-1709					1	0	0	0	1	0	0	0	0
1710-1719					0	1	0	0	1	0	0	0	0
1720-1729	12	3	0	15	0	0	0	0	0	2	1	0	3
1730-1739	0	0	0	0	0	1	1	8	10	7	6	2	15
1740-1749	6	4	1	11	0	0	2	0	2	1	0	0	1
1750-1759	12	5	0	17	0	0	0	0	0				
1760-1769	17	4	0	21	2	2	1	0	5	(Records end 1741)			
1770-1779	8	2	0	10	1	1	0	0	2				
1780-1789	0	0	0	0	0	7	1	0	8				
1790-1799	1	0	1	2	(No cases after 1788)								
1800-1809	1	0	0	1									
Total	57	18	2	77	6	14	7	8	35	10	8	2	20

TABLE VI (*Continued*)

FORNICATION CASES IN REPRESENTATIVE CHURCHES, BY DECADES (1640-1809) AND SEX OF OFFENDER, EXCLUSIVE OF ACQUITTALS

	READING				SALEM FIRST CH.					SUTTON				
	C	W	M	T	C	W	M	?	T	C	W	M	?	T
1660-1669	(No cases before				0	1	0	0	1	(Records begin				
1670-1679	1680)				1	3	2	1	7	1728)				
1680-1689	0	1	0	1	0	1	0	0	1					
1690-1699	0	2	2	4	0	3	1	0	4					
1700-1709	0	0	1	1	0	4	0	0	4					
1710-1719	2	2	0	4	5	1	1	0	7					
1720-1729	1	1	1	3	0	4	0	0	4	0	0	0	0	0
1730-1739	7	1	1	9	2	5	1	0	8	1	0	3	0	4
1740-1749	2	1	1	4	2	8	1	0	11	9	1	3	0	13
1750-1759	5	0	2	7						4	0	2	0	6
1760-1769	1	0	0	1	(No more cases)					1	1	0	0	2
1770-1779	2	0	0	2						0	3	2	0	5
1780-1789	2	0	0	2						0	0	0	1	1
1790-1799	0	0	0	0						0	1	0	0	1
1800-1809	0	1	0	1						0	1	0	0	1
Total	22	9	8	39	10	30	6	1	47	15	7	10	1	33

	WESTFIELD				
	C	W	M	?	T
	(Records begin 1707)				
1700-1709	0	1	0	0	1
1710-1719	0	1	0	0	1
1720-1729	3	4	0	1	8
1730-1739	8	2	5	0	15
1740-1749	9	5	2	0	16
1750-1759	11	10	4	0	25
1760-1769	13	6	0	0	19
1770-1779	14	7	2	2	25
1780-1789	7	8	0	0	15
1790-1799	2	2	0	0	4
1800-1809	0	1	0	0	1
Total	67	47	13	3	130

TABLE VII

CASES OF ALCOHOLISM (INTOXICATION OR INTEMPERANCE), BY COUNTY, PERIOD, AND OFFENDER'S SEX

PERIOD	NUMBER OF YEARS	PLYMOUTH			BARNSTABLE			NORFOLK		
		W	M	T	W	M	T	W	M	T
1620-1689	70	0	1	1	0	0	0	0	0	0
1690-1729	40	2	12	14	2	0	2	2	4	6
1730-1769	40	3	2	5	4	0	4	0	9	9
1770-1809	40	4	15	19	0	5	5	0	0	0
1810-1839	30	0	8	8	0	9	9	0	0	0
Total	220	9	38	47	6	14	20	2	13	15

PERIOD	NUMBER OF YEARS	SUFFOLK			ESSEX			MIDDLESEX		
		W	M	T	W	M	T	W	M	T
1620-1689	70	7	45	52	1	6	7	1	0	1
1690-1729	40	8	26	34	6	13	19	0	0	0
1730-1769	40	3	7	10	2	13	15	3	15	18
1770-1809	40	0	0	0	2	5	7	0	2	2
1810-1839	30	0	0	0	12	6	18	2	4	6
Total	220	18	78	96	23	43	66	6	21	27

PERIOD	NUMBER OF YEARS	WORCESTER			HAMPSHIRE			BERKSHIRE		
		W	M	T	W	M	T	W	M	T
1620-1689	70	0	0	0	0	0	0	0	0	0
1690-1729	40	0	1	1	1	6	7	0	0	0
1730-1769	40	0	4	4	3	11	14	0	5	5
1770-1809	40	0	6	6	2	18	20	9	26	35
1810-1839	30	0	2	2	3	19	22	5	33	38
Later									2[a]	2[a]
Total	220	0	13	13	9	54	63	14	64	78

[a] Not included in total.

TABLE VIII

CASES OF ALCOHOLISM (INTOXICATION OR INTEMPERANCE), BY PERIOD AND OFFENDER'S SEX

PERIOD	NUMBER OF YEARS	WOMEN	MEN	TOTAL
1620-1689	70	9	52	61
1690-1729	40	21	62	83
1730-1769	40	18	66	84
1770-1809	40	17	77	94
1810-1839	30	22	82 [a]	104 [a]
Total	220	87	339 [a]	426 [a]

[a] Includes one man in Bristol County not included in Table VII.

TABLE IX

NUMBER OF PERSONS DISCIPLINED BY SEVEN CHURCHES, 1690-1809, BY FORTY-YEAR PERIODS

CHURCH	1690-1729			1730-1769			1770-1809		
	F	O	T	F	O	T	F	O	T
Plymouth	6	22	28	19	12	31	11	12	23
Barnstable [a]	0	1	1	10	20	30	7	7	14
Boston Second	8	33	41	2	7	9	2	0	2
Bradford	9	9	18	38	4	42	12	0	12
Danvers	17	10	27	39	0	39	24	2	26
Reading	15	5	20	36	19	55	9	7	16
Westfield	13	11	24	116	46	162	68	4	72

[a] East and West.

TABLE X

CONFESSIONS MADE OR CENSURES IMPOSED IN EIGHT CHURCHES INFLUENCED BY THE GREAT AWAKENING, 1730-1749

	PLYMOUTH		ROXBURY [a]		MARBLEHEAD [b]		READING		SUTTON		NORTHAMPTON		DEERFIELD		WESTFIELD	
	F	O	F	O	F	O	F	O	F	O	F	O	F	O	F	O
1720's	0	2	0	0	3	0	4	0	0	1	0	0	0	5	11	6
1730	0	0	0	0	2	0	4	0	0	1	0	0	0	0	2	0
1731	5	0	0	0	0	1	0	0	0	1	0	0	0	0	1	1
1732	5	0	0	0	0	0	4	0	1	0	0	0	2	0	5	1
1733	0	4	4	0	0	0	0	0	0	0	0	0	1	0	0	1
1734	0	0	0	2	0	0	0	1	0	0	0	0	2	0	1	1
1735	0	1	0	0	0	0	0	0	2	0	0	0	3	3	5	3
1736	0	0	0	0	0	0	5	1	2	2	0	0	0	0	2	0
1737	0	0	0	0	0	0	3	2	0	3	0	0	4	0	2	2
1738	0	0	0	0	0	0	0	0	0	0	0	0	3	2	2	1
1739	0	0	0	0	0	0	0	1	0	0	0	0	1	0	3	0
1740	0	0	0	0	1	0	0	0	4	1	0	0	0	0	2	1
1741	0	0	5	0	6	0	0	2	2	2	0	1	4	2	6	2
1742	0	0	2	0	4	0	2	1	2	0	0	0	4	0	3	2
1743	0	3	0	0	2	0	0	0	6	0	1	0	3	0	3	1
1744	0	0	2	0	0	0	4	1	2	0	0	0	4	0	0	0
1745	0	1	0	0	0	0	0	0	2	0	0	0	0	1	3	1
1746	0	0	0	0	0	0	0	0	4	0	0	0	1	0	0	1
1747	0	0	2	0	0	0	0	1	0	2	0	0	5	1	3	0
1748	1	0	2	0	0	0	0	2	0	0	0	0	7	0	3	0
1749	0	0	4	0	0	0	0	0	0	0	0	0	3	0	2	1
1750's	1	0	2	0	6	0	12	1	10	3	1	1	23	4	36	2

[a] Roxbury and West Roxbury.

[b] First and Second Churches.

TABLE XI

THE DECLINE OF CHURCH DISCIPLINE: CENSURES IN SEVENTEEN CHURCHES, 1800-1839, BY DECADES[a]

	1800-1809	1810-1819	1820-1829	1830-1839
Amherst	0	3	6	3
Cambridge	2	1[b]	0	....[c]
Chelsea	0	0	0	0
Danvers	4	2	0	8
Falmouth	1	8	21	0[d]
Framingham	2	2	2	....[c]
Haverhill First	....[e]	1	3	1
Lenox	5[f]	1	5	....[g]
Marblehead First	0	0	10	0
Middleborough North	1	0	0	0
Northampton	12	11	0	0[d]
Pittsfield	2	2	15[h]	5[j]
Plymouth	0	3	0	1[k]
Reading	2	2	6	1
Sockbridge	2	1	3	1[l]
Westfield	1	1	3	0[l]
Worthington	5	6[f]	8	9

[a] Exclusive of cases involving conversions to other religious bodies or those arising from schisms.

[b] The George Bethune English heresy case.

[c] Records consulted end 1830.

[d] Records consulted end 1833.

[e] Records for this decade incomplete.

[f] Exclusive of private cases which were settled.

[g] An unspecified number of members, thirteen of whom are listed by name, were accused of absence.

[h] Including seven cases in which the verdict is not recorded.

[j] Including three cases in which the verdict is not recorded.

[k] Confession in a case counted in a previous decade.

[l] Records consulted end 1836.

Notes

Introduction

1. C. F. Adams, "Some Phases of Sexual Morality and Church Discipline in Colonial New England," *Proceedings of the Massachusetts Historical Society,* 2nd Ser., VI (1891), 477-516.
2. O. E. Winslow, *Meetinghouse Hill* (New York, 1952), chap. XI.
3. E.g., Granville East Ch. Recs., I, 68.
4. E.g., Northampton Recs., Vol. I *passim.*
5. E.g., Bradford Recs., I, 57-58, and parts of pp. 15-16.
6. E.g., Boston Hollis St. Ch. Recs., I, 237.
7. E.g., Bradford Recs., I, 1-46 (damaged by heat).
8. E.g., *ibid.,* I, 3-4; Northampton Recs. *passim.*
9. See Billerica Recs., Vol. I (date missing, before 1751).
10. Social Science Research Council, Committee on Historiography, *Theory and Practice in Historical Study* (New York, no date), p. 135.
11. For comparative purposes, the following records are the most useful: Barnstable (East and West), Boston Second Ch., Bradford, Danvers, Plymouth, Reading, and Westfield. Eight churches which were affected by the Great Awakening and which have complete records for the period are: Deerfield, Marblehead, Northampton, Plymouth, Roxbury, Sutton, and Westfield. For the later period, 1800-1839, the most useful records are: Amherst, Cambridge, Chelsea, Danvers, Falmouth, Framingham, Haverhill First Ch., Lenox, Marblehead First Ch., Middleborough North Ch., Northampton, Pittsfield, Plymouth, Reading, Stockbridge, Westfield, and Worthington.
12. Discussions of terminology may be found in P. Miller, *Orthodoxy in Massachusetts* (Cambridge, 1933), pp. 21-23; R. B.

Perry, *Puritanism and Democracy* (New York, 1944), pp. 68-69, 73, 259; and, perhaps the best, in M. M. Knappen, *Tudor Puritanism* (Chicago, 1939), pp. 487-93. Knappen suggests that the term was first used by the Separatists. Note the useful chart on p. 493, and the footnote in five-point type. See J. T. McNeill, *Modern Christian Movements* (Philadelphia, 1954), p. 29; E. L. Goodwin, *The Colonial Church in Virginia* (Milwaukee and London, 1927), p. 7.

13. See E. B. Crane, *History of Worcester County* (New York and Chicago, 1924), I, 456-57, for a discussion of these terms. For the importance of the distinction between church and parish, see Burr v. Parish of Sandwich, 9 Mass. 277 (1815), and Baker v. Fales, 16 Mass. 492 (1820), in which the difference between the two was decisive.

14. Deut. 5:6-21; Exod. 20:2-17. The former is probably the earlier form; the latter may be a post-exilic priestly insertion in the Sinai narrative (R. H. Pfeiffer, *Introduction to the Old Testament* [New York, 1948], pp. 228-29). Calvin, in his *Institutes of the Christian Religion,* II, viii, followed the traditional Hebrew arrangement, which was followed by the LXX, Josephus, and Philo. The Roman and Lutheran churches follow Augustine's rearrangement, which combined the first two commandments and divided the last. See "Decalogue," *The New Schaff-Herzog Encyclopaedia of Religious Knowledge,* and "Decalogue," *Encyclopaedia of Religion and Knowledge.*

15. R. Mather, *Church-Government and Church-Covenant Discussed* (London, 1643), p. 10.

16. The Puritans' congregationalism may seem to be in conflict with their contention that they had not separated from the Church of England. In an ingenious argument, Ames and Bradshaw sought to reconcile the apparent contradiction. This argument is based on the assertion that the Church of England consists of a number of essentially true churches, which had been corrupted by the addition of nonessential elements, including episcopacy. Bishops, for instance, were the king's ecclesiastical agents, and there was no reason why he should not have such agents; the fact that the bishops were priests was mere coincidence. See W. Bradshaw, *Unreasonablenes*

[*sic*] *of the Separation* (n.p., 1640). P. Miller has discussed the subject in *Orthodoxy in Massachusetts* (Cambridge, 1933), chap. IV.

17. L. J. Trinterud, *The Forming of an American Tradition* (Philadelphia, 1949), p. 19. Cf. J. Cotton, *The Keyes of the Kingdom of Heaven* (Boston, 1852; first pub. 1644), p. 17, which comes close to Presbyterianism.
18. See A. C. McGiffert, "The Cambridge Platform of Church Discipline," in H. W. Foote, ed., *The Cambridge Platform of 1648* (Boston, 1949), pp. 107-8.
19. Cf. P. Oliver, *Puritan Commonwealth* (Boston, 1856), p. 156.
20. W. Ames, *The Marrow of Sacred Divinity* (London, 1642), pp. 157, 202; W. Bradshaw, *English Puritanism* (n.p., 1605), pp. 5-6.
21. J. Cotton, *The Keyes of the Kingdom of Heaven,* pp. 44-48.
22. *A Platform of Church Discipline* (Cambridge, 1649), hereafter cited as *Cambridge Platform,* chap. 25.
23. L. J. Trinterud, *The Forming of an American Tradition,* p. 19; F. L. Fagley, "The Narrative of the Cambridge Synod," in H. W. Foote, *The Cambridge Platform of 1648,* p. 17.
24. H. R. Niebuhr, *The Kingdom of God in America* (Chicago and New York, 1927), p. 70; R. Bronkema, *The Essence of Puritanism* (Gocs, Holland, [1930?]), p. 158.
25. E. B. Greene, *Religion and the State* (New York, 1941), pp. 39-41; H. L. Osgood, "The Political Ideas of the Puritans," *Political Science Quarterly,* VI (1891), 23; A. P. Stokes, Church *and State in the United States* (New York, 1950), I, 155-56. See G. C. Atkins, "The Church and the Commonwealth," *Congregational Quarterly,* XXIX (1951), 30; S. E. Morison, *Builders of the Bay Colony* (Boston and New York, 1930), pp. 86, 106; S. M. Reed, *Church and State in Massachusetts, 1691-1740* (Urbana, 1914), p. 20.
26. W. A. Visser't Hooft, *The Background of the Social Gospel in America* (Haarlem, 1928), p. 74. See W. B. Weeden, *Economic and Social History of New England* (Boston and New York, 1890), I, 68-69; T. J. Wertenbaker, *The Puritan Oligarchy* (New York and London, 1947), p. 62; A. P. Stokes, *Church and State,* I, 158; C. E. Merriam, *A History of American Political Theories* (New York, 1903), p. 5.

27. A. P. Stokes, *Church and State,* I, 156; J. A. Doyle, *English Colonies in America* (New York, 1889), II, 109.
28. G. H. Haynes, *Representation and Suffrage in Massachusetts, 1620-1691* (Baltimore, 1894), p. 25.
29. For disabilities suffered by non-members, and for relief from such discrimination, see *ibid.,* pp. 12, 25-29, 48, 57, 64, 72-75; S. M. Reed, *Church and State,* pp. 139-40; and J. C. Meyer, *Church and State in Massachusetts from 1740 to 1833* (Cleveland, 1930), pp. 7, 15-16, 157-58, 197-98. Also see A. P. Stokes, *Church and State,* I, 156, 420-21. The question of freemanship in relation to the general population is discussed in J. G. Palfrey, *History of New England* (Boston, 1859-64), III, 41, n.3; E. B. Greene and V. Harrington, *American Population before the Census of 1790* (New York, 1932), pp. 11-13; and the critical study by B. K. Brown, "Freemanship in Puritan Massachusetts," *American Historical Review,* LIX (1954), 865-83.
30. H. L. Osgood, *American Colonies in the Eighteenth Century* (New York, 1924), III, 127.
31. W. W. Sweet, *Religion in Colonial America* (New York, 1947), pp. 105-8; W. Walker, *History of the Congregational Churches in the United States* (New York, 1894), pp. 170-78.
32. W. Walker, *History of the Congregational Churches,* pp. 170-78.
33. J. Haroutunian, *Piety versus Moralism* (New York, 1932), p. 4; P. Miller, *Jonathan Edwards* ([New York], 1949), pp. 134, 223.
34. G. H. Haynes, *Representation and Suffrage,* pp. 48, 57, 75; J. C. Meyer, *Church and State,* pp. 15-16; S. M. Reed, *Church and State,* p. 139; A. P. Stokes, *Church and State,* I, 421. Also see note 31.
35. A. P. Stokes, *Church and State,* I, 424-27.
36. J. Cotton, letter to Lord Saye and Sele, quoted in T. Hutchinson, *History of the Colony and Province of Massachusetts Bay,* ed. by L. S. Mayo (Cambridge, 1936), I, 414.
37. *Cambridge Platform,* chap. 17, secs. 2, 5. See B. Adams, *The Emancipation of Massachusetts* (2nd ed., Boston and New York, 1893), I, 26, for a statement identifying the town meeting with the church meeting. Such a statement is not in accordance with the facts.

38. *Cambridge Platform,* chap. 17, secs. 3-7.
39. This is the word most often found in the records; terms like *sinful* occur less frequently.
40. *Cambridge Platform,* chap. 14, sec. 1; chap. 17, sec. 5.
41. See Liberties 58-60, in *The Colonial Laws of Massachusetts* (Boston, 1889).
42. Liberty 42, *ibid.*
43. Liberties 59, 60, *ibid.*
44. *Ibid.*, pp. 26-27.
45. H. B. Adams, *The Saxon Tithing-Man in America* (Baltimore, 1883), *passim.* Cf. A. W. Calhoun, *A Social History of the American Family* (Cleveland, 1917-19), I, 74. See A. M. Earle, *The Sabbath in Puritan New England* (8th ed., New York, 1896), p. 76.

Chapter I: The Covenant Owned

1. E.g., A. C. McGiffert, *Protestant Thought before Kant* (New York, 1917), p. 176, to cite but one example. Cf. R. Bronkema, *The Essence of Puritanism* (Goes, Holland, [1930]), pp. 96-98, for an example of the distinction between Calvinism and Puritanism. This subject will be discussed at greater length below.
2. See D. B. Thompson, "An Historical Reconstruction of Melanchthonianism and the German Reformed Church, Based Upon Confessional and Historical Evidence" (unpublished Ph.D. dissertation, Columbia University, 1953). Dr. Thompson observes that Melanchthon was "no more Lutheran than Crypto Calvinist. He was a Melanchthonian." *Ibid.*, p. 2.
3. No one person can be named as having made *the* definitive contribution to Anglican theology. The editors of the Prayer Books, Richard Hooker, and at a later date the Tractarians came close to it, but no Anglican would ever ascribe to them the position which Calvinists ascribe to Calvin, or Lutherans to Luther.
4. J. Calvin, *Institutes of the Christian Religion,* III, xxi, xiii-xiv; xxv, 12; IV, i, 2, 7-8, 16, 20; G. Harkness, *John Calvin,*

the Man and His Ethics (New York, 1931), p. 73; G. P. Fisher, *History of Christian Doctrine* (Edinburgh, 1908), pp. 299-303, 308-9; L. J. Trinterud, *The Forming of an American Tradition* (Philadelphia, 1949), p. 173.

5. Cf. L. J. Trinterud, "The Origins of Puritanism," *Church History,* XX (1951), 37-57. Professor Trinterud presents an unusually persuasive argument against the traditional explanation of the origin of Puritanism. His argument is based on the evidence of Continental influences which antedated Calvin. According to Trinterud, the main currents of English Puritanism came not from Geneva, but from the Rhineland; not from Calvin, but from theologians like Zwingli, Bullinger, Oecolampadius, Capito, Bucer, and Peter Martyr Vermigli. Tyndale and Frith adhered to the Augustinian, not the Calvinist, doctrine of predestination; Hooper's theology was based on that of Zurich; the Great Bible of 1539 disregarded Calvinist influences altogether. During the reign of Edward VI, Peter Martyr and Bucer visited England; Calvin never crossed the Channel. Finally, when Protestantism was restored after the Marian reaction, the Geneva party lost its bid for power. During the Elizabethan period the English Puritans paid little attention to Calvin's writings and preferred the Covenant Theology, and during the religious chaos marking the period of the civil wars and Interregnum, the Covenant Theology was of invaluable aid to the Independents. In sum, Professor Trinterud's thesis is that the Covenant Theology of the English Puritans is not a modification of Calvinism, but a distinct and separate movement. While Trinterud considers Puritanism an indigenous English movement, Professor Marshall M. Knappen, in *Tudor Puritanism* (Chicago, 1939), pp. 4-5, treats it as an Anglo-Saxon variety of a Continental theological movement. Bronkema, in *The Essence of Puritanism,* pp. 2, 3, concludes that the specifically Puritan characteristics lie in the English character itself, but that Puritanism was influenced by Calvinism via John à Lasco. (Also see *ibid.,* pp. 100-124.) Professor Jerald Brauer, in a recent article ("Reflections on the Nature of English Puritanism," *Church History,* XXIII [1954], 99-108), concurs in Trinterud's finding that the Puritans' adoption of the Covenant Theology dis-

tinguishes them from both Anglicanism and Calvinism, and agrees with Knappen and Woodhouse that English Puritanism is a distinct historical entity. In *The History and Character of Calvinism* (New York, 1954), Professor John T. McNeill holds that Bucer and Bullinger were Calvin's heralds during the reign of Edward VI, in which "most of what was embraced by the word 'Calvinism' had been introduced to the English mind through the influence of Bucer and Bullinger." (Quoted from p. 309, by permission of the Oxford University Press.) Professor McNeill maintains, however, that English Puritanism was indebted to influences other than Calvinism as well: Lutheranism, Bucer, à Lasco, and Bullinger all had a share in shaping Puritanism (J. T. McNeill, *Modern Christian Movements* [Philadelphia, 1954], pp. 24-28). What *may* perhaps be a clue is found in William Ames, *Marrow of Sacred Divinity* (London, 1642), p. 166. Discussing the difference between "ordinary" and "extra ordinary" ministers (the latter being prophets), Ames states that Wyclif, Luther, and Zwingli are not to be considered "extraordinary" ministers. No mention at all is made of Calvin in this context.

6. Gen. 2:16-17 (Adam), 7:1-4 and 6:18-21 (Noah), 15:11-16 and 17:4-14 (Abraham). Since the covenants with Adam and Noah presented difficult theological problems, the Covenant Theologians usually cited the covenant with Abraham. L. J. Trinterud, "The Origins of Puritanism," *Church History,* XX, 42.
7. G. P. Fisher, *History of Christian Doctrine,* pp. 347-50, and L. J. Trinterud, *The Forming of an American Tradition,* pp. 172-73, cite Heb. 8:10 and 9:15-16 as the basis of this. Cf. S. Burrell, "Kirk, Crown, and Covenant" (unpublished Ph.D. dissertation, Columbia University, 1953), pp. 206-7, who ascribes this to Pauline sources.
8. P. Miller, *The New England Mind: The Seventeenth Century* (New York, 1939), p. 407. Professor Miller's statement that the persons of the Trinity formed a "corporation" is a less satisfactory metaphor and can scarcely be reconciled with Christian doctrine.
9. *Cambridge Platform,* chap. IV.
10. See C. Mather, *Ratio Disciplinae Fratrum Nov-Anglicorum*

(Boston, 1726), p. 10. Also see *Diary of Cotton Mather* (Boston, 1911-12), I, 86, for a private covenant between Mather and God. This, however, is a unilateral pledge rather than a mutual agreement.

11. S. Burrell, "Kirk, Crown, and Covenant," p. 207; P. Y. De Jong, *The Covenant Idea in New England* (Grand Rapids, 1945), pp. 17-18.
12. G. Schrenk, *Gottesreich und Bund im älteren Protestantismus* (Guetersloh, Germany, 1923), pp. 37-43.
13. S. Burrell, "Kirk, Crown, and Covenant," pp. 207-8.
14. C. Burrage, *The Church Covenant Idea* (Philadelphia, 1904), pp. 13-15.
15. G. Schrenk, *Gottesreich und Bund,* Part II, chap. II, *passim;* E. T. Jones, "The Church Covenant in Classical Congregationalism," *The Presbyter,* VII, No. 4 (1949), 10.
16. Browne's genetic role in the history of Congregationalism is no longer accepted. See V. D. Morey, "History Corrects Itself; Robert Browne and Congregational Beginnings," *Bulletin of the American Congregational Association,* V (1954), 9-19.
17. S. Burrell, "Kirk, Crown, and Covenant," pp. 211-18; J. T. McNeill, *The History and Character of Calvinism,* p. 307.
18. P. Miller, "The Marrow of Puritan Divinity," *Publications of the Colonial Society of Massachusetts,* XXXII (1937), 247-300; S. Burrell, "Kirk, Crown, and Covenant," p. 208; M. M. Knappen, *Tudor Puritanism,* p. 395; G. P. Fisher, *History of Christian Doctrine,* pp. 348-49; R. T. Jones, "The Church Covenant," *The Presbyter,* VII, no. 4 (1949), 10; J. T. McNeill, *Modern Christian Movements,* pp. 31-32.
19. R. Baxter, *A Christian Directory* (London, 1673), p. 688.
20. *Ibid.*
21. *Ibid.,* p. 689. It would be interesting to know whether the clause was intended to be restrictive or not; we cannot be sure in view of the punctuation of the time. Certainly the Puritans were not Manichaeans.
22. *Ibid.* Note the emphasis on intention. The covenant has an almost sacramental character.
23. *Ibid.*
24. P. Miller, *The New England Mind: The Seventeenth Century,* p. 389-400; R. P. Stearns, "Assessing the New England Mind,"

Church History, X (1941), 250-51. See P. Miller, "The Marrow of Puritan Divinity," *Publications of the Colonial Society of Massachusetts,* XXXII (1937), 262-63.

25. For an example of extreme disagreement, see P. Y. De Jong, *The Covenant Idea,* p. 195, and G. D. Henderson's review of L. J. Trinterud's *The Forming of an American Tradition,* in *Journal of Ecclesiastical History,* II (1951), 240-42. De Jong denies that the New England Congregationalists can be considered Calvinists. Professor Henderson, on the other hand, rejects Professor Trinterud's contention that the Federal Theology is incompatible with Calvin's doctrine of the Church. For Henderson, the Covenant Theology and Presbyterianism are two aspects of "the Geneva Tradition with the Calvinistic doctrine." Professor Burrell, in "Kirk, Crown, and Covenant," pp. 290-94, comes much closer to Henderson's position than to De Jong's, and emphasizes that the Scottish theologians of the Stuart period were Calvinists. R. B. Perry, in *Puritanism and Democracy* (New York, 1944), p. 93, considers the Covenant Theology to be "a form of Calvinism," and denies that the New England divines repudiated Calvinism, while Professor Sidney Mead, in *Nathaniel William Taylor* (Chicago, 1942), p. ix, states that the Federal Theology "greatly modified" Calvinism. Professor McNeill holds that Cocceius "changed the emphasis in Calvinism, bringing into the foreground the divine undertaking in the covenant of grace prefigured in the Old Testament and fully revealed in the New, and relegating to the background the concept of unilateral decrees. Like Arminianism and Amyraldism, it tended to modify the harshness of Calvinism." *The History and Character of Calvinism,* p. 266, quoted by permission of the Oxford University Press. Also see *ibid.,* p. 335, and W. A. Visser't Hooft, *The Background of the Social Gospel in America* (Haarlem, 1928), p. 69.
26. P. Miller, *Jonathan Edwards* ([New York], 1949), pp. 75-76.
27. F. H. Foster, *A Genetic History of the New England Theology* (Chicago, 1907), pp. 37-39, 51; L. J. Trinterud, *The Forming of an American Tradition,* pp. 181-82.
28. J. Haroutunian, *Piety versus Moralism* (New York, 1932), p. 103; P. Miller, *Jonathan Edwards,* p. 33.
29. F. H. Foster, *A Genetic History,* pp. 60-61; F. A. Christie, "The

Beginnings of Arminianism in New England," *Papers of the American Society of Church History,* 2nd Ser., III (1912), 169. For the narrative of Edwards's controversy with his church, see J. R. Trumbull, *History of Northampton* (Northampton, 1902), II, 195-228. The conflict resulted in Edwards's dismissal.

30. J. Edwards, "A Dissertation concerning the End for Which God Created the World," *The Works of President Edwards* (New York, 1829), III, 5-23, 82-83; "Careful and Strict Enquiry into the Modern Prevailing Notion of That Freedom of the Will," *ibid.,* II, 11-300 *passim,* esp. pp. 280-89; "The Great Christian Doctrine of Original Sin Defended," *ibid.,* II, 309-583 *passim.* F. H. Foster, *A Genetic History,* chap. III; P. Miller, *Jonathan Edwards,* pp. 221-22; C. H. Faust and T. H. Johnson, *Jonathan Edwards, Representative Selections* (New York, 1935), pp. xxiv-xxx, xxxv.
31. F. H. Foster, *A Genetic History,* pp. 78-80.
32. J. Haroutunian, *Piety versus Moralism,* pp. xx-xxii, 8-10; S. Mead, *Nathaniel William Taylor,* pp. vii-ix, 97-98; Cf. W. B. Selbie, *Congregationalism* (London, 1927), p. 157.
33. See S. E. Mead, *Nathaniel William Taylor,* pp. 97-101.
34. F. H. Foster, *A Genetic History,* pp. 113-14; J. Haroutunian, *Piety versus Moralism,* pp. 160-66. M. M. Knappen, in *Tudor Puritanism,* p. 392, quotes the saying, "We are all Calvinists when we pray, but all Arminians when we preach."
35. F. H. Foster, *A Genetic History,* chap. V *passim.*
36. *Ibid.,* pp. 178-80; J. Haroutunian, *Piety versus Moralism,* pp. 56-71.
37. J. Haroutunian, *Piety versus Moralism,* p. 127; F. H. Foster, *A Genetic History,* p. 218.
38. J. Haroutunian, *Piety versus Moralism,* p. 71; cf. pp. 281-82.
39. *Ibid.,* pp. 95, 180.
40. S. E. Mead, *Nathaniel William Taylor,* pp. 99-101, 173-76; S. P. Parker, "History of the Episcopal Church in Berkshire," *Collections of the Berkshire Historical and Scientific Society,* II, 84. Cf. W. A. Visser't Hooft, *The Background of the Social Gospel in America,* p. 97. The divergence in thought is well illustrated by resolutions adopted within ten years of each other by two churches. In 1780 the First Church of Salem voted to invite "all members of other churches" to

partake of the Lord's Supper (Salem Recs., IV, 38). Ten years later the Sutton church condemned the Halfway Covenant as unscriptural and decided against the admission of persons to halfway membership (Sutton Recs., I, 51). At the time of the Unitarian "departure" the Salem church became Unitarian, while that in Sutton remained in the Christian tradition.

41. W. E. Barton, *Congregational Creeds and Covenants* (Chicago, 1917), pp. 9, 14, 210.
42. Palmer Recs., I, 7.
43. Quoted in O. Winslow, *Meetinghouse Hill* (New York, 1952), p. 22.
44. See A. Guiterman, "Notations on a Lease," *The New Yorker,* March 6, 1943, p. 62. But whatever a landlord may think of himself, he is not God.
45. But cf. the short covenant adopted by a Trinitarian church in 1759, in Stockbridge Recs., I, 3. Examples of covenants may be found in W. E. Barton, *Congregational Creeds and Covenants*, Part I, chap. X *passim.*
46. Salem Recs., I, 1-4.
47. *Ibid.,* IV, 63-64.
48. W. E. Barton, *Congregational Creeds and Covenants,* p. 10.
49. W. Walker, *The Creeds and Platforms of Congregationalism* (New York, 1893), p. 244; H. L. Osgood, *American Colonies in the Eighteenth Century* (New York, 1924), I, 294.
50. M. M. Knappen, *Tudor Puritanism,* p. 120.
51. Quoted in W. Walker, *Creeds and Platforms,* p. 40.
52. *Cambridge Platform,* chap. III, secs. 1, 3.
53. *Ibid.,* chap. III, sec. 2.
54. C. Mather, *Ratio Disciplinae,* pp. 90-91.
55. *Ibid.,* p. 81; T. Hooker, *A Survey of the Summe of Church Discipline* (London, 1658), p. 60.
56. See H. R. Niebuhr, *The Kingdom of God in America* (Chicago and New York, 1937), p. 71.
57. Cambridge Recs., I, 121-22.
58. Medford Recs., I, 4.
59. Hull Recs., I, 4 (1734). Other cases in which the practice was made optional are found in Brewster Recs., I, 59 (1738); Lynnfield Recs., I, 161 (1784); Quincy Recs., I, 47 (1742); see also Dedham Recs., VIII, 94-95 (1793).

60. Natick Recs., I, 6.
61. Salem North Ch. Recs., II, 130 (1773). Public confessions of faith, but not necessarily of practice of public propounding, were abolished or made optional in at least three other churches: Barnstable East Ch. Recs., I, 97 (1780); Salem Recs., IV, 38 (1781); Boston Brattle St. Ch. Recs., I, 43 (1792).
62. J. Edwards, "An Humble Inquiry," *Works,* IV, 314-20, and Part II *passim.* In 1689 the Danvers church voted to accept written confessions from applicants who suffered from a major impediment in speech. Danvers Recs., I, 3.
63. Danvers Recs., I, 49. In Palmer, the majority of church members opposed a proposal to repeal the requirement, but no formal vote was taken. Palmer Recs., Vol. I (1812).
64. Walpole Recs., I, 12.
65. Becket Recs., II, 25-26 (1808); Charlemont Recs., I, 56 (1817).
66. Boston Brattle St. Ch. Recs., I, 43 (1792); Chelsea Recs., III, 15 (1798); Concord Recs., I, 209 (1795); Pittsfield Recs., I, 318 (1797); Sheffield Recs., II, 229 (1798); Worthington Recs., I, 32 (1799); and, belatedly, Westminster Recs., I, 2 (1815).
67. All baptized persons: Plymouth Recs., I, 230-31 (1726); Westfield Recs., I, 178 (1728); Lanesborough Recs., I, 56 (1772); Egremont Recs., I, 13 (1775); Framingham Recs., I, 181 (1780); Pittsfield Recs., I, 306 (1794). Only covenanted persons (presumably including members by virtue of the Halfway Covenant): Millbury Recs., II, 27 (1777). Ambiguous resolutions: Bradford Recs., I, 20-23 (1720-30?); Haverhill First Ch. Recs., I, 54 (1721). See Westfield Recs., I, 182 (1737), declaring that baptized persons who had not owned the covenant were amenable to the church. If the vote of 1737 was intended to replace the one of 1728, the church obviously did not construe "baptised members" to include those who had not subsequently owned the covenant. On the other hand, the later vote may have been declaratory, defining the intention of the earlier resolution.
68. Salem First Ch. Recs., I, 235-36 (1661).
69. Sutton Recs., I, 28 (1756).
70. Stockbridge Recs., I, 70, 72 (1764, 1768).
71. Barnstable West Ch. Recs., Vol. I (1683); Hatfield Recs., I, 17

(1778); Otis Recs., I, 51 (1817); Plymouth Recs., I, 252 (1783). See Millbury Recs., II, 27 (1777).

72. Northampton Recs., I, 21 (1714).
73. *Cambridge Platform,* chap. 13, sec. 4. See C. Mather, *Ratio Disciplinae,* pp. 138-40.
74. Roxbury Recs., I, 77 (1632 or soon thereafter).
75. Boston Third Ch. Recs., I, 305-6 (1699).
76. Plymouth Recs., I, 146 (1670); Barnstable West Ch. Recs., I, 57 (1684).
77. Lanesborough Recs., I, 78-79 (1805); Plymouth Recs., II, 567-68 (1818). See West Springfield Recs., II, 120-21 (1847).
78. Deerfield Recs., I, 33-34 (1818).
79. Palmer Recs., II, 154 (1838).
80. Dorchester Recs., I, 85 (1681). The pastor was elected by the church, subject to the concurrence of the parish. The member involved was entitled to vote in the parish meeting, but not in the church meeting.
81. Sutton Recs., I, 11 (1737).
82. Salem Recs., I, 492 (1721).

Chapter II: The Covenant Broken

1. J. Cotton, *A Defence of Mr. John Cotton from the Imputation of Self-Contradiction* (1658), p. 71, quoted in P. Miller, *Orthodoxy in Massachusetts* (Cambridge, 1933), p. 197.
2. E. C. Blackman, "The Biblical Idea of the Covenant," *The Presbyter,* VII, No. 4 (1945), 3-9. The quotation is from p. 5.
3. Slade's Case, 4 Rep. 92b (1603), quoted in T. F. T. Plucknett, *A Concise History of the Common Law* (4th ed., London, 1948), p. 609.
4. R. P. Stearns, "Assessing the New England Mind," *Church History,* X (1941), 251; P. Miller, *The New England Mind: The Seventeenth Century* (New York, 1939), pp. 375-76.
5. R. Bronkema, *The Essence of Puritanism* (Goes, Holland, [1930?]), pp. 17, 124; T. C. Hall, *The Religious Background of American Culture* (Boston, 1930), p. 39.
6. R. B. Perry, *Puritanism and Democracy* (New York, 1944), p. 58,

chap. IX *passim*. See J. Edwards, "A Dissertation concerning the Nature of Virtue," *Works* (New York, 1829), III, 109.

7. R. B. Perry, *Puritanism and Democracy*, pp. 225-26.
8. *Ibid.*, p. 87. See R. T. Jones, "The Church Covenant in Classical Congregationalism," *The Presbyter*, VII, No. 4 (1945), p. 10.
9. This outline of the pilgrimage theme is based on L. J. Trinterud, *The Forming of an American Tradition* (Philadelphia, 1949), p. 174.
10. E. K. Trefz, "A Study of Satan, with Particular Emphasis upon His Role in the Preaching of Certain New England Puritans" (MS Th.D. dissertation, Union Theological Seminary, 1952), chaps. III, V, VII, VIII *passim*.
11. *Ibid.*, pp. 296-99. Increase Mather, in *Practical Truths Tending to Promote the Power of Godliness* (Boston, 1682), p. 198, observed that people were not drowsy before or after services, but only while the preacher was at work (cited by E. K. Trefz, "A Study of Satan," pp. 297-98). In view of what we know about Puritan homiletics, Mather's observation is not surprising.
12. E. K. Trefz, "A Study of Satan," pp. 314-16.
13. *Ibid.*, pp. 133, 280-85. Quoted by permission of Dr. Trefz.
14. J. Cotton, *The Keyes of the Kingdom of Heaven* (Boston, 1852, first pub. 1644), p. 25.
15. W. Ames, *The Marrow of Sacred Divinity* (London, 1642), p. 190.
16. C. Mather, *Ratio Disciplinae Fratrum Nov-Anglicorum* (Boston, 1726), p. 144. See Tertullian on Repentance, chap. IX, in *The Ante-Nicene Fathers*, ed. by A. Roberts and J. Donaldson (New York, 1896, or Grand Rapids, 1952), III, 664; O. D. Watkins, *A History of Penance* (London, 1920), I, 193; J. T. McNeill, *A History of the Cure of Souls* (New York, 1951), pp. 91-96.
17. C. Mather, *Ratio Disciplinae*, p. 156. That every offender must be given an opportunity to repent was reaffirmed in 1685 by the Bradford church (Bradford Recs., I, 2.)
18. C. Mather, *Ratio Disciplinae*, pp. 151-52, 157. See Middleborough First Ch. Recs., I, 28 (1734).
19. C. Mather, *Ratio Disciplinae*, p. 145; T. Hooker, *A Survey of*

the Summe of Church Discipline (London, 1658), p. 36. For express enactments of this principle see Sutton Recs., I, 15 (1741); Mattapoisett Recs., I, 77 (1772); Stockbridge Recs., I, 75 (1772); Lenox Recs., Vol. I (1775); Granville West Ch. Recs., I, 9 (1784); South Hadley Recs., Vol. I (1791); Pittsfield Recs., I, 343 (1809); *ibid.*, II, 120-21 (1825?); Otis Recs., I, 32 (1841).

20. W. Ames, *The Marrow of Sacred Divinity*, p. 192.
21. J. Cotton, *The Keyes of the Kingdom of Heaven*, p. 39. See J. Calvin, *Institutes of the Christian Religion*, IV, xii, 3, 6.
22. T. Hooker, *Church Discipline*, p. 37. See J. Calvin, *Institutes*, IV, xii, 2, 4.
23. C. Mather, *Ratio Disciplinae*, p. 43. See J. Calvin, *Institutes*, IV, xii, 6.
24. J. T. McNeill, *The History and Character of Calvinism* (New York, 1954), pp. 163-66. Temporal law enforcement and church discipline were much more closely related in Geneva than in Massachusetts.
25. Salem Recs., I, 481 (1718): "No informations were given concerning any members under church censure, or who live in Scandalous Sins, att [*sic*] this Church meeting."
26. T. Lechford, *Plain Dealing or News from New England*, ed. by J. H. Trumbull (Boston, 1867, first pub. 1642), pp. 29-36.
27. T. Hooker, *Church Discipline*, pp. 36-38.
28. J. Cotton, *The Keyes of the Kingdom of Heaven*, pp. 49-55. See the introduction by Goodwin and Nye, *ibid.*, p. 11.
29. Chelsea Recs., Vol. III.
30. C. Mather, in *Ratio Disciplinae*, p. 124, observed that the elders had become almost wholly extinct by 1670. He noted that in patristic writings, elders and pastors were the same persons exercising different functions. Hence the desuetude of the eldership was justified. See [L. Woods], *Report on Congregationalism* (Boston, 1846), pp. 27-28, where the distinction between the ruling elder and the teaching elder is discussed. For the decline of the office, see I. N. Tarbox, "Ruling Elders in the Early New England Churches," *Congregational Quarterly*, XIV (1872), 401-16.
31. See Farnsworth v. Storrs, 5 Cush. (59 Mass.) 412 (1847), in which the court observed that "the proceedings of the church are *quasi judicial*."

32. See F. L. Fagley, "The Narrative of the Cambridge Synod," in H. W. Foote, ed., *The Cambridge Platform of 1648* (Boston, 1949), p. 8.
33. Westfield Recs., I, 184 (1737).
34. Northampton Recs., I, 23 (1748).
35. *Ibid.*, I, 24 (1749).
36. "The most criminal part of the charge," Groton Recs., II, 35 (1803); "a material witness," Amherst Recs., I, 126 (1807); "a Citation," Northampton Recs., I, 24 (between 1771 and 1781); "sentence," Hatfield Recs., I, 8, 95 (1773, 1842). A citation analogous to a subpoena *duces tecum* is found in Mattapoisett Recs., I, 88-89 (1821-23), which also implies an order to show cause.
37. Hatfield Recs., I, 38 (1800); Granville West Ch. Recs., I, 21 (1814); Pittsfield Recs., II, 80 (1822).
38. Hatfield Recs., I, 40 (1800).
39. South Hadley Recs., Vol. I (1767 and 1791).
40. Lenox Recs., Vol. I (1781); Millbury Recs., II, 38 (1783).
41. Haverhill First Ch. Recs., I, 68-69 (1731). The first mention of a standing committee on disciplinary matters is found in Salem First Ch. Recs., I, 240 (1661). Between 1699 and 1822 twenty-four churches appointed a total of thirty-one such committees, as distinguished from *ad hoc* committees appointed to deal with one or more particular cases. The last standing committee of this nature was appointed in Sheffield in 1841 (Sheffield Recs., II, 336).
42. Medford Recs., II, 54 (1818).
43. Northampton Recs., I, 23 (1748).
44. C. Mather, *Ratio Disciplinae,* pp. 155-61, 175. Delegates to councils were elected by their churches in response to letters missive. The pastor usually nominated the delegates, but the church members were jealous of their rights and felt free to nominate persons as delegates. Judging from the records, elections in the colonial period bore no resemblance to the so-called elections in some of the more "respectable" churches of today.
45. *Cambridge Platform* (Cambridge, 1649), chap. 10, sec. 6; J. Cotton, *The Keyes of the Kingdom of Heaven,* pp. 41-43.
46. C. Mather, *Ratio Disciplinae,* pp. 164-67. The requirement

that a council must be convened before a pastoral relationship could be dissolved was affirmed in Thompson v. Catholic Congregational Society of Rehoboth, 5 Pick. (22 Mass.) 471 (1827). The only other officer was the deacon, who was censured like any other member.

47. North Andover Recs., Vol. I (1733); Lenox Recs., Vol. I (1771); Wilbraham Recs., Vol. II (1821). The North Andover resolution was repealed in 1735.
48. Cf. J. Calvin, *Institutes,* IV, xii, 2, where the three forms of censure are *private* admonition, rebuke in the presence of witnesses, and excommunication. C. E. Park, in "Excommunication in the Colonial Churches," *Transactions of the Colonial Society of Massachusetts,* XII (1911), 328, lists public rebuke, public admonition, and excommunication. The second, he states, entailed suspension. The church records do not support this statement. Cf. the Savoy Declaration of 1658, chap. XIX, in J. Schaff, *The Creeds of Christendom* (New York and London, 1919), III, 727, which mentions admonition and excommunication only. In some cases it seems that the suspension was not so much a censure as an act analogous to an indictment. The suspended person's status was therefore analogous to that of a defendant held for trial in a detention prison, or one admitted to bail. Like a defendant awaiting trial, a suspended person might be deprived of certain liberties, but the deprivation was not punitive and did not imply guilt. Often, however, the suspension was definitely punitive and followed the conviction.
49. C. Mather, *Ratio Disciplinae,* pp. 145-48.
50. Plymouth Recs., I, 225 (1684). For the abolition of public confessions in cases involving sexual transgressions, see chapter VII.
51. Beverly Recs., I, 149.
52. Groton Recs., I, 54; Lenox Recs., Vol. I.
53. Granville West Ch. Recs., I, 18 (1803); Windsor Recs., I, 60-61.
54. Chelsea Recs., III, 4 (1759); Falmouth Recs., II, 125 (1790); North Andover Recs., Vol. I (1790); Weston Recs., II, 57 (1778); Amherst Recs., II, 135 (1838).
55. Mattapoisett Recs., I, 77 (1772); Pittsfield Recs., I, 314-15 (1783); Charlemont Recs., I, 30 (1797); Sutton Recs., I, 63

(1822); Great Barrington Recs., I, 234 (1826); Danvers Recs., I, 128 (1832). Also see Sutton Recs., I, 17 (1745); Leominster Recs., II, 22 (1763); Stockbridge Recs., I, 80 (1778).

56. C. Mather, *Ratio Disciplinae,* p. 149.
57. J. Cotton, *The Keyes of the Kingdom of Heaven,* p. 254. See J. Calvin, *Institutes,* IV, i, 22; IV, xii, 1.
58. C. Mather, *Ratio Disciplinae,* p. 150; R. Mather, *Church-Government and Church-Covenant Discussed* (London, 1643), p. 10; T. Hooker, *Church Discipline,* pp. 45-46; J. Cotton, *The Keyes of the Kingdom of Heaven,* pp. 14-15.
59. C. Mather, *Ratio Disciplinae,* pp. 154-55.
60. Thus in T. J. Wertenbaker, *The Puritan Oligarchy* (New York, 1947), p. 64.
61. Cf. J. Calvin, *Institutes,* IV, xii, 4-6.
62. Bradford Recs., I, 5.
63. C. Mather, *Ratio Disciplinae,* pp. 151-52. Cf. J. Calvin, *Institutes,* IV, xii, 5, stating three reasons for excommunication: to prevent the dishonoring of God on the part of Christians and to keep the Eucharist from being defiled, to keep the church members from corruption by association with the wicked, and to induce the sinner to repent.
64. Bradford Recs., II, 13 (1825).
65. Barnstable East Ch. Recs., III, 7 (1821).
66. Sutton Recs., I, 51 (1790). See J. Calvin, *Institutes,* IV, xii, 10. Cf. Sutton Recs., I, 296 (1675), for a vote that a person who had neglected a number of summonses to appear before the church was "a Non-member of this Church."
67. *Cambridge Platform,* chap. 14, sec. 6.
68. W. Ames, *The Marrow of Sacred Divinity,* p. 191; H. M. Dexter, *Congregationalism: What It Is, Whence It Is, How It Works* (Boston, 1865; based on traditional principles), p. 234. This suggests that membership, like baptism, had an indelible character.
69. *Cambridge Platform,* chap. 14, sec. 6.
70. *Ibid.,* chap. 14, sec. 5. Cf. I Cor. 5:9-11.
71. C. Mather, *Ratio Disciplinae,* pp. 155-56. See Lanesborough Recs., I, 81 (1806), in which this principle was enacted by a church.
72. But in one instance a church warned its members against un-

due familiarity with three persons who had been placed under censure. Stockbridge Recs., I, 77 (1774).

73. Marblehead First Ch. Recs., Vol. I.
74. The Second Commandment must have been very broadly construed; the First or Third would seem more logical.
75. I Cor. 5:5, which, in the A.V., reads: "[You are] to deliver such an one unto Satan for the destruction of the flesh, that the spirit may be saved in the day of the Lord Jesus."
76. Marblehead First Ch. Recs., Vol. I. The passages in quotation marks, which have been added, represent the text of the planned announcement of the excommunication; the rest is the record of the events at the meeting, and of the unrehearsed and unprepared conversation. Italics in the original.

Chapter III: The First Table of the Law: Sins of Omission

1. Gen. 2:1-3; Exod. 20:8-11; 34:21.
2. G. Harkness, *John Calvin: the Man and His Ethics* (New York, 1931), p. 119.
3. C. E. Whiting, *Studies in English Puritanism from the Restoration to the Revolution, 1660-1680* (London, 1931), p. 443.
4. B. B. James and J. F. Jameson, eds., *Journal of Jasper Danckaerts* (New York, 1913), p. 274. See C. E. Whiting, *Studies in English Puritanism,* p. 443, and R. Bronkema, *The Essence of Puritanism* (Goes, Holland, [1930]), pp. 161-69. For general discussions of the Puritan Sabbath, see S. Fleming, *Children and Puritanism* (New Haven, 1933), pp. 18-21, and especially A. M. Earle, *The Sabbath in Puritan New England* (New York, 1891), *passim.*
5. W. Brigham, ed., *The Compact, with the Charter and Laws of the Colony of New Plymouth* (Boston, 1836), p. 93.
6. *Ibid.,* p. 123.
7. Mass. Code, 1660, p. 26, in *The Colonial Laws of Massachusetts* (Boston, 1889), p. 148.
8. Mass. Stats., I Geo. III, c. 1, in *ibid.,* p. 392.
9. Northampton Recs., I, 5 (1661).
10. C. Mather, *Diary of Cotton Mather* (Boston, 1911-12), II, 10.
11. Chelsea Recs., Vol. II (1749).

12. Chelmsford Recs., I, 112-13; II, 294 (1746-62).
13. *Ibid.*, I, 112-13 (1746-64).
14. Granville West Ch. Recs., I, 22 (1815); Billerica Recs., I, 106 (1815).
15. Bradford Recs., Vol. I (page number obscured); Longmeadow Recs., I, 46 (1715); Canton Recs., I, 47 (1736); Needham Recs., Vol. I (1765); Southwick Recs., I, 77-78 (1779); Lynnfield Recs., I, 42 (1784); Granville East Ch. Recs., I, 81 (1809); Barnstable East Ch. Recs., IV, 1 (1820). See Danvers Recs., I, 6 (1690).
16. These numbers are not entirely accurate. Some records mention one or two persons by name and indicate that an unspecified number of other members were also charged.
17. The text was Heb. 10:25: "Let us not neglect meeting together as some do, but let us encourage one another, let us arouse ourselves to rival one another's love and good deeds." Salem Recs., I, 238-42.
18. Merrimac Recs., Vol. I (1743).
19. *Ibid.*
20. *Ibid.*
21. Millbury Recs., II, 15-18, 21 (1768); Northampton Recs., I, 29 (1778), 31 (1780) (two cases), 43 (1798); Plymouth Recs., I, 354-57 (1780); Worthington Recs., I, 31 (1797-98); Kingston Recs., I, 27-29 (1799). The thirty-five cases listed were disposed of as follows: restorations, eight; admonitions, two; suspensions, six; unknown, nineteen.
22. Dalton Recs., I, 14, 19-21 (1802).
23. Chelmsford Recs., I, 66-67 (1809).
24. Wilbraham Recs., Vol. II.
25. *Ibid.*, Vol. II (1824-28).
26. Falmouth Recs., II, 164-74.
27. Lenox Recs., Vol. I (1835). Thirteen of the delinquent members are mentioned by name.
28. Pittsfield Recs., II, 149, 159-60, 171.
29. See Appendix, Tables I-III.
30. See Appendix, Tables II-III.
31. Boston Second Ch. Recs., Vol. IV (1699).
32. Haverhill First Ch. Recs., I, 57 (1726); Framingham Recs., II, 287 (1816); *ibid.*, II, 297 (1818); Sheffield Recs., II, 241 (1825); *ibid.*, II, 225 (1841); Otis Recs., I, 83 (1825); Pittsfield Recs., II, 27-29 (1827); Monterey Recs., Vol. I (1829); Windsor Recs.,

I, 64 (1830); South Hadley Recs., Vol. II (1831); Palmer Recs., II, 148-51 (1838). For women accused of both offenses, see Dorchester Recs., I, 92 (1684); Boston First Ch. Recs., II, 215 (1732); Plymouth Recs., I, 332 (1769).

33. Weston Recs., I, 28 (1716); Plymouth Recs., I, 374 (1769); Groton Recs., II, 35 (1803). For a man accused of both offenses, see Lenox Recs., Vol. I (1801).
34. Haverhill First Ch. Recs., I, 52 (1726); Needham Recs., I, 24 (1734); Bradford Recs., II, 19 (1828).
35. Mattapoisett Recs., I, 70 (1757).
36. Dedham Recs., II, 3-5 (1724); Deerfield Recs., II, 67 (1759); Monterey Recs., Vol. I (1822).
37. Otis Recs., I, 69 (1820).
38. Lanesborough Recs., I, 94 (1824).
39. Lenox Recs., Vol. I (1819); Westfield Recs., I, 18 (1841); West Springfield Recs., II, 119 (1843).
40. Roxbury Recs., I, 212 (1674).
41. North Andover Recs., Vol. I (1729-31).
42. Dalton Recs., I, 20-22, 26 (1807); Becket Recs., II, 66-69 (1824).
43. Canton Recs., I, 55-56 (1741); Peru Recs., I, 145 (1797).
44. *Cambridge Platform,* chap. 14, sec. 9. See Calvin, *Institutes of the Christian Religion,* IV, i, 12.
45. Salem Recs., Vol. III (date uncertain, probably between 1737 and 1740). Similar cases may be found in Boston First Ch. Recs., II, 58 (1696); Barnstable West Ch. Recs., Vol. I (1744); Otis Recs., I, 30 (1813). For such a case, resulting in an excommunication, see Sutton Recs., I, 31-42, 49 (1766-91).
46. Great Barrington Recs., I, 225 (1756); Falmouth Recs., I, 125-26 (1787); Canton Recs., I, 186 (1792).
47. Kingston Recs., I, 24 (1792).
48. Millbury Recs., II, 40-41 (1785).
49. Hatfield Recs., I, 30-33 (1788).
50. Kingston Recs., I, 28-29 (1812-19).
51. Chelsea Recs., II, 5 (1717-18). A similar case may be found in Barnstable East Ch. Recs., I, 94 (1775).
52. Concord Recs., I, 96-102, 114-15 (1760-67).
53. Merrimac Recs., Vol. I (1749).
54. Chelsea Recs., I, 249 (1742). A similar case, in which eighteen years elapsed between censure and restoration, is found in Truro Recs., I, 5, 16 (1756, 1774).

55. Boston First Ch. Recs., I, 95 (1651).
56. Plymouth Recs., I, 351.
57. Barre Recs., I, 18-21 (1778).
58. Groton Recs., II, 33-34 (1803).
59. Brewster Recs., I, 46-48 (1734).
60. Danvers Recs., I, 118-19 (1808).
61. Merrimac Recs., Vol. I (1745).
62. Ipswich First Ch. Recs., I, 8-9, 12 (1782-90).
63. Rochester Recs., I, 76-77 (1824).
64. Weston Recs., II, 56 (1766). This case differs from that of Mrs. Kelley in that the latter had not been formally censured; hence the church's instructions to the pastor did not involve a delegation of authority to restore offenders. In the Weston case the offender had been found guilty by the church.
65. Marblehead Second Ch. Recs., I, 225 (1784).
66. Medford Recs., II, 104-11 (1798-99).
67. Amherst Recs., I, 61 (1748).
68. Becket Recs., I, 26-27 (1802).
69. These contributions were distinct from the taxes levied by the government for the support of the ministry.
70. Amesbury Recs., II, 477-79 (1736); Becket Recs., I, 26-27 (1802); Lenox Recs., loose sheet of paper (1835); Merrimac Recs., Vol. I (1751); *ibid.*, Vol. I (1802); Wilbraham Recs., I, 18-21 (1841).
71. Salem Recs., Vol. III. See J. B. Felt, *The Ecclesiastical History of New England* (Boston, 1855-62), I, 380, for what is probably the same case.
72. Barnstable West Ch. Recs., Vol. I (1642).
73. Chelsea Recs., III, 5-6 (1762).
74. Barre Recs., I, 24-26 (1783).
75. Plymouth Recs., I, 379-81 (1793).
76. Otis Recs., I, 65, 74-77 (1821).
77. Sutton Recs., I, 29 (1757).

Chapter IV: The First Table of the Law: Sins of Commission

1. See S. Fleming, *Children and Puritanism* (New Haven, 1933), pp. 18-21, and especially A. M. Earle, *The Sabbath in Puritan New England* (New York, 1891), *passim.*
2. G. G. Coulton, *Medieval Panorama* (Cambridge and New

York, 1946), pp. 181-85; M. M. Knappen, *Tudor Puritanism* (Chicago, 1939), pp. 447-50; A. H. Lewis, *A Critical History of Sunday Legislation* (New York, 1888), p. 71. Cf. G. Harkness, *John Calvin: The Man and His Ethics* (New York, 1931), p. 122, who stresses the post-Calvinist influence, and G. F. Willison, *Saints and Strangers* (New York, 1945), p. 47.

3. H. Bettenson, ed., *Documents of the Christian Church* (New York and London, 1947), pp. 389-91.
4. Boston First Ch. Recs., II, 44; Canton Recs., I, 54.
5. W. Brigham, ed., *The Compact, with the Charter and Laws of the Colony of New Plymouth* (Boston, 1836), pp. 92, 114, 199; Plymouth Revised Laws 1671, c. 3, s. 9, in *ibid.*; Mass. Code, 1660, p. 69, in *The Colonial Laws of Massachusetts* (Boston, 1889), p. 189; Mass. Stats., 4 Wm. & Mary c. 8, and 1 Geo. III, c. 1, in *Acts and Laws of His Majesty's Province of the Massachusetts Bay in New England* (Boston, 1759).
6. In Suffolk County, for instance, seventeen persons were convicted of Sabbath-breaking between 1671 and 1680: *Records of the Suffolk County Court, 1671-1680* (Boston, 1933), *passim*. The violations varied greatly, including the sale of liquor and trading (p. 83), drying sails (p. 307), drinking or being in a tavern (pp. 389, 435, 561, 1018), doing "servile work" (p. 867), entertaining (p. 958). But two men were acquitted when they showed cause for transporting persons on the Lord's Day (p. 117), and one case was dismissed (p. 305). Also see pp. 340, 586-87 for thefts committed on the Sabbath.
7. O. Winslow, *Meetinghouse Hill* (New York, 1952), p. 180.
8. D. W. Howe, *The Puritan Republic of Massachusetts Bay in New England* (Indianapolis, 1899), p. 163.
9. Boston Second Ch. Recs., III, 38 (1691); Palmer Recs., Vol. I (1817).
10. Middleboro First Ch. Recs., I, 39.
11. Merrimac Recs., I, 9-10 (1728); Brewster Recs., I, 81 (1745).
12. Amherst Recs., III, 77 (1823); Stockbridge Recs., II, 221-23 (1833).
13. Restored after confession: Stockbridge Recs., I, 82 (1781); Pittsfield Recs., II, 59 (1819); Otis Recs., I, 78 (1822); Windsor Recs., I, 63 (1825). Excommunicated for impenitence: Lenox Recs., Vol. I (1819); West Springfield Recs., II, 119 (1843).
14. Bradford Recs., II, 19, 21 (1828-29).

15. Boston First Ch. Recs., I, 93, 100 (1649); *ibid.,* II, 46 (1691); Westfield Recs., I, 146 (1743); Wilbraham Recs., I, 19 (1841); and a woman in Plymouth Recs., II, 514-19 (1789).
16. Lanesborough Recs., I, 62-63 (1779).
17. Mattapoisett Recs., I, 81 (1782).
18. Northampton Recs., I, 25 (1698). Taylor was restored in 1711.
19. *Ibid.,* I, 25.
20. Boston Hollis St. Ch. Recs., Vol. II (1738).
21. Great Barrington Recs., I, 228 (1797).
22. Boston First Ch. Recs., III, 12 (1639).
23. Plymouth Recs., I, 211 (1710).
24. Plymouth Revised Laws 1671, c. 7, s. 13, in W. Brigham, ed., *The Compact, with the Charter and Laws of the Colony of New Plymouth.*
25. Bradford Recs., I, 15 (1723).
26. Weston Recs., I, 31 (1726).
27. Westfield Recs., I, 180 (1733); *ibid.,* I, 194 (1735).
28. Concord Recs., I, 104-11 (1762-65).
29. Restored: Quincy Recs., I, 487 (1724). Occasional communion denied: Haverhill First Ch. Recs., I, 89-90 (1749).
30. Concord Recs., I, 104-11 (1762-65).
31. Great Barrington Recs., I, 225-26 (1758, 1773).
32. A Harwich case, recorded in Brewster Recs., I, 122-23 (1763).
33. Medway Recs., Vol. I (1743-48).
34. Barnstable West Ch. Recs., I, 151 (1726).
35. The entire narrative is recorded in a minute dated August 22, 1739. The earlier meetings were not separately recorded. Falmouth Recs., Vol. I. For the restoration, *ibid.,* Vol. I (1759).
36. Additional cases, not discussed below, may be found in Charlestown Recs., I, xi (1670-72); Boston First Ch. Recs., I, 145 (1647); Deerfield Recs., II, 141 (1754); Barnstable East Ch. Recs., I, 253 (1811, 1820); Great Barrington Recs., I, 232 (1821); Monterey Recs., Vol. I (1822).
37. Barnstable West Ch. Recs., Vol. I, partly on unnumbered pages, also pp. 122-25 (1747, 1754).
38. Truro Recs., I, 17 (1775). The date of the entry is April 30. The "scandalous insult" may have reference to some incident in the Revolutionary War.

39. Barre Recs., I, 27-29, 36-38 (1783-91).
40. Barnstable West Ch. Recs., II, 97-99, 169 (1785). No record of a confession has been found.
41. Lynnfield Recs., I, 163-64 (1805).
42. The man who desired to eject the minister from the pulpit: Great Barrington Recs., I, 226 (1774). Other cases: Plymouth Recs., I, 257 (1685), cf. I, 60; Quincy Recs., I, 490 (1722); Concord Recs., I, 141-42 (1744).
43. Reading Recs., I, 3 (1655).
44. Canton Recs., I, 72-74 (1745).
45. Reading Recs., I, 179-81 (1820).
46. Two other cases, not discussed below, may be found in Westfield Recs., I, 128 (1686), and Chelmsford Recs., Vol. I (1748).
47. In the year 1652; in J. B. Felt, *The Ecclesiastical History of New England* (Boston, 1855-62), II, 60-62. The nature of the alleged heresy is not mentioned.
48. Bradford Recs., I, 22, 25 (1727-28).
49. Kingston Recs., I, 12-13 (1732-35).
50. Canton Recs., I, 66-72 (1744-45). "Civil court" refers to a non-ecclesiastical body. The case was obviously of a criminal nature. A parallel tort action is mentioned in the church records, but the outcome is not indicated.
51. *Ibid.*, I, 76.
52. Haverhill First Ch. Recs., I, 126-28 (1832).
53. *Ibid.*, I, 129-35 (1832-35).
54. Haverhill North Ch. Recs., I, 10-11 (1833).
55. Barnstable West Ch. Recs., II, 41 (1649).
56. Quincy Recs., I, 482 (1677).
57. Boston Second Ch. Recs., III, 45 (1685).
58. Plymouth Recs., I, 258 (1686).
59. Deerfield Recs., II, 65 (1639); Westfield Recs., I, 181-87 (1737-38); *ibid.*, II, 67 (1759).
60. Canton Recs., I, 48-49 (1736). There is no record of a confession or excommunication.
61. Mattapoisett Recs., I, 70-71 (1757-62). Similar cases, but less fully recorded, may be found in Dedham Recs., II, 3-5 (1724); Concord Recs., I, 143-47, 164-65, 178-79, 192-97 (1774-91); Sterling Recs., I, 143-45 (1788); and Hatfield Recs., I, 24-30 (1786).

62. E. K. Trefz, "A Study of Satan, with Special Reference to His Influence on the Preaching of Certain New England Puritans" (unpublished Th.D. dissertation, in the Library of the Union Theological Seminary, New York, 1952), pp. 253, 260-61, 332-34.
63. *Ibid.*, p. 277. Quoted by permission of Dr. Trefz.
64. J. Hale, "A Modest Inquiry into the Nature of Witchcraft," in G. L. Burr, ed., *Narratives of the Witchcraft Cases* (New York, 1914), pp. 409-10; J. Fiske, *Witchcraft in Salem Village* (New York and Boston, 1903), pp. 11-13.
65. C. Mather, "Memorable Providences, relating to Witchcraft and Possessions," in G. L. Burr, ed., *Narratives of the Witchcraft Cases,* pp. 100-126; J. Hale, "A Modest Inquiry," in *ibid.,* pp. 412-13; J. Fiske, *Witchcraft in Salem Village,* pp. 15-20.
66. D. Lawson, "A Brief and True Narrative," in G. L. Burr, *Narratives of the Witchcraft Cases,* pp. 152-54; R. Calef, "More Wonders of the Invisible World," in *ibid.,* pp. 341-43; J. Hale, "A Modest Inquiry," in *ibid.,* pp. 413-14; J. Fiske, *Witchcraft in Salem Village,* pp. 22-26; J. B. Felt, *Annals of Salem* (Salem, 1827), pp. 303-14.
67. J. Fiske, *Witchcraft in Salem Village,* pp. 28-29. For Tituba's confession see J. Hall, "A Modest Inquiry," in G. L. Burr, *Narratives of the Witchcraft Cases,* p. 415. A good summary of the arrests and subsequent proceedings may be found in J. B. Felt, *Annals of Salem,* II, 475-82. Only those cases which concern church members whose names have been found in the records are discussed here.
68. The hearings are discussed in D. Lawson, "A Brief and True Narrative," in G. L. Burr, *Narratives of the Witchcraft Cases,* pp. 154-59, and in R. Calef, "More Wonders of the Invisible World," in *ibid.,* pp. 343-45. Sharp criticism was voiced in a letter by T. Brattle (1692), in *ibid.,* pp. 170-72, where the test of touching the victims is mentioned. See J. Fiske, *Witchcraft in Salem Village,* pp. 36-37.
69. E. K. Trefz, in "A Study of Satan," suggests that, given the assumption that the devil can assume any shape except that of an innocent man, it is logical to conclude that any person accused of witchcraft was guilty. Hence, if a victim testifies that he has seen a spectre in some person's likeness, the accused must be guilty, since the devil cannot appear in the like-

ness of an innocent person. "Thus accusation is tantamount to conviction. There is no defense against this type of attack" (p. 260). This argument overlooks the possibility of willful perjury on the part of the deponent. Dr. Trefz gives credit to Cotton Mather for arresting the epidemic by arguing that Satan *could* appear in the shape of an innocent person (pp. 266-68, 275-76).

70. The most exhaustive primary report of the trials is in R. Calef, "More Wonders of the Invisible World," in G. L. Burr, *Narratives of the Witchcraft Cases,* pp. 344-67. A defense of the procedure, with a suggestion that permissible practices may have been misapplied, is found in J. Hale, "A Modest Inquiry," in *ibid.,* pp. 422-23; cf. the critical statement in Brattle's letter, *ibid.,* pp. 182-84. A good review is found in J. Fiske, *Witchcraft in Salem Village,* pp. 38-46. See Brattle's letter, in G. L. Burr, *Narratives of the Witchcraft Cases,* pp. 171, 176; R. Calef, "More Wonders of the Invisible World," in *ibid.,* pp. 346-47.
71. Letter of T. Brattle, in G. L. Burr, *Narratives of the Witchcraft Cases,* p. 182.
72. J. Fiske, *Witchcraft in Salem Village,* pp. 41-46; J. B. Felt, *Annals of Salem,* II, 482. On Giles Corey, see R. Calef, "More Wonders of the Invisible World," in G. L. Burr, *Narratives of the Witchcraft Cases,* p. 367, and R. and L. Boas, *Cotton Mather, Keeper of the Puritan Conscience* (New York and London, 1928), p. 112.
73. M. Starkey, *The Devil in Massachusetts* (New York, 1949), pp. 29-30, 146; J. Fiske, *Witchcraft in Salem Village* pp. 48-49; W. S. Nevins, *Witchcraft in Salem Village* (Salem, 1892), p. 245; J. B. Felt, *Annals of Salem,* II, 482.
74. Salem Recs., I, 347 (1692).
75. *Ibid.,* I, 345 (1691).
76. *Ibid.,* I, 349 (1692).
77. Danvers Recs., I, 12 (1692). Cf. J. B. Felt, *Annals of Salem,* II, 480.
78. Danvers Recs., I, 10-11 (1692); R. Calef, "More Wonders of the Invisible World," in G. L. Burr, *Narratives of the Witchcraft Cases,* p. 342; M. Starkey, *The Devil in Massachusetts,* p. 31.
79. Danvers Recs., I, 24-25 (1694). The record includes a great

deal of procedural matter. The substantive portion is irrelevant in this connection, except for Parris's proposed confession, which was intended to pacify the withdrawing members. No actual confession on the Parris is found in the Danvers records.

80. R. Calef, "More Wonders of the Invisible World," in G. L. Burr, *Narratives of the Witchcraft Cases,* pp. 386-87, n.
81. Danvers Recs., I, 47.
82. *Ibid.*
83. Salem Recs., I, 411 (1712).
84. *Ibid.,* I, 212-13 (1712).
85. Milton Recs., I, 40 (1718).
86. Fortunetelling was sinful because it mocked God, who had foreordained all things. M. M. Knappen, *Tudor Puritanism,* p. 439.
87. Boston Second Ch. Recs., Vol. IV; Danvers Recs., I, 74 (1746).

Chapter V: "False Doctrine, Heresy, and Schism"

1. G. Harkness, *John Calvin: The Man and His Ethics* (New York, 1931), p. 109.
2. N. Ward, *Simple Cobbler of Aggawam* (1647), quoted in T. J. Wertenbaker, *The Puritan Oligarchy* (New York, 1947), p. 212.
3. M. M. Knappen, *Tudor Puritanism* (Chicago, 1939), pp. 367-68.
4. B. M. Levy, *Preaching in the First Half Century of New England History* (Hartford, 1945), p. 49. See R. Bainton, *Travail of Religious Liberty* (Philadelphia, 1951), pp. 17, 211.
5. In the year 1631; in J. B. Felt, *The Ecclesiastical History of New England* (Boston, 1855-62), I, 151-52.
6. Dorchester Recs., I, 168 (1657). In England any person not a member of a dissenting body is automatically a parishioner (though not necessarily a communicant) of the local branch of the Established Church.
7. *Ibid.,* I, 27 (1668).
8. F. W. Maitland and F. C. Montague, *A Sketch of English Legal History* (New York and London, 1915), p. 145; 2 Hen. IV, c. 15; 29 Car. II, c. 9. See H. L. Osgood, *American Colonies in the Seventeenth Century* (New York, 1904-7), I, 221.

9. Plymouth Revised Stats., 1771, c. 2; c. 3, s. 11-12, in W. Bringham, ed., *The Compact, with the Charter and Laws of the Colony of New Plymouth* (Boston, 1836); Mass. Code, 1660, pp. 8, 33-35, in *The Colonial Laws of Massachusetts* (Boston, 1889), pp. 128, 153-55. The laws against the denial of the canonicity of the biblical books were rather milder in Plymouth.
10. C. F. Adams, *Three Episodes of Massachusetts History* (2nd. ed., Boston and New York, 1892), I, 367, ascribes the prosecution to social, intellectual, and political developments. Cf. S. E. Morison, *Builders of the Bay Colony* (Boston and New York, 1930), p. 120, who stresses the religious aspects, and A. P. Stokes, *Church and State in the United States* (New York, 1950), I, 172-73, who treats it as a fundamentally religious issue with political overtones.
11. C. F. Adams, *Three Episodes,* I, 395, 407-11.
12. *Ibid.,* I, 443-45.
13. *Ibid.,* I, 468-74; J. A. Doyle, *English Colonies in America* (New York, 1889), II, 133; A. P. Stokes, *Church and State,* I, 178. The actions of the synod are recorded in Winthrop's "Short Story," in C. F. Adams, ed., *Antinomianism in the Colony of Massachusetts Bay* (Boston, 1894), pp. 95-124.
14. C. F. Adams, *Three Episodes,* I, 448, 478-81, 496-508; R. B. Morris, *Fair Trial* (New York, 1952), chap. I *passim.;* S. H. Cobb, *The Rise of Religious Liberty in America* (New York, 1902), p. 191; C. M. Andrews, *The Colonial Period of American History* (New Haven, 1934), I, 482. Brooks Adams, in *The Emancipation of Massachusetts,* (2nd ed., Boston, 1886), p. 65, called the court which convicted Anne Hutchinson "the ghastliest den of human iniquity."
15. C. F. Adams, ed., *Antinomianism in the Colony of Massachusetts Bay* (Boston, 1894), which contains the record of the church trial (hereafter cited as *Antinomian Trial*), pp. 297-98. It is quite clear that Anne Hutchinson's heresy had nothing to do with that of John Agricola, the prototype of Antinomians. See C. M. Andrews, *The Colonial Period,* I, 475; W. Walker, *Ten New England Leaders* (New York, 1901), p. 81; J. A. Doyle, *English Colonies in America,* II, 139.
16. *Antinomian Trial,* p. 295.
17. *Ibid.,* pp. 298-99.

18. *Ibid.*, p. 304.
19. *Ibid.*, p. 305.
20. *Ibid.*, pp. 309-10, 314-17. For the text of the admonition see pp. 310-14.
21. *Ibid.*, pp. 320-21.
22. *Ibid.*, pp. 321, 330-32.
23. P. Miller, *Orthodoxy in Massachusetts* (Cambridge, 1933), pp. 163-65.
24. Boston First Ch. Recs., III, 9.
25. Roxbury Recs., I, 78-79 (1633), 81 (1633).
26. *Ibid.*, I, 79, 187 (1635?-42).
27. Boston First Ch. Recs., I, 83, 86 (1646).
28. *Ibid.*, III, 17. For a conviction for Pelagianism by a civil court see J. B. Felt, *Ecclesiastical History*, I, 422 (1640).
29. Barnstable West Ch. Recs., Vol. I. (Date of excommunication uncertain; restoration probably in 1670's.)
30. Brewster Recs., I, 61 (1738).
31. Mattapoisett Recs., I, 63-64 (1751). No record of a formal censure has been found.
32. Haverhill First Ch. Recs., I, 92-96 (1753).
33. Reading Recs., I, 90-93, 105 (1741, 1761).
34. Brewster Recs., I, 39. The selection of this text was curiously inept.
35. *Ibid.*, I, 65. For Uzziah's sin, see II Chron. 26:16-23, a more relevant selection.
36. The date is obscured.
37. Brewster Recs., I, 92-93.
38. Concord Recs., I, 90-92 (1759).
39. Lenox Recs., Vol. I (1775).
40. Danvers Recs., I, 138-39 (1836).
41. Middleborough North Ch. Recs., I, 18, 22 (1751).
42. Great Barrington Recs., I, 227 (1774).
43. Hatfield Recs., I, 54-57 (1819-20).
44. Kingston Recs., I, 24 (1785).
45. Amesbury Recs., II, 480 (1731); Granville West Ch. Recs., I, 57 (1799); Pittsfield Recs., II, 11 (1824); Amherst Recs., II, 117-20 (1835); Wilbraham Recs., I, 11 (1838).
46. G. B. English, *The Grounds of Christianity Examined* (Boston, 1813), p. 84.

47. *Ibid.*, p. 94.
48. *Ibid.*, pp. 112-14.
49. *Ibid.*, pp. 156-57.
50. S. Cary, *Review of a Book Entitled . . .* (Boston, 1813).
51. E. Everett, *A Defence of Christianity against the Work of George B. English, A.M.* (Boston, 1814).
52. Cambridge Recs., I, 389-94 (1814).
53. "George Bethune English," *Dictionary of American Biography* (New York, 1931), VI, 165.
54. Canton Recs., I, 185-86 (1792).
55. Granville East Ch. Recs., I, 99-103 (1817).
56. J. B. Felt, *Ecclesiastical History,* I, 486. Cf. Salem Recs., I, 13.
57. W. H. Clark and D. L. Marsh, eds., *The Story of Massachusetts* (New York, 1938), I, 129.
58. Plymouth Recs., I, 146 (1670).
59. Charlestown Recs., I, i-vii; R. Frothingham, *The History of Charlestown* (Charlestown, 1845-49), pp. 165-69.
60. Boston Second Ch. Recs., III, 19-24, 43 (1665, 1683). An excellent narrative of the case may be found in O. Winslow, *Meetinghouse Hill* (New York, 1952), pp. 187-89.
61. Mattapoisett Recs., I, 78 (1773); S. L. Blake, *The Separates or Strict Congregationalists of New England* (Boston and Chicago, 1902), pp. 134-35.
62. Middleborough North Ch. Recs., I, 21-31 (1751-52).
63. Kingston Recs., I, 27-28 (1779).
64. Barnstable West Ch. Recs., I, 104 (1808); Falmouth Recs., I, 129 (1808); Reading Recs., I, 150 (1808); Hanover Recs., I, 58 (1810); Kingston Recs., I, 28 (1812); Leominster Recs., III, 17 (1817); Needham Recs., I, 54-59 (1817); Sandisfield Recs., I, 59-64 (1817); Otis Recs., I, 59-64 (1818); Westminster Recs., I, 7, 15 (1818, 1830); Barnstable East Ch. Recs., II, 11 (1821); Framingham Recs., I, 308 (1827); Windsor Recs., I, 64 (1827); Sheffield Recs., II, 240 (1831); Wilbraham Recs., I, 22 (1842).
65. Falmouth Recs., I, 129 (1808).
66. Sheffield Recs., II, 240 (1831).
67. Reading Recs., I, 150 (1808).
68. Needham Recs., I, 54-59 (1817).
69. Windsor Recs., I, 64 (1827).
70. Dalton Recs., I, 26 (1815).

71. Barnstable East Ch. Recs., II, 11 (1821).
72. Rochester Recs., I, 97 (1834).
73. W. Brigham, ed., *The Compact, with the Charter and Laws of the Colony of New Plymouth,* pp. 104, 114, 122, 130.
74. Mass. Code, 1660, pp. 35-36, in *The Colonial Laws of Massachusetts,* pp. 155-56.
75. E. Russell, *The History of Quakerism* (New York, 1942), pp. 37-43, 108-9.
76. A. P. Stokes, *Church and State,* I, 421.
77. Boston First Ch. Recs., II, 211 (1669).
78. Excommunicated: Salem Recs., I, 375 (1703), and three persons mentioned in J. B. Felt, *Ecclesiastical History,* II, 291 (1662). No further record found: Salem Recs., I, 342 (1685) (two persons); *ibid.,* I, 376 (1703). An abjured Quaker who had been baptized in the First Church of Salem made a confession of his heresy before admission to full communion: *ibid.,* I, 563 (1718).
79. Plymouth Recs., I, 54-60.
80. Sutton Recs., I, 9-10 (1736-37).
81. Canton Recs., I, 73-74, 85, 95. Similar apathy was shown by the church when another member converted to Anglicanism. *Ibid.,* I, 101-2 (1764).
82. Sheffield Recs., II, 242-45 (1831); *ibid.,* II, 58 (1844).
83. *Otis Recs.,* I, 52-58 (1818, 1829); *ibid.,* I, 55-58 (1818, 1846). The sixth case is in Peru Recs., II, 23 (1828).
84. Marblehead Second Ch. Recs., I, 270-74 (1790-93); Pittsfield Recs., I, 357 (1811); Reading Recs., I, 186-88 (1821); Otis Recs., I, 89 (1829).
85. Barnstable East Ch. Recs., II, 7-11 (1821). Similar cases of termination of membership, without dismission or excommunication, are found in Worthington Recs., I, 38 (1810); Pittsfield Recs., I, 357 (1811); Truro Recs., I, 23-24 (1817); Pittsfield Recs., II, 58 (1818); Wilbraham Recs., I, 15 (1819); Reading Recs., I, 198 (1824); and Peru Recs., II, 21-24 (1826).
86. Otis Recs., I, 65-69 (1819).
87. Danvers Recs., I, 158 (1842); F. H. Foster, *A Genetic History of the New England Theology* (Chicago, 1907), p. 190. Two women favored Universalism but did not join the denomination: Worthington Recs., I, 48-49 (1823).
88. Westfield Recs., I, 226-28 (1798). No claims to revelations:

Lenox Recs., Vol. I (1783); Granville East Ch. Recs., I, 88, 92 (1813); Reading Recs., I, 194-98 (1823); Egremont Recs., I, 31-35 (1827); Wilbraham Recs., I, 7, 11-13 (1835). One convert recanted: Lanesborough Recs., I, 84-85 (1811, 1822).

89. Reading Recs., I, 202 (1827); *ibid.*, I, 194-95 (1823).
90. *Ibid.*, I, 154-62 (1809).
91. Rochester Recs., I, 33, 56-58 (1814-15).
92. Westminster Recs., I, 12 (1826).
93. South Hadley Recs., Vol. II (between 1832 and 1834).
94. Billerica Recs., I, 110-11 (1820).
95. Peru Recs., I, 89, 114-17 (1785-90).
96. South Hadley Recs., Vol. II (1834).
97. *Ibid.*
98. Framingham Recs., II, 300-301 (1821).
99. Lincoln Recs., I, 16.
100. Reading Recs., I, 124-26.
101. Rochester Recs., I, 31 (1798).
102. Plymouth Recs., II, 567-77 (1825).
103. Westminster Recs., I, 19.
104. Boston Third Ch. Recs., I, 539-40, 587. A photostat of the sentence of excommunication is at the Massachusetts Historical Society Library, Boston.
105. Westfield Recs., I, 196-98, 202 (1750-54, 1762).
106. Worthington Recs. I, 25-27 (1782).
107. Danvers Recs., I, 118-19 (1808-9).
108. Lanesborough Recs., I, 78-82.
109. Peru Recs., I, 157; II, 5.
110. Boston Third Ch. Recs., I, 12-21, 25-27. The subject is briefly treated in A. W. M'Clure, *The Lives of John Wilson John Norton, and John Davenport* (Boston, 1846), pp. 288-93, and in I. M. Calder, *The New Haven Colony* (New Haven, 1934), pp. 256-58. Also see Salem Recs., I, 276-78.
111. Boston Third Ch. Recs., I, 27-28, 31.
112. *Ibid.*, I, 29-41. In early Congregational practice a minister was ordained to the pastorate of a particular church. If he took another church, he was reordained.
113. *Ibid.*, I, 42-49.
114. *Ibid.*, I, 52-57.
115. *Ibid.*, I, 57-60.

116. *Ibid.*, I, 60-66.
117. *Ibid.*, I, 63-73.
118. *Ibid.*, I, 76, 79.
119. *Ibid.*, I, 81-87, 94, 113.
120. Salem Recs., II, 81, 87-96 (1736-40); C. S. Osgood and H. M. Batchelder, *Historical Sketch of Salem* (Salem, 1879), p. 83. At least two churches supported the council and withdrew from fellowship with the First Church of Salem. Chelsea Recs., Vol. II (1735); Canton Recs., I, 43 (1735). The custody of the records presented a problem. Fiske walked off with the books. On his death they passed to General John Fiske, who was willing to surrender them to the First Church. Perhaps it was mere lethargy which kept the church from taking custody of the volumes. Upon the general's death the records came into the possession of the Reverend William Bentley, who refused to surrender them to Fiske's heirs. In 1811 the First Church made a last effort to reclaim the documents. Reluctantly Bentley turned them over to Fiske's heirs, who in turn delivered them to the church. Salem Recs., IV, 45-46.
121. Concord Recs., I, 4-12 (1739-40).
122. *Ibid.*, I, 13-18.
123. *Ibid.*, I, 23-28, 36-42. The majority of secessionists returned to the church. No further action was taken by the church until 1765, when the few remaining schismatics were restored without demand of confession. *Ibid.*, I, 110.
124. Boston Second Ch. Recs., Vol. VI.
125. Hull Recs., I, 6-7 (1743). Nothing is known of the schism save that it existed.
126. Chelmsford Recs., I, 694-97 (1743-46, 1772).
127. Sutton Recs., I, 19-48 (1747-86, 1791).
128. Westfield Recs., I, 194-95 (1749). The Second Church of Framingham may have had its origin in a schism, but the evidence does not justify a definite conclusion. See Framingham Recs., I, 126-27, 129, and W. Barry, *A History of Framingham* (Boston, 1847), p. 116.
129. Barre Recs., I, 4-5 (1767); *A Memorial of the One Hundredth Anniversary of the Town of Barre* (Cambridge, 1875), pp. 57-61.
130. Salem Recs., II, 102-3 (1772).
131. Pittsfield Recs., I, 344-50, 355-57 (1810-11).

CHAPTER VI: DOMESTIC AND MARITAL RELATIONS

1. Gen. 2:18; M. Weber, *The Protestant Ethic and the Spirit of Capitalism,* tr. by T. Parsons (New York, 1948), p. 158. See J. T. McNeill, *Modern Christian Movements* (Philadelphia, 1954), p. 22.
2. J. Calvin, *Institutes of the Christian Religion,* II, viii, 41-42; G. Harkness, *John Calvin: The Man and His Ethics* (New York, 1931), pp. 135-37, 143-44
3. J. Calvin, *Institutes,* IV, xix, 34; G. E. Howard, *A History of Matrimonial Institutions* (Chicago, 1904), II, 127-40; C. L. Powell, *English Domestic Relations, 1487-1653* (New York, 1917), pp. 37-44, 53-54; R. B. Morris, *Studies in the History of American Law* (New York, 1930), pp. 126-28. After 1688 marriages were increasingly often solemnized in churches, but they remained contracts and did not become sacraments.
4. E. Morgan, *The Puritan Family* (Boston, 1944), pp. 12-27.
5. G. E. Howard, *A History of Matrimonial Institutions,* II, 144.
6. E. Morgan, *The Puritan Family,* p. 42; M. M. Knappen, *Tudor Puritanism* (Chicago, 1939), p. 42.
7. J. Cotton, *The Keys of the Kingdom of Heaven* (Boston, 1852; first pub. 1644), p. 12.
8. C. L. Powell, *English Domestic Relations,* pp. 3-4.
9. G. E. Howard, *A History of Matrimonial Institutions,* I, 376.
10. C. L. Powell, *English Domestic Relations,* pp. 41-44.
11. Framingham Recs., II, 279 (1795).
12. Charlemont Recs., I, 17-26 (1789-92).
13. G. E. Howard, *A History of Matrimonial Institutions,* II, 178.
14. *Ibid.,* II, 177. Incest was a felony in Massachusetts; for a brief period it was a capital crime. Usually construed to refer to relations by persons within the forbidden degrees of consanguinity, incest technically also includes sexual relations within the forbidden degrees of affinity. See *ibid.,* II, 127, and 31 C. J. 374.
15. Quincy Recs., I, 658 (1692).
16. Middleborough First Ch. Recs., I, 10 (1716).
17. Dalton Recs., I, 7 (1787); Mattapoisett Recs., I, 80 (1781).

18. Lenox Recs., Vol. I.
19. Haverhill First Ch. Recs., I, 83-84.
20. Plymouth Recs., I, 302-3, 331-32 (1756).
21. Charlemont Recs., I, 27. Cf. G. E. Howard, *A History of Matrimonial Institutions,* II, 96.
22. Barnstable West Ch. Recs., II, 40.
23. Great Barrington Recs., I, 226 (1774).
24. Stockbridge Recs., I, 78-80; [J. Huntington], *A Plea before the Ecclesiastical Council at Stockbridge in the Case of Mrs. Fisk* (Boston, 1782), pp. 30-31.
25. *Ibid.,* p. 8.
26. *Ibid.,* p. 11.
27. *Ibid.,* pp. 13, 26.
28. *Ibid.,* pp. 24-25.
29. S. West, *A Vindication of the Principles and Conduct of the Church in Stockbridge* (Hartford, 1780), pp. 36-37, 42, 67.
30. [J. Huntington], *A Plea,* pp. 31-32.
31. Stockbridge Recs., I, 81-82.
32. G. E. Howard, *A History of Matrimonial Institutions,* III, 333. See A. W. Calhoun, *A Social History of the American Family* (Cleveland, 1917-19), I, 146.
33. G. E. Howard, *A History of Matrimonial Institutions,* II, 87; C. L. Powell, *English Domestic Relations,* pp. 80-93; R. B. Schlatter, *The Social Ideas of Religious Leaders, 1660-1688* (Oxford, 1940), p. 26.
34. Marblehead First Ch. Recs., Vol. I (1721).
35. Sandisfield Recs., I, 5 (1801).
36. Palmer Recs., Vol. I (1818).
37. Worthington Recs., I, 50 (1828).
38. Pittsfield Recs., I, 190-91 (1858).
39. Canton Recs., I, 51 (1738).
40. Worthington Recs., I, 47-48 (1813-14, 1822).
41. Rockport Recs., I, 30 (1756); Falmouth Recs., Vol. I (1784).
42. Westfield Recs., I, 193 (1743-46?); Sandisfield Recs., I, 3 (1800).
43. Sandisfield Recs., I, 3 (1800).
44. Otis Recs., I, 69-75 (1820). See Amherst Recs., I, 119 (1785), and Barnstable West Ch. Recs., I, loose leaf of paper (no date), for similar cases, in which, however, the information is inadequate.

45. E. Morgan, *The Puritan Family,* p. 10; G. B. Schlatter, *The Social Ideas of Religious Leaders,* pp. 19-22.
46. C. J. Hilkey, *Legal Development in Massachusetts, 1630-1686* (New York, 1910), p. 131.
47. Mattapoisett Recs., I, 7-71 (1757).
48. Dorchester Recs., I, 88 (1682).
49. Merrimac Recs., Vol. I (1729-34).
50. Mattapoisett Recs., I, 64 (1751); Pittsfield Recs., II, 116-17 (1824).
51. Pittsfield Recs., I, 307.
52. *Ibid.*
53. *Ibid.,* I, 308.
54. *Ibid.,* I, 309.
55. Marblehead First Ch. Recs., Vol. I (1703).
56. Quincy Recs., I, 485-86 (1713).
57. Cambridge Recs., I, 126.
58. Lanesborough Recs., I, 75 (1801). Similar cases, in which the records are not informative, are found in Westfield Recs., I, 155 (1735); Merrimac Recs., Vol. I (1746); Worcester Recs., Vol. I (1757); Hatfield Recs., I, 68-73 (1826). A suspension is found in Sandisfield Recs., I, 3-4 (1800), while Concord Recs., I, 152 (1775), mentions the appointment of a committee to inquire into an unspecified quarrel between husband and wife.
59. Boston First Ch. Recs., I, 124 (1668); *ibid.*, I, 140 (1672); Roxbury Recs., I, 85 (1644); Salem Recs., I, 317 (1679). The Roxbury offender was later restored.
60. Plymouth Recs., I, 258, 269 (1686).
61. Deerfield Recs., II, 139 (1762); Millbury Recs., II, 34-35 (1780).
62. Sandisfield Recs., I, 5 (1801).
63. The minister used I Cor. 16:2 as his text: "Upon the first day of the week let every one of you lay by him in store, as God hath prospered him, that there be no gatherings when I come." (A.V.)
64. Using Ephes. 5:33 as his text: "Nevertheless let every one of you in particular so love his wife even as himself; and the wife see that she reverence her husband." (A.V.)
65. "Therefore as the church is subject unto Christ, so let the wives be [subject] to their own husbands in every thing." Ephes.

5:24, A.V. A mixture of admirable theology of lasting value and dubious sociology of temporary value.

66. Barnstable West Ch. Recs., I, 31-32 (1683).
67. Mass. Code, 1660, p. 9, in *The Colonial Laws of Massachusetts* (Boston, 1889), p. 129; Plymouth Revised Stats. 1771, c. 2, ss. 13-14, in W. Bringham, ed., *The Compact, with the Charter and Laws of the Colony of New Plymouth* (Boston, 1836), pp. 244-45.
68. Plymouth Recs., I, 251 (1683).
69. Boston First Ch. Recs., II, 81 (1707); Deerfield Recs., II, 67 (1767).
70. Boston Second Ch. Recs., Vol. V (1733); Chelsea Recs., I, 237-38 (1731); Westfield Recs., I, 156 (1741); Lincoln Recs., I, 51-52 (1765); Canton Recs., I, 112-13 (1777).
71. Westfield Recs., I, 129, 135-36 (1697, 1712).
72. Boston First Ch. Recs., I, 116 (1664); Westfield Recs., I, 140 (1712).
73. Norton Recs., I, 79 (1827); Quincy Recs., I, 488-90 (1735).
74. Monterey Recs., Vol. I (1779).
75. Boston First Ch. Recs., III, 8.
76. *Ibid.*, III, 9 (1638).
77. Granville East Ch. Recs., I, 68-70 (1802).
78. Falmouth Recs., Vol. I (1747).
79. Framingham Recs., I, 22 (1720); Plymouth Recs., I, 332 (1769).
80. The same was true in Calvin's Geneva (G. Harkness, *John Calvin,* pp. 152-53).

Chapter VII: Extramarital Relations

1. J. Calvin, *Institutes of the Christian Religion,* II, viii, 41-43.
2. Adultery and fornication were clearly distinguished whenever either term was used. In the records of the Middleborough North Church (I, 12, 1749), the pastor first recorded that a woman had "made a Confession of her being guilty of adultery." The word *adultery,* however, was crossed out and *fornication* interlined, in the same ink and handwriting as the rest of the record, and no effort was made to obscure the first entry. Exactly the reverse of this may be found in Amherst Recs., III, 75.

3. E.g., Concord Recs., I, 35-36 (1743); Amesbury Recs., II, 477 (1773).
4. E.g., Granville East Ch. Recs., I, 35-36 (1797); Salem Recs., I, 295, 309-11 (1674-78); *ibid.*, I, 297, 309-11 (1675-78).
5. N. B. Shurtleff, ed., *Records of the Governor and Company of the Massachusetts Bay* (Boston, 1853-54), IV, Part II, 143.
6. Dorchester Recs., I, 19.
7. See Appendix, Tables IV and V.
8. The Middlesex County figures are: 85 couples, 42 men, 16 women, 66 sex unknown. If 42 or less of the 66 were women, the couples have a plurality.
9. Four couples and four women.
10. G. E. Howard, *A History of Matrimonial Institutions* (Chicago, 1904), II, 193. The penalties varied. In Massachusetts, compulsory marriage, fine, or whipping were permissible punishments for fornication (Mass. Revised Laws 1660, p. 33, in *The Colonial Laws of Massachusetts* [Boston, 1889], p. 153). In Plymouth the standard fine was ten pounds, with whipping and imprisonment as alternatives. If the culprits married, the fine was to be divided between them; if they were betrothed at the time of the act, the fine was reduced to fifty shillings each (Plymouth Revised Stats. 1671, in W. Brigham, *The Compact, with the Charter and Laws of the Colony of New Plymouth* [Boston, 1836], p. 246).
11. G. E. Howard, *A History of Matrimonial Institutions*, II, 188.
12. *Ibid.*, II, 193.
13. Barnstable East and West Chs., Boston First and Second Chs., Bradford, Brewster, Canton, Danvers, Deerfield, Dorchester, Framingham, Plymouth, Quincy, Reading, Salem First Ch., Sutton, and Westfield.
14. Decreases are found in the Barnstable and Boston First Ch. records. Increases are prominent in the Dorchester and Boston Second Ch. records.
15. The eight churches, all but one of which have records from 1700 to 1769, are: Plymouth, Barnstable East and West, Quincy, Boston Second, Bradford, Danvers, Reading, and Westfield. The Westfield records begin in 1707.
16. The figures for the seven decades are: 1700-1709, 6; 1710-19, 11; 1720-29, 36; 1730-39, 55; 1740-49, 40; 1750-59, 45; 1760-69, 35. See Appendix, Table VI.

17. The twelve churches are: Barnstable East and West, Boston Second, Bradford, Brewster, Canton, Danvers, Framingham, Plymouth, Quincy, Reading, Salem First, and Westfield.
18. See Chapter XV.
19. H. B. Parkes, "Morals and Law Enforcement in Colonial New England," *The New England Quarterly,* V (1932), 442.
20. C. Mather, *Ratio Disciplinae Fratrum Nov-Anglicorum* (Boston, 1726), p. 143. For instances in which the rule was taken for granted, see Cambridge Recs., I, 278-80 (1788); Groton Recs., II, 32 (1803); Leominster Recs., II, 27 (1795); Salem Recs., IV, 50 (1779).
21. Plymouth Recs., I, 251 (1683).
22. Haverhill First Ch. Recs., I, 55 (1725); *ibid.,* I, 71-73 (1732); Plymouth Recs., I, 245-46 (1732); *ibid.,* I, 256 (1684); Salem Recs., I, 522 (1733); Dedham Recs., I, 11 (1729).
23. Boston Second Ch. Recs., Vol. IV (1701).
24. Haverhill First Ch. Recs., I, 95-96 (1754). A similar case is found in Peru Recs., I, 117-18 (1788).
25. Haverhill First Ch. Recs., I, 97 (1756).
26. Dorchester Recs., I, 137 (1722).
27. Haverhill First Ch. Recs., I, 55-57 (1725). Upon confession the couple were admitted to full communion. *Ibid.,* II, 60.
28. Pittsfield Recs., II, 148, 156 (1837-38).
29. Sheffield Recs., II, 246-51 (1838-39). A committee appointed to inquire into Sophia West's morals reported in 1842 that her conduct was "not inconsistent" with Christian standards. *Ibid.,* II, 256.
30. C. Mather, *Ratio Disciplinae,* p. 143.
31. Dedham Recs., I, 11 (1729); Haverhill North Ch. Recs., I, 75 (1759).
32. Deerfield Recs., II, 138 (1750).
33. Barre Recs., I, 16-18 (1778); Deerfield Recs., II, 141 (1784).
34. Falmouth Recs., Vol. I (1756).
35. Northampton Recs., I, 30 (1780).
36. Bradford Recs., I, 52 (1772).
37. Milton Recs., I, 41 (1726).
38. Haverhill First Ch. Recs., I, 99-100 (1762-63).
39. Billerica Recs., I, 55-56 (1771).
40. Boston First Ch. Recs., I, 114-15 (1664); Westfield Recs., I, 161 (1779).

41. Plymouth Recs., I, 251 (1683); Westfield Recs., I, 157 (1749).
42. Barnstable East Ch. Recs., I, 79 (1742).
43. Groton Recs., II, 9 (1761-63); Lenox Recs., Vol. I (1807).
44. Boston First Ch. Recs., I, 103 (1655); Hatfield Recs., I, 95 (1842).
45. Deerfield Recs., I, 66 (1743).
46. Millbury Recs., II, 30-32 (1743).
47. Otis Recs., I, 91 (1829).
48. Boston Second Ch. Recs., III, 37-38.
49. Westfield Recs., I, 156 (probably 1742).
50. Barnstable West Ch. Recs., Vol. I (probably before 1641).
51. Groton Recs., I, 21-24.
52. C. Mather, *Ratio Disciplinae,* p. 144.
53. Groton Recs., I, 41.
54. Salem Recs., IV, 41.
55. Milton Recs., II, 8-9. Similar resolutions are found in Sheffield Recs., II, 229 (1794); Leominster Recs., II, 27 (1795); Palmer Recs., Vol. I (1812); and for the Dedham Church, in C. F. Adams, "Some Phases of Sexual Morality and Church Discipline," *Proceedings of the Massachusetts Historical Society,* 2nd Ser., VI (1891), 495. In other churches public confessions were abolished without specific reference to sexual offenses. In the votes here mentioned, the exemption was confined to cases of fornication and adultery.
56. Billerica Recs., Vol. I (probably before 1751).
57. Beverly Recs., I, 194 (1674). For similar cases, see *ibid.,* II, 3, 155, 160, 303 (1714, 1729).
58. Merrimac Recs., Vol. I (1733).
59. Lenox Recs., Vol. II (1853).
60. Haverhill First Ch. Recs., I, 71-78, 81-84 (1732-43).
61. Boston First Ch. Recs., I, 51-52 (1689).
62. Danvers Recs., I, 49 (1710).
63. Canton Recs., I, 28-29 (1730-31).
64. Salem Recs., I, 453 (1716).
65. Canton Recs., I, 28 (1730). The text reads: "If any man come to me, and hate not his father, and mother, and wife, and children, and brethren, and sisters, yea, and his own life also, he cannot be my disciple." (A.V.)
66. Granville East Ch. Recs., I, 58 (1799).
67. Canton Recs., I, 30-31 (1731).

68. Sutton Recs., I, 52-53, 58 (1793-1800).
69. C. F. Adams, "Some Phases of Sexual Morality," *Proceedings of the Massachusetts Historical Society,* 2nd Ser., VI, 493; A. W. Calhoun, *A Social History of the American Family* (Cleveland, 1917-19), I, 132.
70. Beverly Recs., I, 156-57 (1716). See Marblehead Second Ch. Recs., I, 213 (1775), for the expression "spurious child." In Chelsea Recs., III, 61 (1766), the bastardy of a child is indicated by the absence of the father's name in the baptismal record.
71. Hatfield Recs., I, 8-9.
72. Hanover Recs., I, 68-70.
73. West Roxbury Recs., I, 45-99 *passim.*
74. Salem Recs., I, 453-574 *passim.*
75. Marblehead First Ch. Recs., Vol. I (1702).
76. Plymouth Recs., I, 212 (1712).
77. Scituate Recs., I, 45; Brewster Recs., I, 159; Plymouth Recs., I, 374-75.
78. Cambridge Recs., I, 279-80.
79. Truro Recs., I, 20.
80. Plymouth Recs., I, 196, 240-82 *passim,* 328-75 *passim.*
81. Sharon Recs., I, 8-23 *passim.*
82. Deerfield Recs., I, 65-68.
83. Danvers Recs., I, 46-141 *passim.*
84. Wilbraham Recs., I, 26. For other late confessions, see Great Barrington Recs., I, 234 (1825); Otis Recs., I, 86-87 (1827); Sheffield Recs., II, 247 (1842).
85. Hatfield Recs., I, 95. For other late excommunications, see Stockbridge Recs., II, 134-39 (1821); Lanesborough Recs., I, 2 (1835).
86. C. F. Adams, "Some Phases of Sexual Morality," *Proceedings of the Massachusetts Historical Society,* 2nd Ser., VI, 506. See H. R. Stiles, *Bundling; Its Origin, Progress, and Decline in America* (Albany, 1871), p. 67.
87. Canton Recs., I, 61-62 (1742).
88. See H. R. Stiles, *Bundling,* pp. 13, 75.
89. Brewster Recs., I, 37.
90. Boston First Ch. Recs., I, 89; Dorchester Recs., I, 70, 79-85 (1676).

91. Worthington Recs., I, 33-36 (1800).
92. Charlemont Recs., I, 37-38 (1800).
93. Rochester Recs., I, 32.
94. Stockbridge Recs., II, 141-44 (1828).
95. Otis Recs., I, 79-81 (1822).
96. C. F. Adams, "Some Phases of Sexual Morality," *Proceedings of the Massachusetts Historical Society,* 2nd Ser., VI, 509-10.
97. Boston First Ch. Recs., I, 100, 106 (1653-56); Roxbury Recs., I, 98 (1694).
98. MS in Stockbridge Library.
99. G. E. Howard, *A History of Matrimonial Institutions,* III, 169-77; H. B. Parkes, "Morals and Law Enforcement," *The New England Quarterly,* V, 445. In the early decades of Massachusetts, adultery was a capital crime (*The Colonial Laws of Massachusetts,* p. 8). In Plymouth, adultery was "to be punished," but this provision appeared under the heading "Offenses Capital" (W. Brigham, ed., *The Compact, with the Charter and Laws of the Colony of New Plymouth,* pp. 12-13). Whipping and the wearing of a letter were prescribed in 1650 (*ibid.,* p. 113). Under the Second Charter, the death penalty was abolished. Convicted adulterers were to sit under the gallows, with the rope around their necks, for an hour. They were then to be taken to jail to be whipped up to forty times. For the rest of their lives they were to wear the letter *A,* two inches in length and in contrasting color, on their arms or backs. If caught without the letter, they were to receive fifteen lashes (Mass. Stats., 6 Wm. and Mary, c. 4, in *Acts and Laws of His Majesty's Province of the Massachusetts Bay in New England* [Boston, 1759]).
100. In addition to the cases discussed below, seven persons were excommunicated for adultery in the seventeenth century: Boston First Ch. Recs., I, 59, 68, 75-76, 82, 110; Boston Second Ch. Recs., Vol. IV. See *Diary of Cotton Mather* (Boston, 1911-12), I, 261, n.
101. Boston First Ch. Recs., III, 12, 18.
102. *Ibid.,* III, 13 (1640).
103. Boston Second Ch. Recs., III, 29 (1678).
104. Salem Recs., I, 340 (1688).

105. Boston Second Ch. Recs., Vol. IV (1699). Nothing more is said about Mills in the records.
106. Stockbridge Recs., I, 76 (1773); Mattapoisett Recs., I, 81-82 (1780); Lenox Recs., Vol. I (1793).
107. Westfield Recs., I, 195-97, 202 (1750, 1761).
108. Haverhill First Ch. Recs., I, 64-66 (1730); Merrimac Recs., Vol. I (1732); Westfield Recs., I, 156, 159, 188-89 (1739, 1769); Boston Hollis St. Ch. Recs., Vol. I (1742); West Roxbury Recs., Vol. I (1742); Natick Recs., I, 11-12 (1744); Middleborough First Ch. Recs., I, 38 (1751); Canton Recs., I, 85 (1752); Truro Recs., Vol. I (1757); Dalton Recs., I, 6-7 (1787); Barnstable East Ch. Recs., I, 172-73 (1792); Lenox Recs., Vol. I (1793).
109. Haverhill First Ch. Recs., I, 65-66 (1730-31).
110. North Andover Recs., Vol. I (1731).
111. Pittsfield Recs., I, 309 (1772).
112. Egremont Recs., I, 5-7, 10 (1770-71). The witnesses were called into the room severally and were asked to point out the man who had taken their room.
113. Pittsfield Recs., I, 313-15.
114. Groton Recs., II, 33-35 (1803).
115. Hatfield Recs., I, 48-51, 67 (1811); Falmouth Recs., I, 186 (1819); Dalton Recs., I, 24-26 (1822); Amherst Recs., II, 73-76 (1823). Also see the cases in note 20.
116. Pittsfield Recs., II, 138 (1853); *ibid.,* II, 176 (1853).
117. Westfield Recs., I, 16-17 (1831).
118. Pittsfield Recs., II, 171.
119. *Ibid.,* II, 175-76.
120. *Ibid.,* II, 178-79.
121. *Ibid.,* II, 181-82.
122. *Ibid.,* II, 183-85.
123. Boston Second Ch. Recs., Vol. IV (1696).
124. Reading Recs., I, 8 (date missing, probably between 1664 and 1670).
125. Montague Recs., Vol. I.
126. Boston First Ch. Recs., I, 119-21 (1666). Bates was later restored. Statutory rape was unknown in Massachusetts and the law did not recognize the rape of a girl under ten. In England, however, statutory rape existed since the thirteenth century, when Parliament enacted that "the King prohibiteth

that none do ravish nor take away by Force, any Maiden within Age (neither by her own Consent, nor without) nor any Wife or Maiden of full Age, nor any Woman against her will." 3 Edw. I, c. 13. By the statute of 18 Eliz., c. 7, s. 4, any sexual relations with a girl under ten years of age constituted rape.

127. H. B. Parkes, "Morals and Law Enforcement," *The New England Quarterly*, V, 445.
128. Roxbury Recs., I, 212. The nature of crime is not mentioned in the record but may be inferred from the sermon mentioned below.
129. S. Danforth, *Cry of Sodom Enquired Into* (Cambridge, 1674), pp. 13-15, 25.
130. A. C. Kinsey, et al., *Sexual Behavior in the Human Male* (Philadelphia and London, 1948), p. 550.
131. A. C. Kinsey, et al., *Sexual Behavior in the Human Female* (Philadelphia and London, 1953), p. 287.
132. *Ibid.*, pp. 304-7, 321-24; A. C. Kinsey, *Sexual Behavior in the Human Male*, pp. 483-87, 553.

Chapter VIII: "The Affected Bottle" and Its Consequences

1. J. A. Krout, *The Origins of Prohibition* (New York, 1925), pp. 13, 27-28, 51-54, 90; G. Harkness, *John Calvin: The Man and His Ethics* (New York, 1931), pp. 27-28, 159-61; C. E. Whiting, *Studies in English Puritanism from the Restoration to the Revolution, 1660-1688* (London, 1931), p. 445.
2. W. Brigham, ed., *The Compact, with the Charter and Laws of the Colony of New Plymouth* (Boston, 1836), pp. 47, 84; Plymouth Revised Stats, 1671, c. 3, s. 25, in *ibid.*
3. Mass. Code, 1660, pp. 44-45, 67, in *The Colonial Laws of Massachusetts* (Boston, 1889), pp. 164-65, 187.
4. Westfield Recs., I, 180-84 (1737); Plymouth Recs., I, 357, 360 (1780).
5. Boston Second Ch. Recs., III, 39 (1681). See Westfield Recs., I, 235 (1813), in which the question of whether a particular case of intoxication was public or private was litigated in church.
6. See Appendix, Tables VII and VIII.

7. For an interesting comment on this point, see J. R. Oliver, *Foursquare* (New York, 1929), p. 116.
8. Plymouth Recs., I, 153, 255.
9. In the year 1675; in E. D. Hanscom, *The Heart of the Puritan* (New York, 1917), pp. 177-78.
10. Mather observed that the wine was from God, the drunkard from the devil. I. Mather, *Wo to Drunkards* (Cambridge, 1673), p. 4, cited in K. Murdock, *Increase Mather* (Cambridge, 1925), p. 103.
11. C. Mather, *Diary of Cotton Mather* (Boston, 1911-12), II, 51.
12. *Ibid.,* II, 65.
13. *Ibid.,* II, 762.
14. Longmeadow Recs., I, 48 (1715); *ibid.,* I, 95; Haverhill First Ch. Recs., I, 59 (1727); Cambridge Recs., I, 128-29 (1735).
15. Brewster Recs., I, 36-37 (1730).
16. Sheffield Recs., II, 330 (1824); Becket Recs., II, 69 (1828).
17. Lenox Recs., Vol. I (1829); Rochester Recs., I, 94 (1829); Westfield Recs., I, 239 (1834); Falmouth Recs., II, 175-76 (1839). See Norton Recs., I, 75-76 (1821). The investigation took place in Falmouth.
18. Salem Recs., I, 342 (1689). The alcoholic left for New Jersey, and the case was held in abeyance until 1703, when he returned to Salem and was restored. *Ibid.,* I, 378.
19. Boston Second Ch. Recs., Vol. IV (1707).
20. M. E. Perley, history of the Congregational Church, Boxford (MS at the Essex Institute, Salem), II, 4.
21. Plymouth Recs., I, 2-3 (1706-8); *ibid.,* II, 564 (1815). The first was a minister in Middleborough, the latter in Barnstable.
22. Falmouth Recs., Vol. I (1773).
23. Otis Recs., I, 76-77 (1821).
24. Westfield Recs., I, 136, 149-50 (1712, 1714, 1720). Another voluntary confession is found in Middleborough First Ch. Recs., I, 60 (1804).
25. Plymouth Recs., I, 237-40 (1728-29).
26. Canton Recs., I, 59 (1742).
27. Worthington Recs., I, 48 (1818).
28. Sutton Recs., I, 54 (1800). Hayden had made a confession of intoxication in 1786. *Ibid.,* I, 47, 51.
29. In addition to the cases cited below, see Middleborough First Ch. Recs., I, 7, 13, 18-21 (1720).

30. Salem Recs., I, 250 (1664).
31. *Ibid.*, I, 254, 266 (1665).
32. Sutton Recs., I, 11-13, 210 (1737-41).
33. Roxbury Recs., I, 93, 202 (1664, 1678); Boston Second Ch. Recs., II, 39 (1683); Boston First Ch. Recs., III, 15 (1640); *ibid.*, I, 36, 100 (1640); Dorchester Recs., I, 223, 227 (1711, 1726); Westfield Recs., I, 136, 151 (1714); Middleborough First Ch. Recs., I, 13 (1720); Plymouth Recs., I, 237-40, 290 (1728-33); Sutton Recs., I, 14 (1739); Pittsfield Recs., I, 306 (1785); Otis Recs., I, 32, 50 (1814, 1817); Worthington Recs., I, 56 (1805); Falmouth Recs., I, 137 (1820).
34. Excommunicated: Boston First Ch. Recs., I, 131 (1670); *ibid.*, I, 123 (1668); *ibid.*, II, 19, 38, 63, 215 (1687-97); *ibid.*, I, 148, 154 (1675-79); Peabody Recs., I, 6-9 (1800); Mattapoisett Recs., I, 83-85 (1791, 1808); Danvers Recs., I, 128, 140 (1832, 1836). Died: Middleborough First Ch. Recs., I, 39, 51 (1806). Conclusion not recorded: Danvers Recs., I, 48 (1709); Sutton First Ch. Recs., I, 7 (1729, 1736); Falmouth Recs., I, 126-27 (1803-5); Ipswich First Ch. Recs., II, 14-18, 27-30 (1815-17); Worthington Recs., I, 24 56 (1823-24).
35. Boston First Ch. Recs., I, 93, 100-101, 120 (1649, 1653, 1666).
36. *Ibid.*, II, 65-66, 81-82 (1698, 1707, 1715); Brewster Recs., I, 33, 45-46 (1729, 1733); Deerfield Recs., II, 65 (1735, 1738, 1741); Lenox Recs., I (1797, 1801-2, 1810); and the case mentioned in note 37.
37. Falmouth Recs., II, 127 (1805).
38. See O. E. Winslow, *Meetinghouse Hill* (New York, 1952), p. 181.
39. Dorchester Recs., I, 75, 80-83 (1677-79).
40. Marblehead First Ch. Recs., Vol. II (1823-26). The two other women, presumably not reformed, were excommunicated.
41. Dorchester Recs., I, 75, 80-83 (1677-79); Reading Recs., I, 73-77, 90-94 (1737-49); Mattapoisett Recs., I, 84-85 (1807-8); Worcester Recs., III (1820-24); Amherst Recs., I, 130-31 (1814 or 1817); Marblehead First Ch. Recs., Vol. II (1823-26) (two cases).
42. Cambridge Recs., I, 132, 208-11 (1737); Natick Recs., I, 11-12 (1744-45); Ipswich First Ch. Recs., I, 20-24 (1761-64); Worcester Recs., Vol. III (1822-24); Becket Recs., II, 669-70 (1829).
43. Rochester Recs., I, 70, 76-77 (1822-24).
44. Plymouth Recs., II, 235-36, 552 (1799-1804).

45. Salem First Ch. Recs., I, 322-23 (1681-82).
46. Plymouth Recs., II, 574, 587-88 (1816, 1834).
47. Ipswich First Ch. Recs., II, 14-18, 27, 30 (1814-17, 1827).
48. Marblehead Second Ch. Recs., I, 211-12 (1774).
49. Canton Recs., I, 96 (1758); Stockbridge Recs., I, 88 (1789); Lanesborough Recs., I, 74 (1789).
50. Falmouth Recs., Vol. I (1746).
51. *Ibid.,* Vol. I (1762).
52. Truro Recs., I, 1.
53. Plymouth Recs., I, 157.
54. B. M. Levy, *Preaching in the First Half Century of New England History* (Hartford, 1945), p. 44.
55. C. Mather, *Diary of Cotton Mather,* I, 213-15.
56. The 61 persons include 48 men and 13 women. Of these, 5 women and 14 men were simultaneously charged with drunkenness and profanity. The acquittal is found in Peru Recs., I, 143 (1797).
57. Hatfield Recs., I, 68, 71-72 (1828).
58. Deerfield Recs., II, 65 (1738).
59. Egremont Recs., I, 17 (1784).
60. Beverly Recs., II, 22-25 (1676).
61. Marblehead First Ch. Recs., Vol. I (1727).
62. Falmouth Recs., Vol. I (1751).
63. Truro Recs., I, 15-16 (1774).
64. Lanesborough Recs., I, 76-77 (1801).
65. Canton Recs., I, 80 (1747); Stockbridge Recs., I, 73 (1769).
66. Reading Recs., I, 3 (1653?).
67. *Ibid.,* I, 13 (probably between 1678 and 1685).
68. Lanesborough Recs., I, 76-77 (1801). Another excommunication, but probably incurred by a more serious offense also charged, is found in *ibid.,* I, 67-69 (1781).
69. Canton Recs., I, 80 (1747); Stockbridge Recs., I, 73 (1769).
70. South Hadley Recs., Vol. I (1823).
71. T. F. T. Plucknett, *A Concise History of the Common Law* (4th ed., London, 1948), pp. 347-48.
72. Boston First Ch. Recs., II, 12-15 (1639).
73. Confessions: Westfield Recs., I, 157, 193 (1746); Pittsfield Recs., I, 305, 314 (1768, 1782); Millbury Recs., II, 22-24, 150 (1774). Offense disregarded: Otis Recs., I, 65-68 (1820).

74. Worthington Recs., I, 38 (1810) (two persons dealt with as one case); Lenox Recs., Vol. I (1822).
75. Cambridge Recs., I, 371-75. The respondent was excommunicated in 1808 and restored, after a confession, in 1813. *Ibid.*, I, 388.
76. Danvers Recs., I, 129-31 (1832).
77. Great Barrington Recs., I, 231 (1820).
78. Lanesborough Recs., I, 76-78 (1801-2).
79. J. B. Felt, *The Ecclesiastical History of New England* (Boston, 1855-62), I, 380.
80. Canton Recs., I, 112-13, 177-78, 184 (1777-92).
81. Amherst Recs., I, 124-25 (1799).
82. Boston Second Ch. Recs., Vol. IV (1713).
83. Deerfield Recs., II, 65, 134, (1739).
84. Haverhill First Ch. Recs., I, 69-71 (1730); North Andover Recs., Vol. I (1731-35); Boston Hollis St. Ch. Recs., Vol. II (1738); Canton Recs., I, 52 (1739); *ibid.*, I, 98 (1760); Sutton Recs., I, 24 (1752); Stockbridge Recs., I, 70-71 (1764); Pittsfield Recs., I, 905 (1797).
85. Barnstable West Ch. Recs., Vol. I (1737); Middleborough First Ch. Recs., I, 38-39 (1760).
86. In addition to the cases discussed below, see Barnstable East Ch. Recs., I, 77-80 (1743); Middleborough First Ch. Recs., I, 36 (1747).
87. Weston Recs., II, 46 (1758); Cambridge Recs., I, 126, 133 (1733-38).
88. Windsor Recs., I, 61-63 (1815).
89. Lanesborough Recs., I, 67-69 (1781).
90. Palmer Recs., Vol. I (1816).
91. See J. A. Krout, *The Origins of Prohibition*, p. 27.

Chapter IX: The Sixth Commandment: Offenses against the Person

1. See J. Calvin, *Institutes of the Christian Religion,* I, xiv, 22; II, viii, 39-40.
2. J. Winthrop, *History of New England,* ed. by J. K. Hosmer (New York, 1908-9), I, 310-18; F. L. Weis, *The Colonial*

Churches and the Colonial Clergy of New England (Lancaster, Mass., 1936), p. 76.

3. Charlestown Recs., I, vii-viii, xii (1667, 1674-76).
4. Boston First Ch. Recs., II, 81 (1707).
5. Peru Recs., II, 17-19 (1814, 1821-22).
6. Lenox Recs., Vol. I (1781).
7. Haverhill First Ch. Recs., I, 64-66, 69-70 (1730-32).
8. Peru Recs., I, 121-24 (1793).
9. Plymouth Recs., I, 265-66, 269 (1689).
10. Mattapoisett Recs., I, 82 (1782).
11. Stockbridge Recs., I, 89-92 (1792-96).
12. Canton Recs., I, 54 (1741).
13. Barnstable West Ch. Recs., I, 52 (1769).
14. Falmouth Recs., II, 137 (1820).
15. Westfield Recs., I, 158 (1751).
16. Barnstable West Ch. Recs., I, 149 (1737); Northampton Recs., I, 25 (1697).
17. In addition to the cases already mentioned and those involving servants and slaves, which are treated below, see Boston Second Ch. Recs., Vol. IV (1709); Merrimac Recs., I, 11 (1729); Sutton Recs., I, 23-25, 210 (1752); Westfield Recs., I, 159 (1760); Deerfield Recs., II, 150-51 (1789).
18. Roxbury Recs., I, 85-87, 187 (1643).
19. Boston First Ch. Recs., I, 77-78, 81-82 (1645-46). The only reference to the case in the courts which has been found states that the cause was remanded for a new trial (N. B. Shurtleff, ed., *Records of the Governor and Company of the Massachusetts Bay* [Boston, 1853-54], II, 71).
20. Barnstable West Ch. Recs., II, 40 (1651).
21. Worthington Recs., I, 51-52. See Norton Recs., I, 97-98 (1843), for a statement concerning "the awful sin of slavery." No disciplinary action was involved.
22. J. Winthrop, *The History of New England,* I, 335-36. For the execution, see *Records of the Court of Assistants of the Colony of the Massachusetts Bay* (Boston, 1904), II, 78.
23. Roxbury Recs., I, 207 (1668); *Diary of Cotton Mather* (Boston, 1911-12), I, 164 (two cases); II, 569.
24. Boston First Ch. Recs., I, 63 (1642); *ibid.,* III, 19 (1642).
25. Roxbury Recs., I, 95-96 (1681-83).

26. *Ibid.*, I, 3 (1653). See R. B. Schlatter, *The Social Ideas of Religious Leaders, 1660-1688* (Oxford, 1940), p. 137.
27. Canton Recs., I, 38 (1732). Fenno was later tried for perjury, but was acquitted. Still later he made a confession of drunkenness (*ibid.*, I, 83, 95 [1750, 1757]). Dueling was prohibited in 1719, but three earlier cases resulted in common law prosecutions. A Massachusetts statute of 1728 (2 Geo. II, c. 5) provided that the convict was to be carried in a cart to the gallows, where he was to sit for an hour, with the rope around his neck. See E. B. Greene, "The Code of Honor in Colonial and Revolutionary Times, with Special Reference to New England," *Publications of the Colonial Society of Massachusetts,* XXVI (1926), 367-88.
28. Lanesborough Recs., I, 94-95 (1824).
29. See S. Fleming, *Children and Puritanism* (New Haven, 1933), pp. 38, 45.
30. *The Colonial Laws of Massachusetts* (Boston, 1887), p. 137. (This statute has not been found in the 1889 edition of the Massachusetts laws, which has usually been cited.)
31. Roxbury Recs., I, 95.
32. Salem Recs., I, 417 (1712).
33. S. Williams, MS diary (typescript copy at the Congregational Church, Longmeadow), II, 72. The entry is dated August 3, 1716.
34. Falmouth Recs., II, 136 (1818-19).

Chapter X: Bearers of False Witness

1. J. Calvin, *Institutes of the Christian Religion,* II, viii, 47-48.
2. T. F. T. Plucknett, *A Concise History of the Common Law* (4th ed., London, 1945), pp. 455, 461-63; W. S. Holdsworth, *A History of English Law* (London, 1924), VIII, 361-67.
3. W. Brigham, ed., *The Compact, with the Charter and Laws of the Colony of New Plymouth* (Boston, 1836), p. 129.
4. Mass. Code, 1660, p. 51, in *The Colonial Laws of Massachusetts* (Boston, 1889), p. 171.
5. Mass. Code, 1660, p. 51, in *ibid.*, p. 171; W. S. Holdsworth, *A History of English Law,* V, 206-7; R. B. Morris, "Massachu-

setts and the Common Law; The Declaration of 1646," *American Historical Review,* XXVI (1926), 451.

6. But in thirty-nine cases (or slightly more than half), the record does not specify the nature of the alleged slander.
7. Barnstable West Ch. Recs., II, 41 (1649).
8. Boston Second Ch. Recs., III, 39 (1682); Dorchester Recs., I, 112 (1696).
9. Salisbury Recs., I, 95 (1731).
10. Canton Recs., I, 52 (1739); Peabody Recs., I, 19-20 (1806).
11. Worthington Recs., I, 47 (1813); Brewster Recs., I, 66 (1740); Salisbury Recs., I, 94 (1731).
12. Haverhill First Ch. Recs., I, 59-60 (1727). In another case the revival of an issue settled privately was likewise held to be slanderous: North Andover Recs., Vol. I (1731-32).
13. Worthington Recs., I, 36-37 (1806-7).
14. Plymouth Recs., I, 199-200 (1704).
15. *Ibid.,* I, 195 (1703); Lincoln Recs., I, 51-53 (1765); Peabody Recs., I, 22-25 (1807-8).
16. North Andover Recs., Vol. I (1748).
17. Boston First Ch. Recs., III, 16 (1640).
18. Groton Recs., II, 10-11 (1769).
19. Boston First Ch. Recs., Vol. IV (1699). Mills was excommunicated, but the censure was doubtless influenced by the fact that he was also convicted with absence, gaming, adultery, and incest.
20. Canton Recs., I, 44-47 (1735-36).
21. Danvers Recs., I, 138-45 (1836-37).
22. Boston Second Ch. Recs., Vol. IV (1697).
23. Lincoln Recs., I, 51-53 (1765).
24. Bradford Recs., I, 11 (date missing, probably about 1720).
25. Marblehead First Ch. Recs., Vol. I (1727).
26. Haverhill First Ch. Recs., I, 62-68 (1729-31). For a somewhat similar case, see Danvers Recs., I, 48 (1710).
27. Reading Recs., I, 71 (1736); Pittsfield Recs., I, 317 (1790).
28. Falmouth Recs., Vol. I (1741).
29. Canton Recs., I, 18-19, 31-32, 36 (1729-31).
30. Egremont Recs., I, 10-12 (1771).
31. Granville East Ch. Recs., I, 34-36 (1797). A similar case is found in Otis Recs., I, 48 (1817).

32. Reading Recs., I, 90 (1747).
33. Boston Second Ch. Recs., III, 33 (1777); Pittsfield Recs., I, 313 (1781).
34. Reading Recs., I, 151-52 (1808).
35. Plymouth Recs., I, 156-57 (1681); Salisbury Recs., I, 45-47 (1688); Westfield Recs., I, 205 (1768); South Hadley Recs., Vol. I (1795).
36. The case involving the published libel is in Reading Recs., I, 4 (1658).
37. In addition to cases discussed above, see Northampton Recs., I, 25 (1740); Sutton Recs., I, 31-49 (1760-91); Westfield Recs., I, 207-21 (1772-77); Concord Recs., I, 143-47, 164-65, 178-79, 192-97 (1774-90).
38. Chelsea Recs., II, 2 (1719); Boston Hollis St. Ch. Recs., Vol. II (1735-36); Salisbury Recs., I, 92-96 (1737); Middleborough First Ch. Recs., I, 36-37 (1748-49); Westfield Recs., I, 200-201 (1757-61); Egremont Recs., I, 16-17 (1781); Danvers Recs., I, 123 (1822).
39. T. P. Oakley, *English Penitential Discipline and Anglo-Saxon Law in Their Joint Influence* (New York, 1923), pp. 141-42, 159, 199.
40. 32 Hen. VIII, c. 9, s. 3.
41. Plymouth Revised Laws of 1671, c. 2, s. 11, in W. Brigham, ed., *The Compact, with the Charter and Laws of the Colony of New Plymouth.*
42. Thus in the printed record. No reason is suggested why Clark should have testified falsely that his son-in-law had been "committed for murder."
43. Roxbury Recs. I, 203-5 (1665-66).
44. Beverly Recs., I, 203-5 (1677-80).
45. Sutton Recs., I, 30 (1761).
46. Dorchester Recs., I, 112 (1696).
47. A case before the Malden church, in Chelsea Recs., I, 204 (1713).
48. Billerica Recs., I, 20-23 (1757-59).
49. Haverhill First Ch. Recs., I, 90-91 (1749); Canton Recs., I, 83 (1750); *ibid.*, I, 84 (1751); Framingham Recs., I, 136-37 (1766); Amherst Recs., I, 126 (1807); Worthington Recs., I, 52-64 (1832).

50. Framingham Recs., I, 137-38 (1767).
51. Canton Recs., I, 84 (1751).
52. Dorchester Recs., I, 135-37 (1722) (Record of the council).
53. Barnstable East Ch. Recs., I, 80 (1743).
54. Brewster Recs., I, 122-34, 138-39 (1763-67, 1770).
55. O. E. Winslow, *Meetinghouse Hill* (New York, 1952), p. 191.
56. Thirty-two persons were found guilty of denying their guilt of another offense. Twelve cases occurred in the seventeenth century, fourteen in the eighteenth, and six in the nineteenth. One person was acquitted of sexual immorality and denying his guilt (Canton Recs., I, 61-62 [1742]). A confession for denying the existence of a contract is found in Reading Recs., I, 79-80 (1741), while Middleborough First Ch. Recs., I, 39, 59 (1769, 1803), mentions an excommunication for impenitence after conviction for denying the existence of an agreement.
57. Quincy Recs., I, 483-84 (1683).
58. Charlemont Recs., I, 37-38 (1800); Westfield Recs., I, 195-97, 202 (1750).
59. Boston Second Ch. Recs., III, 37-38 (1678).
60. Boston First Ch. Recs., III, 9 (1638).
61. Westfield Recs., I, 200-202 (1758-61); *ibid.*, I, 208-10 (1773); Pittsfield Recs., I, 309 (1773); Stockbridge Recs., I, 51-58 (1773); Plymouth Recs., I, 345-50 (1775-76); Great Barrington Recs., I, 230 (1813).
62. Brewster Recs., I, 77-78, 111-14 (1743, 1758-59). No further action is mentioned. Between the two cases the member made a public confession of intoxication.
63. South Hadley Recs., Vol. I (1792). In one case the complaint was withdrawn: Lenox Recs., Vol. I (1801).
64. In addition to the cases discussed below, see Barnstable West Ch. Recs., II, 41 (1640); Westfield Recs., I, 153 (1728); Sutton Recs., I, 29-30 (1759); Peru Recs., I, 149-50 (1799) for restorations. The rejected applicant is found in Worthington Recs., I, 25-27 (1781-82), and the forgotten case in Sutton Recs., I, 23-24 (1752). The excommunications are found in Northampton Recs., I, 25 (1709-11); Stockbridge Recs., I, 81 (1779); Granville West Ch. Recs., I, 23-24 (1816).
65. In addition to the cases discussed below: Charlestown Recs., I, xi (1672); Salisbury Recs., I, 98 (1731); Billerica Recs., I, 9, 12 (1750-52).

66. Worthington Recs., I, 30 (1786).
67. Rochester Recs., I, 66 (1820). The case originated in Abington; only the record of the council is available.
68. Great Barrington Recs., I, 231-32 (1820).
69. *Ibid.*, I, 216, 232-34 (1821-25). In September, 1825, the church reconsidered a vote to accept a confession made in 1824. There is no reference to this confession in the abridged record. The votes of 1824 and 1825 may refer to an altogether different offense, or to a reopened case again Pitkin for his earlier lies. In one place the abridged copy of the record states "See records." The complete records of the Great Barrington church, reported by the pastor to be extant, were not made available.

Chapter XI: Business Ethics and Property Rights

1. Ecclus. 11:20. From the American Standard Version. Also see Ecclus. 11:21.
2. T. J. Wertenbaker, *The Puritan Oligarchy* (New York, 1947), pp. 184-92.
3. *Ibid.*, pp. 192-203.
4. *Ibid.*, p. 203; J. Dorfman, *The Economic Mind in American Civilization* (New York, 1946), I, 42-44; R. B. Perry, *Puritanism and Democracy* (New York, 1944), pp. 193, 297-314, 333 n.; R. H. Tawney, *Religion and the Rise of Capitalism* (London, 1931), chap. IV *passim;* E. Troeltsch, *The Social Teaching of the Christian Churches* (tr. by O. Wyon, New York, 1931), pp. 602-17; M. Weber, *The Protestant Ethic and the Spirit of Capitalism* (tr. by T. Parsons, New York, 1948), pp. 98-128. For a searching critique of Weber, see H. M. Robinson, *Aspects of the Rise of Economic Individualism: A Criticism of Max Weber and His School* (Cambridge, 1933), pp. 15-17, 164-67. See J. Haroutunian, *Piety versus Moralism* (New York, 1932), p. xiv; J. Calvin, *Institutes of the Christian Religion,* III, x, 6; J. T. McNeill, *Modern Christian Movements* (Philadelphia, 1954), pp. 33-34, 39-41.
5. R. B. Perry, *Puritanism and Democracy,* p. 301. See J. Calvin, *Institutes,* II, viii, 46, 49-50; III, vii, 9; G. Harkness, *John Calvin: The Man and His Ethics* (New York, 1931), pp. 171-72.

6. J. Dorfman, *The Economic Mind,* I, 13, 42; M. M. Knappen, *Tudor Puritanism* (Chicago, 1939), pp. 346-47.
7. M. M. Knappen, *Tudor Puritanism,* p. 418; J. Dorfman, *The Economic Mind,* I, 12; E. Troeltsch, *The Social Teaching,* p. 648; G. Harkness, *John Calvin,* pp. 201-9.
8. 37 Hen. VIII, c. 9. Also unenforced was the act of 13 Eliz., c. 8, providing for the forfeiture of interest of less than 10 percent, and for the ecclesiastical and temporal punishment of persons taking more than 10 percent. See J. F. Stephen, *A History of the Criminal Law of England* (London, 1883), III, 198.
9. 21 Jas. I, c. 17; 17 & 18 Vic. c. 90.
10. *The Colonial Laws of Massachusetts* (Boston, 1889), p. 78. The maximum rate in 1623 was 8 percent. Pretended legislation of the Commonwealth, reducing the rate to 6 percent, was enacted in 1660 (12 Car. II, c. 13), and a further reduction to 5 percent followed in 1713 (12 Ann. c. 16).
11. R. B. Morris, *Government and Labor in Early America* (New York, 1946), pp. 57-61, 70-74; J. Dorfman, *The Economic Mind,* I, 44-46.
12. J. Winthrop, *The History of New England* (ed. by J. K. Hosmer, New York, 1908-9), I, 315-18; II, 8; J. Dorfman, *The Economic Mind,* I, 47; B. M. Levy, *Preaching in the First Half Century of New England History* (Hartford, 1945), p. 63. See J. Calvin, *Institutes,* II, viii, 45-46. The text of the sermon was I Cor. 5:11: "But now I have written unto you not to keep company, if any man that is called a brother be a fornicator, or covetous, or an idolater, or a railer, or a drunkard, or an extortioner; with such an one, no, not to eat." (A.V.)
13. J. Winthrop, *The History of New England,* I, 317-18; Boston First Ch. Recs., III, 12-14 (1640). Winthrop's reference to a later excommunication (I, 386, n.) is not found in the church records.
14. Boston First Ch. Recs., III, 13 (1640); Roxbury Recs., I, 83, 187 (1642).
15. Boston First Ch. Recs., I, 89-90 (1648).
16. *Ibid.,* I, 69, 78 (1644-46); *ibid.,* I, 78, 82 (1645-46).
17. Reading Recs., I, 97-99 (1752-53). See Millbury Recs., II, 64 (1829), for a suspension for "divers acts of dishonesty," which

could mean anything, and Framingham Recs., I, 159-66 (1770). Also see Needham Recs., I, 23 (1738), for an appropriation of twenty shillings for a flagon, concluding: "No usury to be paid."

18. Reading Recs., I, 28 (1702); Sutton Recs., I, 8-9 (1737).
19. Peru Recs., I, 109-14 (1783-85); Pittsfield Recs., I, 315 (1784).
20. Worthington Recs., I, 50 (1829).
21. Danvers Recs., I, 135-36 (1834). Similar cases, but not as clearly described, are in Montague Recs., Vol. I (1816-18); Pittsfield Recs., II, 59-62 (1818-19); Lenox Recs., Vol. I (1835); Palmer Recs., II, 146 (1835); Worthington Recs., I, 57 (1836).
22. Lenox Recs., Vol. I (1774). There is a sudden break in the record, perhaps because of the Revolution.
23. Worthington Recs., I, 36-37 (1806).
24. Peru Recs., II, 22-23 (1826-27).
25. North Andover Recs., Vol. I (1740-43); Lenox Recs., Vol. I (1809); Charlemont Recs., Vol. I (1809).
26. Pittsfield Recs., II, 28-32, 73-76 (1821-22).
27. Boston Second Ch. Recs., III, 25-28 (1675).
28. Westfield Recs., I, 127 (1685).
29. Sutton Recs., I, 210 (1757).
30. Boston First Ch. Recs., II, 65 (1698).
31. Worthington Recs., I, 19-24, 37-38 (1789-90, 1806, 1811).
32. Becket Recs., I, 22 (1772).
33. Danvers Recs., I, 144-45 (no date, probably about 1840).
34. In addition to the cases discussed below, see Barnstable West Ch. Recs., II, 41 (1644-46), and Boston First Ch. Recs., I, 81 (1646), which resulted in excommunications, and *ibid.*, I, 107 (1657), resulting in an admonition. Also see Beverly Recs., II, 27 (1677); Roxbury Recs., I, 99 (1686); Boston Second Ch. Recs., Vol. IV (1697), and *ibid.*, Vol. IV (1698), for thefts later in the century.
35. Boston First Ch. Recs., III, 9.
36. *Ibid.*, I, 72-76 (1644-45).
37. *Ibid.*, I, 91 (1683); *ibid.*, I, 15 (1692).
38. In addition to the cases discussed below, see Dorchester Recs., I, 88-89 (1682), for the excommunication of an impenitent horse thief.
39. Beverly Recs., II, 16-17 (1668).

40. Salem Recs., I, 258, 279-80 (1657-79).
41. Danvers Recs., I, 4-5 (1690).
42. Quincy Recs., I, 483-84 (1683).
43. In addition to the cases discussed below, the following cases involve thieves: Middleborough First Ch. Recs., Vol. I (1713); Westfield Recs., I, 154 (1731); *ibid.,* I, 154 (1742) (a couple); *ibid.,* I, 159 (1765); Quincy Recs., I, 487 (1728); *ibid.,* I, 498 (1733) (a Negro woman); Scituate Recs., I, 44 (1748); Northampton Recs., I, 25 (1765).
44. Haverhill First Ch. Recs., I, 57-58 (1726). No further record has been found.
45. Kingston Recs., I, 17-18 (1756-57).
46. Sutton Recs., I, 12 (1737); Haverhill First Ch. Recs., I, 101 (1763).
47. See notes 44 and 45; also Reading Recs., I, 82 (1742); Great Barrington Recs., I, 225 (1757).
48. Boston Hollis St. Ch. Recs., Vol. II (1748). Lewdness and lying may have aggravated the guilt incurred by the theft.
49. Chelsea Recs., I, 203-4 (1719). See *ibid.,* I, 204, for a complaint by Skinner alleging perjury. The record is vague and mentions no verdict.
50. Great Barrington Recs., I, 225 (1753).
51. Deerfield Recs., II, 65-67, 140.
52. Millbury Recs., II, 23-26, 32 (1774-79).
53. Framingham Recs., II, 281 (1795).
54. Sutton Recs., I, 41 (1777); Millbury Recs., II, 151 (1778); Deerfield Recs., II, 67 (1782); Northampton Recs., I, 32 (1789); Worthington Recs., I, 9 (1798); Sandisfield Recs., I, 3 (1799).
55. Sutton Recs., I, 50 (1791).
56. Barnstable East Ch. Recs., I, 95 (1775-76).
57. Sheffield Recs., II, 232-33 (1799-1800).
58. Peabody Recs., I, 22-25 (1807); Granville West Ch. Recs., I, 19-21 (1813-14).
59. Bradford Recs., I, 19-21 (1828-29).
60. *Ibid.,* II, 12-13 (1825); Danvers Recs., I, 145-47 (1837); Falmouth Recs., II, 129, 136, (1810, 1819).
61. Charlemont Recs., I, 36-38 (1800); Amherst Recs., II, 136-37 (1838).
62. Stockbridge Recs., II, 125-27 (1820); Pittsfield Recs., II, 108, 123 (1823-28).

63. Falmouth Recs., II, 129 (1810); Danvers Recs., I, 121 (1817); Barre Recs., I, 164 (1843).
64. Egremont Recs., I, 9 (1771).
65. Boston First Ch. Recs., II, 45.
66. Boston Second Ch. Recs., VI, 28-29 (1743).
67. Sutton Recs., I, 45-50 (1784-91); Brewster Recs., I, 159 (1780).
68. Sutton Recs., I, 21, 30 (1750, 1761).
69. Roxbury Recs., I, 95-96 (1681-83).
70. Amherst Recs., I, 131-37 (1838).
71. A half century before these cases arose, Cotton Mather preached against runaway slaves and urged the return of such fugitives to their masters. *Diary of Cotton Mather* (Boston, 1911-12), I, 177.
72. Westfield Recs., I, 156-57, 193.
73. *Ibid.*, I, 157, 193.

Chapter XII: The Churches as Courts of Law

1. I Cor. 6:1. From the Revised Standard Version of the Bible, copyrighted 1946 and 1952.
2. J. Calvin, *Institutes of the Christian Religion,* IV, xx, 18.
3. J. B. Felt, *The Ecclesiastical History of New England* (Boston, 1855-62), I, 236.
4. Boston First Ch. Recs., I, 93.
5. Kingston Recs., I, 18 (1757).
6. Concord Recs., I, 96-98 (1760).
7. Barnstable East Ch. Recs., II, 95-96 (1780).
8. Pittsfield Recs., I, 316.
9. Charlemont Recs., I, 39 (1804). The question arose when a church member brought suit against a brother. After deciding that he might bring an action because it was not unlawful for Christians to sue their brethren in the courts, the church adopted a resolution, without specific reference to this case, permitting lawsuits. Thus we have a situation, apparently unique in the Massachusetts church records, in which ecclesiastical case law was affirmed, as it were, by ecclesiastical statute law.
10. Lenox Recs., Vol. I.

11. From the standpoint of the churches all state courts, whether of civil or criminal jurisdiction, were "civil courts."
12. C. J. Hilkey, *Legal Development in Massachusetts* (New York, 1910), p. 70; J. Goebel, Jr., "King's Law and Local Custom in Seventeenth Century New England," 30 Col. L. Rev. 437; E. Washburn, *Sketches of the Judicial History of Massachusetts from 1630 to 1775* (Boston, 1840), pp. 48, 61-62; R. B. Morris, *Studies in the History of American Law* (New York, 1930), pp. 49-51. Some idea of the chaotic state of law in seventeenth-century New England may be had from a case cited by Professor Morris. In 1645 a Maine farmer brought an action of *trover* for the unlawful *detention* of land. The jury returned a verdict confirming the plaintiff's title in the property! (*Ibid.*, p. 52.)
13. Salisbury Recs., I, 296-97 (1688).
14. Billerica Recs., I, 43-44, 53 (1764-70).
15. Dalton Recs., I, 24 (1809).
16. Lanesborough Recs., I, 82-83 (1808).
17. Westfield Recs., I, 180. In pre-Commonwealth England, suits for breach of promise to marry were litigated in the ecclesiastical courts. After 1660 assumpsit lay in such cases, but the church courts retained concurrent jurisdiction until the statute of 26 Geo. II, c. 33, s. 13.
18. Falmouth Recs., Vol. I (1738-39).
19. Lincoln Recs., I, 61-62 (1765).
20. Amesbury Recs., II, 479-80 (1757).
21. Pittsfield Recs., I, 309 (1775).
22. Amherst Recs., I, 43-44.
23. Falmouth Recs., I, 114-27 (1785-87).
24. Middleborough First Ch. Recs., I, 39, 59 (1769-1803); *ibid.*, I, 39 (1772); Groton Recs., II, 11-12 (1770); Stockbridge Recs., I, 82 (1781); Plymouth Recs., I, 265-66 (1785); Charlemont Recs., I, 42 (1808).
25. Peru Recs., II, 19-20 (1823).
26. Salem Recs., I, 325 (1683).
27. Reading Recs., I, 13 (between 1670 and 1685); Charlestown Recs., I, xiv (1688); Kingston Recs., I, 11 (1721); Sutton Recs., I, 31 (1766); Weston Recs., II, 48 (1766); Plymouth Recs., I, 339-40, 356-62 (1771-82); *ibid.*, II, 160 (1824); Worthington

Recs., I, 29-31 (1786-87); *ibid.*, I, 38 (1810); *ibid.*, I, 48 (1820); *ibid.*, I, 48 (1821); Granville East Ch. Recs., I, 109-10 (1820-21).

28. Brewster Recs., I, 89 (1748); Concord Recs., I, 152 (1775); Sutton Recs., I, 47 (1785).
29. Barre Recs., I, 8 (1768).
30. Pittsfield Recs., I, 307 (1769); Amherst Recs., I, 117 (1788).
31. Merrimac Recs., Vol. I (1732-33).
32. Complaints dismissed: Concord Recs., I, 6 (1740); Stockbridge Recs., I, 82-84 (1781). Application refused: Sutton Recs., I, 49-50 (1736).
33. Verse 1 reads: "Behold, how good and how pleasant it is for brethren to dwell together in unity." (A.V.)
34. Needham Recs., I, 26-27 (1736).
35. Westfield Recs., I, 125-26 (1682).
36. Salisbury Recs., I, 22-23 (1702); Canton Recs., I, 45-46 (1736); Lanesborough Recs., I, 63-64 (1779). Cf. Canton Recs., I, 55-56 (1741), where the church first voted, over the pastor's objection, to try a title, but then refused to take jurisdiction. See Westfield Recs., I, 192 (1743), an almost illegible record concerning a land question.
37. Reading Recs., I, 7-8 (1663); Natick Recs., I, 8-9 (1731).
38. An Edgartown case, in Barnstable East Ch. Recs., I, 51 (1748).
39. Boxford Recs., II, 31-36 (1743-52).
40. Sutton Recs., I, 24-27 (1753-55).
41. Stockbridge Recs., I, 93 (1807).
42. Peru Recs., I, 151-55 (1801-2).
43. Amherst Recs., III, 64.
44. The entire case to this point is recorded in *ibid.*, III, 53-73 (1821).
45. *Ibid.*, III, 85-97 (1825-28).
46. *Ibid.*, III, 102 (1833). Another possibility is this: the church rejected the council's recommendation and waited five years for Smith to make a more extensive confession, or Smith refused to make the confession recommended by the council and, after five years, was excommunicated.
47. Lanesborough Recs., I, 100 (1827).
48. Hatfield Recs., I, 99-104 (1843). No further record of this case is found for the period to 1853.

49. Plymouth Recs., I, 380-81 (1793). The records fail to indicate the final result. The case may have been settled privately.
50. Other than assault and slander, which are discussed separately.
51. Needham Recs., I, 21-23 (1728-30).
52. But see T. F. T. Plucknett, *A Concise History of the Common Law* (4th ed., London, 1948), p. 640, on common law actions for specific performance.
53. South Hadley Recs., Vol. I (1790-91). The church accepted the council's advice. Probably the officer made the required confession; his name is subsequently found as a member in good standing.
54. *Ibid.*, Vol. I (1744-45).
55. Lanesborough Recs., I, 63-72 (1779-82).
56. Needham Recs., I, 33 (1749); Northampton Recs., I, 38 (1791); Peru Recs., I, 111-12, 117-20 (1784-92).
57. Concord Recs., I, 81-85 (1754-55).

Chapter XIII: The Churches and the State

1. S. Brockunier, *The Irrepressible Democrat* (New York, 1940), pp. 41-57; M. Calamadrei, "Neglected Aspects of Roger Williams' Thought," *Church History,* XXI (1952), 239-56; P. Miller, *Roger Williams* (Indianapolis and New York, 1953), p. 19; P. Miller, *Orthodoxy in Massachusetts* (Cambridge, 1933), pp. 157-59.
2. C. M. Andrews, *The Colonial Period of American History* (New Haven, 1934), I, 472.
3. S. Brockunier, *The Irrepressible Democrat,* pp. 58-65, 76. The official record of the sentence, found in N. B. Shurtleff, ed., *Records of the Governor and Company of the Massachusetts Bay* (Boston, 1853-54), I, 160-61, is vague. Williams was convicted of writing defamatory letters which he would not recant, and of "dyvers newe and original opinions," which could mean anything.
4. P. Miller, *Roger Williams,* p. 93.
5. M. Calamandrei, "Neglected Aspects of Roger Williams' Thought," *Church History,* XXI, 242, 256; P. Miller, *Roger Williams,* pp. 27-28, 254-57.

6. P. Miller, *Roger Williams, passim,* esp. pp. 19, 32-48, 53-56, 82, 85, 106, 169, 194-95, 255; M. Calamandrei, "Neglected Aspects of Roger Williams' Thought," *Church History,* XXI, 254.
7. M. Calamandrei, "Neglected Aspects of Roger Williams' Thought," *Church History,* XXI, 247, 252-53; P. Miller, *Roger Williams, passim,* esp. pp. 29, 83, 107-10, 118, 139, 145, 169-70, 245, 256; J. Dorfman, *The Economic Mind in American Civilization* (New York, 1946), I, 70. Ironically, the danger which Williams saw in the church-state relationship in Massachusetts is now a cause of concern to some members of the church from which Williams first turned away. See C. F. Garbett, *Church and State in England* (London, 1950), pp. 314-16.
8. S. Brockunier, *The Irrepressible Democrat,* pp. 83-85.
9. A Salem case, in Plymouth Recs., I, 65 (date not mentioned but known to be 1638); J. B. Felt, *The Ecclesiastical History of New England* (Boston, 1855-62), I, 380.
10. In civil cases, jurors could be challenged *for cause.* C. J. Hilkey, *Legal Development in Massachusetts* (New York, 1910), p. 78.
11. Salem Recs., Vol. III (between 1637 and 1640).
12. Dorchester Recs., I, 51-52 (1666); *ibid.,* I, 69 (1675).
13. Roxbury Recs., I, 93 (1678).
14. Boston Second Ch. Recs., Vol. IV.
15. *Ibid.,* Vol. IV (1711).
16. Framingham Recs., I, 159-66 (1770).
17. Reading Recs., I, 129.
18. Becket Recs., I, 22-23 (1775). The offensive sermon was delivered in July, 1774, but the case was not tried until October, 1775. Crane's confession implies a breach of the Sabbath, but the underlying issue was the Bliss-Hunn problem.
19. A. M. Baldwin, *The New England Clergy and the American Revolution* (Durham, 1928), pp. 170-71.
20. Groton Recs., II, 14 (1775); S. A. Green, *Three Historical Addresses at Groton* (Groton, 1908), pp. 55-56; F. L. Weis, *The Colonial Churches and the Colonial Clergy of New England* (Lancaster, Mass., 1936), p. 68.
21. Plymouth Recs., I, 349.
22. The entire case is recorded in *ibid.,* I, 345-52.

23. *Ibid.*, I, 353.
24. Lanesborough Recs., I, 60-61 (1779). Another confession, in Kingston Recs., I, 20 (1781), merely alludes to "some matters of a civil and political nature."
25. Barre Recs., I, 29-43 (1787-91). The record does not expressly mention Shays's Rebellion or the Petersham incident, in which General Lincoln dispersed the rebellious mob, but mentions "a disturbance of last winter relative to our public affairs." This, together with the confession, clearly points to Shays's Rebellion. Unfortunately it was not possible to locate the Petersham records for that period. In his confession Mills said, in part: "I would wish to do everything in my power . . . to heal the difficulties among us—and am willing to confess that in matters of Government and of a civil nature I have acted with too great a degree of Zeal as I should not do if I was to act the part again." *Ibid.*, I, 43.
26. Canton Recs., I, 186.
27. Pittsfield Recs., II, 75 (1822).

Chapter XIV: The Enjoyment of Time and Worldly Pleasures

1. J. Calvin, *Institutes of the Christian Religion,* III, x, 1-6.
2. W. Brigham, ed., *The Compact, with the Charter and Laws of the Colony of New Plymouth* (Boston, 1836), p. 64; Mass. Code, 1660, pp. 3, 38, in *The Colonial Laws of Massachusetts* (Boston, 1889), pp. 123, 158. New England was not alone in enacting such laws; the manpower shortage was felt in other colonies as well. See R. B. Morris, *Government and Labor in Early America* (New York, 1946), pp. 5-8; T. J. Wertenbaker, *The Puritan Oligarchy* (New York, 1947), pp. 167-68.
3. C. Mather, *Diary of Cotton Mather* (Boston, 1911-12), I, 584.
4. *Ibid.*, II, 80.
5. J. Calvin, *Institutes,* II, viii, 45; I. Mather, *The Doctrine of Divine Providence Proved* (Boston, 1684), p. 98; J. T. McNeill, *Modern Christian Movements* (Philadelphia, 1954), pp. 42-43.
6. Quoted in E. D. Hanscom, *The Heart of the Puritan* (New York, 1917), p. 263.
7. Barnstable West Ch. Recs., II, 41.

8. Boston First Ch. Recs., I, 105.
9. North Andover Recs., Vol. I (1729).
10. Concord Recs., I, 143-47, 164-65, 178-79, 192-97 (1774-91).
11. Otis Recs., I, 43-47 (1814-16).
12. C. E. Whiting, *Studies in English Puritanism from the Restoration to the Revolution, 1660-1688* (London, 1931), pp. 444-45; M. M. Knappen, *Tudor Puritanism* (Chicago, 1939), p. 437; J. T. McNeill, *Modern Christian Movements,* pp. 43-48.
13. Quoted in E. D. Hanscom, *The Heart of the Puritan,* p. 182. C. E. Whiting, in *Studies in English Puritanism,* p. 445, portrays the Puritan as thoroughly hostile to the theatre; M. M. Knappen, in *Tudor Puritanism,* pp. 439-40, takes a more moderate view. For a sociological rather than theological interpretation of the Puritan position on amusements, see T. C. Hall, *The Religious Background of American Culture* (Boston, 1930), pp. 89-90.
14. Boston First Ch. Recs., III, 12 (1639).
15. M. M. Knappen, *Tudor Puritanism,* pp. 437-38.
16. J. T. McNeill, *A History of the Cure of Souls* (New York, 1951), p. 264.
17. W. B. Weeden, *Economic and Social History of New England* (Boston and New York, 1890), I, 423; II, 696.
18. C. Mather, *Diary of Cotton Mather,* II, 144.
19. Mass. Code, 1660, p. 33, in *The Colonial Laws of Massachusetts,* p. 153.
20. W. Brigham, ed., *The Compact, with the Charter and Laws of the Colony of New Plymouth,* p. 101.
21. *Ibid.,* p. 64; Mass. Code, 1660, p. 38, in *The Colonial Laws of Massachusetts,* p. 158.
22. H. B. Parkes, "Morals and Law Enforcement in Colonial New England," *New England Quarterly,* V (1932), 438.
23. J. Cotton to R. Levett, in E. D. Hanscom, *The Heart of the Puritan,* p. 177.
24. I. Mather, *A Testimony against Several Prophane and Superstitious Customs* (Boston, 1688).
25. C. Mather, *Diary of Cotton Mather,* I, 202.
26. Deerfield Recs., II, 135.
27. Boston Second Ch. Recs., Vol. IV (1669).
28. Confessions: Charlemont Recs., I, 30 (1797); Plymouth Recs.,

II, 535-36 (1799). No further action: Plymouth Recs., II, 535-36 (1799-1819).

29. Pittsfield Recs., II, 59-62; II, 160-61.
30. Becket Recs., II, 66-69.
31. M. M. Knappen, *Tudor Puritanism,* pp. 437-38; J. Cotton to R. Levett, in E. D. Hanscom, *The Heart of the Puritan,* p. 177. See J. T. McNeill, *Modern Christian Movements,* pp. 46-47.
32. W. R. Bliss, *Side Glimpses from the Colonial Meeting House* (Boston and New York, 1894), pp. 134-35. The text reads:

    The Lord said:

    "Because the daughters of Zion are haughty,
    and walk with outstretched necks,
    glancing wantonly with their eyes,
    Mincing along as they go,
    tinkling with their feet;
    The Lord will smite with a scab
    the heads of the daughters of Zion,
    and the Lord will lay bare their private parts."

    From the Revised Standard Version of the Bible, copyrighted 1946 and 1952.
33. Quoted in E. D. Hanscom, *The Heart of the Puritan,* p. 179.
34. T. J. Wertenbaker, *The Puritan Oligarchy,* pp. 176-77.
35. Stockbridge Recs., I, 80 (1778). See Great Barrington Recs., I, 233 (1825), for a vote concerning "the amusements of the ballroom." The complete record was not made available.
36. Stockbridge Recs., I, 83, 88 (1782-90). See Isaac Marsh's tavern record (MS, Stockbridge Library) for this entry: "To pint of rum by Mrs. Morgan—2s6d, 25 Nov. 1782." Perhaps the rum was consumed at this dance.
37. Great Barrington Recs., I, 226 (1772-74).
38. Danvers Recs., I, 151-54.
39. Boston First Ch. Recs., III, 13 (1646); Roxbury Recs., I, 95 (1681).
40. Otis Recs., I, 31-32.
41. Dedham Recs., I, 6-7, 24-25, 28.
42. J. B. Felt, *The Ecclesiastical History of New England* (Boston, 1855-62), I, 380.
43. Roxbury Recs., I, 95-98 (1683), resulting in a confession; Boston

First Ch. Recs., II, 45 (1691), resulting in excommunication; Westfield Recs., I, 154.

44. Boston Second Ch. Recs., Vol. IV.
45. Barnstable East Ch. Recs., I, 171.
46. See B. M. Levy, *Preaching in the First Half Century of New England History* (Hartford, 1945), p. 42.
47. J. Edwards, "Some Thoughts concerning the Present Revival of Religion," *Works* (New York, 1829), IV, 185-86.

Chapter XV: The Unattained Utopia

1. T. J. Wertenbaker, *The Puritan Oligarchy* (New York, 1947), p. 177; G. B. Boardman, *A History of the New England Theology* (New York, 1899), p. 19. See B. Levy, *Preaching in the First Half Century of New England History* (Hartford, 1945), p. 54.
2. T. J. Wertenbaker, *The Puritan Oligarchy,* pp. 180-82.
3. Quoted in S. Fleming, *Children and Puritanism* (New Haven, 1933), p. 11. Quoted by permission of the Yale University Press.
4. C. Mather, *Diary of Cotton Mather* (Boston, 1911-12), I, 214-15.
5. Plymouth Recs., I, 274 (1692).
6. *Ibid.,* I, 336-37 (1770).
7. Egremont Recs., I, 12-13 (1775).
8. See Appendix, Table IX. The numbers in fornication cases deviate from those in Table VI because they represent *persons* censured, rather than the number of *cases.* In Table IX cases involving couples were counted as involving two persons.
9. See Appendix, Table X.
10. S. Fleming, *Children and Puritanism,* p. 143.
11. Parts of the records have been mutilated and some extant entries are illegible or severely faded. Another reason for the absence of cases (except two) between 1730 and 1749 may be the fact that the church voted in 1740 to delegate disciplinary authority to a committee, and all such authority was delegated to a committee created in 1748. These committees may have kept separate records.

12. J. Tracy, *A History of the Revival of Religion in the Time of Edwards and Whitefield* (Boston, 1845), p. 186.
13. *Ibid.,* p. 91.
14. *Ibid.,* p. 93.
15. *Ibid.,* pp. 162-65; F. G. Beardsley, *A History of American Revivals* (Boston and New York, 1904), p. 28.
16. F. G. Beardsley, *A History of American Revivals,* p. 28.
17. J. Tracy, *A History of the Revival,* p. 142.
18. *Ibid.,* p. 101.
19. The large number of cases in Canton (Appendix, Table VI) cannot be evaluated in relation to the Great Awakening, since the records begin in 1727 and hence cannot be compared with those of a sufficient number of years before the Awakening. The records of the other churches affected by revivals are either too incomplete to permit a reliable analysis or are incomplete or missing for the relevant years.
20. See Appendix, Table VI; Quincy Recs. *passim.* Note that the minister's record ends in 1744; the few cases of later dates are recorded in the parish records, which have been published along with those of the church.
21. C. F. Adams, "Some Phases of Sexual Morality and Church Discipline in Colonial New England," *Proceedings of the Massachusetts Historical Society,* 2nd Ser., VI (1891), 497-503. It should be noted that Adams made no claim to be able to prove this point. He offered it as a working hypothesis and conceded his inability to substantiate it.
22. H. B. Parkes, "Sexual Morality and the Great Awakening," *The New England Quarterly,* III (1930), 133-35.
23. H. B. Parkes, "Morals and Law Enforcement in Colonial New England," *ibid.,* V (1932), 431-52.
24. As stated in the latter article.
25. Westfield Recs., I, 156 (1741 or 1742).
26. C. F. Adams, "Some Phases of Sexual Morality," *Proceedings of the Massachusetts Historical Society,* 2nd Ser., VI, 502.
27. W. Walker, *A History of the Congregational Churches in the United States* (New York, 1894), p. 319. Cf. S. Fleming, *Children and Puritanism,* pp. 13-14.
28. See Appendix, Table VIII.
29. See Appendix, Table II.

30. See Appendix, Tables I-III.
31. S. Fleming, *Children and Puritanism,* pp. 14-16. For an interesting first hand narrative of the effects of the revival on one church, see the Reverend Oliver Cobb's "Account of the Reformation, 1807-8," Rochester Recs., I, 8-19 (1810).
32. See Appendix, Table III.
33. See Appendix, Table XI.
34. Chelsea Recs., III, 71.
35. Plymouth Recs., II, 586-88 (1816, 1834).
36. Middleborough North Ch. Recs., III, 11.
37. I.e., Barnstable, Essex, Middlesex, Norfolk, Plymouth, and Suffolk counties. No records for this period have been found in Bristol County, and none at all in Dukes and Nantucket counties.
38. Falmouth Recs., II, 137 (1820).
39. Haverhill First Ch. Recs., II, 115-20; Marblehead First Ch. Recs. *passim*; Danvers Recs., I, 118-50 *passim.*
40. Danvers Recs., I, 115-17 (1837), and I, 135-36 (1834).
41. *Ibid.,* I, 151-52 (1840), and I, 158 (1842); Haverhill First Ch. Recs., I, 129-35 (1832-35).
42. Cambridge Recs., I, 351; *ibid.,* I, 389-94.
43. Reading Recs., I, 207-8.
44. *Ibid.,* I, 153.
45. Northampton Recs., I, 44-49; Amherst Recs., II, 77; *ibid.,* II, 131-37.
46. Worthington Recs., I, 50 (1828).
47. Pittsfield Recs., II, 161.
48. *Ibid.,* II, 119 (1837); II, 159-60 (1840); II, 171 (1853).
49. Lenox Recs., Vol. I (1853).
50. Pittsfield Recs., II, 171, 183-85 (1853); *ibid.,* I, 190-91 (1858).
51. MS in Stockbridge Library.
52. J. Mitchell, *A Guide to the Principles of the Congregational Churches of New England* (Northampton, 1838), pp. 75-137 *passim.*
53. These manuals are listed in the bibliographical essay.
54. [L. Woods], *Report on Congregationalism* (Boston, 1846).
55. *Ibid.,* p. 37.
56. P. Cummings, *A Dictionary of Congregational Usages and Principles* (Boston, 1853), p. 2.

57. A. H. Ross, *A Pocket Manual of Congregationalism* (Chicago, 1883), pp. 94-101.
58. G. M. Boynton, *The Congregational Way* (New York, etc., 1903), pp. 78-80.
59. W. E. Barton, *The Law of Congregational Usage* (Chicago, 1916), pp. 331-36.
60. O. E. Maurer, ed., *Manual of the Congregational Christian Churches* (Boston, 1951), p. 54.
61. Remington v. Congdon, 2 Pick. (19 Mass.) 310, at 313 (1824).
62. Farnsworth v. Storrs, 5 Cush. (59 Mass.) 412 (1847). In York v. Pease, 2 Gray (68 Mass.) 282 (1854), an action brought against the respondent in a church trial, who had attempted to show that the plaintiff in the civil suit bore a grudge against the defendant, the court followed the Farnsworth case. See Barros v. Bell, 7 Gray (73 Mass.) 301 (1856), in which the right of medical society to hear complaints against members was upheld on the strength of Farnsworth v. Storrs.
63. Fitzgerald v. Robinson, 112 Mass. 371 (1873). In this case, an action against a Roman Catholic priest who had announced an excommunication, the trial court sustained the defendant's demurrers. The judgment was sustained in part, but three counts, wherein the plaintiff alleged that the priest had accused the plaintiff of maintaining a house of prostitution, were held valid. See Morasse v. Brochu, 151 Mass. 526 (1890), affirming a trial court's judgment for $1,500 against a Roman Catholic priest who, in announcing an excommunication, had inflicted professional injury on the excommunicate, a physician, and had referred to him as "vermin."
64. Bouldin v. Alexander, 15 Wall. 131 (1872). Cf. First English Lutheran Church of Oklahoma City v. Evangelical Lutheran Synod of Kansas and Adjacent States, 135 F. 2d 701 (C.C.A. 10th, 1943), and Taylor v. Jackson, 273 F. 345 (App. D.C., 1921). A classical case on the subject is Watson v. Jones, 13 Wall. 679 (1871), but it should be remembered that no Federal question was raised in the case; the Federal courts derived jurisdiction from diversity of citizenship. See Shannon v. Frost, 2 B. Monroe (Ky. App., 1842), which was cited by the Supreme Court in the opinion in the Watson case.
65. U. S. ex rel. Johnson v. First Colored Baptist Church, 13 F. 2d

296 (App. D.C., 1926). See also the cases in notes 64 and 66, and Carter v. Papineau, 222 Mass. 464 (1916), in which the court, relying on the Farnsworth case, ruled that the exclusion of a communicant of the Episcopal Church from receiving Holy Communion was not actionable. Suits against the local rector and the bishop of Western Massachusetts were dismissed.

66. Satterlee v. U. S. ex rel. Williams, 20 App. D.C. 393 (1902). The Episcopal bishop of Washington had convened a court pursuant to canon law for the trial of Gilbert F. Williams, presbyter, on charges of what amounted to rape. Convicted by the court and deposed by the bishop, Williams petitioned for a writ of certiorari, requiring the ecclesiastical body to submit the record of the trial for review. Justifying its decision in a fantastic opinion, the court issued the writ. The decision was reversed by an appellate court, which ordered the court below to dismiss the petition on the ground that a civil court of common law jurisdiction had no authority to review an ecclesiastical judgment on certiorari.

67. See J. Haroutunian, *Piety versus Moralism* (New York, 1932), pp. 89-90; T. C. Hall, *The Religious Background of American Culture* (Boston, 1930), p. 99.

68. J. Calvin, *Institutes of the Christian Religion,* I, i; J. T. McNeill, *The History and Character of Calvinism* (New York, 1954), pp. 138-39, 214-18; J. T. McNeill, *Modern Christian Movements* (Philadelphia, 1954), p. 12.

69. See S. F. Bayne, Jr., *The Optional God* (New York, 1953), pp. 126-29, for an excellent discussion of the conflict between the church spirit and the sect spirit. See E. Morgan, *The Puritan Family* (Boston, 1944), pp. 94, 101.

70. The terminology found in the records offers a clue in this connection. The usual statement closing a case in which the offender made a confession is "he was restored," or an equivalent phrase. There are, however, *particularly in the seventeenth century,* several statements like "he was absolved," or "the sentence of absolution [was pronounced]," which imply reconciliation with God rather than restoration to some status in a visible society. Such expressions are found in Charlestown Recs., I, iii (1664), v (1670), xi (1671), xii (1674); Salem Recs., I, 268 (1666); Roxbury Recs., I, 209 (1781), and I, 93

(1682); Beverly Recs., IV, 25 (1676); Dorchester Recs., I, 114 (1697); Quincy Recs., I, 482 (1698); Milton Recs., I, 26 (1701); Danvers Recs., I, 47 (1707); Northampton Recs., I, 25 (1711); and Westfield Recs., I, 136 (1712). An unexpected late use of this term appears in Northampton Recs., III, 34 (1782). The use of these terms is not particularly surprising. Alexander Henderson, in *Government and Order of the Church of Scotland* (Edinburgh, 1641), p. 45, refers to "the sentence of absolution," and in early Scottish practice the pastor said to the penitent: "I absolve thee." Such absolution, however, was dependent on sincere repentance and was not a merely mechanical act. See J. T. McNeill, *A History of the Cure of Souls* (New York, 1951), pp. 250, 326.

71. See R. Bronkema, *The Essence of Puritanism* (Goes, Holland, [1930?]), pp. 139-45; H. R. Niebuhr, *The Kingdom of God in America* (Chicago and New York, 1937), pp. 62-63. Cf. J. T. McNeill, *Modern Christian Movements* (Philadelphia, 1954), p. 39.
72. See J. A. Doyle, *English Colonies in America* (New York, 1889), II, 3; R. B. Perry, *Puritanism and Democracy* (New York, 1944), p. 243.
73. M. B. Johnstone, *When God Says "No"* (New York, 1954), pp. 135, 160. Quoted by permission of Mrs. Johnstone.
74. *Ibid.*, p. 160. The biblical passage read by Mrs. Johnstone was Matt. 7:1-5, from the Revised Standard Version.
75. Barnstable West Ch. Recs., Vol. I (date missing, probably before 1641).
76. Egremont Recs., I, 5 (1770).
77. J. Shepard, *Two Sermons Preached at Lynn* (1711), pp. 9, 57, quoted in O. Winslow, *Meetinghouse Hill* (New York, 1952), p. 96.
78. See V. L. Parrington, *Main Currents in American Thought* (New York, 1927), I, 107-11. Parrington thought that Cotton Mather was "an attractive subject for the psychoanalyst."
79. C. Mather, *Diary of Cotton Mather* (Boston, 1911-12), *passim.*
80. H. R. Niebuhr, *The Kingdom of God in America,* p. 171. Professor Richard Niebuhr also observes that Mather identified the kingdom of God with the institutional church, and that for him Christ's reign had become a habit. *Ibid.,* p. 171.

81. C. Mather, *Diary of Cotton Mather,* I, 338.
82. From the exposition of Luke 18:10-14, by George Arthur Buttrick, in *The Interpreter's Bible* (New York and Nashville, 1952), VIII, 308-10. By permission of the Abingdon Press.
83. *Ibid.,* VIII, 309.
84. S. F. Bayne, *The Optional God,* p. 141. By permission of the Oxford University Press.
85. H. R. Niebuhr, *The Kingdom of God in America,* p. 172. See J. T. McNeill, *Modern Christian Movements,* p. 21.
86. P. Miller, *The New England Mind: The Seventeenth Century* (New York, 1939), p. 45; M. M. Knappen, *Tudor Puritanism* (Chicago, 1939), p. 342.
87. This was not an exclusively Puritan notion. On rigorism in the early Church see K. E. Kirk, *The Vision of God* (London, 1931), pp. 229-334. A limerick, found in A. L. Drummond, *Story of American Protestantism* (Edinburgh and London, 1949), p. 183, n., may be relevant here:

    There was a young lady of Lynn,
    Who was deep in original sin.
      When they said, "Do be good!"
      She said, "Would if I could,"
    And straightway was at it again.

88. G. Aulen, *The Faith of the Christian Church* (translated from the 4th Swedish ed. by E. H. Wahlstrom and G. E. Arden, Philadelphia, 1948), p. 102.
89. Luther to Melanchthon, August 1, 1521, in *Briefwechsel* (Weimar, 1931), II, 370 (no. 424). A translation into English, via German, may be found in J. Koestlin, *The Theology of Luther* (translated from the 2nd German ed. by C. E. Hay, Philadelphia, 1897), II, 470. See D. F. Kaltenbusch, "Luthers pecca fortiter," *Studien zur systematischen Theologie* (Tubingen, 1918), pp. 50-72, and K. Holl, *Gesammelte Aufsätze zur Kirchengeschichte* (Tubingen, 1921), 200, n., and 201, n. Holl translates *fortiter* as *herzhaft,* heartily.
90. H. W. Schneider, *The Puritan Mind* (New York, 1930), pp. 36, 74.
91. See T. J. Wertenbaker, *The Puritan Oligarchy,* pp. 340-42; E. Morgan, *The Puritan Family* (Boston, 1944), p. 94.

Bibliographical Essay

A. Church Records

The most valuable source of information for the study of church discipline is without doubt the records of the churches. Some of the problems involved in the search for, and the use of, these records have been discussed in the introduction. In this section, the records consulted are listed, and certain situations which require fuller explanation are discussed.

Unfortunately there is no bibliography of the records of the Congregational and Unitarian churches in Massachusetts. The provincialism and ancestor worship of New England have, however, stimulated the production of hundreds of local histories. These are for the most part antiquarian chronicles, largely consisting of quotations from older books, letters, and records, held together by a line or two of comment. Nearly every church which can claim colonial origin has been honored by some sort of publication, often a reprint of an "historical discourse" which would lull the average listener of today to sleep. Nevertheless, these chronicles and discourses are sometimes useful in furnishing clues to the old records. A helpful bibliography of these writings is C. A. Flagg, *A Guide to Massachusetts Local History* (Salem, 1907), which makes no attempt, however, to furnish a complete list of church records or histories. Some bibliographical and statistical data on the churches in Essex County may be found in *Contributions to the Ecclesiastical History of Essex County* (Boston, 1865). Perhaps the most useful, if antiquated and not now entirely accurate, guide is R. T. Swain, "Churches, Parishes, Precincts, and Religious Societies,

Past and Present, in Massachusetts," in the *Tenth Report of the Commissioner of Public Records* (Boston, 1898).

Published and typescript copies of records have been freely used whenever they appeared to be accurate and complete. For the sake of clarity, no distinction has been made in the footnote references, but the exact nature of the records used may be ascertained from the following list. Among the unpublished collections of church records, the Cooke collection in the Berkshire Athenaeum, Pittsfield, deserves special mention. During the last decade of the nineteenth century Robert Hilyer Cooke, a resident of the Berkshires, copied a variety of local records, including those of churches in western Massachusetts. These copies, now the property of the Berkshire Athenaeum, were transcribed by WPA typists, whose products may be consulted in the local history room of the Athenaeum. Extensive notes based on the original records of the churches in Lenox, Sheffield, and Stockbridge, carefully compared with the Cooke copies and the WPA typescripts, indicate that the latter are complete and accurate, save for an occasional typing error in the WPA copies. In cases of doubt or of unlikely typing errors, the WPA copies, which follow the pagination of the Cooke copies, have been compared with the latter. The one exception is the Great Barrington records. The Cooke manuscript in this case is an abstract rather than a transcript. A request to consult the original records, reportedly extant, was denied.

In the case of some especially useful and well-preserved records, a special note has been added. Particular mention must be made of the records of the Second Church of Boston. Complete for the period since 1673, they are now housed in the library of the Massachusetts Historical Society, Boston. The collection is exceptionally complete and exhaustive, the volumes are carefully numbered, and a rough index is available at the church office. Since these books are the property of the Second Church, permission of the church authorities must be obtained before the custodians will make them available to readers.

In the lists below, the name of the town is stated first, followed by the name or names of the church or churches whose records were consulted. Volumes found to consist entirely of registers, lists, accounts, parish (as distinguished from church) minutes, or other information irrelevant for this project are not listed. The date following the name of the church indicates the year in which the church was founded.[1] Because churches are not always known by their official designation, and because names may be misleading as to a church's denomination,[2] the letters *C* and *U*, following the name of the church, have been used to designate Congregational and Unitarian churches, respectively. Churches now extinct are indicated by the letter *E*.

Under the heading of the church appear the items consulted and cited, the Roman numeral indicating the particular volume. Thus a footnote to the text reading "Boston Second Ch., III, 14," refers to page 14 in the volume indicated by the Roman numeral III under the heading of "Second Church" in the list of Boston churches. No attempt has been made in the notes to assign page numbers in the case of records whose pages were not thus numbered. The years following the designation of the source indicate the scope of the records included in the particular volume, except that in the case of volumes containing minutes extending beyond the period encompassed by this study, the last year for which the volume has been consulted appears in parentheses. Haphazard methods of record-keeping make it impossible to define the scope of all volumes accurately; unless otherwise indicated, the years represent the first and last minutes of church meetings consistently entered.

The absence of any indication concerning the ownership or location of the records indicates that the records are the property of the church and that they are in the custody of the minister, church clerk, secretary, or some other officer. In such cases application for permission to consult the records should be made to the minister, who usually knows where the records are kept. Unless other-

[1] The dates are taken from the Congregational and Unitarian yearbooks. In the few instances where these dates conflicted with information found elsewhere, the best available evidence was followed.

[2] In the case of Marblehead, for instance, a visitor who asked a resident for the location of the Second Congregational Church (which is Unitarian) by its official name might well find himself directed to the First Congregational Church, which is Trinitarian and, therefore, "Congregational" in the popularly accepted sense of the word. To take an even more confusing example, until about 1930 the Congregational Church in Rehoboth was officially known by the impressive name of "The Catholic Congregational Church and Society in the Second Precinct of the Town of Rehoboth," which doubtless stems from the days when, in popular thought, *Catholic* did not connote *Roman* Catholic, and when a Protestant could be a member of the Catholic Church, since *Protestant* and *Catholic* were neither opposites nor mutually exclusive.

wise indicated, volumes which are not in the custody of the church are the property of its custodian. Published records are listed in the customary manner.

Following the list of records consulted are brief comments, arranged by counties, on some of the more important records which are known to be lost, or which could not be located or were not made available. Primary sources other than church records are discussed immediately thereafter.

An asterisk following the description of a source indicates a WPA typescript copy of a manuscript copy by Robert H. Cooke, in the Berkshire Athenaeum, Pittsfield.

AMESBURY. FIRST CHURCH (E). 1618.

I. Extracts from second volume of records, in D. W. Hoyt, *The Old Families of Salisbury and Amesbury, Mass.* (Providence, 1897), Vol. II. Votes, 1733-36, 1757. Most disciplinary cases have been deliberately omitted (*ibid.*, II, 380). The records used by Hoyt are now lost; the earlier ones were missing in 1897 (*ibid.*, I, 28).

——SECOND (Rock Hill) CONGREGATIONAL CHURCH: See Merrimac.

AMHERST. FIRST CONGREGATIONAL CHURCH (C). 1739.

I. "A Book of Church Records," 1741-1820. Church property; at Jones Library, Amherst.

II. Records, 1820-35. Church property; at Jones Library, Amherst.

ANDOVER: See North Andover.

BARNSTABLE. EAST CHURCH (Unitarian Congregational Society) (U). 1725.

I. "Records of the East Parish Congregational Church," 1725-1816 (lacuna: 1797-1809). Church property; in custody of County Treasurer, Barnstable.

II. "Records of the Church in the East Precinct of Barnstable," 1820-(35). Church property; in custody of County Treasurer.

——WEST CHURCH (Congregational Church) (C). 1613.[3]

I. "Records of the West Parish of Barnstable," 1668-1807. Photo-

[3] This date, understandably enough, seems preposterous. It is, however, recognized by the yearbook of the Congregational Churches and by the particular church itself, and is based on the date of the gathering of a church in Europe, whose direct successor the Barnstable church claims to be.

stat. Copies available at New York Historical Society and Boston Public Library.

II. Extracts from "Scituate and Barnstable Church Records," 1634-1702, *New England Historical and Genealogical Register,* X, 37-43, 345-51.

BARRE. FIRST PARISH (U). 1753.

I. Records, 1768-1827.

II. Records, 1827-44.

BECKET. FIRST CONGREGATIONAL CHURCH (C). 1758.

I. "A Book of Records," 1758-1805 (lacuna: 1776-92).*

II. "Records of the Church of Christ in Becket, vol. 22 [*sic*]," 1806-50.*

BEVERLY. FIRST CHURCH (U). 1667.

I. "The First Church Records," 1667-1776, in *Essex Institute Historical Collections,* XXXV, 177-211.

II. *Ibid.,* XXXVI, 141-60, 297-324.

III. *Ibid.,* XLI, 199-226.

IV. "Copy of the First Book of Records." At Essex Institute, Salem.

BILLERICA. THE FIRST PARISH (U). 1663.

I. "A Church Book," 1747-1835. Typescript copy in possession of A. W. Stearns, M.D., of Tufts College, Medford.

II. Records, 1747-1842 (overlapping with I). Typescript copy in possession of Dr. Stearns.

BOSTON (Also see Charlestown, Dorchester, Roxbury, and West Roxbury). FIRST CHURCH (U). 1630.

I. "Records," 1630-87. A copy. Office of City Registrar, Boston.

II. "Records of the First Church, Boston," 1630-1745. A copy. Office of City Registrar.

III. "First Church, Boston. Records," 1630-79. A copy, containing some entries not found in I and II. Massachusetts Historical Society, Boston.

——SECOND (Old North) CHURCH (U). 1649.

All save the current records of this church are at the Massachusetts Historical Society, Boston. They are church property, and permission of the church must be obtained before they may be consulted. This is an exceptionally useful collection; the volumes are systematically numbered, and a rough index is available at the church office. The numbers assigned to the volumes by their custodians have been followed throughout in the footnotes. Volume I was irrelevant and hence is not listed.

II. "Cotton Mather's Book." A copy of III.

III. Records, 1673-85.

IV. Records, 1689-1716.

V. Records, 1717-41.

VI. Records, 1741-1816.

——THIRD (Old South) CHURCH (C). 1669.

I. Records, in H. A. Hill, *History of the Old South Church* (Boston, 1890), Vol. I. A photostat of the sentence of excommunication of Nathaniel Wardel is at the Massachusetts Historical Society, Boston.

——HOLLIS STREET (Eighth) CHURCH (E). 1732.

I. "Records, Hollis Street Church, Boston," 1733-1847. A copy. Office of the City Registrar, Boston.

II. "The Records of the New Church at the South End of Boston," 1732-53. Church property; at Massachusetts Historical Society, Boston.

III. "Records of the Church in Hollis Street," 1753-89. Church property; at Massachusetts Historical Society.

BRADFORD. FIRST CHURCH (C). 1682.

I. "A Church Book," 1682-1824 (lacuna: 1801-24).

II. "Records of the First Church of Christ in Bradford," 1824-(30).

BRAINTREE: See Quincy.

BREWSTER. THE FIRST PARISH (U). 1700.

I. *Records of the Brewster Congregational Church,* 1700-1792. (Privately printed, 1911. One of the twenty-five copies is at the Essex Institute, Salem.)

CAMBRIDGE. FIRST CONGREGATIONAL SOCIETY (U). 1632.

I. *Records of the Church of Christ at Cambridge in New England, 1632-1830,* edited by S. P. Sharples (Boston, 1906). Editor noted that the early records were incomplete.

CANTON. THE FIRST CONGREGATIONAL PARISH (U). 1717.

I. "Records belonging to the Church of Christ in *Canton.*" 1717-(1830). Copied from earlier records now presumed lost.

CHARLEMONT. FIRST CONGREGATIONAL CHURCH (C). 1785.

I. Records, 1788-1823.

CHARLESTOWN. FIRST CHURCH (C). 1632.

I. *Records of the First Church in Charlestown, Massachusetts, 1632-1789* (Boston, 1880). Includes minutes, 1658-1724. The original records, owned by the church, are at the Congregational Library, Boston, but contain no minutes not found in the printed volume.

CHELMSFORD. FIRST CONGREGATIONAL SOCIETY (U). 1655.

I. "A Book of Records of the Church of Christ in Chelmsford, 1741," in W. Waters, *History of Chelmsford* (n.p., 1917) Contains votes, 1743-76. Waters does not mention any earlier records.

CHELSEA. RUMNEY MARSH CHURCH (E). 1715.

I. Records, 1715-1802, in M. Chamberlain, *A Documentary History of Chelsea* (2 vols., Boston, 1908).

II. "Rumny [*sic*] Marsh Church-Book," 1715-57. Boston Museum of Fine Arts.[4]

III. "Records of the Church at Chelsea," 1757-1801. Boston Museum of Fine Arts.

IV. "Records of the Church in Chelsea," 1801-38. Boston Museum of Fine Arts.

CONCORD. FIRST PARISH (U). 1636.

I. "Records of the First Church in Concord," 1739-(1835). Copy at Free Public Library, Concord. The librarian reports that the earlier records are believed missing.

DALTON. CONGREGATIONAL CHURCH (C). 1791.

I. "Records of the Congregational Church," 1791-(1830).*

[4] The Chelsea church records were turned over to the Boston Museum of Fine Arts along with the Revere silverware when the church dissolved. The later volumes include the records of Horatio Alger.

DANVERS. FIRST CONGREGATIONAL CHURCH (C). 1682.

I. "Records, First Church Danvers," 1689-1845. This exceptionally well-preserved and carefully treated volume contains numerous cases of interest, even if the witchcraft cases are disregarded.

DEDHAM. FIRST CHURCH AND PARISH (U). 1638.

I. "The Record of Baptism, Marriages, and Deaths, and Admissions to the Church and Dismissals Therefrom." Includes votes, 1638-71. In *Dedham Historical Record Series* (Dedham, 1888), Vol. II.

The following records, church property, are on deposit at the Dedham Historical Society, but are available only on application to the church clerk. The records for 1671-1724 are lost.

II. "Dedham Church Book Began [*sic*] May 6th 1724." 1724-31.

III. "Records, Dedham First Parish," 1731-63, including a few votes.

IV. "Church Records," 1792-1803.

DEERFIELD. THE FIRST CHURCH (C and U). 1688.

I. "Records of the Church in Deerfield," 1688-1733. A copy.

II. "Records," 1733-1803.

DORCHESTER. THE FIRST PARISH CHURCH (U). 1630.

I. *Records of the First Church at Dorchester . . . 1636-1734* (Boston, 1891). The original records, as well as the later ones, which are church property, are located in a bank vault in Boston. Although the minister gave generously of his time in an attempt to make them available, access to the records was rendered impossible by the illness of the church official who had custody of the key to the vault.

EGREMONT. CONGREGATIONAL CHURCH (C). 1770.

I. "Records of the Congregational Church," 1770-91.*

FALMOUTH. FIRST CONGREGATIONAL CHURCH (C). 1708.

I. "Falmouth Church Records," 1731-90. The earlier records are presumed lost.

II. "The Records of Falmouth," 1790-1830.

FRAMINGHAM. THE FIRST PARISH CHURCH (U). 1701.

I. "First Parish Church of Framingham. Records," 1717-1830. A WPA typescript copy. Vol. I.

II. *Ibid.,* Vol. II.

GRANVILLE. EAST CHURCH (Federated First Congregational Church) (C). 1747.

I. "Records of the First Church of Christ in Granville." 1791-1821.*

——WEST CONGREGATIONAL CHURCH (C). 1781.

I. "Records of the Congregational Church." 1811-(30).*

GREAT BARRINGTON. CONGREGATIONAL CHURCH (C). 1743?

I. Abstract of records, 1753-(1835).* Permission to consult the original records, reported to be extant, was denied.

GROTON. FIRST CHURCH OF CHRIST (U). 1664.

I. "The Earliest Book of Church Records," 1706-60, in S. A. Green, ed., *Groton Historical Series,* Vol. I, No. 10 (Groton, 1887).

II. Records, 1761-1830, in *ibid.,* Vol. IV, No. 1 (Groton, 1899).

HANOVER. FIRST CONGREGATIONAL CHURCH (C). 1728.

I. L. V. Briggs, ed., *History and Records of the First Congregational Church, Hanover, Massachusetts, 1727-1865* (Boston, 1895). Consulted through 1830.

HATFIELD. CONGREGATIONAL CHURCH (C). 1670.

I. "Records of the Church of Christ in Hatfield." 1722-(1850). Church property; in custody of Town Clerk. Earlier records could not be located.

HAVERHILL. THE FIRST CHURCH (U). 1641.

I. "Records of the First Parish." 1720-1840 (lacuna: 1769-84). Notarized typescript copy in Haverhill Public Library. The title of the volume is misleading.

——NORTH PARISH CONGREGATIONAL CHURCH (Second Church) (C). 1730.

I. "Records of the North Parish Congregational Church." 1730-(1835). Typescript copy in Haverhill Public Library.

HULL. (Name not located) (E). 1670.

I. "Hull Church Records." 1725-67. New England Historic Genealogical Society, Boston. Note on cover states that earlier records are lost.

IPSWICH. FIRST AND SOUTH CONGREGATIONAL CHURCH (C). 1634.

I. "Records of the First Church of Christ in Ipswich," 1739-1805. Copied from "a copy of more ancient records, taken from the book of records belonging to the feoffees of the Grammar School in Ipswich."

II. "Records, First Congregational Church, Ipswich," 1806-29.

——SECOND OR SOUTH CONGREGATIONAL CHURCH (C). 1747.

I. "South Church Records, Ipswich," 1747-1848. A copy, with a note showing that some disciplinary cases were not recorded.

KINGSTON. FIRST CONGREGATIONAL PARISH (U). 1717.

I. "Books 1 and 2 of the First Parish Records of Kingston," including church records, 1717-1812. WPA typescript copy at Town Clerk's office.

LANESBOROUGH. FEDERATED CONGREGATIONAL CHURCH (C). 1764.

I. "Records of the Church of Christ in . . . Lanesborough," 1746-(1840).*

LENOX. CONGREGATIONAL CHURCH (C). 1769.

I. Records, 1771-1846.

II. "Records of the Congregational Church, Lenox," 1846-72. Consulted only to follow up cases not concluded in I.

LEOMINSTER. FIRST CHURCH (U). 1763.

I. Records, 1763-1806.

II. Records, 1806-(35).

LINCOLN. CONGREGATIONAL CHURCH (C). 1747.

I. "Lincoln Church Records," 1747-1827. Microfilm.

LYNNFIELD. FIRST CHURCH (E). 1720.

I. "First Book of Records of the First Church of Lynnfield," 1734-1819, *Essex Institute Historical Collections,* XXXIV, 117-93. Other records have been published in *ibid.,* but were irrelevant here.

MARBLEHEAD. FIRST CHURCH OF CHRIST (C). 1684.
I. "First Book Containing the Records of the First Congregational Church of Marblehead," 1684-1800.
II. "Second Book Containing the Records of the First Congregational Church in Marblehead," 1740-1837.
——SECOND CONGREGATIONAL CHURCH (U). 1716.
I. "Unitarian Records Book #1," 1716-92. Church property; in custody of Town Clerk.
II. "A Book of Records," with votes, 1794-1811. Church property; in custody of Town Clerk.

MATTAPOISETT. FIRST PRECINCT CHURCH (C). 1736.
I. "Records of the Second Church in Rochester," 1737-1832.

MEDFORD. FIRST PARISH (U). 1712.
I. "Records of the First Church, Medford," 1712-73. Town Clerk's Office.
II. "Records of the First Church, Medford," 1774-1823. Town Clerk's Office.

MEDWAY. EAST (First) CHURCH (E). 1715.
I. Loose pages of notes, letters, sermons, and some records. Congregational Library, Boston.

MERRIMAC. CONGREGATIONAL CHURCH (C). 1726.
I. "Pain Wingate, his Book. Records of the Second Church in Amesbury," 1726-82. Church property; in custody of First National Bank, Merrimac.

MIDDLEBOROUGH. FIRST CONGREGATIONAL CHURCH (C). 1694.
I. "The Book of Church Records," 1707-1820.
——NORTH CONGREGATIONAL CHURCH (C). 1784.
I. "The Records of the Church of Christ, in the Joining Borders of Bridgewater and Middleborough," 1748-54.
II. "Records of the Congregational Church, Titicut Parish," 1756-85.
III. "A Book of Church Records," 1787-1850.

MILLBURY. FIRST CONGREGATIONAL CHURCH (formerly Second Church in Sutton) (C). 1717.
I. "Records of the Second Church in Sutton," 1747-63. American Antiquarian Society, Worcester.

II. "The Records of the 2nd Church in Sutton," 1764-1830 (lacuna: 1792-1827). American Antiquarian Society, Worcester.

MILTON. THE FIRST CONGREGATIONAL CHURCH (U). 1678.
I. "Milton Church Records," 1681-1754. Photostat. Milton Public Library.
II. "Milton Church Records," 1797-(1835). Photostat of volume compiled in 1797 from fragments. Milton Public Library.

MONTAGUE. FIRST CONGREGATIONAL CHURCH, TRINITARIAN (C). 1752.
I. "First Congregational Church in Montague," 1812-(40). The earlier records are reported lost.

MONTEREY. CONGREGATIONAL CHURCH (C). 1750.
I. "Church Records," 1750-1835 (fragmentary, 1750-80; lacuna, 1780-1810). In part copied from older records now lost.

NATICK. (Name not located) (E). 1730.
I. Records, 1730-44. At New England Historic Genealogical Society, Boston.

NEEDHAM. THE FIRST PARISH (U). 1711?
I. "The Records of the Church in Needham." 1720-(1835). Church property; in vault of Historical Society, at Public Library, Needham.

NORTHAMPTON. FIRST CONGREGATIONAL CHURCH (C). 1661.
I. Records, containing minutes, 1661-1833. The entries between 1793 and 1834 are largely illegible, and parts of the book are badly mutilated.

NORTH ANDOVER. THE NORTH PARISH CHURCH (formerly First Church of Andover) (U). 1645.
I. Records, containing votes, 1630-1810.

NORTH READING: See Reading.

NORTON. THE CONGREGATIONAL PARISH (U). 1710.
I. "Records of the First Congregational Church in Norton." Disciplinary cases 1715-28 only. A copy, perhaps incomplete, from older records which could not be located.

NORWOOD. CONGREGATIONAL CHURCH (C). 1736.
I. Records, 1736-1844, printed with Dedham Records, Vol. I.

OTIS. CONGREGATIONAL CHURCH (C). 1779?
I. "Record of Votes and Proceedings." 1813-(35).*

PALMER. FIRST CONGREGATIONAL CHURCH (C). 1730.
I. "Records of the Church in the Town of Palmer," 1811-27.
II. "A Church Register," 1827-40.
This church was Presbyterian until 1811. The records for the Presbyterian period could not be located.

PEABODY. SOUTH CONGREGATIONAL CHURCH (C). 1713.
I. "Record Book," 1794-1840. Church property; in custody of Peabody Institute Library. The parish records go back to 1711; the early church records could not be located.

PERU. CONGREGATIONAL CHURCH (C). 1770.
I. Records, containing votes 1783-1810.*
II. Records, 1814-(35).*

PITTSFIELD. FIRST CHURCH OF CHRIST (C). 1764.
I. "Church Book of Pittsfield," 1764-1817.*
II. "Church Book of Pittsfield," 1817-50.*

PLYMOUTH. THE FIRST PARISH (U). 1630.
I. "Plymouth Church Records, 1620-1859," *Publications of the Colonial Society of Massachusetts* (Boston, 1920), Vol. XXII.
II. *Ibid.*, Vol. XXIII.

QUINCY. FIRST CONGREGATIONAL SOCIETY (formerly Braintree North Precinct Church) (U). 1639.
I. Minister's record, 1673-1744, in C. F. Adams, "Some Phases of Sexual Morality and Church Discipline in Colonial New England," *Proceedings of the Massachusetts Historical Society*, 2nd Ser., VI (1891), 477-516.

READING. NOTE: The first Church in the township of Reading, gathered in 1644, became the church in Wakefield, which was set off from Reading. The Second Parish, created in 1713, later became North Reading. The Third Parish, set off in 1770, is the present town of Reading. The source listed below is presumably a copy of the records of the church originally known as the First Church of Reading, but now known as the First Church in Wakefield. See D. H. Hurd, *History of Middlesex County* (Philadelphia, 1890), II, 794-96.

I. "Church Records of the Old Town of Reading, Massachusetts, and of the First Parish of Reading and South Reading," 1648-1846. Typescript copy, probably by WPA, in Reading Public Library.

ROCHESTER. FIRST CONGREGATIONAL CHURCH (C). 1703.

I. Records, 1798-(1840). The earlier records are lost. This volume is mutilated: one leaf is missing and four lines are obliterated with this explanation: "Expunged by order of the Church as a relic of barbarism."

ROXBURY. THE FIRST CHURCH (U). 1631.

I. "The Rev. John Eliot's Record," including disciplinary cases to 1686, in City of Boston, *Report of Record Commissioners* (Boston, 1884), Vol. VI. The later records, presumably extant, were not made available for examination.

SALEM. THE FIRST CONGREGATIONAL SOCIETY (U). 1629.

I. "Records of the First Church of Salem," 1629-1736. A copy, by Mrs. McSwiggin of the Essex Institute, on loose sheets. Essex Institute, Salem.

II. "Records of the First Church in Salem," 1660-1776. A copy by the Reverend Thomas Barnard, overlapping with Vol. I. Essex Institute, Salem.

III. "Records of the First Church of Salem," 1736-(1835). Typescript copy by WPA, at the First Church.

SALISBURY. FIRST CHURCH (E). 1638.

I. "Church Records," 1687-1752. Massachusetts Historical Society library, Boston.

SANDISFIELD. CONGREGATIONAL CHURCH (C). 1756.

I. "Records of the Sandisfield Church—2nd Book," 1799-(1835) (lacuna: 1801-16).* Copyist observed loss of earlier records.

SCITUATE. CONGREGATIONAL CHURCH (C). 1635.

I. "Scituate First Parish Records," 1707-91. A copy. American Antiquarian Society, Worcester.

SHARON. FIRST CONGREGATIONAL PARISH (U). 1741.

I. Records, 1742-97, in *Publications of the Sharon Historical Society*, No. 5 (Sharon, 1908).

SHEFFIELD. CONGREGATIONAL CHURCH (C). 1733.

I. Records, 1735-1855. A copy. Original records lost.

II. "Records of the Church of Christ," 1814-(50).

SOUTH HADLEY. THE FIRST CONGREGATIONAL CHURCH (C). 1733.

I. "Church Records," 1743-1824 (lacuna: 1795-1823). Church property; at Mount Holyoke College library, South Hadley.

II. "Church Records," 1824-35. Church property; at Mount Holyoke College library.

SOUTHWICK. CONGREGATIONAL CHURCH (C). 1773.

I. Records, 1773-1831, perhaps fragmentary.*

STERLING. FIRST CHURCH (formerly Second Church in Lancaster) (U). 1742.

I. "Book of Records of the Second Church of Lancaster," 1746-88. Photostat at American Antiquarian Society, Worcester.

STOCKBRIDGE. CONGREGATIONAL CHURCH (C). 1734.

I. "Records of the Church of Christ in Stockbridge," 1759-1819. A copy. Original records lost.

II. "Records of the Church of Christ in Stockbridge," 1819-(35).

SUTTON. FIRST CONGREGATIONAL CHURCH (C). 1720.

I. "A Book of Records," 1728-1811. Eight pages missing.

——SECOND CHURCH: See Millbury.

TRURO. FIRST CONGREGATIONAL CHURCH (C). 1711.

I. Records, 1753-1832. Church property; in custody of Town Clerk, Truro.

WAKEFIELD: See Reading.

WALPOLE. (Name not located) (E). ?

I. Fragment of old records, with vote of 1729. At New England Historic Genealogical Society, Boston.

WESTFIELD. FIRST CONGREGATIONAL CHURCH (C). 1679.

I. "The Publick Records of the Church," 1679-1836. Some parts are mutilated, others are illegible, but the volume is still among the most useful and interesting. Church property; in custody of Westfield Athenaeum, Westfield.

WESTMINISTER. FIRST CHURCH (C). 1742.
I. Records containing some votes, 1815-(33).

WESTON. FIRST PARISH (U). 1709.
I. Town of Weston, *Church Records, 1709-1825* (Boston, 1901).

WEST SPRINGFIELD. FIRST CONGREGATIONAL CHURCH (C). 1698.
I. "Church Records and Registry," containing minutes, 1843-52. The earlier records are lost.

WILBRAHAM. CONGREGATIONAL CHURCH (C). 1741.
I. "Book of Records," 1801-28.
II. Records, 1832-(50).

WINDSOR. CONGREGATIONAL CHURCH (C). 1733.
I. "Records of the Church of Christ in Windsor," 1773-(1835).*

WORCESTER. FIRST (Old South) CHURCH (C). 1716.
I. Records, 1747-61, in a folder.
II. "Church Records Began [*sic*] Oct. 13, 1820."
The church secretary reports that no other records of the colonial period exist.

A NOTE ON CHURCH RECORDS NOT CONSULTED OR LOST

Barnstable County. The Chatham and Sandwich records were destroyed by fire; those of the Harwich church are all but inaccessible. The Wellfleet records have come into the possession of a woman who has no title to them but refuses to permit even the minister to consult them. The early Yarmouth records could not be located; the later ones contain no minutes. The Provincetown church was extinct by 1714, must have been revived, and was again dissolved in 1950. There is no trace of its records.

Bristol County. The early records of the churches in Attleborough, Dighton, Easton, New Bedford, and Taunton are reported as lost. Those of the church until recently known as the Catholic Congregational Society of Rehoboth were stolen by a minister who, in about 1810, was dismissed after he and his daughter brought suit against a sometime boarder who had broken his promise to marry the parson's daughter. The minister, who took the records and plate with him, held separatist services and was awarded a judgment for arrears of salary. The chalice was restored to the church in 1900; the records are still missing. The churches in Fall River, Freetown, Mansfield, and Seekonk became extinct at an early date; the records have not been found.

Dukes County. The curator of the Dukes County Historical Society reports that the old records of Edgartown and Tisbury are lost. What purports to be a copy of the "Ancient Records of the Church of Tisbury, Mass.," 1700-1819, in the West Tisbury *Sea Gull,* January, 1890, is actually an extract from the parish and town records. The church in Chilimark and the Indian church in Gayhead became extinct at early dates; their records are lost.

Essex County. No information concerning the records of the First Church in Boxford was available, but the Essex Institute owns the manuscript of Mary Ellen Perley's "History of the First Congregational Church, Boxford, Mass., 1699-1912," which is based on church records. The West Boxford records, reportedly in the town vault, are inaccessible. The Lynn records were lost in a fire. Those of the Groveland church, once listed as being the property of the Congregational Library, could not be found, and a thorough search of the stacks of the Essex Institute failed to locate the records of the Second Church in Salem, reportedly at the Institute. A request to consult the records of the Tabernacle Congregational Church, Salem, brought no reply. The Cape Ann Association, Gloucester, has the records of two old churches in Gloucester, but arrangements could not be made to consult them. Fragments of the Wenham records, at the Congregational Library, contain no disciplinary cases.

The records of the First Church in Newbury are almost entirely lost; only mutilated fragments remain. The Third Church of Newbury, which became the First Church of Newburyport, is extinct; the records appear to be lost. The Second and Fourth churches of Newbury became the First and Second churches of West Newbury. No information concerning the records of the church now known as the First Church of West Newbury was available; the pre-1815 records of the present Second Church of

West Newbury, allegedly at the Essex Institute, could not be located.

Franklin, Hampden, and Hampshire counties. The early records of one of the oldest churches in the area, that in Hadley (1659), were lost in a fire. Those of the Greenfield church are believed to be lost. A cursory inspection of a trunk filled with old papers of the church in Springfield (1637) did not at first glance disclose any minutes; a more thorough examination of its contents was not permitted. The early Longmeadow records could not be located; some information on the life of the church may be found in the unpublished diary of the Reverend Stephen Williams, a WPA copy of which is at the church.

Middlesex County. The Newton records were destroyed by fire. Those of the churches in Lexington and Wilmington, presumably extant, could not be located, and there appears to be no trace of the Malden First Church and Watertown records. Lists of baptisms and the like are all that have been found for the churches in Acton (extinct), Marlborough, and Sudbury. The ministers of the Arlington and Waltham churches report that their records contain no disciplinary cases.

Nantucket County. The minister of Nantucket and the Nantucket Athenaeum report that the old church records are no longer extant.

Norfolk County. The records of the First Church of Braintree and of the Westwood church were destroyed by fire. Those of Brookline could not be found, and no information was available concerning the Weymouth records.

Plymouth County. The First Congregational Society of Bridgewater felt that it would be unwise to make their old records available, and the minister dreaded the adverse publicity which might arise from a study of disciplinary action taken against ancestors of persons now living in the town. The minister of Wareham's First Church reported that his records contained no disciplinary cases. The Hingham records could not be located.

Suffolk County. The published records of the Brattle Square Church in Boston contain no references to discipline; the published portions of the ministers' diaries, which originally included a good many church records, deal exclusively with the diarists' private lives. The other parts of the diaries have not been found. The

New South (Sixth), New Brick (Seventh), Lynde Street (Ninth), and Eleventh churches are extinct and their records have disappeared. Those of the New North (Fifth) Church, supposedly at the office of the City Clerk, Boston, could not be located, while those of the extinct Tenth Church are known to be lost.

The Third Church of Roxbury (1672), in Jamaica Plain, is extinct, and its records have vanished. The First Parish in Brighton had a gathered church by 1734, but it was not fully organized until 1783. The records of the Arlington Street Church, which was Presbyterian until the Revolution, at which time it became Unitarian, are presumed to have been taken back to Scotland by a disgruntled Loyalist minister. King's Chapel, now Unitarian, was Anglican until the Revolution.

Worcester County. The old church records of Brookfield and Petersham could not be found, although there are numerous parish records in the Brookfield Town Hall. No information could be had concerning the records of the oldest church in the county, the First Church of Lancaster (1653). In the case of the Harvard church, the writer was referred to the New England Historic Genealogical Society, which does not have the records of that church.

B. Other Primary Sources

Three indispensable narratives by early New England Puritans are William Bradford's classic, which has been made available in modern English by G. F. Willison, entitled *History of Plymouth Colony, 1606-1646* (New York, 1949); John Winthrop's *History of New England from 1630 to 1649,* edited by J. Savage (Boston, 1883) or by J. K. Hosmer (New York, 1908-9); and Cotton Mather's *Magnalia Christi Americana* (2 vols., Hartford, 1820), first published in London in 1702. An important diary is that of Cotton Mather, which covers the period from 1681 to 1724 (Boston, 1911-12).

The statutes of the Plymouth Colony cited herein have been taken from *The Compact, with the Charter and Laws of the Colony of New Plymouth,* edited by W. Brigham (Boston, 1836). The early Massachusetts statutes may be found in *The Colonial Laws of Massachusetts, reprinted from the edition of 1660, with supplements to 1672, containing also the Body of Liberties of 1641* (Boston, 1889), and in *Colonial Laws of Massachusetts, reprinted from the edition of 1672, with supplement through 1686* (Boston, 1887), both of which contain facsimile reprints of the edition of 1660, which is also available separately.[5] The later statutes are found in *Acts and Laws of His Majesty's Province of the Massachusetts Bay in New England* (Boston, dated 1759, but containing statutes to 1761). Whenever possible statutes have been cited in the customary manner in order to minimize confusion. Unfortunately, however, the early Massachusetts statutes were not published by regnal years and chapter numbers, with the result that the modern historical investigator is confronted by a mass of statutes in chaotic condition. W. B. Shurtleff's edition of the *Records of the Governor and Company of the Massachusetts Bay* (5 vols. in 6, Boston, 1854) is an invaluable collection of source materials.

It is impossible to present here anything approximating a complete list of writings by the Puritan divines. An excellent bibliography of such writings may be found in A. E. Dunning, *Congregationalism as Seen in Its Literature* (New York, 1880), a good revision of which would be helpful. In the field of church polity, W. Walker, ed., *The Creeds and Platforms of Congregationalism* (New York, 1893) is an indispensable source book, which includes, among other documents, the Cambridge Platform, the Halfway Covenant, the Savoy Declaration, and the documents of the Reform Synod of 1679-80. The most important original American writings on this subject are John Cotton's *The Keyes of the Kingdom of Heaven* (Boston, 1852), first published in 1644; Thomas Hooker's *A Survey of the Summe of Church Discipline* (London, 1658), first published in 1648; and, most useful of all, Cotton Mather's *Ratio Disciplinae Fratrum Nov-Anglicorum* (Boston, 1726), which is a combination of a handbook on polity and a liturgical manual, a sort of eighteenth-century Puritan *Didache*. In some respects these three works are analogous to the great works on English law by Glanvil, Bracton, Littleton, Coke, and Blackstone: each is based on the actual application of discipline and the practice of church

[5] The 1889 edition has been cited in most cases, rather than that of 1887. The statute concerning the burial of suicides, however, though enacted in 1660, was not found in the 1889 edition, but was located in the 1887 publication.

government, but was written as a guide for the ministers of the time. Other important discussions of the polity of American Congregationalism are Richard Mather's *Church-Government and Church-Covenant Discussed* (London, 1643), and John Cotton's *The Way of the Congregational Churches Cleared* (London, 1648), which is an attack on Presbyterianism. An important English work is Richard Baxter's *A Christian Directory* (London, 1673), consisting of over a thousand folio pages. While Baxter represents the English position, Alexander Henderson, in *The Government and Order of the Church of Scotland* (Edinburgh, 1641), states the Scottish point of view.

Moralistic writings of the period include Urian Oakes, *New England Pleaded With* (Cambridge, 1673), and Cotton Mather, *The Sailor's Companion* (Boston, 1709). Some comment on the use of liquor may be found in Increase Mather's *Wo to Drunkards* (Boston, 1673), and in his *Testimony against Several Prophane and Superstitious Customs* (Boston, 1688). Samuel Danforth's polemic on bestiality, *Cry of Sodom Enquired Into* (Cambridge, 1674) may be consulted in the Rare Book Department of the Boston Public Library.

The classical attack on religious persecution by a contemporary writer is Roger Williams's *The Bloudy Tenent of Persecution for Cause of Conscience* (London, 1644), which initiated an exchange of arguments. John Cotton's plea in answer to Williams's declaration is found in *The Bloudy Tenent Washed and Made White in the Bloud of the Lambe* (London, 1647). Williams's replication, "The Bloudy Tenent Yet More Bloody by Master Cottons Attempting to Wash It White with the Blood of the Lambe" (1652), has been reprinted in the *Publications of the Narragansett Club* (Providence, 1870), Vol. III. Cotton's death in 1652 prevented him from writing a rejoinder to Williams's second publication on the subject. The argument of an intervenor, Nathaniel Ward, is stated in "Simple Cobbler of Aggawam" (1647), a satire on religious liberty, which is most readily found in Peter Force's *Tracts,* Vol. III, No. 8.

An objective firsthand account of church discipline in the first decade of Massachusetts history is included in Thomas Lechford's *Plain Dealing, or News from New England* (Boston, 1867), first published in London in 1642. The records of the "Antinomian" trials, including Winthrop's "Short Story," the friendlier account included in Hutchinson's history, the transcript of the church trial, and relevant extracts from the writings of John Cotton and Robert Keayne, have been published in Charles Francis Adams's edition of *Antinomianism in the Colony of Massachusetts Bay, 1636-1638* (Boston, 1849).

Calvin's *Institutes of the Christian Religion* are available in numerous translations and editions; the seventh American edition, translated by J. Allen, has been used (Philadelphia, 1936). Jonathan Edwards's works have been published in eight volumes (Worcester, 1809) and in ten volumes (New York, 1829-30); the latter edition has been used.

The Puritans, edited by P. Miller and T. H. Johnson (New York, etc., 1938), is an excellent one-volume collection of readings in the Puritan writings, while in *The Heart of the Puritan* (New York, 1917) Professor Elizabeth Deering Hanscom has collected some delightful extracts from the letters and journals of the Puritans.

C. Secondary Sources

THE BACKGROUND

The general background is discussed in every volume which deals with the colonies in general, or with New England in particular. It is impossible to present here anything approximating a complete bibliography of the subject. The best general works on the colonial period are C. M. Andrews, *The Colonial Period in American History* (4 vols., New Haven, 1934), which, in the first volume, has several superb essays on the history of institutions; J. A. Doyle, *English Colonies in America* (3 vols., New York, 1889); and H. L. Osgood, *The American Colonies in the Seventeenth Century* (3 vols., New York, 1904-7) and *The American Colonies in the Eighteenth Century* (4 vols., New York, 1924).

The most useful works on the history of New England or Massachusetts are B. Adams, *The Emancipation of Massachusetts* (2nd ed., Boston and New York, 1886); C. F. Adams, *Three Episodes of Massachusetts History* (5th ed., 2 vols., Boston and New York, 1896); J. T. Adams, *The Founding of New England* (Boston, 1921);

S. E. Morison, *Builders of the Bay Colony* (Boston and New York, 1930); W. B. Weeden, *Economic and Social History of New England, 1620-1789* (2 vols., Boston and New York, 1890); T. J. Wertenbaker, *The Puritan Oligarchy* (New York, 1947); and G. F. Willison, *Saints and Strangers* (New York, 1945). Older, but still useful, are J. G. Palfrey, *History of New England* (3 vols., Boston, 1859-64), and T. Hutchinson, *History of the Colony and Province of Massachusetts Bay,* edited by L. S. Mayo (3 vols., Cambridge, 1936).

Among the older and now largely superseded works are E. H. Byington, *The Puritan as Colonist and Reformer* (Boston, 1899); G. E. Ellis, *The Puritan Age and Rule in the Colony of Massachusetts Bay* (Boston and New York, 1888); and R. G. Usher, *The Pilgrims and Their History* (New York, 1918). J. Fiske's *The Beginnings of New England* (Boston and New York, 1889) is a vivid narrative but overemphasizes the religious factors in the motivation of the Puritans. C. W. Elliott, *The New England History* (New York, 1857); J. A. Goodwin, *The Pilgrim Republic* (Boston, 1888); and D. W. Howe, *The Puritan Republic of Massachusetts Bay in New England* (Indianapolis, 1899) are of little use save to the antiquarian. W. H. Clark and D. L. Marsh, *The Story of Massachusetts* (4 vols., New York, 1938) is a beautifully printed but useless and undocumented compendium. *The Commonwealth History of Massachusetts,* edited by A. B. Hart (5 vols., New York, 1927-30), while possibly useful, contains nothing of help which is not found elsewhere.

In the field of American church history, P. G. Mode, *Sourcebook and Bibliographical Guide for American Church History* (Menasha, Wisconsin, 1921) is still the best (and only) book of its kind, and is badly in need of republication in an up-to-date edition. W. W. Sweet, the dean of American church historians, has provided the scholar with valuable background information. His *Story of Religion in America* (New York, 1950), a revision of his *Story of Religions in America* (New York and London, 1930), is still the best one-volume work on the subject, although it is unduly influenced by the Turner hypothesis. Also relevant are his *Religion in Colonial America* (New York, 1942), and *Religion in the Development of American Culture, 1765-1840* (New York, 1952); the latter contains an excellent bibliography. A recent publication worthy of note is J. C. Brauer, *Protestantism in America* (Philadelphia, 1953), which is especially good on the broad currents of religious thought crossing denominational boundaries, but which is marred by a lack of documentation and by too brief a bibliography. A. L. Drummond, *Story of American Protestantism* (2nd ed., Boston, 1951), an English work, is well written and interesting but contains a goodly number of errors. L. A. Weigle, *American Idealism* (New Haven, 1928), which forms Vol. X in the *Pageant of American History* series, has good pictorial material.

Three other volumes, interpretive rather than narrative, must be mentioned: T. C. Hall, *The Religious Background of American Culture* (Boston, 1930); W. A. Visser't Hooft, *The Background of the Social Gospel in America* (Haarlem, 1928); and H. R. Niebuhr, *The Kingdom of God in America* (New York and Chicago, 1937). All three provide helpful insights, although Puritanism is treated only briefly.

CONGREGATIONAL HISTORY AND POLITY

The English background of American Congregationalism is discussed, *inter alia,* in two indispensable works: W. Haller, *The Rise of Puritanism* (New York, 1938), which discusses Puritan leaders and their writings from 1570 to 1643, and M. M. Knappen, *Tudor Puritanism* (Chicago, 1939), an excellent book written with a priceless sense of humor. D. Neal, *The History of the Puritans . . . from 1517 to . . . 1688* (rev. ed., 2 vols., New York, 1844) is still useful for some factual information. B. Hanbury's three-volume edition of *Historical Memorials Relating to the English Independents* (London, n.d.) contains useful extracts from the writings of the Puritans but is deplorably edited. A. E. Dunning, *Congregationalism as Seen in Its Literature* (New York, 1880), consisting of twelve pompous lectures, largely on English Congregationalism, has an excellent bibliography listing hundreds of Puritan writings. Now outdated are G. Punchard, *History of Congregationalism* (Boston, 1880-1), the fourth and fifth volumes of which deal with American Congregationalism, and L. Bacon, *Genesis of the New England Churches* (New York, 1874), an apologetic treatise beginning with the year one.

More modern publications include H. H. Henson, *Puritanism in England* (New York and London, 1912); C. Burrage, *The Early*

English Dissenters in the Light of Recent Research, (Cambridge, 1912), which includes a chapter on "The Churches of New England until About 1641"; and L. Pullan, *Religion since the Reformation* (Oxford, 1923), which devotes some space to Puritanism. A significant recent contribution is L. J. Trinterud, "The Origins of Puritanism," *Church History,* XX (1951), 37-57. On the larger subject of Calvinism, J. T. McNeill's *The History and Character of Calvinism* (New York, 1954) is an indispensable work by an eminent Calvin scholar. Professor McNeill also has devoted a chapter of *Modern Christian Movements* (Philadelphia, 1954) to English Puritanism, and the contribution of the Puritans to the movement for Church unity are discussed in a chapter on "The Ecumenical Movement in Historical Perspective."

More specialized discussions of some interest here are W. Schenk, *The Concern for Social Justice in the Puritan Revolution* (London, 1940); C. E. Whiting, *Studies in English Puritanism from the Restoration to the Revolution, 1660-1689* (London, 1931); and R. B. Schlatter, *The Social Ideas of Religious Leaders, 1660-1688* (Oxford, 1940). J. C. Dow, "Hebrew and Puritan," *Jewish Quarterly Review,* III (1891), 52-84, deserves mention because of its fantastic comparison between Cromwell's deliverance of the Puritans from the Laudian regime and Judas Maccabeus' deliverance of the Jews from Antiochus Epiphanes.

The best general history of American Congregationalism is G. C. Atkins and F. L. Fagley, *History of American Congregationalism* (Boston and Chicago, 1942), which although well written and useful, devotes relatively little space to the colonial period. Older but still useful is W. Walker, *A History of the Congregational Churches in the United States* (New York, 1894). The equivalent of Professor Haller's *Rise of Puritanism* for American Puritan thought remains to be written. American Unitarianism is treated in E. M. Wilbur, *A History of Unitarianism in Transylvania, England, and America* (Cambridge, 1952); the older work by G. W. Cooke, *Unitarianism in America* (Boston, 1902), is still useful.

Among the important writings on special topics in the history of American Congregationalism are S. L. Blake, *The Separates or Strict Congregationalists of New England* (Boston, 1902); H. W. Foote, ed., *The Cambridge Platform of 1648* (Boston, 1949); B. Levy's prize-winning dissertation, *Preaching in the First Half*

Century of New England History (Hartford, 1945); A. M. Baldwin, *The New England Clergy and the American Revolution* (Durham, 1928); S. E. Mead, *Nathaniel William Taylor, 1786-1858* (Chicago, 1942), important for the development of religious thought in the early nineteenth century; M. L. Gambrell, *Ministerial Training in Eighteenth Century New England* (New York, 1937); C. K. Shipton, "The New England Clergy of the 'Glacial Age,'" *Publications of the Colonial Society of Massachusetts,* XXXII (1937), 24-54; and H. B. Adams, *The Saxon Tithing Man in America* (Baltimore, 1883). The literature of the period is discussed in K. B. Murdock, *Literature and Theology in Colonial New England* (Cambridge, 1949); R. E. Spiller, *et al., Literary History of the United States* (3 vols., New York, 1946), Vol. I, Chaps. 5-6; and M. C. Tyler, *A History of American Literature* (Ithaca, 1949; first published in 1878), while A. L. Drummond, *The Churches in English Fiction* (Leicester, 1950) treats religion in English imaginative literature.

The churches in Massachusetts are discussed in J. B. Felt, *The Ecclesiastical History of New England* (Boston, 1855-62), an uncritical, unscholarly, and undocumented work, but not wholly useless and far from uninteresting. J. S. Clark, *A Historical Sketch of the Congregational Churches in Massachusetts from 1620 to 1858* (Boston, 1858) draws heavily on Felt but provides a useful guide to local churches. F. L. Weis, *The Colonial Clergy and the Colonial Churches of New England* (Lancaster, 1936) is a useful biographical directory, while W. B. Sprague, *Annals of the American Pulpit* (New York, 1865) provides some eulogistic sketches of the lives of prominent ministers. Among the more valuable local church histories are A. B. Ellis, *History of the First Church in Boston* (Boston, 1881); H. A. Hill, *History of the Old South Church* (2 vols., Boston, 1890); and six sermons by S. K. Lothrop, *A History of the Church in Brattle Square, Boston* (Boston, 1851). J. Winsor, ed., *The Memorial History of Boston* (4 vols., Boston, 1880-81) contains some helpful information in Vol. II, Chap. 6; Vol. III, Chap. 7; and Vol. VIII, Chap. 11. Some other histories of churches which contain reliable reprints of colonial records have been listed with the primary sources.

For the student of American Congregational polity, W. E. Barton, *Congregational Creeds and Covenants* (Chicago, 1917) is indispensable, and W. Walker, *The Creeds and Platforms of Congregation-*

alism (New York, 1893), in addition to being a useful sourcebook, contains numerous helpful observations. Some discussion of the office of elder is found in I. N. Tarbox, "Ruling Elders in the Early New England Churches," *Congregational Quarterly,* XIV (1872), 401-16. The numerous handbooks and manuals, although of little use to the student of the colonial period, disclose the adaptation of Congregational principles to modern trends. In chronological order these are J. Mitchell, *A Guide to the Principles of the Congregational Church* [*sic*] *of New England* (Northampton, 1838); E. Hall, *The Puritans and Their Principles* (New York, 1846), containing equally vitriolic blasts against both Canterbury and Rome; L. Woods's anonymously published *Report of Congregationalism* (Boston, 1846); P. Cummings, *A Dictionary of Congregational Usages and Principles* (Boston, 1851); J. E. Roy, *A Manual of the Principles, Doctrines, and Usages of the Congregational Churches* (Chicago, 1849); H. M. Dexter, *Congregationalism: What It Is, Whence It Is, How It Works* (Boston, 1865); A. H. Ross, *A Pocket Manual of Congregationalism* (Chicago, 1883); G. N. Boardman, *Congregationalism* (Chicago, 1889); L. W. Bacon, *The Congregationalists* (New York, 1904); G. M. Boynton, *The Congregational Way* (New York, 1904); W. E. Barton, *The Law of Congregational Usage* (Chicago, 1916); F. L. Fagley, *The Congregational Churches* (Boston and Chicago, 1925); and O. E. Maurer, ed., *Manual of the Congregational Christian Churches* (Boston, 1951). Also see G. Punchard, *A View of Congregationalism* (Salem, 1840).

THEOLOGY

Two useful works for the non-technical student of the history of Christian doctrine are R. Seeberg, *Textbook of the History of Christian Doctrine,* translated by C. E. Hay (2 vols. in 1, Grand Rapids, 1952), which has extensive quotations from the sources, but which, like a number of similar works, stops with Luther, Calvin, and Tridentine Roman Catholicism, and G. P. Fisher, *History of Christian Doctrine* (Edinburgh, 1908), which contains fewer quotations but is more interpretive and devotes some space to Arminianism, the Covenant Theology, and American doctrinal thought. A. C. McGiffert, *Protestant Thought before Kant* (New York, 1917) is useful and devotes some space to Calvinism and

Puritanism, but fails to make the slightest distinction between the two. P. Schaff, *The Creeds of Christendom* (New York and London, 1919) is indispensable, particularly Vol. I, "The History of the Creeds," and Vol. III, "The Evangelical and Protestant Churches."

Among the numerous works on Calvin and Calvinism are G. Harkness, *John Calvin: The Man and His Ethics* (New York, 1931); A. M. Hunter, *The Teaching of Calvin* (2nd ed., London, 1950); W. Walker, *John Calvin: The Organiser to Reformed Protestantism, 1509-1564* (New York and London, 1906); and B. Breckenridge, *Calvin and Calvinism* (New York, 1931). A brief but excellent discussion of Calvin's Institutes may be found in J. T. McNeill, *Books of Faith and Power* (New York and London, 1947), whose *The History and Character of Calvinism* (New York, 1954) has already been noted.

The Covenant Theology is discussed in C. Burrage, *The Church Covenant Idea* (Philadelphia, 1904), a scissors-and-paste work with long but useful quotations. G. Schrenk, *Gottesreich und Bund im älteren Protestantismus* (Guetersloh, 1923) traces the covenant in Continental theology and devotes some pages to William Ames. E. C. Blackman, "The Biblical Idea of Covenant," *The Presbyter,* VII, No. 4 (1945), 3-9, and R. T. Jones, "The Church Covenant in Classical Congregationalism," *ibid.,* pp. 9-22, are of interest. S. Burrell, "Kirk, Crown, and Covenant" (unpublished Ph.D. dissertation, Columbia University, 1953) is an important work on the political implications and uses of the covenant in Scotland. P. Y. De Jong, *The Covenant Idea in New England Theology, 1620-1847* (Grand Rapids, 1945) discusses the Covenant Theology in America.

The difference between Calvinism and Puritanism is treated in H. Bronkema, *The Essence of Puritanism* (Goes, [1930]), and P. Miller, in "The Marrow of Puritan Divinity," *Publications of the Colonial Society of New England,* XXXII (1937), 247-300, maintains that the American Puritans of the seventeenth century were not Calvinists. In *Orthodoxy in Massachusetts* (Cambridge, 1933) Professor Miller discusses the Ames-Bradshaw concept of nonseparatist Congregationalism. Other useful contributions by Miller are "The Half-Way Covenant," *The New England Quarterly,* VI (1933), 676-715; "Solomon Stoddard," *Harvard Theological Review,* XXXIV (1941), 277-320; and "Declension in a Bible Commonwealth," *Proceedings of the American Antiquarian Society,*

New Series, LI (1941), 37-94. His most comprehensive works are *The New England Mind: The Seventeenth Century* (New York, 1939), and *The New England Mind: From Colony to Province* (New York, 1953). Professor Miller is inclined to state theological matters in down-to-earth language, which in a number of instances leads to a distorted oversimplification, if not downright error. As indispensable as the latter works is R. B. Perry, *Puritanism and Democracy* (New York, 1944), a superb book.

W. Walker, *Ten New England Leaders* (New York, etc., 1901) contains biographical sketches of some prominent Puritans, including Jonathan Edwards, Increase Mather, and Charles Chauncy, and offers helpful information concerning their theology, while his *Creeds and Platforms of Congregationalism* (New York, 1893), already noted, is a valuable source book. Standard histories of the New England Theology, beginning with Edwards and ending with the Oberlin school of theology, are G. N. Boardman, *A History of New England Theology* (New York, 1899), and F. H. Foster, *A Genetic History of the New England Theology* (Chicago, 1907), which covers the same ground; both books fail to distinguish between traditional Calvinism and the Covenant Theology. The Arminian slant of Boardman and Foster is counterbalanced by J. Haroutunian in *Piety versus Moralism* (New York, 1932), an excellent but controversial work featuring a blast against the moralism of the later Edwardeans. "The Beginnings of Arminianism in New England" are discussed by F. A. Chambers in *Papers of the American Society of Church History*, 2nd Series, III (1912), 153-72. For a discussion of the Covenant Theology in American religious thought, see L. J. Trinterud, *The Forming of an American Tradition* (Philadelphia, 1949).

Jonathan Edwards's thought is discussed in P. Miller, *Jonathan Edwards* ([New York], 1949), a philosophical and difficult discussion. A. C. McGiffert, *Jonathan Edwards* (New York and London, 1932) is a good introduction to the divine's life, while A. V. G. Allen, *Jonathan Edwards* (Boston and New York, 1894) is an older biography. An interesting and good biography, free from excessive philosophical discussion, is O. E. Winslow, *Jonathan Edwards, 1703-1758* (New York, 1941).

The penitential system of the early Church and of Roman Catholicism is discussed in O. D. Watkins, *A History of Penance*

(2 vols., London, 1920), and H. C. Lea, *History of Auricular Confession and Indulgences* (3 vols., Philadelphia, 1896), both of which are objectively written. The subject is also discussed in J. T. McNeill, *A History of the Cure of Souls* (New York, 1951), while his earlier work, *The Celtic Penitentials* (Paris, 1923), contains useful information on penance in England. Also of some interest is T. P. Oakley, *English Penitential Discipline and Anglo-Saxon Law in Their Joint Influence* (New York, 1923).

PURITAN LIFE AND THOUGHT

In addition to the general background literature already mentioned, Puritan society and thought are discussed in S. E. Morison, *The Puritan Pronaos* (New York, 1836), a series of essays on the intellectual history of seventeenth-century New England. O. E. Winslow, *Meetinghouse Hill* (New York, 1952) is an excellent description of Puritan church life, with a good chapter on church discipline, and H. W. Schneider, *The Puritan Mind* (New York, 1930), written by a philosopher with a Christian point of view, discusses Puritan thought and the relationship of their theology to their ethics. H. Wish, *Society and Thought in Early America* (New York, 1950) and M. Savelle, *The Seeds of Liberty* (New York, 1948) contain some pages on Puritan thought; the latter is marred by an animus against religion. V. L. Parrington, *The Colonial Mind, 1620-1800,* which forms the first part of *Main Currents in American Thought* (New York, 1927), is not only an indispensable classic of historical writing but is also magnificent literature. Other relevant discussions may be found in C. A. Beard, "On Puritans," *The New Republic,* XXV, No. 1 (December 1, 1920), 15-17, and G. M. Stephenson, *The Puritan Heritage* (New York, 1952).

The most important relevant biographies are W. King, *Unafraid: A Life of Anne Hutchinson* (Boston and New York, 1930), an undocumented and rather emotional study, and somewhat weak on theology; S. H. Brockunier, *The Irrepressible Democrat* [Roger Williams] (New York, 1940); and J. Ernst, *Roger Williams: New England Firebrand* (New York, 1932). A revisionist approach to Williams is found in P. Miller, *Roger Williams: His Contribution to the American Tradition* (Indianapolis, 1953) and M. Calamandrei, "Neglected Aspects of Roger Williams' Thought," *Church History,* XXI (1952), 239-56. R. and L. Boas, *Cotton*

Mather, Keeper of the Puritan Conscience (New York and London, 1928) is a good and readable biography.

Family life and sexual relations are discussed in A. W. Calhoun, *A Social History of the American Family* (3 vols., Cleveland, 1917-19), an excellent but poorly documented work, and in the more detailed study by G. E. Howard, *A History of Matrimonial Institutions* (3 vols., Chicago, 1904), which contains detailed analyses of marriage, sex, and divorce in colonial Massachusetts, based largely on court records. E. Morgan, *The Puritan Family* (Boston, 1944) is a useful and charming contribution on social history, while S. Fleming, *Children and Puritanism* (New Haven, 1933) takes a more theological approach and is perhaps a bit too optimistic in its view of human nature. L. L. Schuecking, *Die Familie im Puritanismus* (Leipzig, 1929) contributes little to our knowledge of Puritan life. Equally devoid of any significant contribution is A. P. James, "Domestic Relations in Colonial New England" (unpublished M.A. essay, University of Chicago, 1912). The English background is ably treated in C. L. Powell, *English Domestic Relations, 1487-1653* (New York, 1917). Domestic life in the colonial period is discussed by A. M. Earle in *Home Life in Colonial Days* (New York, 1898) and in *Customs and Fashions in New England* (New York, 1896), both of which are allegedly based on true incidents but are undocumented, and in G. F. Dow, *Domestic Life in New England in the Seventeenth Century* (Topsfield, 1925), which adds little of importance.

Sexual morality is discussed in H. B. Parkes, "Sexual Morals and the Great Awakening," *The New England Quarterly,* III (1930), 133-35, and "Morals and Law Enforcement in Colonial New England," *ibid.,* V (1932), 431-52, in which Parkes takes issue with the thesis stated by C. F. Adams in "Some Phases of Sexual Morality and Church Discipline in Colonial New England," *Proceedings of the Massachusetts Historical Society,* 2nd Ser., VI (1891), 477-516. G. May, *Social Control of Sex Expression* (New York, 1930) is of some use. H. R. Stiles, *Bundling: Its Origin, Progress, and Decline in America* (Albany, 1871), is entertaining but of doubtful scholarly value.

The Puritan Sabbath is treated in A. H. Earle, *The Sabbath in Puritan New England* (8th ed., New York, 1896), a delightful but undocumented book based on allegedly true incidents. R. R.

Hinman, *The Blue Laws* (Hartford, 1838) is a good guide to the Sabbath legislation of the Puritans but emphasizes Connecticut. Less useful are A. H. Lewis, *A Critical History of Sunday Legislation* (New York, 1888) and G. Myers, *Ye Olden Blue Laws* (New York, 1921), which is unoriginal and undocumented.

The Puritans' economic theories are discussed by J. Dorfman in his outstanding history of American economic thought, *The Economic Mind in American Civilization* (3 vols., New York, 1946), which devotes chapters 3 and 7-9 of the first volume to Puritanism. Sociological studies include M. Weber, *The Protestant Ethic and the Spirit of Capitalism,* translated from the German by T. Parsons (New York, 1930); E. Troeltsch, *The Social Teaching of the Christian Churches,* translated from the German by O. Wyon (New York, 1931); and R. H. Tawney's classic, *Religion and the Rise of Capitalism* (New York and London, 1926). A searching critique of the Weber thesis is found in H. M. Robertson, *Aspects of the Rise of Economic Individualism: A Criticism of Max Weber and His School* (Cambridge, 1933). Two articles of narrower scope are A. W. Griswold, "Three Puritans on Prosperity," *The New England Quarterly,* VII (1934), 481-92, based on the writings of Cotton Mather, Benjamin Franklin, and Timothy Dwight; and R. Niebuhr, "Puritanism and Prosperity," *Atlantic Monthly,* CXXXVII (1926), 721. In "Calvinism and Capitalism," *Harvard Theological Review,* XXI (1928), 163-95, K. Fullerton discusses the Calvinist doctrine of vocation.

The political theories of the Puritans are discussed in almost every work on New England history. The only worth-while contribution specifically on this subject is H. L. Osgood, "The Political Ideas of the Puritans," *Political Science Quarterly,* VI (1891), 1-28, 201-31. C. E. Merriam, *A History of American Political Theories* (New York, 1903), devotes some pages to the subject.

History, theology, and law overlap in several volumes devoted to the witchcraft trials. Almost every history of the period discusses these proceedings at some length. The most up-to-date work is M. L. Starkey, *The Devil in Massachusetts* (New York, 1949), which is written like an excellent novel but is based on exhaustive research. The best collection of sources is G. L. Burr, ed., *Narratives of the Witchcraft Cases, 1648-1706* (New York, 1914). J. Fiske,

Witchcraft in Salem Village (Boston and New York, 1903), a reprint from *New France and New England,* gives an excellent brief treatment of the subject, while W. S. Nevins, *Witchcraft in Salem Village* (Salem and Boston, 1892) is interesting because of its psychological approach.

The exercise of church discipline is discussed by C. F. Adams in "Some Phases of Sexual Morality and Church Discipline in Colonial New England," which has already been mentioned, and a good general description is found in chapter XI of O. Winslow, *Meetinghouse Hill* (New York, 1952). Excommunication is discussed in C. E. Park, "Excommunication in Colonial Churches," *Transactions of the Colonial Society of Massachusetts,* XII (1908-9), 321-32. H. W. Johnson, "Moral Discipline in Early New England Churches" (unpublished B.D. thesis, University of Chicago, 1915) contains very little information which is not available elsewhere. The records of the trials of Anne Hutchinson have been edited by C. F. Adams in *Antinomianism in the Colony of Massachusetts Bay, 1636-1638* (Boston, 1894), and the civil trial is brilliantly narrated in chapter I of R. B. Morris, *Fair Trial* (New York, 1952).

For the study of the Great Awakening in Massachusetts, *The Christian History* (Boston, 1744), a periodical devoted to the news of the revivals, is an indispensable source. The anti-revivalist viewpoint is expressed in C. Chauncy, *Seasonable Thoughts* (Boston, 1743). J. Tracy, *A History of the Revival of Religion in the Times of Edwards and Whitefield* (Boston, 1842) is vivid and entertaining. Other relevant literature includes F. G. Beardsley, *A History of American Revivals* (New York, 1904), favoring revivalism, and E. E. White, "Decline of the Great Awakening in New England, 1741 to 1746," *The New England Quarterly,* XXIV (1951), 35-52, which is more objective. The relationship between the Awakening and morality is discussed in the articles by C. F. Adams and H. B. Parkes, cited above.

In *The Origins of Prohibition* (New York, 1925), J. A. Krout discusses the Puritan view on alcoholic beverages. Dueling is treated in E. B. Greene, "The Code of Honor in Colonial and Revolutionary Times, with Special Reference to New England," *Publications of the Colonial Society of Massachusetts,* XXVI (1926), 367-88.

LAW AND LEGAL HISTORY

Useful introductions to the history of English law are T. F. T. Plucknett, *Concise History of the Common Law* (4th ed., London, 1948), and E. Jenks, *A Short History of English Law* (6th ed., London, 1949), or the briefer work by F. W. Maitland and F. C. Montague, *A Sketch of English Legal History* (New York and London, 1915). The criminal side of the law is treated in Sir J. F. Stephen, *A History of the Criminal Law of England* (London, 1883), while the more patient reader will find invaluable information in W. S. Holdsworth's monumental and indispensable thirteen-volume work, *A History of English Law* (London, 1903-38).

C. J. Hilkey, *Legal Development in Massachusetts, 1630-1686* (New York, 1910) is descriptive, informative, and dry, while an older work, E. Washburn, *Sketches of the Judicial History of Massachusetts from 1630 . . . to . . . 1775* (Boston, 1840), suffers from superficiality, provincialism, and miserable documentation. Much more rewarding reading is R. B. Morris, *Studies in the History of American Law* (New York, 1930), the first chapter of which is especially relevant. The adoption of the common law in the colonies is discussed by J. Goebel, Jr., in "King's Law and Local Custom in Seventeenth Century New England," 30 *Columbia Law Review* (1931), 416, and by P. S. Reinsch in "The English Common Law in the Early American Colonies," *Select Essays in Anglo-American Legal History* (3 vols., Boston, 1907-8). Other relevant contributions in these volumes are those by Wigmore, Stephen, Holdsworth, Holmes, Langdell, Wilson, and Stubbs. R. Pound has devoted a chapter of *The Spirit of the Common Law* (Boston, 1921) to "Puritanism and the Law," but overemphasizes the Puritans' love for common law and their hatred of equity. M. D. Howe, *Readings in American Legal History* (Cambridge, 1949) and his *Cases on Church and State in the United States* (Cambridge, 1952) contain some cases which are relevant to the study of Puritanism.

Among the more specialized studies are F. G. Gray, "Remarks on the Early Laws of Massachusetts Bay," *Collections of the Massachusetts Historical Society,* 3rd Ser., VIII, 191, which contains nothing not said in the more thorough works; R. B. Morris, "Massachusetts and the Common Law: The Declaration of 1646,"

American Historical Review, XXVI (1926), 443-53, and R. C. Pittman, "The Colonial and Constitutional History of the Privilege against Self-Incrimination in America," 21 *Virginia Law Review* (1935), 763. Some information on procedure in colonial Massachusetts may be found in the introduction to the *Records and Files of the Quarterly Courts of Essex County* (Salem, 1911), II, vi.

Church-state relations are discussed in the first volume of A. P. Stokes, *Church and State in the United States* (New York, 1950), an outstanding contribution to the subject. Also useful are S. H. Cobb's narrative study, *The Rise of Religious Liberty in America* (New York, 1902); E. B. Greene's interpretive work, *Religion and the State* (New York, 1941); and E. F. Humphrey, *Nationalism and Religion in America* (Boston, 1924). The student of statute law will find some relevant information in P. E. Lauer, *Church and State in New England* (Baltimore, 1892), and G. H. Haynes, *Representation and Suffrage in Massachusetts, 1620-1691* (Baltimore, 1894). Much more interesting are S. M. Reed, *Church and State in Massachusetts, 1691-1740* (Urbana, 1914), and J. C. Meyer, *Church and State in Massachusetts from 1740 to 1833* (Cleveland, 1930). A recent article of importance is B. K. Brown, "Freemanship in Puritan Massachusetts," *American Historical Review,* LIX (1954), 865-83. E. Buck, *Massachusetts Ecclesiastical Law* (Boston, 1868) is of some use, especially for the national period. P. Oliver, *Puritan Commonwealth* (Boston, 1856), purporting to be "an historical review of Puritan government in Massachusetts in its civil and ecclesiastical relations," is a miserably written Anglican polemic against "those wicked Puritans," and reads like something from the seventeenth century.

The problem of religious toleration is discussed in R. Bainton, "The Puritan Theocracy and the Cambridge Platform," in H. W. Foote, ed., *The Cambridge Platform of 1648* (Boston, 1949). M. S. Bates has a section on Puritanism in *Religious Liberty: An Inquiry* (New York and London, 1945), and Professor Bainton's *Travail of Religious Liberty* (Philadelphia, 1951), although not directly relevant, offers some helpful insights.

Index